Exploring *Downto*

Exploring
Downton Abbey

Critical Essays

Edited by
SCOTT F. STODDART

McFarland & Company, Inc., Publishers
Jefferson, North Carolina

ISBN (print) 978-0-7864-7688-6
ISBN (ebook) 978-1-4766-3220-9

LIBRARY OF CONGRESS CATALOGUING-IN-PUBLICATION DATA ARE AVAILABLE

BRITISH LIBRARY CATALOGUING DATA ARE AVAILABLE

Front cover images © 2018 iStock

Printed in the United States of America

*McFarland & Company, Inc., Publishers
Box 611, Jefferson, North Carolina 28640
www.mcfarlandpub.com*

Table of Contents

The Servants' Hall

Acknowledgments

"Exploring Downton Abbey" has been a part of my life for as long as the series ran. Given that this project has, finally, found its way into your hands, I would like to take the time to thank those who helped me along as I struggled to complete this worthwhile venture.

I want to thank my new academic home, Saint Peter's University, for supporting a dean in his efforts to remain current in his field. President Eugene Cornacchia, Dr. Frederick Bonato, Professor John Walsh, and Dr. Gerard O'Sullivan helped me to balance my administrative efforts and my scholarship so I could remain a better role model for my faculty in the College of Arts and Sciences. In addition, my thanks go out to professors Paul Almonte, Anna Brown, Andrea Bubka, Jill Callahan, John Hammett, Lisa O'Neill, Alp Tuncaci, Rachel Wifall, Jeanette Wilmanski and Wei Dong Zhu for their collegiality and support this past year.

Thanks go to my administrative colleagues who support my work: Dr. Joseph Doria, Dr. Bruce Rosenthal, Dr. Mary-Kate Naatus, Dr. Lauren O'Hare and Elizabeth Kane inspire me daily. My thanks go as well to Fr. Rocco Danzi, Leah Leto, and Anthony Skevakis—each one helps me to maintain balance during complicated times.

The College of Arts and Sciences at Saint Peter's University is run like a well-oiled machine because of my team: my thanks to Dr. Nicole Houser, Mark Median, and especially Ruth Vazquez and Kilolo Kumanyita, who take on many more responsibilities than necessary because they believe in my efforts.

The contributors to this volume have suffered along with me—we have all felt like Lady Edith at one time or another, thinking the end result would never come in time—my thanks for their patience and fortitude.

My extended family grounds me in a variety of ways. My thanks and love to Stuart Parman and Rebecca Meyer; Sarah and Al Griffith; Praveen Chaudhry and Souziena Mushtaq and Kurt Cartensen.

Dr. Bill Mooney has long been a champion of my work, and I love and respect his efforts to meet with me every other week to be certain that I am on-task and properly lubricated.

Michael Samuel, one of the contributors, has never ceased to amaze me with his kind nature, his thoughtful approach to his work, and his tireless ability to be there just when I need him most.

My partner, Travis Wicklund, strengthens me every day with his grace, his charm, his endless ability to be kind and his boundless energy. He continues to inspire me because he has such faith in my abilities. I owe him so very much.

Finally, I dedicate *"Exploring Downton Abbey"* to my mother, Jeanne F. Black, who fostered a love of Hollywood classics in me from an early age, and who helped me to translate that passion to "quality" television, watching event series like *Masterpiece Theatre*, *Roots*, *The Adams Chronicles*, *Beacon Hill* and countless serial dramas with me, and making me talk with her about what I saw and learned from them. She never knew it, but those conversations became the basis of my pedagogical philosophy, teaching me to read closely and to articulate my ideas. Her love of all things Victorian, costume dramas, and art left a lasting impression on me, and her example continues to inspire me daily.

Introduction

Scott F. Stoddart

When the news from across the pond broke in December 2013, that Matthew Crowley—the long-suffering love interest of Lady Mary Crowley—and the beloved character of millions of fans on the BBC/PBS series *Downton Abbey*—was going to die in the final episode of Series Three, the response was far from positive. Not only did major news agencies—like the *New York Times*, the AP, Reuters, and the *Wall Street Journal*—report his tragic death in a manner befitting a real hero, but fans turned to the blogosphere to respond—some with great sadness: MSN reported that the news coming before Christmas in England "nearly ruined Boxing Day" across the country. And in America, where bloggers take their affinities to television characters quite seriously, some promised to stop watching the series after Series Three—some even vowing to never patronize another vehicle starring Dan Stevens, the actor who dared to "try something new" after appearing in this series that has formed an emotional bridge between the Empire and her former colony.

The passion that has made *Downton Abbey* one of the most popular series ever to run on ITV/PBS has mystified almost any critic of series television. Unlike other successful series, such as *The Sopranos* (1999–2007) and *Breaking Bad* (2008–2013), it does not violently engage its audience with foul-talking wiseguys; unlike *The West Wing* (1999–2006) or *Homeland* (2011–), it does not use its global politics for intrigue; unlike the *CSI* (2000–) or the *Law & Order* series (1990–2010), it does not bill itself as a modern parable of life "ripped from the pages of major-new stories"; and unlike *Mad Men* (2007–2014), it does not use its focus on the historical past to expose the limits of nostalgia. Instead of a catchy web presence, with interactive party games, avatars, and gossipy backstories, *Downton* "has become a sensation in the old-fashioned way: Based on word-of-mouth" (Lowey), telling its tales of upstairs and downstairs in a simply elegant manner, engaging its audiences through carefully constructed storylines involving fully realized characters.

Why has this British series about life in a country estate at the turn of the twentieth century grabbed the hearts of its viewers with such passion? Why have critics and industry professionals rewarded this series with over 200 award nominations including fifteen Emmy Awards, three Golden Globe Awards, four Screen Actors Guild Awards and three BAFTAs? Why do spectators gather together weekly to screen the series "like the Super Bowl"? Why have designers, inspired by the fashions and decors, turned down hem-lines and fostered a palette of softer pastels to showcase the frippery of *objet d'art*? Why have sales of books on Edwardian England—from the time, historical treatises and cookbooks—sky-rocketed over the past three years? Why has this episodic drama caught the popular culture zeitgeist so forcefully, spawning everything from paper dolls to parodies on stage and screen? These are only a few of the questions *Exploring* Downton Abbey hopes to answer.

The genesis of the series is found in a conversation between two old friends. The plan, as recorded by creator, writer and executive producer Julian Fellowes, was to produce a mini-series fit for *Masterpiece Theatre* that would return the writer to a time similarly captured in his Oscar-winning screenplay for Robert Altman's *Gosford Park* (2001). However, he was reluctant at first: "It would be like trying to make lightening strike in the same place twice" (266). Further conversations with producing partner, Gareth Neame, an executive at Carnival Films, "planted a seed" that it might be done: Neame recalls,

> I thought that as an episodic serial you'd have a timescale to get right inside the lives of everyone above and below stairs, in a way that you can't in a film. I knew it would play to the strengths of television and had a hunch it would be very popular. With Julian writing it, I knew it would be authentic [266].

Fellowes took up the challenge and decided to "retreat twenty years to 1912" to visit a time significantly different from our own, but rendered familiar "with cars and trains and telephones"—forming "a bridge from the old world into the new" (World 8).

With moderate press, the first episode aired on 26 September 2010 in the United Kingdom to some nine million viewers (*World* 297). When the second episode was broadcast to an audience of over three million more, Fellowes and crew knew they had tapped a nerve, and the final episode of Series One, when Lord Grantham halts the festivities of high British tea to announce that England is at war, set the stage for a continuing drama of epic proportions: "Television—or rather, a television series, with its open-endedness, with its unlimited time to develop any character—held possibilities that the space allowed for a film narrative could not offer" (*World* 7). So a series was to the manor born!

Interestingly enough, in charting the course of his characters, Fellowes freely admits that he owes much to American drama series. "I think the Americans, with *West Wing* and *NYPD Blue* and *ER* and *Chicago Hope*—this tremendously energized, multi-narrative, multilevel show—I think that was a reinvention of television that has affected us all." Critics hypothesize that American episodic drama for television found its roots in *Masterpiece Theatre* series such as *Upstairs Downstairs* (1971–1975; 2010–2012), but Fellowes' desire to infuse energy into a series that "goes at the speed of a snail" is crucial to his method of engaging his audience. Taking the best of both worlds—the prestige of the British and the vitality of the Americans—Fellowes "made the decision to treat every character, the members of the family and the members of their staff, equally, in terms of their narrative" (*Chronicles* 6). Fellowes believes that his series is distinctive because of the medium, which allows space for character development—to build audience connection—and energy to push his characters into the realities of the modern world—facing new technologies and modernizations that threaten the community of the family and country in a manner similar to our own time.

The plot of the drama follows the lives of two classes at the turn of the twentieth century who inhabit one country estate in England. Lord Robert and Lady Cora Crawley, the Earl and Countess of Grantham, the proprietors of the estate, have raised their three daughters, Lady Mary, Lady Edith, and Lady Sybil, in a manner suited to the nobility with the assistance of a capable staff of butlers, footmen, ladies' maids and cooks—all under the persistently watchful eye of their grandmother, the Dowager Countess, Lady

Violet. Their way of life is threatened when the heir to the estate (and presumed fiancé to Lady Mary), Patrick Crawley, perishes with his father aboard the HMS *Titanic*, sailing to America during its maiden voyage. With his death, the estate falls victim to laws of entailment, which prohibits female primogeniture, and the plot intensifies as the new heir, the unknown cousin Matthew, comes to Downton with his mother, Isobel, to take up the mantle of his inheritance.

While the basics of the plot—focusing on the travails of the nobles upstairs and the servants down—appear similar in scope to Britain's famous export in the 1970s, *Upstairs Downstairs*, Fellowes acknowledges that the real inspiration for the series is based in his reading of the period, and the tales of his own family history. At the time that he was completing his work on *Gosford Park*, Fellowes was reading Carol Wallace's *To Marry an English Lord* (2010), an historical account of the so-called Buccaneers—daughters of wealthy Americans who traveled to England during the later 1800s in search of single British men of noble birth. In essence, similar to Cora Levinson's marriage to Lord Grantham, these wealthy American brides would hold the key to salvaging the estates of the British noble class, whose agrarian way of life was bankrupting the estates at the time. For instance,

> at Welbeck Abbey, the Duke of Portland had more than 60 staff in the house, with a further 200 laboring away in the stables, gardens and home farm. In today's Britain, that number of employees would be—categorized as a big business—Welbeck's annual Servants' Ball was so huge and so grand that an orchestra and 50 waiters had to be brought in from London [*Daily Mail*].

As detailed in 1:2, Matthew learns how the one class relies on the other for its livelihood. The maintenance of the estate was crucial to this way of life, necessitating the need to marry money.

Critics have been hard on the series—mainly because its success has caught off-guard those who believe that the adult drama is nothing more than a soap opera. Its defenders are actually few, and these readers show that despite the nay-sayers, there is something of value to appreciate in the series. *Downton*'s combination of using history and romance to tell its story appears to fill a void that contemporary television drama is not able to fulfill. Gordon Hauser of *The Mennonite* believes that it is a simple case of well-written melodrama—providing characters to cheer and ones to see succeed. While many liberal critics want to scoff at the popularity of the series, many television critics wrack their minds to figure out what might be at the root of its popularity. For instance, *Forbes*' Jerry Bowyer believes that *Downton Abbey*'s message is one factor:

> The fact is that the spirit of the critics is hard left, and maybe that's why *Downton Abbey* makes them so angry, because the success of the series shows that this group does not speak for America. It also shows something equally important to the future of our culture: that there is no inherent need for good TV to be left of center. Stories sympathetic to virtue, preservation of property and admiration of nobility and of wealth can be told beautifully and to wide audiences, and I suspect they will be more and more in the future.

In a similar take, Matt Zoller Seitz believes that Fellowes' plot design helps contemporary audiences understand our own changing world:

> Since 1945 "recession" to us has meant "doing less well." That was until the economy collapsed near the end of George W. Bush's second term and we all started to wonder if the fairy tale had ended. Fear was in the air. Banks were failing. The auto industry was dying. Everyone I knew was unemployed or barely employed. When you've recently endured that sort of national reality check, the

scenes of *Downton's* servants quaking at the prospect of losing their jobs over illness, pregnancy, workplace politics, or turmoil higher up the food chain can hit you in a deep place—as can the scenes of the family flipping out over the prospect of having to sell their family home or begging an American relative for a bailout.

America is evolving in ways that many older citizens find alarming, and they've responded like the Earl of Grantham, by digging in their heels. The US shifted from a manufacturing economy to an information-and-war-based one in less than three decades. Gays and lesbians have new rights. Marijuana is on the path to being a controlled legal substance. We have a black president. In light of such changes, it's easy to translate the sight of aristocrats learning to accept a daughter's marriage to an Irish Catholic, or deciding to be all right with an unwed mother serving them food, into 21st-century American specifics. Old eras end, new ones start, and you have to bend or else you'll break. On some level, we get this—and as we view *Downton Abbey*, watching characters in another time and place experiencing a version of America's present reality, we're reassured that somehow we'll all muddle through. "When I think what the past ten years have brought," Violet marveled in the season three Christmas special. "God knows what we're in for now."

In zeroing in on why people watch the series, these critics take seriously the efforts of the writers and producers of the series to tap into the nerve of their viewers. For as the essays in this volume reveal, *Downton Abbey* does more than simply entertain—it is, in fact, a series devoted to wrestling with the complexities of change.

Interestingly enough, *Downton Abbey* has become a cultural bell-weather in a manner similar to *Mad Men*, influencing everything from fashion collections and home décor to books and jigsaw puzzles. Late-night television comedians poke fun at the series, and *Downton* paper doll collections permit the entire family to play at being Lady Violet— by far, everyone's favorite character.

In fact, the series appears to have generated a market for older brands of entertainment, even bringing families and friends together for screening parties. While young adults gathered to revel in boy-band fever and vampire and zombie fetishes, groups of middle-class viewers calling themselves "Abbey Acolytes," "Abbey Addicts" and "Downton Divas" gathered on Sunday nights in various parts of Boston, New York City and other cities to watch the show together and discuss it afterwards (Heyman 12/16/11). It's almost like the series, harkening back to a time before the Internet fragmented audience attention, bringing together groups in a community to commune in a more civilized manner. Hypothesizing a reason for this phenomenon, Rebecca Eaton, a self-proclaimed "Abbey Acolyte" says, "In spite of the fact it's about the 1% and its tremendous eye candy potential, I think Julian Fellowes has written a group of people who are actually trying to do the right thing…. They're heroes of the romantic and political variety. It's also a fabulous adult soap opera" (3). The soap opera angle is an important one, as the continuing drama, rooted in the tradition of the sprawling Victorian novels of Dickens and Eliot, giving way to the tradition of the mini-series—such as *Roots* (1977) and *The Winds of War* (1983)—which birthed the night-time soaps of the 1980s such as *Dallas* (1978–1991), *Dynasty* (1981–1989), *Falcon Crest* (1981–1990) and *Knots Landing* (1979–1993)—appears to be feeding a need for adult television that is not sustained by the likes of current continuing dramas— such as *Grey's Anatomy* (2005–), *The Good Wife* (2009–2016) and *Scandal* (2012–).

The popularity of the series infiltrates a variety of areas. Highclere Castle, where the series was shot, has become a Mecca of sorts—a highly lucrative tourist destination that hosted 1,500 visitors a day in 2012, spending $27 for an admission fee, $14.50 for a guidebook to the 1,000-acre estate, and $23 for polo shirts emblazoned with Lady Violet's image.

The publishing world experienced a true boon in books that help clarify the world of Downton. When Julian Fellowes told the *New York Times* that one inspiration for the series was in reading Carol Wallace's *To Marry an English Lord*, sales of the book flourished at Amazon.com. Subsequently, publishers have rushed back into print such classics as the Countess of Carnarvon's *Lady Almina and the Real Downton Abbey: The Lost Legacy of Highclere Castle*; Rosina Harrison's *Rose: My Life in Service to Lady Astor*; and Charles Todd's *A Bitter Truth*, a history of World War I. Julie Bosman reports that many publishers took to Twitter to suggest titles related to the time period of *Downton Abbey*, hoping for a spike in sales. Bookstores took to hosting events that showcase books on "the British aristocracy, the Titanic and World War I" (11 Jan. 2012)—even classic novels written at the turn of the twentieth century, just to feed a need between series.

Fellowes himself joined the foray, assisting his daughter Jessica with the publication of many books, including *The World of Downton Abbey*, *The Chronicles of Downton Abbey*, *A Year in the Life of Downton Abbey*, *Downton Abbey: A Celebration*, all top sellers on Amazon. The publication of *Downton Script Book* for Series One, Two and Three, in addition to a plethora of décor and cookbooks, reveals how popular the series is for the reading public in addition to the television audience. Promising "never before seen material, incisive commentary, and color photos that completely immerse fans in the world of *Downton Abbey*" (Jessica Fellowes, *The World*), the volumes have proven to be big sellers at Amazon, feeding a desire for *Downton* discourse.

Of course in the theatre, parody is considered the highest of compliments, and if that is true, *Downton* is considered golden indeed by the profession. *Late Night with Jimmy Fallon* has paid the compliment endlessly, staging riotous parodies playing up the stiffly class-conscious brood in skits employing many of the actors from the series. One, titled "Breaking *Downton*," features Hugh Bonneville (Lord Grantham), Rob James-Collier (Thomas) and Jim Carter (Mr. Carson) playing exaggerated versions of themselves as if on the violent series *Breaking Bad*. In the skit, Downton is a cover for a crack cocaine den, and Carson's delivery of "tea" is actually the product being sold to a bevy of gangsters who want it for the street. The genius of the parody is that Lord Gratham, Thomas and Carson continue to speak in very proper tones using American slang they pretend not to fully understand, revealing how ludicrous the series appears ... particularly in comparison to the Grand Guignol antics of *Breaking Bad*.

In another parody, available on YouTube, 54 Below in New York City staged *Downton: The Musical*, a musical review billed as a sneak peak at Series Four. Featuring many of Broadway's best, the ten-minute mini-feature is entertainingly narrated by a mincing Julian Fellowes, sipping tea and deliciously dishing about how he is only going to reveal a few secrets of the next series through this musical episode. Of course, the fun lies in the exaggerated performances of the cast, both in performing the clever songs and in providing faux backstage commentary about the supposed new season.

Beyond the performative, *Downton Abbey* has found itself in the midst of a marketing bonanza, offering up a variety of items that put the series at the forefront of the advertising world. Fashion designer Ralph Lauren used *Downton Abbey* as the inspiration of his fall 2012 collection, featuring actress Jessica Chastain in a series of photos modeling long, romantic gowns and hunting togs, all situated to appear as if on the series. *Downton* jigsaw puzzles and paper dolls add a sense of whimsy to these more old-fashioned entertainments—a reminder of how *Downton* plays off of some consumers' sense of nostalgia ... simple entertainments of a by-gone age.

In fact, that appears to be the real dichotomy in respect to *Downton Abbey*. While recollecting the past through its gorgeous costumes, its sumptuous art direction, and its use of history, *Downton Abbey* is not simply a series about celebrating the romantic past; it is a series about change: how families—both upstairs and downstairs—cope with new technologies and modern philosophies. It is this aspect of the series that I believe is the real reason *Downton* has caught on with viewers in both the United Kingdom and the United States. While change is exhilarating, it is also frightening—certainly making life easier, but also complicating it in newly exciting and fearfully paralyzing ways. Emphasizing change, *Downton* forms a bridge between the past and our own time, making us feel secure in our own complex society.

I titled this collection *Exploring Downton Abbey* because I wanted to allow the reader a chance to examine with my contributors the complexities of this series that appears, on its surface, to be all surface—with no depth. The first section, "The Main House: The Contexts of Downton," sets the structure of this volume as it uses the architecture of a country home as its foundation, allowing the reader to experience these probing analyses as if strolling through the manor house, pausing to savor each nuance of the production as an element of importance. In fact, the first essay, "'Even Elizabeth Bennet paid to see what Pemberley looked like inside': The Manor House as Character," written by Michael Samuel and myself, looks at how Highclere Castle—the real Downton Abbey—figures into the story of the Grantham family. Looking at the history of manor homes in literature and film, particularly Forster's *Howards End*, Austen's Pemberley (from *Pride and Prejudice*), and Fellowes' own *Gosford Park*, we argue that the series "is indicative of the wider conversations regarding character, social class, and heritage culture in the United Kingdom, which is capitalized on nationally as well as internationally." After looking at the tradition of how manor homes shape the stories of their respective protagonists, we seek to answer a particular question regarding *Downton Abbey*: "In what ways does the shifting role and ever-changing function of the house through the eras (as a home, convalescent center and as a tourism destination) impact on the dynamic of life within it for the occupants?"

In her essay "Revisiting *Gosford Park*: *Downton Abbey*, American Audiences and the British Heritage Genre," Gayle Sherwood Magee looks at Fellowes' collaboration with Robert Altman—which produced the Academy Award–winning film *Gosford Park* (2002)—as the real beginning of what became *Downton Abbey*. Realizing that both creations "were built on the Indiewood-era British heritage film and television model" helps us to understand the series' appeal in America. Looking at both the film and the series in detail, Magee provocatively argues that "a large part of the appeal of the British heritage genre [including the popularity of *Downton Abbey*] exists in the American mindset because 'the cultural myth of Englishness' of tradition, stability, and fair play that exists outside TV drama only in the historic imaginary."

The essays in the second section, titled "The Entrance Hall: Understanding History and *Downton Abbey*," relate the series to historical trends and theories that help put the show in a broader cultural context. Looking closely at the historical connections in Series Two, Elizabeth Fitzgerald's "Series Two of *Downton Abbey*: War! What Are We Good For?" argues that the series' focus on World War I allowed viewers to feel a timely synergy with the fictional characters of the *Abbey*: "Most of the characters in *Downton Abbey* spend their time worrying about how useful and necessary they are. And as is the case with many Americans today, they can't help but measure their use, and also their personal value, by their work." Looking at the series' use of World War I, she posits how times of war permit people to "experience a crisis where they reevaluate what they do and strive to prove to themselves or others that there is need for them."

Jennifer Poulos Nesbitt's provocative "'There's always something': Representing Race" examines two instances where race plays a large role in the series. The first looks at Series One's entrance (and abrupt exit) of Kemal Pamuk and his affair with Lady Mary; the second focuses on Lady Rose MacClare's dalliance with Jack Ross in Series Five. Examining mainstream reactions to both seasons playing of the race card—one through assault, the other through mutual desire—Nesbitt argues that "the series carefully manages the relationship" where race is concerned:

> *Downton's* presentation of birth control masks an underlying anxiety about English racial purity as a sign of national fitness…. *Downton* capitalizes on the indeterminacy and flexibility of race as a category to maintain racial boundaries without rendering whiteness visible, and thus contestable, as an element of Englishness.

In an essay that focuses on Series Four, Ellen Hernandez looks in particular at how American Jazz influenced British high society. "*Downton Abbey*, the Jazz Age and Adaptation to Change" examines, in particular, the real-life counterpart of Jack Ross and whether there are elements of historical truth in his presentation. In looking at how jazz pervaded the cultural landscape of Europe and then England, Hernandez hypothesizes that "connection" is the element that has drawn American audiences to the series, and that "the shared cultural changes of the Jazz Age, and its impact on economics, politics and social reforms" has much to do with the way Americans consume the show.

The essays that comprise the third section, "The Library: The Man's Domain," focus on the men of *Downton Abbey*, and pose questions regarding the changing role of women as the times and the series progress.

In a tightly focused essay, Anthony Guy Patricia looks at the charged online response to Thomas in "'Not family friendly': *Downton Abbey* and the Specter of Male Same-Sex Kissing." Drawing on queer theory and linguistic analysis, Patricia argues that the audience response following the seminal moment in Series One, revealing the clandestine relationship between Thomas and the visiting Duke of Crowbourough, and a single kiss they share prior to their falling out, "reflects larger societal and cultural trends connected with the depiction of non-normative male erotic realities in the medium of television." Looking at a variety of fan-sites, the essay parses the language used by spectators in an effort to understand the visceral response to Thomas' "queer tenure" on the series.

In "Wearing the Trousers: 'Female' Voices in 'Male' Spaces," Joy E. Morrow writes that the Edwardian period was a moment of significant "radical" change, "mostly brought about by new technologies which were affecting the ways people lived their day to day lives. Shifts in the economy were opening up new opportunities…. Ideological value shifts also brought significant political changes," and this forms the basis of her linguistic discussion of how the series renders female voice in spaces once believed to be male. Her conclusion argues that "gendered spaces are arbitrary" and that "the women of the higher class can do and wield more power than a viewer might initially expect" making us to comprehend the plight of the Edwardian woman all the more.

The women of *Downton* make up the fourth section, "M'Lady's Chamber: The Women of *Downton Abbey*," showing how the evolution of the Crawley sisters, Lady Mary, Lady Edith and Lady Sybil, evolve from their sheltered lives as debutantes to their becoming traditional wives and mothers, while embracing their emerging roles as working women. Jennifer Harrison's "Feminist Tendencies" argues that it is the stories of the women tied to the estate that helped guide the series to such international acclaim. Looking at the plights of Lady Mary in Series One and Lady Sybil in Series Three, she argues, "This essay will not go so far as to imply a blatant display of feminism during Series One, Two and Three; however, *Downton Abbey* demonstrates subtle feminist tendencies" throughout. Applying feminist theories to the Crawleys proves that the series is an "intersection" at best, between classist and feminist tendencies, particularly when the stories of the Crawley daughters are aligned with those of the women below stairs, in particular the stories of Gwen and Ethyl.

Examining the dynamics of events occurring in Series One, Rachel L. Carazo's "'Damaged' First, Romance Later: The Patterning of Courtship on Lady Mary Crawley" focuses on Lady Mary and her seemingly endless struggle to find a love that will satisfy her spiritually. Closely examining marital customs from the Victorian and Edwardian period, Carazo looks at how Mary struggles to find a rewarding relationship after her brief affair with Kamal Pamuk (which ends in a tragically abrupt manner) with first, Matthew Crawley and ultimately, with Henry Talbot. Focusing on her "damaged" condition, Carazo argues that "relationships [in the series] begin with a damaged phase, whether physical, emotional, or both, and progress to a romantic phase, during which characters receive their happy endings." This seems to be the norm for the Abbey as this is the pattern for Lady Edith and Lady Sybil and for most of the servants below stairs, including for Anna and Bates and for Carson and Mrs. Hughes.

Mary Ruth Marotte examines the significance of Series Three in "Lady Sybil Must Die: Class and Gender Constraints." Marotte's premise is that Lady Sybil's transformation from privileged debutante to female activist, wife, mother and, ultimately, a memory when she passes away in childbirth, a result of eclampsia, and that these transformations make her "a palpable threat" because of her "destabilized" state. "Unlike so many around her who are bound to a system that constrains and constricts them, Sybil has no allegiance to a system that privileges few at the expense of many. In short, she is a socialist even before her interactions with Branson, before she really understands the meaning of the term." In essence, Sybil is doomed to her early death because of the constant disruptions she creates.

In "'We are allies, my dear': Defining British and American National Identity," Melissa Wehler looks at the relationship between Lady Violet Crawley and Lady Cora Crawley and examines how the politics of each season develop the rich texture of their strange alliance as they work together to marry the three Crawley daughters. Wehler sees this "special relationship" as a "interesting microcosm" of the relations between American and Great Britain since colonial days, "to better understand how and why this British television series has found its own powerful allies in the American viewing public."

The final section, "The Servants' Hall," focuses on the lives of the servants at *Downton*, and the way that the series uses class to critique the British economy. Focusing on the servant's quarters, Courtney Pina Miller examines the place of the female servants in particular. Her essay, "The Downstairs Domestic: Servant Femininity," looks primarily at the roles Mrs. Hughes, Mrs. Patmore, Anna Bates and Daisy Mason play, and argues that "the series depicts domestic labor as a social, spatial, and embodied force that shapes and determines certain understandings of post–Edwardian servant femininity." In focusing on these characters, she shows how the series not only looks at the occupations they represent, but "its detailed look at the women beneath the aprons" as well.

In her essay titled "'Education is for everyone': Education and the American Dream," Katrin Suhren focuses on the character of Daisy Mason, and her efforts in the series' later seasons to advance socially through her educational efforts. Suhren sees this plotline to be highly connected to the American success of the series "which essentially feeds the American dream of upward social mobility that is enabled through hard work and determination." Being a decidedly American value, the education Daisy experiences would not have made a significant difference to one of her class and station in Edwardian England; consequently, she hypothesizes, this involved storyline must be present to draw American viewers into the story.

Finally, Gill Jamieson draws on recent British political history to underscore the parallels between Edwardian England and the recent conservative rejuvenation with both David Cameron and Theresa May's conservative agendas. "'We're all in this together': Big Society Themes" looks at the government established by Lloyd George in the early twentieth century and compares its agenda to Cameron's "Big Society" efforts during the run of the series. Her essay proposes "the first detailed examination of the series in light of coalition political philosophy and policy during that pivotal five-year period." Extending the work of Bryne, Tincknell and Nesbitt in particular, she argues "the various ways in which the series intersects with and frames, contemporary public debates in the UK about spending, consumption, equality, welfare provision and personal responsibility."

It is difficult to know what the overall effect of *Downton Abbey* will be, now that it has ended its six season run, but rumors in the mainstream press about a forthcoming *Downton Abbey* film has the hearts and minds of its legion of fans aflutter. As I expressed earlier, I hope that this collection of essays will help us to understand the singular achievement of this series at this difficult time where the world, once more, seems in need of a return to simple civility in the face of great change. In the final conversation between Isobel Crawley and Lady Violet, the Dowager Countess, the words ring true for both their worlds, and our own:

> Isobel: It makes me smile, the way we drink every year to what the future may bring. For it shows the more adaptable we are.
> Violet: If only we had the choice.

Works Cited

Bosman, Julie. "If You're Mad for Downton, Publishers Have a Reading List for You." *New York Times*, 11 January 2012.

Boyer, Jerry. "Down on Downton Abbey: Why the Left Is Torching Downton Abbey." *Forbes*, 14 February 2013.

Carnarvon, Countess Fiona. *Lady Almina and the Real Downton Abbey: The Lost Legacy of Highclere Castle.* New York: Broadway, 2011.

Fellowes, Jessica. *The Chronicles of Downton Abbey: A New Era.* New York: St. Martin's, 2012.

_____. *Downton Abbey: A Celebration.* New York: St. Martin's, 2014.

_____. *The World of Downton Abbey.* New York: St. Martin's, 2011.

_____. *A Year in the Life of Downton Abbey: Seasonal Celebrations, Traditions, and Recipes.* New York: St. Martin's, 2015

Harrison, Rose. *Rose: My Life in Service to Lady Astor.* New York: Penguin, 2011.

Hauser, Jerry. "Why Is Downton Abbey So Popular?" *The Mennonite*, 1 March 2013.

Seitz, Matt Zoller. "Season Three of Downton Abbey Teaches an Unlikely Lesson in Austerity." *New York Magazine*, 31 December 2012.

Todd, Charles. *A Bitter Truth.* New York: William Morrow, 2012.

Wallace, Carol. *To Marry an English Lord: Tales of Wealth and Marriage, Sex and Snobbery.* Ed. Gail MacColl. New York: Workman, 2012.

Cast of Characters

Central Characters

Upstairs

Thomas Branson — Allen Leech

Cora Crawley (née Levinson),
    Countess of Grantham — Elizabeth McGovern

Isobel Crawley (née Turnbull) — Penelope Wilton

Lady Edith Crawley — Laura Carmichael

Lady Mary Crawley — Michelle Dockery

Lady Sybil Crawley Branson — Jessica Brown Findlay

Matthew Crawley — Dan Stevens

Robert Crawley, Earl of Grantham — Hugh Bonneville

Violet Crawley, h
    Dowager Countess of Grantham — Maggie Smit

Lady Rose MacClare — Lily James

Downstairs

Thomas Barrow — Rob James-Collier

Anna Bates (née Smith) — Joanne Froggatt

Mr. John Bates — Brendan Coyle

Phyllis Baxter — Raquel Cassidy

Mr. Charles Carson — Jim Carter

Gwen Dawson — Rose Leslie

Ms. Elsie Hughes — Phyllis Logan

James Kent — Ed Speleers

Daisy Mason (née Robinson) — Sophie McShera

William Mason — Thomas Howes

Joseph Molesely — Kevin Doyle

Alfred Nugent — Matt Milne

Sarah O'Brien — Siobhan Finneran

Ethel Parks — Amy Nuttall

Mrs. Beryl Patmore — Lesly Nicol

Ivy Stuart — Cara Theobold

Recurring Characters

Daniel Aldridge, Lord Sinderby	James Faulner
Ephraim Atticus Aldridge	Matt Barber
Rachel Aldridge, Lady Sinderby	Penny Downie
Archbishop of York	Michael Culkin
Audrey	Victoria Emslie
Mrs. Barlett	Clare Higgins
Vera Bates	Maria Doyle Kennedy
May Bird	Christine Lohr
Charles Blake	Julian Ovenden
Edna Braithwaite	MyAnna Buring
Simon Bricker	Richard E. Grant
Major Charles Bryant	Daniel Pirrie
Daphne Bryant	Christine Mackie
Horace Bryant	Kevin R. McNally
Sir John Bullock	Andrew Alexander
Sarah Bunting	Daisy Lewis
Sir Richard Carlisle of Morningside	Iain Glen
Mr. Clarkham	Mark Penfold
Dr. Richard Clarkson	David Robb
Craig	Jason Furnival
Davis	Stephen Ventura
Mr. Dawes	Patrick Brennan
Gladys Denker	Sue Johnston
Dent	Karl Haynes
Margie Drewe	Emma Lowndes
Timothy Drewe	Andrew Scarborough
Duchess of Yeovil	Joanna David
Durrant	Neil Bell
Laura Edmunds	Antonia Bernath
The Hon. Mabel Lane Fox	Catherine Steadman
Anthony Foyle, Viscount Gillingham	Tom Cullen
Alex Green	Nigel Harman
Michael Gregson	Charles Edwards
Amelia Grey (née Cruikshank)	Phoebe Sparrow
Richard Grey, Baron Merton	Douglas Reith
Charles Grigg	Nicky Henson
Prince Igor Kuragin	Rade Sherbedgia
Henry Lang	Cal MacAninch
Martha Levinson	Shirley MacLaine
Lucy	Hayley Jayne Standing
Mr. Lynch	Andrew Westfield
Hugh "Shrimpie" MacClare	Peter Egan
Mr. Mason	Paul Copley
Jane Moorsum	Clare Calbraith
George Murray	Jonathan Coy
The Hon. Evelyn Napier	Brendan Patricks
Lady Rosamund Painswick	Samantha Bond

Paparazzo	Jake Rowley
Andrew Parker	Michael Fox
John Pegg	Joncie Elmore
Herbert Pelham	Harry Hadden-Paton
Prudence, Dowager Lady Shackelton	Harriet Walter
Miss Reed	Lucille Sharp
Charlie Rogers	Sebastian Dunn
Jack Ross	Gary Carr
Count Nikolai Rostov	Christopher Rozycki
Dr. Ryder	Richard Teverson
Terence Sampson	Patrick Kennedy
Mr. Skinner	Paul Putner
Septimus Spratt	Jeremy Swift
Sir Anthony Strallan	Robert Bathurst
Lavinia Swire	Zoe Boyle
Henry Talbot	Matthew Goode
Taylor	Lionel Guyett
Rev. Albert Travis	Michael Cochrane
Turner	Ged Simmons
Inspector Vyner	Louis Hilyer
Mrs. Wigan, Postmistress	Helen Sheals
Sergeant Willis	Howard Ward

Guest Stars

Lady Anne Acland	Charlotte Hamblin
The Hon. Madeleine Allsopp	Poppy Drayton
William Allsopp, Baron Aysgarth	James Fox
Dowager Lady Anstruther	Anna Chancellor
Arsene Avignon	Yves Aubert
Mrs. Bates	Jane Wenham
Rita Bevan	Nichola Burley
Billy	Christos Lawton
Kieran Branson	Ruairi Conaghan
Mr. Bromidge	Sean McKenzie
Joe Burns	Bill Fellow
Lord Chamberlain	Alastair Bruce
Neville Chamberlain	Rupert Frazer
Diana Clark	Alice Patten
Kitty Colthrust	Louise Calf
Lt. Edward Courtenay	Lachlan Nieboer
Sir John Darnley	Adrian Lukis
John Drake	Fergus O'Donell
Mrs. Drake	Cathy Sara
Duke of York	Jonathan Townsend
Mrs. Elcot	Naomi Radcliffe
Evans	Dean Ashton
Mr. Fairclough	Mark Morrell
Mr. Finch	Martin Walsh

George V	Guy Williams
Maj. Patrick Gordon	Trevor White
The Hon. Larry Grey	Charlie Anson
The Hon. Timothy Grey	Ed Cooper Clarke
John Harding	Philip Battley
Mr. Henderson	Rick Bacon
Lord Hepworth	Nigel Havers
Jarvis	Terence Harvey
Princess Irina Kuragin	Jane Lapotaire
Harold Levinson	Paul Giamatti
Susan MacClare,	
Marchioness of Flintshire	Phoebe Nicholls
Lady Manville	Sarah Crowden
Terence Margadale	Edward Baker-Duly
Mavis	Emma Keele
McCree	Ron Donachie
Mead	Edmund Kente
Nellie Melba	Kiri Te Kanawa
William Molesley	Bernard Gallagher
Mr. Moore	Trevor Cooper
Nield	Kenneth Bryans
Kermal Pamuk	Theo James
Miranda Pelham	Patricia Hodge
Philip, Duke of Crowborough	Charlie Cox
Photographer	John Voce
Prince of Wales	Oliver Dimsdale
Queen Mary	Valerie Dane
Receptionist	Devon Black
Sir Michael Reresby	Ronald Pickup
General Robertson	Jeremy Clyde
Marigold Shore	Sharon Small
Basil Shute	Darren Machin
Ethan Slade	Michael Slade
Captain Smiley	Tom Feary-Campbell
Inspector Stanford	Tony Turner
Sergeant Stevens	Peter McNeil O'Connor
Sir Mark Stiles	James Greene
Stowell	Alun Armstrong
Sir Herbert Strutt	Julian Wadham
Sir Philip Tapsell	Tim Pigott-Smith
Sam Thawley	Jonathan Howard
Jos Tufton	John Henshaw
Freda Dudley Ward	Janet Montgomery
John Ward	Stephen Critchlow
Nanny West	Di Botcher
Wilkins	Simone Lahbib
Virginia Woolf	Christina Carty

"Even Elizabeth Bennet paid to see what Pemberley was like inside"

The Manor House as Character

MICHAEL SAMUEL *and* SCOTT F. STODDART

Episode six of the final season of *Downton Abbey* opens with a scene that depicts two villagers from the fictional town of Downton looking at a poster attached to a public notice board. The poster reads, "OPEN HOUSE AT DOWNTON ABBEY. SATURDAY 6TH JUNE. A RARE OPPORTUNITY TO VIEW THE STATE ROOMS OF DOWNTON ABBEY. IN AID OF DOWNTON HOSPITAL TRUST. 6d. ADMISSION. BRING ALL THE FAMILY."[1]

The event comes in response to the major storyline running through Season Six regarding the future of Downton's hospital, and the open house tour is a means for the committee—of which the Lady Cora Grantham is the chair—to raise money. In succession, the opening sequence is composed of several scenes in which the Crawley family and the staff of the Downton Abbey estate discusses the opportunity and the need to open the house to the public, and how the general visitors' experience of the house and estate is to be planned and managed. In one scene, a bed-ridden Lord Grantham, recovering from an earlier incident involving the eruption of a stomach ulcer, is engaged in a discussion with Lady Mary and Tom Branson. The baffled Lord Grantham is curious as to why anyone would want to visit Downton, to which Lady Mary and Tom explain the fascination such houses hold for the masses:

> LORD GRANTHAM: What are they paying to see, we have nothing to show them?… They'd do better taking a train to London and visiting the Tate.
> TOM: That's not the point.
> LADY MARY: People want to see a different type of home; it's not the things in it.
> LORD GRANTHAM: How the other half lives.
> TOM: There's a curiosity about these places and this way of life.

Meanwhile, in another scene, a similar discussion between the Dowager Countess and Isobel Crawley invites similar curiosities, not only illustrating the divide between the traditional attitudes of one generation from those of the younger, but highlighting the attitudes toward class and status unearthed under public scrutiny. In the scene the Dowager is curious as to why anyone would wish to pay to see what she refers to as "an ordinary house," to which Isobel replies, "Not everyone lives in a house like Downton

Abbey.... People have always tipped the butler to look around the house. Even Elizabeth Bennett paid to see what Pemberley was like inside."

Immediately, these separate opening conversations underscore the impact of tourism upon the families who occupy historical locations—in this scene in particular, the way that tourism affects, or threatens to affect the lives of the fictional Crawley family at Downton Abbey. Moreover, their scripted conversations echo the sentiments of those who occupy the real-life estate that the series uses—the Carnarvon family at Highclere Castle in Berkshire, England. The conflicting opinions expressed by certain members of the Crawley family throughout the episode bring to the fore the tensions between the aristocracy's want for things to remain as they are, and the public's growing curiosity to see, as Grantham puts it, "how the other half lives," which, as expressed in the episode, can leave the families and occupants of such historical locales feeling exposed. The popularity of the series indicates both the public as well as audience's fascination with the lives of the aristocracy, which comes through frequently in discussions concerning so-called "heritage films."

Considering the manor house as a distinct character, this essay examines the ways that this episode of *Downton Abbey* (and arguably the series in general) is indicative of the wider conversations regarding character, social class and heritage culture in the United Kingdom, which is capitalized on nationally as well as internationally, particularly in the United States. After reflecting on the way the manor house has been used to delineate conversations regarding character and class in both literature and film, it seeks to answer the question—in what ways does the shifting role and ever-changing function of the house through the eras (as a home, convalescent center and as a tourism location) impact on the dynamic of life within it for the occupants?

The Heritage Film

The fascination with depictions of British heritage onscreen (in cinema and television dramas alike), and the use of a national iconography to reinstate a right-wing nostalgia for yesteryear (i.e., country houses, period costumes and upper-middle class activities) formed the basis of Andrew Higson's notion of the heritage film and the study of a cycle of perceived quality costume dramas and literary adaptations to emerge from the UK in the late 1980s and 1990s, particularly under the Thatcherite government (1979–90). These films included many Merchant Ivory Productions, such as *A Room with a View* (1986), *Maurice* (1987) and *Howard's End* (1992) as well as other non–Merchant-Ivory productions, such as *Chariots of Fire* (Hudson, 1981), *Passage to India* (Lean, 1984), *Sense & Sensibility* (Lee, 1995), *Emma* (Lawrence, ITV, 1996) and *Shakespeare in Love* (Madden, 1998). Heritage films, Higson writes,

> are set in the past, telling stories of manners and proprieties, but also the often transgressive romantic entanglements of the upper and upper middle-class English, in carefully detailed and visually splendid period reconstructions. The luxurious country-house settings, the picturesque rolling green landscapes of southern England, the pleasures of period costume, and the canonical literary reference points are among the more frequently noted attractions of such films—although there are of course exceptions, costumes dramas or period films that eschew such attractions [1].

Higson's cross-examination of British heritage in cinema interrogated the universally presented portrait of middle to upper-middle class rural Englishness, which dominated period dramas, and though it is concerned with films and period costume television dramas, it belongs to a wider body of research that examined the climate of the late 1980s and early 1990s, in which popular culture was saturated with patriotic iconography and content. Moreover, the work of heritage critics like Higson, and also Patrick Wright and Robert Hewison, viewed the deployment of heritage and its function, in terms of nation building, as a divisive part of Thatcher's political agenda, which aimed to reassert a sense of Britishness and restore a firm, rural, middle to upper-middle class in the UK. Considering the heritage climate in the UK in the 1980s, the aforementioned critics Wright and Hewison established the context that the heritage films were a part of, in the process identifying "what they saw as the consolidation of a heritage industry," in which there was "a potent marketing of the past as part of a new enterprise culture" (2).

Higson's concept of the heritage film explored the ways that heritage inspired the kinds of historical dramas that were being made for cinema and television during the specific period of the 1980s and 1990s in the UK, contributing to, as well as igniting, new debates about what we mean by, and how we understand, heritage in the present-day. Higson's initial investigation addressed growing concerns over the distinct version of Britishness, specifically Englishness, that was being communicated during this period, and his critique continues to be adapted to the study of contemporary heritage films and television dramas that continue to circulate nationally and transnationally, on big and small screens alike. Recent examples of successful "heritage films" include *The King's Speech* (Hooper, 2010), *The Imitation Game* (Tyldum, 2014) and *A Royal Night Out* (Jarrold, 2015). Meanwhile on television, series such as *Downton Abbey* (ITV/PBS, 2010–15), *Call the Midwife* (BBC/PBS, 2012–), *Mr Selfridge* (ITV/PBS, 2013–), *Wolf Hall* (BBC/PBS, 2015), *Indian Summers* (Channel 4/PBS, 2015–16), *War and Peace* (BBC/PBS, 2016) and *The Crown* (Netflix, 2016), a 10-part Queen Elizabeth II drama written by Peter Morgan, who wrote the West End and Broadway play *The Audience* (2013 and 2015), as well as the screenplays for contemporary heritage films *The Queen* (Stephen Frears, 2006) and *The Other Boleyn Girl* (Justin Chadwick, 2008) could be likened to heritage films.[2] These texts prove that there is an appetite in the UK, as well as in the U.S., for British heritage dramas on the small screen. Indeed, at present it would seem that, if anything, this appetite is growing, evidenced by numerous series that premiered in the UK in late 2016, such as the Victorian serial killer miniseries *Dark Angel* (ITV, 2016), the World War II drama *The Halcyon* (ITV, 2016), the second season of *Poldark* (BBC, 2015–), and the eight-part dramatization of the early life of Queen Victoria (*Victoria*, ITV, 2016–).[3] These titles are not only limited to British and American production companies and broadcast channels, however, as on-demand platforms, such as Amazon Prime Instant and Netflix, have started to produce or acquire heritage drama series.

Heritage and Howards End

James Ivory and his long-time producing partner, Ishmael Merchant, were, almost, single-handedly responsible for the birth of the heritage movement. The pair started out creating "costume" or "period" films in the 1970s, but with the production of *A Room with a View*, they found themselves in the forefront of a movement that "connects the period film to a network of cultural and industrial practices that relate to the construction of a collective cultural memory" (Vidal 3). Stunning in its attention to detail, Ruth Prawer

Jhabvala's meticulous screenplay brings Forster's engagingly witty story of Lucy Honey-church (Helena Bonham Carter) and her self-discovery among the antiquities of Italy to life. The film was nominated for eight Oscars and won three: for its screenplay, and its costume and production design. When it came time for a follow-up, Merchant—Ivory settled on another Forster classic, *Howards End*, uniting their efforts with another Jhab-vala screenplay (for which she would win a second Oscar), and establishing what has become the "heritage movement." Focusing on two families, the old-moneyed Wilcoxes and the middle-class Schlegels, *Howards End* becomes a struggle for the future of Britain via a home.

Forster's novel never fully describes Howards End; the genius is that the glimpses we get of Ruth Wilcox's family home provide an impression to the reader, allowing us to feel the home first, and experience it only when the time is right. For instance, the novel opens with a letter from Helen Schlegel to her sister Margaret, who describes the house through her observations of Mrs. Wilcox:

> It is old and little, and altogether delightful—red brick. We can scarcely pack in as it is, and the dear knows what will happen when Paul (younger son) arrives to-morrow. From hall you go right or left into dining-room or drawing-room. Hall itself is practically a room. You open another door in it, and there are the stairs going up in a sort of tunnel to the first-floor. Three bed-rooms in a row there, and three attics in a row above. That isn't all the house really, but it's all that one notices—nine windows as you look up from the front garden.
>
> Then there's a very big wych-elm—to the left as you look up—leaning a little over the house, and standing on the boundary between the garden and meadow. I quite love that tree already.... Why did we settle that their house would be all gables and wiggles, and their garden all gamboge-coloured paths? I believe simply because we associate them with expensive hotels—Mrs. Wilcox trailing in beautiful dresses down long corridors, Mr. Wilcox bullying porters, etc. We females are that unjust.... Oh, the beautiful vine leaves! The house is covered with a vine. I looked out earlier, and Mrs. Wilcox was already in the garden. She evidently loves it. No wonder she sometimes looks tired. She was watching the large red poppies come out. Then she walked off the lawn to the meadow, whose corner to the right I can just see. Trail, trail, went her long dress over the sopping grass, and she came back with her hands full of the hay that was cut yesterday—I suppose for rabbits or something, as she kept on smelling it. The air here is delicious [21–22].

What is most striking about Helen's detail is that she has characterized the Wilcox marriage, showing us how to think about them through the house itself. The sisters had imagined Howards End through the lens of Mr. Wilcox, characterizing it through his "bullying porters" as a house of ostentation, "all gables and wiggles, and their garden all gamboge-coloured paths." It's Mr. Wilcox's desire to be associated with "expensive hotels" because he is defined through his profession. On the other hand, Helen's depiction of Mrs. Wilcox shows that they were quite wrong. The family home is hers, and we feel instantly the magic of the home, and, in essence, of Ruth herself because "she evidently loves it," its "delightful" floor-plan at one with the countryside, its gardens comprised of the "wych-elm" and wild "poppies" and "lawn" linked to the "meadow" where Mrs. Wilcox strolls in "her long dress over the sopping grass" returning at last with "her hands full of the hay ... for the rabbits or something." She is one with nature here at Howards End, and, therefore she is the spirit of the house that imbues it with loving qualities.

We feel this even more after Ruth and Margaret rekindle their friendship in London. Ruth, sensing a spiritual connection to Margaret, tells her of her house:

> "His father gave him a car for a wedding present, which for the present is being stored at Howards End."

"I suppose you have a garage there?"

"Yes. My husband built a little one only last month, to the west of the house, not far from the wych-elm, in what used to be the paddock for the pony."

The last words had an indescribable ring about them.

"Where's the pony gone?" asked Margaret after a pause.

"The pony? Oh, dead, ever so long ago."

"The wych-elm I remember. Helen spoke of it as a very splendid tree."

"It is the finest wych-elm in Hertfordshire. Did your sister tell you about the teeth?"

"No."

"Oh, it might interest you. There are pigs' teeth stuck into the trunk, about four feet from the ground. The country people put them in long ago, and they think that if they chew a piece of the bark, it will cure the toothache. The teeth are almost grown over now, and no one comes to the tree."

"I should. I love folklore and all festering superstitions."

"Do you think that the tree really did cure toothache, if one believed in it?"

"Of course it did. It would cure anything—once."

"Certainly I remember cases—you see I lived at Howards End long, long before Mr. Wilcox knew it. I was born there."

The conversation again shifted. At the time it seemed little more than aimless chatter. She was interested when her hostess explained that Howards End was her own property [76].

As the friendship develops between the two women, Ruth realizes that Margaret is a kindred spirit—the most genuine she knows.

But the friendship does not last long; Mrs. Wilcox goes to hospital and dies, the narrator revealing to us that she has left her Howards End to Miss Schlegel, leaving a note "in pencil" as a codicil. The irony is that she recognizes in Margaret the very spirit necessary to preserve the goodness in the Wilcoxes—a goodness similar in her own spirit, but one trampled by Henry and their entrepreneurial children. Soon thereafter, Henry meets with his family, and they, together, destroy Ruth's letter of bequest, agreeing to never mention the note thereafter.

When Henry meets Margaret again, after two years, he falls in love with her, and proposes to her amidst the grandeur of his London flat. But it is Howards End she desires to see, and he takes her there on the way to his newest purchase, a castle at Oniton, where Margaret will assist with the marriage of Henry's daughter, Evie. Margaret's first glimpse of the home is our own first glance; we experience it through Margaret so as to understand why the country home is so sacred.

There were the greengage-trees that Helen had once described, there the tennis lawn, there the hedge that would be glorious with dog-roses in June, but the vision now was of black and palest green. Down by the dell-hole more vivid colours were awakening, and Lent Lilies stood sentinel on its margin, or advanced in battalions over the grass. Tulips were a tray of jewels. She could not see the wych-elm tree, but a branch of the celebrated vine, studded with velvet knobs, had covered the porch. She was struck by the fertility of the soil; she had seldom been in a garden where the flowers looked so well, and even the weeds she was idly plucking out of the porch were intensely green. Why had poor Mr. Bryce fled from all this beauty? For she had already decided that the place was beautiful.

Desolation greeted her. Dirty finger-prints were on the hall-windows, flue and rubbish on its unwashed boards. The civilization of luggage had been here for a month, and then decamped. Dining-room and drawing room—right and left—were guessed only by their wall-papers. They were just rooms where one could shelter from the rain. Across the ceiling of each ran a great beam. The dining-room and hall revealed theirs openly, but the drawing-room's was match-boarded—because the facts of life must be concealed from ladies? Drawing-room, dining-room, and hall—how petty the names sounded! Here were simply three rooms where children could play and friends shelter from the rain. Yes, and they were beautiful.

Then she opened one of the doors opposite—there were two—and exchanged wall-papers for whitewash. It was the servants' part, though she scarcely realized that: just rooms again, where friends might shelter. The garden at the back was full of flowering cherries and plums. Farther on were hints of the meadow and a black cliff of pines. Yes, the meadow was beautiful....

She paced back into the hall, and as she did so the house reverberated.

"Is that you, Henry?" she called.

There was no answer, but the house reverberated again.

"Henry, have you got in?"

But it was the heart of the house beating, faintly at first, then loudly, martially. It dominated the rain.

It is the starved imagination, not the well-nourished, that is afraid. Margaret flung open the door to the stairs. A noise as of drums seemed to deafen her. A woman, an old woman, was descending, with figure erect, with face impassive, with lips that parted and said dryly:

"Oh! Well, I took you for Ruth Wilcox."

Margaret stammered: "I—Mrs. Wilcox—I?"

"In fancy, of course—in fancy. You had her way of walking. Good-day."

And the old woman passed out into the rain [179–180].

Seeing Howards End through Margaret permits us to understand the bond between the women better, and allows us insight into how the homestead, now properly transferred via marriage, represents the future. At this point, Margaret sees herself as a bridge between the two families—two distinct philosophies—and this visit becomes spiritual as she recognizes the importance of her position: "She forgot the luggage and the motor-cars, and the hurrying men who knew so much and connect so little. She recaptured the sense of space, which is the basis of all earthly beauty, and starting from Howards End, she attempted to realize England" (213–214). As she sees more clearly what it will mean for her to accept Henry's hand in marriage, she comes back to reflect on the active role Howards End will play in her life: "Her only ally was the power of Home. The loss of Wickham Place had taught her more than its possession. Howards End had repeated the lesson" (232).

Margaret and Henry's courtship and subsequent marriage reveals how he takes the spirit of women and molds them to suit his own view of the world. Margaret, more spirited, caring more for "books and literature," becomes "Mrs. Wilcox" despite Henry's confession for having "known" Mrs. Bast in Cypress, causing a rift between she and Helen. While some critics scoff at a strong woman's decision to succumb to the will of the patriarchy, Forster does not want us to see Margaret's decision in tragic terms. Instead, he wants us to understand Margaret's fortitude in resolving to bring the likes of the Wilcoxes and the Schlegels together—this will be her singular triumph.

Forster paints the new marriage in terms of battle-lines being drawn for some penultimate confrontation. Henry, the "warrior" assumes that his bride "cannot win the real battle" when it comes to the real things in life, outside of her reading and her society discussions. However, Henry's fatal flaw is in his underestimation of Margaret, who certainly "claps the book up" when called upon, but who relishes a more advantageous role in the family than the sickly Ruth could. When she returns to Howards End to supervise the storage of her family's belongings, she learns that Mrs. Avery, the caretaker who mistook her for Ruth Wilcox, has subsequently unpacked the Schlegel belongings and furnished the home with them. Margaret is struck with how right everything feels, knowing full well Mrs. Avery's confusion involves more than simply the furniture: "In the house Margaret had wondered whether she quite distinguished the first wife from the second" (286). Forster opened the novel with a simple epigram, "Only connect"—it is this desire that maintains Margaret through the subsequent battle, serving as the maternal force that will unite her own siblings with Henry and his tenacious clan.

Helen returns from Germany about this time to reclaim her belongings, seven months pregnant—a result of her solace with Leonard Bast, who Henry humiliated at Ointon. Margaret asks Henry leave to stay the night at Howards End to reason with Helen; when Henry refuses, he forces Margaret to take sides, and her response shows her understanding that Henry will not assist her in bringing the families together. She uses his language, asking, "Will Helen's condition depreciate the property?" realizing that connection is the only thing that can preserve order. Margaret's decision, inspired by her love of preserving the homestead, is key to understanding what becomes her collective feminine weapon:

> She was transfigured. "Not any more of this!" she cried. "You shall see the connection if it kills you, Henry! You have had a mistress—I forgave you. My sister has a lover—you drive her from the house. Do you see the connection? Stupid, hypocritical, cruel—oh, contemptible!—a man who insults his wife when she's alive and cants with her memory when she's dead. A man who ruins a woman for his pleasure, and casts her off to ruin other men. And gives bad financial advice, and then says he is not responsible. These, man, are you. You can't recognize the, because you cannot connect" [322–323].

Margaret's decision to defend not only Helen but Ruth Wilcox and Jackie Bast, along with the repeated use of the word "connection" shows her ability to see the entire picture, her desire to serve as the mediator in this *battle royale* becoming clearer as she seeks to "connect" the warring factions of Britain's social fabric.

Of course, while Margaret wins this battle, at first, she seemingly loses the war. Leonard Bast arrives at the End to see Helen the following morning, and Charles Wilcox, defending the honor of the family, brashly beats him with the Schlegel family sword, killing the slight clerk, and bringing ruin on the Wilcox name. Margaret leaves Henry to help Helen raise her child, and their decision to reside at Howards End seems fitting: "To what ultimate harmony we tend she did not know, but there seemed a great chance that a child would be born into the world, to take the great chances of beauty and adventure that the world offers" (345–346). In remaining married to Henry, and becoming a second mother to Helen's child, Margaret succeeds in "connecting"; two years later, she takes the shattered Henry in and reconstitutes a new family order; Forster ends the novel with the aged Henry signing a new will that leaves Howards End to Margaret; the house becoming the site of a maternal empowerment which re-connects the two worlds of England under the roof of harmonious domesticity.

In making the decision to screen *Howards End*, Merchant and Ivory looked for a locale that would mirror Forster's vision of a house that could represent connection. They found it in Oxfordshire, near Henley-on-the-Thames; named Peppard Cottage, it belonged to Roger and Caroline Shapland, at the time friends of the film's production designer, Luciana Arrighi. Originally belonging to Lady Ottoline Morrell, a member of the Bloomsbury crowd, the house is much larger in scale than that conceived by Forester. Ivory cheated the angle to only screen the front and one end, to convey the charming majesty of Howards End. The Shaplands moved into the large H-shaped back end of the home with stars Emma Thompson (Margaret) and Anthony Hopkins (Henry), who lived there together during the three-month shoot. Arrighi redecorated the front rooms and supervised the landscaping of the front lawns, replacing the plants with trees, vegetation, and wild flowers suited to the period.

Shortly after the release of the film, crowds of tourists from London descended on the little village, hoping to catch a glimpse of the cottage at the center of the film. "It wasn't that bad," says Mrs. Shapland. "People did come and look at it, but they weren't really intrusive. It didn't particularly bother us because we were right on the common so people could walk past anyway."

Jane in Austenland

In 1995, a *Masterpiece Theatre* production of *Pride and Prejudice*, directed by Simon Langton, brought the plight of the Benet sisters to the small screen in the UK and in the States, and Ang Lee and Emma Thompson brought *Sense and Sensibility* to the big screen, ushering in an era of Austenmania that persists today. Film versions of all Austen's novels followed over the next few years, including *Emma* (McGrath, 1996 and O'Hanlon, 2009), *Northanger Abbey* (Jones, 2007), and *Persuasion* (Michell, 1995 and Shergold, 2007) and *Love and Friendship*, based on *Lady Susan* (Stillman, 2016). Novels as diverse as Karen Fowler's romantic *The Jane Austen Book Club* (2005) and Seth Grahame-Smith's send up *Pride & Prejudice and Zombies* (2009) entertained Austen enthusiasts, including Helen Fielding, who wrote her own *Bridget Jones' Diary* (and its subsequent sequels) in 1999 after watching *Pride and Prejudice* on *Masterpiece Theatre*.

It's safe to say that the *Masterpiece Theatre* mini-series is largely responsible for this cottage industry that has translated into tourist packages for anyone interested in seeing "where it all began." This is keenly shown in Jerusha Hess' *Austenland* (2013), a light comedy starring Keri Russell and Jennifer Coolidge as devotees of the mini-series, duped into spending their savings on a trip to an English resort catering to Austen-crazed women desiring to "meet their Mr. Darcy." Run by a true entrepreneur, Mrs. Wattlesbrook (Jane Seymour) hires actors to provide a full Regency holiday (complete with closing night ball) designed to fulfill the heightened fantasies of each visitor. Jane Hayes (Russell) has watched the series so many times (in the company of a large cut-out of Colin Firth as Mr. Darcy) that any man she dates runs from her apartment, cringing from comparison. Following the holiday itself, the film critiques the heritage industry's exploitation of the romanticized version of the past, and indeed fictionalized romantic others.

In looking back at the novel, and the miniseries, it is interesting to see just how Austen might have foreseen the future. Seeking a solution to the "truth universally acknowledged" that "a single man in possession of a good fortune, must be in want of a wife" (1), the multi-part series was a smash in both sides of the Atlantic, picking up where the popular *Upstairs Downstairs* (1971–75; 2010–12) left off, feeding a need for high-minded romance in an episodic manner. As in the novel, one of the pivotal moments is Elizabeth Benet's (Jennifer Ehle) visit to Pemberley, the home of the elusive Mr. Darcy (Colin Firth); however, unlike the novel, the scene in this version becomes infamous as a startled Darcy confronts Miss Benet after a dive into a lake on the grounds. He emerges from the fall dripping wet, his shirt clinging to his chiseled chest, gazing with a sense of shy desire as he approaches her. Knowing this was not part of Austen's original, screenwriter Andrew Davies created the scene "to create an amusing moment in which Darcy tries to maintain his dignity while improperly dressed and sopping wet."

While solidifying its place in the pantheon of most romantic moments ever screened (reaching # 3 in a poll taken by *Time* magazine), the sequence comes as a result of Davies' reading Austen carefully for inspiration. In the novel, Elizabeth, the clever, witty Benet sister, is seriously wrong in both her perception and her feelings toward Darcy throughout, misreading his shyness and reserve as haughty condescension. When Elizabeth inadvertently arrives at Pemberley with her aunt and uncle, Mr. and Mrs. Gardiner, in the novel's third act, she immediately recognizes that the stately manor home reveals more about the character of Darcy than she has assumed:

> Elizabeth, as they drove along, watched for the first appearance of Pemberley Woods with some perturbation; and when at length they turned in at the lodge, her spirits were in a high flutter....
>
> Elizabeth's mind was too full for conversation, but she saw and admired every remarkable spot and point of view. They gradually ascended for half-a-mile, and then found themselves at the top of a considerable eminence, where the wood ceased, and the eye was instantly caught by Pemberley House, situated on the opposite side of a valley, into which the road with some abruptness wound. It was a large, handsome stone building, standing well on rising ground, and backed by a ridge of high woody hills; and in front, a stream of some natural importance was swelled into greater, but without any artificial appearance. Its banks were neither formal nor falsely adorned. Elizabeth was delighted. She had never seen a place for which nature had done more, or where natural beauty had been so little counteracted by an awkward taste. They were all of them warm in their admiration; and at that moment she felt that to be mistress of Pemberley might be something!
>
> The housekeeper came; a respectable-looking elderly woman, much less fine, and more civil, than she had any notion of finding her. They followed her into the dining-parlour. It was a large, well proportioned room, handsomely fitted up. Elizabeth, after slightly surveying it, went to a window to enjoy its prospect. The hill, crowned with wood, which they had descended, receiving increased abruptness from the distance, was a beautiful object. Every disposition of the ground was good; and she looked on the whole scene, the river, the trees scattered on its banks and the winding of the valley, as far as she could trace it, with delight. As they passed into other rooms these objects were taking different positions; but from every window there were beauties to be seen. The rooms were lofty and handsome, and their furniture suitable to the fortune of its proprietor; but Elizabeth saw, with admiration of his taste, that it was neither gaudy nor uselessly fine; with less of splendour, and more real elegance, than the furniture of Rosings [156].

It is evident Elizabeth expects Pemberley to reflect its owner, but it is the "real elegance" that catches her off guard. From their first meeting, Elizabeth judged Darcy as "a most disagreeable, horrid man" (10) filled with both "vanity and pride" (14), based solely on their first impressions of one another. However, as the novel moves forward, and Darcy and Elizabeth are brought together by the love shared between Jane, Elizabeth's older sister, and Bingley, Darcy's oldest friend, they begin to appreciate what one another might bring to their own coupledom. The visit to Pemberley solidifies this union of the spirits.

While we are not certain what Elizabeth expects in her visit, we witness first-hand the effect of Darcy's "taste," "neither gaudy nor uselessly fine." Instead, Elizabeth begins to reassess her former pronouncements based on her initial impressions of Pemberley, the manor home assisting in her redefining of Darcy. It is from this moment on that Elizabeth recognizes that her "prejudice" was brought on by her own "pride," casting Darcy's clumsy shyness as snobbery. The rest of the novel, in which Darcy proves himself worthy of the Benet clan, follows Elizabeth and Darcy as they come together at Pemberley, a united front.

Screening Elizabeth's visit to Pemberley "almost usurped the original novel in the minds of the public" remarks Deborah Cantwell, because of Andrew Davies' decision to charge the meeting of Elizabeth and Darcy. "Since it came out, every cultural reference to Jane Austen, and every adaptation, has had much to do with Andrew Davies as it does to Austen." Davis himself credits this with the decision to get adaptation out of the studio and into the great outdoors, much like Merchant and Ivory.

Scouring the countryside to secure the right location for Pemberley proved to be a challenge. "Houses on the scale of Pemberley are few and far between," says location manager Sam Breckman. "It is supposed to be in Derbyshire which would give a distinctive northern look, and it has to be very big and set in stunning scenery. Some people think Jane Austen was thinking of Chatsworth as Pemberley, but in fact Chatsworth was referred to in its own right in the novel." Knowing they had to get this right, the team looked far and wide for just the right location.

They settled on Lyme Park near Manchester for the exteriors, but had to find another set for the interiors when the management company changed and balked at having the film crew inside. The interiors were soon discovered at Sudbury Hall, whose rooms flowed more elegantly, lending the scenes when the housekeeper gives a tour to Lizzy and the Gardiners a more graceful feel, as Elizabeth's prideful heart begins to melt.

Using the lake to humanize Darcy, and making the meeting between Elizabeth and Darcy more comic was the real reason Davies wrote the scene.

> I wanted to make the adaptation very pro–Darcy, so I thought, "Let's start with him and Bingley galloping along on their horses—nobody has ever done that before." And the thing that sets the whole story off: Bingley seeing Netherfield Hall and being rich enough to make the snap decision to rent it for the season. Then I thought, "Let's have Elizabeth on a hillside seeing these two tasty blokes galloping along, and something about them makes her skip down the hill." I can remember writing those first pages and thinking, "This is a bit different from the usual Jane Austen adaptation."

However, the lake scene triggered what is known on the Internet as "Darcymania"— a swooning by women seeking their own romantic Darcy. Davies claims the scene was not set to spark romantic feelings, but was to be a comic way of bringing the couple together:

> When women started pinning Colin's picture to their walls, it was a puzzle and a surprise because I just thought it was a funny scene. It was about Darcy being a bloke, diving in his lake on a hot day, not having to be polite—and then he suddenly finds himself in a situation where he does have to be polite. So you have two people having a stilted conversation and politely ignoring the fact that one of them is soaking wet. I never thought it was supposed to be a sexy scene in any way.

While taking credit for the idea, Davies knows that the scene sparked interest in tourist groups set to capitalize on the miniseries popularity. For instance, the London-based P&P Tours, founded in the wake of the miniseries' popularity, takes visitors to both Lyme Park and Sudbury Hall locations, even though most simply want to see "Darcy's lake."

Downton Abbey *by Way of* Gosford Park

Julian Fellowes recalls that the first time he heard that Robert Altman wanted to travel to England to make *Gosford Park* (2007) was during a conversation with actor Bob Balaban, who told the screenwriter about Altman's desire to "pay homage to the Agatha Christie tradition, by creating a film that was "to examine the relationships between the classes in the context of a party at a large country house" such as those hosted in Christie's *The Mysterious Affair at Styles* (1920), *And Then There Were None* (1939), *The Hollow* (1951) and *The Mousetrap* (1952). Fellowes leaped at the chance even more when he spoke to Altman, who said the film would not be a "Who-Dunnit" but a "Who-Cares-Who-Dunnit," focusing the story on the characters and their relationships, rather than on the mystery itself. The subsequent film, *Gosford Park*, built itself from a class-oriented myth recounted by his aunt about a millionaire shop-owner named William Whitely:

> According to her version of the legend, Whitely used his female employees much as William McCordle is reputed to have used his. These wretched girls were fired if they became pregnant and many fell into lives of prostitution and despair. Many years later, Whitely was told there was a young man waiting to see him in his vast emporium not far from Kensington Palace. He went downstairs. His visitor informed him that he was in fact Whitely's illegitimate son, the child of one of his miserable cast-offs, and stabbed him to death on the spot [165].

This tale moved Fellowes to compose a screenplay that would focus on "characters from both upstairs and down" (164).

The film that developed, partly through Fellowes' script and partly through Altman's improvisational technique, focuses on a weekend at the McCordle Estate where Sir William (Michael Gambon) and his cool wife Lady Silvia (Kristen Scott Thomas) host a large family gathering that ends in Sir William's murder. Avoiding the "cliché of characters whom the audience is instructed to dislike" (165), Fellowes and Altman weave an intricate web of family intrigue upstairs and focus on the downstairs' parsing of events with witty performances from Helen Mirren (Mrs. Wilson), Emily Watson (Elsie), Derek Jacobi (Probert), Richard E. Grant (George), Alan Bates (Jennings) and Eileen Atkins (Mrs. Croft), showing the spectator how to understand the drama unfolding upstairs.

Altman selected Wrotham Park for his Gosford Park, a neo–Palladian English country house in Hertforshire, built in 1754. While other films have been set here, Altman and Fellowes wanted to be certain that the house that would take center stage in the film looked lived in, so as to represent a particular period in English history—the mid–1930s:

> Bob wanted it [the film] to take place as late as possible before the end of the way of life. Of course fragments of it would continue until the present day but, as a nation-wide accepted manner of existence, it was finished by the Second World War so that meant the nineteen-thirties. I was certain that it had to be a shooting party as the rituals of shooting echo the rituals by which they lived their lives and sport was the *raison d'etre* of this existence so that tied us to the winter months. In real life, within seven or eight years the younger servants would be called up. Later most of the younger women, would follow them into war work.... Robert Altman is especially keen, when dealing with a period subject, that one should never lose the sense that these were real people leading real lives. I remember his discussion with Jenny Beavan, the designer: "I want clothes," he said, "not costumes" [169–170].

Fellowes account of the filming at Wrotham Park shows how much he learned about the process of writing dialogue in a natural manner—something that would certainly separate his *Downton Abbey* from other costume dramas. The success of *Gosford Park* continues to this day, as the Byng Family, owners of the home since 1847, opened the home as a commercial venue for heritage-themed weddings and receptions, charging up to £90,000 (roughly $111,753) per day for the 2,500-acre estate.

Downton Abbey

The success of *Downton Abbey* attracts large groups of fans, particularly from America, to its filming locations in the UK, the most famous being the Highclere Castle estate in Berkshire, England, currently home to the Eighth Earl and Countess of Carnarvon.

Downton Abbey is now considered a significant driver in promoting Highclere as a world famous heritage building; as a result of *Downton Abbey*'s popularity, the house has experienced a rapid transformation from "relative obscurity to become one of the UK's most famous stately homes." The rise of this formerly-obscure estate into such a popular landmark is not due to the series alone, but is the result of careful strategies aimed at exploiting the international popularity of British heritage films and television series in America, and commercializing on the house's newly discovered fame and identity as a film tourism location. With regard to the benefits of film-induced tourism upon heritage sites, Lady Carnarvon has spoken candidly, elaborating on the impact that *Downton Abbey* has had upon Highclere Castle. However, Lady Carnarvon is also aware of the temporary nature of the opportunity, joking that her family and staff are "all working jolly hard to make hay while the sun shines." The success of *Downton Abbey*, paired with the careful marketing of Highclere Castle as a location in tandem, has resulted in growing numbers of visitors to the house. *Downton*-related tours to Highclere are generally fully booked during the tourist season when the house is opened to visitors for short periods of time, welcoming over 1200 visitors a day.

Downton's success, and its quantifiable importance for the Highclere estate, is made evident by its relative fortunes before the series' broadcast. Despite the fact that the house had been used as a location for several films and television series since the 1980s, the estate was suffering and unable to generate the kind of financial income needed for preservation, maintenance and running costs. Moreover, before *Downton* put Highclere on the map, the Carnarvon family relied heavily upon the income earned from letting the house out for conferences, weddings and other corporate events, as well as allowing it to be marketed alongside certain brands (for instance, Welsh jewelers *Clogau Gold*'s "Heritage" campaign). The family has publicized the location during several visits to the *Downton Abbey* sets by current members of the British Royal Family, most notably the Duchess of Cambridge, Kate Middleton; the image of the Duchess as a "fan" personally participating in heritage tourism activities has also been instrumental in creating wider-world interest in Highclere Castle, especially where American audiences are concerned. The astonishing popularity of *Downton Abbey* in both the UK and the United States has only added to the location's popularity.

The credit sequence that opens each episode (starting at 1:2; it does not open the Christmas Specials) establishes the manor house as the central concern of the series. As the names of cast members appear and dissolve, a variety of images flash by: a man walking a lively Golden Retriever; a Palladian window draped in damask, the view of a carefully manicured lawn; a tinkling bell swinging, calling for assistance; a box of letters waiting for the post in the foreground, a woman in an apron walking up a flight of stairs in the background; a yellow-rimmed plate with sterling flatware laid on a table, a ruler in the lower right-corner measuring the plate's distance from a knife; a shimmering oil lamp next to a vase of flowers, one or two petals gently falling in slow motion; a feather duster lightly tickling the pendants of a Venetian glass chandelier; each image overlaps one another as John Lunn's score carries the viewer back in time to Edwardian England. The final image before the title card, a crane shot slowly gliding up to reveal the largess of Highclare Castle / Downton Abbey builds a dramatic effect, inviting the viewer into the dual nature of the building, serving as both the Crawley's home and as a workplace for the domestics who reside downstairs. The fact that each image shows an activity in addition to an object illustrates the very invisibility of the servants who wait table, who dust, who set things right, who keep things going. The binary nature of the show is captured in the title card (first appearing in 1:3): an image of Downton in black against a white field, and a reverse image below in white on a field of black, a reflection, of sorts, that illustrates the dual plot lines that will comprise the series, reflecting, in a way, the Victorian multi-plot novels of Dickens, Trollope, Eliot and Thackeray.

Throughout its six seasons, the Downton estate becomes more than a setting. In fact, its fate becomes a character and the overall focus at times. Each time the estate is compromised, the crisis revolves around stories of how the Crawleys will manage to "save" Downton from ruin. In Season One, the death of the Crawley heir, Patrick, affianced to Lady Mary, sets the tone as both Sir Robert and Lady Cora begin to struggle with the idea that a new heir will soon descend on them and their three daughters, who cannot inherit the estate due to an entailment. Having Patrick and his father die aboard the *Titanic* in April 1912, not only sets the show within the actual historical moment, but it helps us to understand the obligation the Crawleys, as well as the servants, face as they acknowledge how their fates are linked to the manor house—a new heir / tenant not only turns the present Crawley family out of the house, but puts the livelihood of the servant class in jeopardy.[4] When Mr. Bates arrives, and witnesses the turmoil Patrick's death causes, he says, "None of this is ours," meaning nothing in and of the house materially belongs to the servants. But the silent glares from the staff, particularly from Mr. Carson, shows that, in fact, a true servant feels the life of the house *is* theirs, and the problems of the family upstairs do, in fact, belong to each one of them.

From the start, the plight of the estate is tied to not only the Crawley women but to the servants, often blurring the boundaries between their roles. For instance, in Season One, one of the main stories is when Lady Sybil takes on the cause of Gwen, the kitchen-maid, who dreams of leaving service to become a secretary. Sybil, already immersed in the suffrage movement, pretty much adopts Gwen, loaning her clothes suitable for an interview, serving as a reference, ultimately driving her to one interview in secret (1:4). This storyline paves the way for Sybil and Branson's ultimate courtship and marriage. The way that the series intertwines the upstairs family with the downstairs crowd becomes a hallmark of the series, perhaps the most obliging nod to American audiences who do not always understand separation based on class and service. Season Two sees Downton transformed in a unique manner as the series focuses on the impact of World War I on the home-front. After a great deal of conversation, the Crawleys convert their home into a convalescent center, complicating their lives as many severely wounded soldiers come to the Abbey as Cora, Lady Edith and Lady Sybil learn that they are made for more than just dressing for afternoon tea and perching on a sofa. The idea came about, Fellowes says, when he heard that "in fact, in real life, Highclere Castle became a hospital" during the war. "The Countess of Carnarvon at that time was a brave, adventurous and vivid figure, and she decided that the proper use of the house was as a hospital, and she paid to kit it out," though the family moved from the premises during that time. Thomas, the scamp, and William, the country-boy, both enlist with Matthew, and all three return wounded—Thomas deliberately maiming himself to go home (2:3); Matthew and William gassed at Amiens in 1918, one of the most brutal battles of the war (2:5). William ultimately dies, his insides rotted by the lethal gas; Matthew crippled (temporarily) after being shot while trying to escape. The war continues to burden the servants on the home-front as Daisy marries William on his deathbed, and Mrs. Patmore learns that her nephew, Archie, is shot as a traitor after being traumatized by the ugliness of war (2:6). As the war comes to a close, and the home's inhabitants try to return to normalcy, Lady Sybil's is the one voice that rebels,

> SYBIL: Doesn't it feel odd to have the rooms back?
> EDITH: And only us to sit in them. I suppose we'll get used to it.
> SYBIL: I don't want to get used to it.
> EDITH: What do you mean?
> SYBIL: I know what it is to work now. To have a full day. To be tired in a good way. I don't want to start dress fittings, or paying calls, or standing behind the guns [379].

However, while Sybil is the one to articulate her desire to stay active, it is obvious that the war changed both Edith and Cora in dramatically positive manners. Edith learned to drive; Cora learned to manage the day-to-day operations of running a hospital. All three of the women from this point forward appear disinterested in returning Downton to its former status. Instead, the war makes the house become a symbol of modern change.

Fellowes touches on this further, admitting that this realization is what sets the tone for Downton's changing role as the series continues:

> For me, this is a key moment. We begin a theme here that we play on through the third and forth series. It is charting the beginning of the decline of these families. After the war, although this way of life did survive—more, in fact, than many people think—nevertheless the writing was on the wall for those who could read it. Despite most of the upper classes going on in the old way until the Second World War, albeit on a reduced scale, there were families that threw in the towel even at this point [315].

The Abbey's fate once more is placed center-stage in Season Three, when it becomes evident that Lord Grantham's investments with a Canadian Railroad put the estate in jeopardy once more. This time, Robert's mismanagement centers the cause in the changing times, when, according to Fellowes, "the vast majority of these houses that stayed in private hands" began to dilute their large staffs after the war, as upward mobility became more doable in England. For the elderly servants, such as Mr. Carson, Mrs. Hughes and Mrs. Patmore, the fate of the Crawleys is, in fact, their fate as well. In a footnote to the script, Fellowes explains why "the fact that this way of life will not go on forever is a theme that trickles throughout the show. Human beings usually assume that the way they live now will see them out and there are periods of history where it's fairly true. What we're not prepared for is absolute change and yet it happens" (216). The series, following historical trends, reflects this moment when many of the large estates faced foreclosure due to poor investments—this was a real threat to most servants' livelihoods.

The arrival of Cora's mother, the American Mrs. Lewinson, causes the household to turn out its best to entice her to invest in the household once more, and the conversations below-stairs mirror those upstairs as the fate of the Abbey becomes a *cause célèbre*. At the dinner welcoming the return of Martha and her millions, the conversation turns to the "excess" of the household and its traditions. To Violet, "nothing succeeds like excess" (3:2), and the efforts of the staff to stage a show is evident as everyone joins in the effort to secure the estate. Mary claims, "the role of houses like Downton is to protect tradition." However, Martha, voicing her good old American Puritanism, states, "Only if you think it's worth it" (106). As Fellowes says, "Mary is trying to evoke in Martha an emotion that the older woman does not share (113). After Martha saves the day with her "picnic," Mary and Violet use the opportunity to commit her to saving the estate:

MARTHA: But of course I'll help you in any way that I can.
MARY: Thank heaven.
VIOLET: Oh, it seems our family owes Downton's survival to the Levinsons not once, but twice.
MARTHA: Oh. I'm sorry, but you've misunderstood me. No, I cannot rescue Downton. It's a shame if it has to go, but I can't.
MARY: But ... why not?
MARTHA: Because your grandpa tied the money down. He felt that the Crawley family had quite enough.
MARY: But you said you'd help us.
MARTHA: I can entertain all of you in Newport and in New York, and I can add to Cora's dress allowance, but that's all. My income might be generous, but I cannot touch the capital. Besides, Mary ... the world has changed. These houses were built for another age. Are you quite sure you want to continue with the bother of it all?
MARY: Quite sure [130].

Before returning to America, Martha takes one more dig at the insecure circumstances, this time with Robert:

ROBERT: Sometimes I feel like a creature in the wilds, whose natural habitat is gradually being destroyed.
Martha: But some animals adapt to new surroundings. Seems a better choice than extinction.
ROBERT: I don't think it is a choice. I think it's what's in you.
MARTHA: Well, let's hope what's in you will carry you through these times to a safer shore [135].

Of course, Matthew's inheritance from his late fiancée's father comes in time to save the home—just in time for Matthew's own untimely death at the end of Season Three, following close on the heels of Lady's Sybil's in childbirth. While the Abbey drowns in sorrow at the end of Season Three, the Crawley's estate is secure to maintain this way of life for a bit longer.[5]

While the tax bill that arrives (4:3) helps stir intrigue, the abrupt death of Matthew places the estate in the hands of the one-year old Master George, Mary only being allowed to act as its ward, making it appear all the more important that Mary marry sooner than she might like. The servants' response to Lady Mary's saga is reflected in their dinner conversations, as they worry about the downsizing of the local estates, wondering when Downton will do the same. The idea that Downton serves as an employer pervades the series, and the Crawleys understand that their success will ensure the future of the locals as well. Opening in 1922, the series for the next two seasons contends with the complexities of the modern world impacting the traditions that make the Abbey a character in its own right.

With Lady Mary in mourning, a parade of suitors begin to descend on Downton, each man hoping for a chance to rescue the young widow from her weeds. It is Mary's plight in Season Four that is the basis of most conversations in the servants' hall because her decisions, regarding marriage and money, affect the fate of them all. When Mary and Tom form the bond to take up the management of the estate, Robert, for the first time, must reckon with the fact that he cannot any longer be in charge. In fact, Mary and Tom's plan for farming even more land for raising more livestock, embracing a more scientific means of farming the estate conflict with Robert's idea: "If you do not respect the past, we cannot build a future" (4:5). But Mary does respect the past, and her willingness to run the estate with Tom by her side, particularly after Matthew's letter is found among his personal items which names her his heir, forces Downton into becoming a modern day organization: "It's time to get used to something different." (4:7). So while Anna deals with surviving an attack by Tony Gillingham's manservant (4:3); Edith contends with a secret pregnancy (4:6); Lady Rose takes up with a black jazz band leader, Jack Ross (4:6); and Robert travels to America to save Cora's brother, Harold, from the Teapot Dome Scandal (4:7), Mary fends off three suitors all trying to remove her from her modern self. And yet, Mary continues to work to "save Downton for George" (4:9) and as Season Five begins, in 1924, the estate appears stable enough to permit the melodrama to proliferate.

By the start of Season Six—set in 1925—the trend in downsizing estates becomes the over-riding fear of the Crawleys; even though the farm appears a success, the changing economy of England puts greater strains on the maintenance of said estates. The fate of the Mallerton estate, auctioned off piece-by-piece, makes for a somber transition. Robert tells his daughters, "This life is over for us ... learn from us" (6:1), just what Mary and Tom have done all along, economizing with attention to detail.

One of the more interesting stories of this season focuses on Daisy, the kitchen maid, who determines to "fix the system" by educating herself to do more than just assist in a kitchen. Even though the Crawleys wander through the estate in a daze, wondering at how Lord Mallerton can sell everything, including his grandmother's portrait, Daisy takes the tour to heart, wanting to defend her father-in-law. After hearing that Mr. Mason was to lose his tenancy on the Mallerton estate, Daisy makes his plight her new cause, facing off with the Hendersons, the new owners, at the estate auction. "So it's you who insists on serving notice to men who have given their whole life to the land... you boot out families who have been here for generations. What gives you the right." She continues, turning to Lord Mallerton: "A man who sells his wedding presents.... Do you know what it meant for a farmer to give half a crown? Or don't you care? Mr. Mason has given his whole life to this farm.... Like his father and his grandfather before him. But where's the gratitude?" Daisy's new found tongue, while spontaneously naïve is honestly sincere in its passion. With her new education, Daisy begins to see that life has other opportunities in store for her, and she understands that her limitations have been foisted upon her by the class system. While Mrs. Patmore refers to her as "Madame Le Farge," Daisy with her new understanding of the class struggle, realizes that the new order will make room for class mobility. In going to the Crawleys to fight for Mr. Mason to take over Yew Tree Farm, Daisy articulates the need of the ruling class to work with the servant class to constitute a new way of doing things.

Which brings us full circle—to the opening of this essay—where Downton Abbey is opened to the public. Much to Lord Grantham's disgust, the Crawleys do put on display for the benefit of the hospital, and the crowds line up for a chance to see what the Crawleys believe to be "a perfectly ordinary house" (6:6). However, spectators of the series know that here is so much more to the transformation of the Abbey into a museum—in fact, the entire series has put on display the inner workings of the house in such a way that the intrigues and celebrations are part of that transformation. Focusing the series on one level (upstairs) or the other (downstairs) would have skewed the experience; bringing both together, and making the house itself the soul of the series invests the audience in a singular way, making Downton's fate *our* fate, teaching us all to be mindful of the past so as to move toward the future together, with grace and dignity for all. In the final episode, when Lady Grantham declares the ending "English," she speaks universally. Happiness is relative, so long as it remains "adaptable."

Notes

1. Taken from episode 6:6. In the brief, "6d" refers to sixpence in pre-decimalized sterling, as British currency was decimalized in 1971.

2. Though the BBC's *War & Peace* was an adaptation of Leo Tolstoy's Russian literary epic and was filmed on location in Russia, Lithuania and Latvia, it was a British/ American-produced series (BBC Cymru Wales, the Weinstein Company and A&E Networks), written for the screen by Andrew Davies—whose credits include several British serial period dramas including *Mr Selfridge*, *Little Dorrit* (BBC, 2008), *Bleak House* (BBC, 2005) and *The Line of Beauty*.

3. *Poldark* and *Victoria* debuted to a particularly high share in audience figures in the UK, with *Poldark* attracting seven million viewers with its 2015 debut, and *Victoria* receiving 6.1 million viewers.

4. According to Julian Fellowes, this was an important decision on his part:
The challenge of an opening episode, as I keep saying, is to give the audience enough information so that they can follow the show. The reason I chose the sinking of the *Titanic* to begin with, was the *Titanic* is an iconic disaster. There are very few people who've never heard of the Titanic and most of us have a fairly accurate idea of when it took place, which is just before the First World War. By sinking two off-screen characters on the *Titanic* is a shorthand way of saying we are in England and it is just before the First World War. These characters are not living in Queen Victoria's reign, but during the aftermath of the long Edwardian summer, in that seemingly placid period just before the war would shake everything up. The audience knows all this because the script contains one word, *Titanic*, or indeed from the moment when Robert opens the newspaper and they see those familiar four funnels [12].

5. About the ending of Season Three, Fellowes writes,
The demonstration of Matthew and Mary's happiness was the scene I wanted to end the episode with. And so I spoke to Dan Stevens. He had been very definite about leaving the show, as we know, but I asked him if he would reconsider, let this episode end happily before coming back in Season Four to be killed, or die in some way, right at the start. He thought about it, but finally just felt he couldn't. I was very sorry, but I also sympathized with what he was trying to do, and so I had quite mixed feelings. Anyway, I knew I had to kill him in the end. Then I woke up one morning and realized that his decision meant we could have a six-month gap between his death and resuming the story the following year. We wouldn't need to have funerals or memorials and Mary reeling at the onset of her grief. We could pick it up again when Mary was beginning to come out of it, which actually had far more dramatic potential than her just sobbing. And so although I was very, very sorry to spoil a lot of Christmas evenings, nevertheless it allowed us a far more interesting role for Mary, both to act and to watch, in Season Four [556].

Works Cited

Austen, Jane. *Pride and Prejudice*. New York: Norton, 1993.

Fellowes, Julian. *Downton Abbey: The Complete Scripts, Season One*. New York: William Morrow, 2012.

_____. *Downton Abbey: The Complete Scripts, Season Two*. New York: William Morrow, 2013.

_____. *Downton Abbey: The Complete Scripts, Season Three*. New York: William Morrow, 2014.

_____. *Gosford Park: The Shooting Script*. New York: Newmarket, 2002.

Forster, E.M. *Howard's End*. Boston: Bedford, 1997.

Revisiting *Gosford Park*

Downton Abbey, *American Audiences* *and the British Heritage Genre*

GAYLE SHERWOOD MAGEE

"Could I ever persuade you to revisit the territory of Gosford Park, but in a multiepisode television environment?"—Gareth Neame, producer of *Downton Abbey*, to Julian Fellowes

In 1999, Bob Balaban approached director Robert Altman to do a project, and the two agreed to develop an Agatha Christie–like British murder-mystery film. Balaban and Altman had met one another over the years, but had never worked together. Balaban, known primarily as an actor for his appearances in *Waiting for Guffman* (1996), *Best in Show* (2000), and the television show *Seinfeld* (1989–96), in which he had a recurring role, had worked as director and producer on smaller projects. As Balaban later recalled, "I thought it would be really, really interesting to put Robert Altman in a very traditional circumstance, which would mean England."[1]

By 1999, the seventy-five-year-old Altman had established a reputation as a maverick filmmaker with an uneven track record dating from his most successful feature, *M*A*S*H* (1970), to a string of critical successes (chief among them *Nashville*, 1975) and misses. The 1990s had been particularly good to Altman after more than a decade in exile from the Hollywood studio system, when films such as *The Player* (1992) and *Short Cuts* (1993) received critical acclaim and re-established his viability at the box office. Both films embody the emerging independent major movement, or Indiewood, which saw art house films financed, marketed, and distributed through increasingly mainstream channels and which fueled the careers of auteurs Quentin Tarantino and Paul Thomas Anderson among others. While his health and career faltered with the disastrous *Ready to Wear* (1994) and uneven *Kansas City* (1996), Altman rebounded with *Cookie's Fortune* (1999), a well-received, high-profile, star-studded semi-independent film that opened the Sundance Film Festival that year. In this context, Balaban's proposal caught Altman's attention, as the project held out the possibility for Altman to further secure his footing by developing a film with broad international and specifically transatlantic appeal.

Altman and Balaban drafted a general idea for their film, which centered on a murder in an English country house during a weekend hunting party, with the aristocratic guests as well as their servants as suspects. The filmmaker may have had, from an early stage, plans to pay homage to Jean Renoir's 1939 film *Le règle du jeu* (*The Rules of the Game*), a longtime favorite of Altman for its large ensemble cast, critique of the aristocracy, self-reflexive perspective, and prescient forebodings of the Second World War.[2] Altman and Balaban commissioned brief treatments from two potential screenwriters interested in fully developing their concept. The first came from Eileen Atkins and Jean Marsh, the co-creators of the BBC television series *Upstairs, Downstairs* (1971–77): as Balaban and Altman acknowledged, they planned to focus their film on the servants and masters of a British manor house, and Atkins and Marsh's highly popular and critically praised series served as one model for their project. But it was the second treatment by Julian Fellowes that Altman and Balaban chose to pursue, and within a few months Fellowes had completed a draft of the screenplay for *The Back of the Tapestry*.[3] (Atkins would be cast as the cantankerous cook, Mrs. Croft, in the final film.) Later, the film was renamed *Gosford Park* and released in 2001, and Fellowes would win an Academy Award for his Best Original Screenplay.

Gosford Park and later Fellowes' own television series *Downton Abbey* (2011–2016) were built on the foundations of the Indiewood-era British heritage film and television model, one of the most commercially and critically successful genres of the previous decade, with proven appeal on both sides of the Atlantic. The genre's defining elements include historical plots based on or inspired by literary sources, as well as elaborate period costumes, luxurious visual design, and historically accurate staging. The heritage genre through the 1990s was marketed as independently produced and valuing cultural over commercial value (although, in fact, many heritage productions were created by major studios as noted below), with the intimate and usually leisurely film style associated with an auteurist aesthetic—all of which represent a close match with Altman's signature directorial style.[4] These elements appear as early as *Chariots of Fire* (Hudson, 1981) and *A Room with a View* (Ivory, 1985), and coalesced with the television miniseries, telefilms, and feature films of the "Austen year" of 1995–96.

The long legacy of the Indiewood-period British heritage genre and its appeal to American viewers informs the multiple correspondences between *Gosford Park* and *Downton Abbey*, as primary source materials from the Robert Altman Archives and close viewings of the film and television series will reveal. First, significant similarities emerge in casting, character, plot, setting, cinematography, and other visual references, particularly in *Downton Abbey*'s premiere episode, reaching beyond these two works to connect with the larger heritage field dating back to the 1990s and the Americanization of several British productions. These similarities as well as differences reflect the changing climate of media production, consumption, and financing, especially for the products' targeted to American markets. Second, a close listening to each soundtrack reinforces the connections between the works and with earlier heritage productions, particularly in the use of specific instrumentation and musical genre in the opening credits; carefully selected diegetic (source) performances and nondiegetic (underscoring); and the blurring of boundaries between these musical modes. A final consideration of the reception of *Gosford Park* and *Downton Abbey* reveals evolving contemporary views concerning class, especially for viewers within the United States in the wake of the global financial recession.

Building Gosford Park *and* Downton Abbey

The closest models for *Gosford Park* and *Downton Abbey* within the heritage genre are the films of the Merchant Ivory production company, consisting of an international team based in New York that included American director James Ivory, Indian producer Ismail Merchant, and German-Polish screenwriter Ruth Prawer Jhabvala. Altman recognized the influence of the company, stating that "had [Merchant Ivory] not done their films, *Gosford Park* wouldn't have been made, as there wouldn't have been a reference," and the same can be said of *Downton Abbey*.[5] Merchant Ivory's earlier films, such as *A Room with a View*, were aimed primarily at audiences in the United Kingdom with only limited art-house releases in the United States. However, the team secured U.S. financing and distribution for their 1992 adaptation of E.M. Forster's novel *Howards End*, which proved economically and critically successful in the United States. Their next film, *The Remains of the Day* (1993), was financed and distributed by Disney/Miramax using the sophisticated tools and substantial resources of a major Hollywood studio. Thus by 1993 Merchant Ivory represented another arm of the mini-major or major-independent experience of Altman, Tarantino, Anderson and others: the takeover of "the art film market … [by] Hollywood majors who either created a classics division or acquired the leading independent art film distributors," according to film scholar Tino Balio.[6]

Merchant Ivory's stateside success, industry consolidation, and the art film/Hollywood hybrid produced a flurry of Jane Austen adaptations of U.S. and UK pedigree, with six new releases in 1995–1996. According to Linda Troost and Sayre Greenfield, although only three of these six originated in Hollywood, "the rest [were] influenced by it."[7] Each of the six films "Americanized" the British heritage film of the previous decade to some extent. Most offered English stars already familiar to U.S. audiences combined with authentic locations, U.S.-based directors, producers, and studios. Columbia's *Sense and Sensibility* (1996), for example, featured stars Emma Thompson and Hugh Grant, director Ang Lee (who received an undergraduate degree from the University of Illinois, Urbana-Champaign, and a graduate degree from New York University), and producer Sydney Pollack, among others. While the highly influential miniseries *Pride and Prejudice* (1995) offered no familiar faces to American audiences, it was co-produced by the BBC with WGBH, the Boston-based, PBS production company that produces content for *Masterpiece Theatre*.[8]

As in these earlier heritage films, both *Gosford* and *Downton* reflect a carefully balanced internationalism in their financing, production history, and casting choices. For *Gosford*, the film faced an uphill battle for investors who found the screenplay puzzling, according to Fellowes: "For the people putting up the money, it was terribly frightening. Here was this film about this very arcane world that nobody knew the rules about. For one thing, the servants took their employers' names downstairs—it was very quirky. The executives couldn't understand it."[9] Balaban recalled that the premise of Altman directing a heritage film "frightened people, the investors, to see Robert Altman directing a movie that you're used to seeing from Merchant Ivory because it had to be respectful and Bob is not respectful."[10] With funding finally in place, Altman traveled to London to meet with actors along with the film's casting director Mary Selway.

At which point the funding fell through, even as actors such as Maggie Smith and Michael Gambon began committing to the project "without dates or a contract or anything else," according to Balaban:

We thought we had the financing lined up. It was enough to get Bob over to London.... And it fell apart. And in between it falling apart and coming back together, we tried everything.... And there [Altman] was in England and practically mortgaging his house, as we were all thinking of doing, and so the strain financially was horrendous.[11]

Despite pressure to replace Fellowes as head writer, to rewrite the script to provide a more satisfying conclusion, and to make the casting and film's premise more accessible to American audiences, Altman "just wouldn't let it happen," as Fellowes recalled.[12] Altman, Balaban, and the film's co-producer David Levy frantically pursued new investors, with little luck. At nearly the last moment, the project received funding from the British Film Council, a fund designed to promote investment in the British filmmaking industry, established by the government and financed by lottery proceeds.

The film is neither predominantly U.S. nor British in terms of its cast, crew, production history, plot, and characters—which served as one of the main obstacles for American investors. On one hand, the director, all of the producers, and most of the pre- and post-production crew were based in Hollywood. Yet the cinematographer, composers (of original and adapted music), most of the actors, and the casting director were British and based in England where the project was filmed in its entirety. As a feature film rather than a television series, *Gosford* made use of its significantly larger budget and compressed production schedule (rehearsals and filming took place in March and April 2001) to hire some of the best known English theatrical and cinematic actors simultaneously familiar to U.S. audiences: Academy Award nominee Kirsten Scott Thomas (Lady Sylvia) from *Four Weddings and a Funeral* (1994), *The English Patient* (1996), and studio-sponsored *The Horse Whisperer* (1998); two-time Academy Award winner Maggie Smith (Countess Trentham) from Merchant Ivory's *A Room with a View* (1986), plus the coeval *Harry Potter and the Sorcerer's Stone* (2001); Emmy Award and Academy Award winner Helen Mirren (Mrs. Parks) from the BBC's *Prime Suspect* series (1991–96), which aired on PBS in the United States; Jeremy Northam (Ivor Novello) from *Emma* (1996, Miramax release); and Derek Jacobi (Probert, the valet) in *Henry V* (1989), *Dead Again* (1991), and *Cadfael* (1994–98), another PBS favorite. Of course, Altman himself was the main drawing card for U.S. audiences, although Bob Balaban would have been known through his recent film and television appearances, as well as earlier character roles in *Midnight Cowboy* (1969) and *Close Encounters of the Third Kind* (1977).

Like *Gosford*, *Downton* struggled to find investors at first, but in this case because of increased competition in the heritage television market. The series began life at Carnival Films, once an independent British film company with a strong track record in heritage drama that had been purchased by American-based media conglomerate NBCUniversal in 2008. *Downton Abbey* was one of the new subsidiary's first projects. Gareth Neame, executive producer and head of Carnival Films, was "looking for a production partner or a broadcaster in the United States" and approached Rebecca Eaton, the executive producer of *Masterpiece Theater*, who initially passed on *Downton Abbey* in favor of a new version of *Upstairs, Downstairs* produced by the BBC.[13] Neame approached HBO, the History Channel, and even Carnival's new parent company NBCUniversal, with no luck. Eventually, Eaton changed her mind and *Downton Abbey* was coproduced by WGBH, by now one of the most established channels for distributing heritage media to American audiences. Thus, while fully immersed in British heritage culture, production talent, writers, and actors, *Downton Abbey*'s foundation rests on American funding and distribution, unlike *Gosford* which depended on British funding for its existence. With episodes costing a million pounds apiece, and that financing coming from American backers directly (through WGBH) and indirectly (through NBCUniversal), the show needed to reach a wide audience within the United States to recoup its considerable investment.[14]

Likewise, Fellowes and his collaborators on *Downton* cast faces familiar to American PBS viewers as well as fans of earlier British heritage pieces. The most notable carryover is Maggie Smith, whose similarly named *Gosford* character of Lady Trentham provides a close model for *Downton*'s Lady Grantham. Additionally, Elizabeth McGovern (Lady Cora Crawley) would be familiar to an older segment of *Downton*'s American viewership from her earlier career in the 1980s, in mainstream films such as *Ordinary People* (Redford, 1980), *Ragtime* (Forman, 1981), *Once Upon a Time in America* (Leone, 1984), and *She's Having a Baby* (Hughes, 1988). A *Vanity Fair* feature on "the transcendently transatlantic" McGovern helped to promote the U.S. premiere of the show in January 2011 while connecting with a larger, more diverse audience, as *Masterpiece Theater* producer Rebecca Eaton recalled:

> The piece meant that *Downton* was going to have huge U.S. visibility in *Vanity Fair*, just weeks before our broadcast. A magazine feature like that for an upcoming TV show is more precious than rubies.... The *Vanity Fair* coverage launched us into a new orbit of media visibility. A large segment of its readership overlaps with our audience, and even better, they skew a little younger.[15]

Many of *Downton*'s other actors had appeared prior to 2010 on British-produced dramas (costume or otherwise) rebroadcast on PBS: Michelle Dockery and Jim Carter in BBC's *Cranford*, 2007–09, for example, and Brendan Coyle in the final installment of the long-running ITV Granada/PBS favorite *Prime Suspect*. Hugh Bonneville had even appeared in several episodes of a short-lived CBS sitcom in 2006, *Courting Alex*. As such, the *Downton* cast was clearly meant to trigger U.S. viewers' memories of heritage dramas of the recent past.

Beyond crucial casting decisions, both *Gosford* and *Downton* share similar characters and storylines, albeit developed differently as appropriate to a feature film versus a six-series (or, in the United States, season) television program. Indeed, Neame initially approached Fellowes with the idea of revisiting the work he had done for *Gosford*. As Neame recalled, "I said [to Fellowes,] 'Could I ever persuade you to revisit the territory of *Gosford Park*, but in a multiepisode television environment, where you can have that whole cast, but week upon week, so that viewers can get to know them and invest in them as characters?'"[16] (Fellowes' initial reaction to the idea was muted, but changed when Neame told him. "I think you could make a lot of money.")[17] Since both consist of newly written material rather than adaptations of literary sources, Fellowes had a fair amount of freedom to invent characters and develop storylines in *Downton* particularly, which makes similarities between the two all the more noticeable, especially in the transposition of the haughty, meddling, disdainful Lady Trentham into Lady Grantham, played by the same high-profile actress in each production. Other similarities abound, including the dignified butler who is hiding a secret (Mr. Carson's background in vaudeville in *Downton*, Mr. Jennings' [Alan Bates] imprisonment as a conscientious objector during the First World War in *Gosford*); the frazzled maid who answers to both the kitchen and the housekeeper (Daisy and Dorothy); an untrustworthy footman (Thomas and George); the three upstairs sisters faced with marrying for title, money, or love (Ladies Mary, Edith, and Sybil compared with Ladies Sylvia, Louisa, and Lavinia); and representatives of the middle-class who are drawn into the stratified world of upstairs aristocracy and downstairs servants, and belonging, at least initially in *Downton* and permanently in *Gosford*, to neither (Matthew Crawley and Mabel Nesbitt).

Yet the series format of *Downton* allowed its plot and characters to grow far beyond the general similarities shared with its predecessor. While the three sisters in *Gosford* have made their choices and live unhappily with them (Lady Sylvia having married the boorish Sir William McCordle for money, Lady Louisa who wed Lord Stockbridge for title, and Lady Lavinia who married the unlucky Colonel Meredith for love), *Downton*'s three ladies follow evolving trajectories that lead in surprising directions (Lady Mary's unexpected widowhood, or Lady Sybil's death in childbirth, for example). And in *Downton* Fellowes introduces original characters who revise the dynamics of *Gosford*, replacing the latter's low-born McCordle with the noble Lord Crawley as head of the family and manor, or counterbalancing the cutting Lady Grantham with Mrs. Isobel Crawley, an educated, independent middle-class woman.

Downton also provided Fellowes, who serves as the creator and head writer of the series, with a greater opportunity to realize his own scripts on screen than in *Gosford*, where Altman was the authority.[18] (Remembering his reaction to Altman overruling his suggestions at times, Fellowes recalled, "We'd have these spats…. We were just two fat men fighting.")[19] One example of this latitude is the more overt representation of homosexuality in *Downton* compared with *Gosford*. Downton Abbey's footman Thomas has various gay relationships over the course of the series, beginning with a somewhat explicit scene of his affair with a Duke in the first episode.[20] By contrast, suggestions of Ivor Novello's homosexuality were written into the *Gosford* script by Fellowes and filmed by Altman, but entirely edited out of the final theatrical version.[21] Instead, only one scene regarding homosexuality survives, portraying an ongoing gay relationship between producer Weissman (Bob Balaban) and Henry Denton (Ryan Phillippe) that is mentioned but not shown.

Perhaps the most important character, however, is the great house itself, the country manor after which both productions are named. Not only do these estates represent the link between master and servant: they stand as physical manifestations of many of the characteristics of earlier heritage films as well, particularly those of the Merchant Ivory films and the Austen adaptations of the mid–1990s. The significance of each is established at the outset—in the opening titles of *Gosford* and the first episode of *Downton*—through visual and musical tropes that telegraph the relationship between each production and the longer history and larger meaning of heritage media.

Downton's *Soundtrack*

From its opening moments, *Downton* explicitly evokes the British heritage genre made familiar to American audiences in previous decades. Indeed, one of the most common means of starting most heritage productions involves an establishing shot of the English country home, whether revealed through the windshield of a vintage car traveling down a lane (*The Remains of the Day*), alongside gamboling sheep and a horse and carriage (*Persuasion*, BBC telefilm, 1995), gentleman galloping through the countryside (*Pride and Prejudice*, BBC television series, 1995), or lit by oil lamps at night (*Sense and Sensibility*). Not only is this imagery deployed in the opening seconds of the first episode of *Downton*; it is accompanied by a soundtrack model established fifteen years earlier and codified in productions since.

Downton, *Gosford*, and the Americanized Austen adaptations prominently feature the same instrument to accompany the estate shot: the piano. *Persuasion* and *Gosford* use solo piano music, with the latter showcasing the first of several songs written by Ivor Novello used in the film, "Waltz of My Heart."[22] Additionally, *Pride and Prejudice*, *Sense and Sensibility*, and *Downton* begin with a piano concerto texture. In the course of these films, the piano concerto efficiently signifying the film's marriage plot, which centers around the threat of losing property, and resolves with its acquisition through romantic union at the close of the work. In *Pride and Prejudice*, the orchestral melody evokes hunting horns immediately visualized in the series' opening images of Bingley and Darcy on horseback discussing the "fair prospect" of a country house, against a fast, light, virtuosic piano solo that is heard as Elizabeth Bennett comes into view. Similar scenes can be found in *Sense and Sensibility*, as Marianne Dashwood's indoor piano performance of their "father's favorite" blends into a piano concerto that accompanies Edward and Elinor's outdoor courting (13:55–17:21).[23] As is common in Austen novels and retained in adaptations, later piano performances explicitly link the piano to the women characters (Marianne Dashwood, Mary and Elizabeth Bennett, Georgiana Darcy et al, Ivor Novello's performances notwithstanding). Meanwhile, the overwhelming majority of nondiegetic (underscore) soundtracks employ orchestras, particularly for outdoor settings in the countryside. As such, the orchestra represents the outdoor spaces of the masculine sphere, the piano for the interior, domestic, feminine sphere, and the piano concerto the perfect merger of both, in the country estate.

When *Downton*'s piano concerto theme features piano and chamber string ensemble to accompany the estate shot, the series continues an established tradition that telegraphs its central storylines aurally as well as visually: saving the estate and all who work in it through marriage, historically (Robert and Cora's union) and contemporaneously (through Mary's primary responsibility to marry the heir). At the opening of the first episode (where the musical soundtrack begins immediately after the train whistle, at 0:13), the expansive triple meter melody, first played in solo piano then joined by violins, creates rhythmic tension against the churning duple meter accompaniment in the remainder of the orchestra.[24] Over the next few moments, the music fades behind dialogue concerning the telegram that will be delivered to the Crawley family, during which time the accompaniment moves into triple meter. By the time of the estate reveal (1:32–1:40), melody and accompaniment are working together in triple meter and, as composer John Lunn mentions, "the harmony completely expands for the first time" to accompany the "this fantastic shot of the house." In fact, these two measures move from the vacillating A minor and F major 7th spaces of the opening to a wider, more open quartal harmony (E-A-D) to a tentative resolution on C major, albeit with a gentle major seventh harmony added.[25] The effect is to establish Downton as a well-oiled machine in which its various parts work together in harmony.

Downton's main theme refers to earlier musical models beyond the piano concerto texture. The writing blends a neo–Romantic sensibility in the piano line with a minimalist aesthetic in the orchestra, replicating not only the closing credits of *Howards End* but also the character of the score of *The Remains of the Day*, both featuring original soundtracks composed by Merchant-Ivory's house composer Richard Robbins.[26] Heard as emblematic of the world of *Downton*, these strata could embody the more leisurely world of upstairs (the piano melody) and the constantly-in-motion downstairs (the pulsing orchestra) that supports and maintains the melody. These divisions are supported by the camerawork accompanying the opening sequence of the first episode, in another nod to *Gosford*, by reinforcing the constant motion and work of the bustling servants through a one-minute tracking shot that follows Daisy and then Thomas as the house awakes (2:31–3:30).[27]

The layered piano concerto underscores the premiere episode's imagery as well, which can be viewed against the backdrop of, and in dialogue with, earlier heritage products: from the locomotive steam and the fresh mown English countryside (0:27–0:40, both salient images in *Howards End*), to the ironing of Lord Crawley's newspaper (4:13-:17 and 5:39-:50, referencing *The Remains of the Day*), and the image of ringing bells labeled by upstairs room on the wall in the servants' area (5:15, 6:06 and elsewhere, from *Sense and Sensibility*), to name only a few. In later episodes, an abridged version of the main theme accompanies intimate images of the estate's inner world, offering in Lucy Elvis' words, "fictionalized spaces … [as] a jumping-off point for the imagination, a place for our minds to begin a search for an ideal home-space through a combination of recollection, lived experience, and shared notions of 'home.'"[28] Together, the credits' soundtrack and visual imagery telegraph key elements of the earlier heritage film into a compressed, thirty-second form, with the same harmonic and rhythmic resolution on the main title and graphic of the estate.

In addition to the music and visuals for the main titles, *Downton Abbey* employs diegetic (or source) music in ways that create continuity, and perhaps commentary, on earlier British heritage films and television series. While source performances are comparatively rare—likely due to the challenges of filming live musical performances on the limited shooting schedule typical of television series—a few scenes use repertoire, performance, and cinematography in ways similar to *Gosford Park*. What follows are discussions of two representative musical moments that build on *Gosford*'s model, which was itself established by Fellowes at Altman's suggestion and stands as a remarkable merger of story, song, and image.

When Fellowes' first screenplay draft was completed in May 2000, under its original title *The Back of the Tapestry*, it contained neither the songs nor the singer that would prove "integral" and "central to the movie," according to Altman. Fellowes added them at Altman's request.[29] As he recalled, Altman made specific suggestions including those regarding the film's music at a meeting in Los Angeles the next month between Fellowes, Altman and Balaban. "At this point Bob Altman suggested adding Ivor Novello to the mix. He was a fan of [Novello's] and he wanted some `live action music' in the movie, not just background scoring, and we both felt it would anchor the film in the period to have one real-life person of the time."[30] Jeremy Northam plays Ivor Novello (1893–1951)— a celebrated British film star, songwriter and playwright—and sings songs once performed by Novello and plays period piano tunes live on set.

Several of Novello's songs act as the perfect accompaniment for a sequence in the middle of the film, when Sir William McCordle (Michael Gambon) is stabbed in the chest while sitting in his library, all while the remaining houseguests and family members enjoy the music and play cards. The song's lyrics work in tandem with the script and cinematography to provide clues, and even identify McCordle's murderers, motivations, methods, and other plot intricacies.[31] In its precise melding of music, drama, and image, the film provides one of Altman's most sophisticated extended musical sequences in his nearly four decade career where he constantly pushed the limits of soundtracks while seeking an innovative integration of speech, sound, and music. In this sequence, Altman and his collaborators used source music as underscoring, with the purpose of having the music reflexively comment on the characters' actions and the film's plot, while using apparently innocuous music hall songs to accompany a shockingly violent act.

Two examples involving Matthew and Mary serve to illustrate how *Downton* uses period, source music in a similar way, moving the soundtrack beyond mere musical performance to offer commentary on the plot.[32] In 2:4, set in the First World War, Matthew and William are missing at the front while the family plans a benefit for wounded soldiers at the manor. Mary, who is distraught at Matthew's status, sings, "If You Were the Only Girl in the World," accompanied by her sister (and usual nemesis) Edith (46:38–48:53). The song, written by London-based American songwriter Nat D. Ayer with words by Clifford Grey and premiered in April 1916 as part of the West End revue *The Bing Boys Are Here*, aimed, in part, at soldiers on leave. The wistful melody and lyrics imagine a world with just two lovers in which "nothing else would matter," longing for "a Garden of Eden just made for two" with "nothing to mar our joy"—aptly remote images perhaps for soldiers and civilians damaged, often beyond repair, by the war.

As Mary sings, the camera pans across the show's various characters, many of whom are struggling with their own romantic challenges (including Daisy, who is concerned about William), and who join the soldiers in singing the chorus. Unexpectedly, Matthew and William enter the hall (47:43), and the soundtrack immediately moves to non-diegetic underscoring as Matthew and Mary make eye contact. The abrupt insertion of underscoring serves to move the narrative immediately out of the public gathering and into the internalized world of the couple's unspoken emotions, suggesting that in this moment Mary and Matthew are, in fact, the only girl and boy in their private world. After an awkward greeting, it is Matthew who resumes the song (48:20), singing, "I would say such wonderful things to you" as he approaches Mary, and she joins the duet with "There would be such wonderful things to do," before the ensemble joins in again (48:31), blurring the public sphere of the concert and in the increasingly intimate space of their developing romance.

Later in 2:8, the soundtrack uses a song to accompany Mary and Matthew's most significant romantic expression up to that moment (18:06–21:37). As Matthew starts a recording of Jerome Kern and B.G. DeSylva's "Look for the Silver Lining" on the Crawley's new phonograph, the editing and cinematography suggest a similar choreography to that used in *Gosford*. Mary looks down on Matthew on the line "Please don't be offended" (18:10,) descends the stairs to meet him on "There's a way" (18:32), and crosses into the room on "Happy little secret of it all," suggesting Mary and Matthew's secret feelings for one another (18:41).

When Mary asks what song is playing, Matthew responds, "Actually, I quite like it. I think it was in a show that flopped—*Zip! Goes a Million* or something" (19:01-:08). After they begin to dance, Mary responds, "We were a show that flopped" (19:31-:33). The song's lyrics underscore the couple's disappointment in love ("clouds appear in the sky," "banish sadness and strife") while building to an optimistic conclusion at the apex of the chorus: "So always look for the silver lining / And try to find the sunny side of life." Yet on the soundtrack, non-diegetic scoring suddenly swells and drowns out the diegetic recording on this crucial line (19:40): essentially, as Strovas and Strovas write, "the audience joins the pair on their emotional journey and shares their all-too-brief moment of emotional satisfaction."[33] As the couple's impromptu dance continues, accompanied by confessions and ending with a passionate kiss, it becomes clear that the two still have feelings for one another despite Matthew's engagement to Lavinia Swire. At Lavinia's unexpected entrance (20:47), the soundtrack transitions back to the diegetic recording, interrupting the sonically reinforced intimacy and continuing the technique used for "If You Were the Only Girl in the World" earlier in the series. A nearly complete hearing of the refrain accompanies Mary's awkward departure and Lavinia's pained conversation with Matthew, asking that she never become a nuisance to him. In fact, the optimistic lyrics of the song may better reflect Lavinia's self-sacrificing character as demonstrated earlier through her desire to care for and marry Matthew after his paralysis, as well as her later actions on her deathbed that will benefit Matthew, Mary, and the entire Crawley family.

Although the song and recording seem a good fit narratively and visually, this soundtrack choice reveals several anachronisms and inaccuracies that Fellowes and Altman generally avoided for the Novello songs used in *Gosford* (with one exception, as noted below). "Look for the Silver Lining" was written for the 1919 musical *Zip! Goes a Million*, as Matthew mentions. Along with several other shows written between 1917 and 1919, *Zip* is grouped with a series of innovative Kern musicals staged at the intimate Princess Theatre in New York, even though it never actually played at the Princess. Unlike the dominant Broadway genre of the revue, which changed periodically to introduce new songs, actors, and topical storylines, Kern's shows emphasized stories and characters while introducing popular Kern hits. Simultaneously, however, the Princess Theatre shows highlighted contemporary plots and young characters exchanging snappy, witty dialogue and plots, setting the stage for the post-war Gershwin-era musical comedy of the 1920s.

The story of *Zip! Goes a Million* is based on the 1902 novel *Brewster's Millions*, perhaps best known for its 1985 film version, directed by Walter Hill and starring Richard Pryor and John Candy and involving the eccentric stipulations of a millionaire's will. Originally titled *Maid O' Money*, *Zip* opened at the Worcester Theatre in Worcester, Massachusetts, on December 8, 1919, some seven months after the timeframe of 2:8, and never made it to Broadway: it closed during out-of-town tryouts in Washington, D.C., a few weeks later.[34] Two of its songs became hits, however: "Look For the Silver Lining" and "Whip-Poor-Will," both of which Kern recycled the following year in *Sally*, a new show that premiered a year after *Zip* closed, on Broadway's New Amsterdam Theatre on December 21, 1920.[35] In fact, the recording heard in 2:8, by singer Marion Harris, clearly identifies the song as being from *Sally* on the shellac disc's original label.[36] The recording was made at the time of *Sally*'s premiere in December 1920, and only released in 1921. It became a hit in the United States the following April, a full two years after *Downton's* 2:8 is set. These chronological missteps—that the original show that flopped premiered months after the episode, and that the recording was made nineteen months later, and only in circulation approximately two years later—overshadow the other possible challenges in accepting the premise of the song's use: that Matthew, who has been bedridden and recuperating from serious war wounds during the previous year, would somehow know the history of the song and its connection to a failed musical not identified on the recording's label.

A similar criticism was made over the inclusion of an as-yet-unwritten song in *Gosford*, which is set in November 1932. Novello's song "Waltz of My Heart" (1939) is used in an instrumental version for the film's credits, and played briefly by Northam/Novello within the film as the character comments that it is "just a little something I'm working on." Fellowes defended his and Altman's decision to incorporate the song into the film, stating,

> We were pretty rigorous…. All the songs [Novello] actually plays are pre–November 1932, with the sole exception of a phrase from "Waltz of My Heart." I had always liked it, and I thought, "well, I'm going to put this in." But of course it hadn't come out, it was years later. And so there's a moment when Sylvia says, "What are you playing? I don't think I know that." And he says, "Oh, it's just something I've been fiddling with." This is the premise, that every composer has a drawer full of ideas that they haven't fully developed. And so that's how I got 'round it.[37]

While critics excoriated Fellowes specifically over these and other anachronisms, as the screenwriter for both and the creator of *Downton*, it is evident that Fellowes took historical accuracy very seriously at all creative levels.[38] For example, in pre-production for *Gosford*, Altman's staff communicated nearly constantly with Fellowes for advice on specific issues: what language luggage or telegrams would use on their labels, how much money Lady Trentham would leave in envelopes for the servants, or how the aristocracy would be addressed by one another as well as by the servants and outsiders, for which he created a detailed list with such information as "Constance, Countess of Trentham … [or] the Dowager Countess of Trentham … [also] 'Lady Trentham.' Above all, she could never be called 'Lady Constance' or 'Lady Constance Trentham.'"[39]

Most importantly, during the script's development, Fellowes insisted on changing the relationship between two key characters. For *Gosford*, Altman asked that Novello be introduced as a cousin of Lady Sylvia. Fellowes responded firmly that, because Novello came from a lower-middle class family, it would be impossible for Novello to be related to high-born Lady Sylvia, and he did not want to "risk a savaging for 'inaccurate research." Instead, he suggested making Novello "a cousin of Sir William's which seems perfectly plausible."[40] Once filming began, "Bob knew enough about what he didn't know to make sure that Julian was on set every second," Balaban recalled. "Of course, by the end of it he wanted to kill Julian, which was no surprise to me."[41] Fellowes remembered, "Bob realized it was kind of a minefield, this whole class thing…. He wanted it to be specific— not BBC servant acting, wandering around with a tray."[42] While this level of detail and control was possible in a two-hour feature film such as *Gosford*, the multiepisode format of *Downton*, Fellowes' various roles as head writer, series creator, and promoter, and the speedy production schedule demanded of a television series offered less time for more thorough research and verification. Then again, Fellowes may have chosen to exercise artistic license by using a song that was appropriate to the character's situation over its chronological accuracy.

A final comparison between *Downton*'s and *Gosford*'s songs suggests another distinction. In 2001, Ivor Novello's name remained familiar to the general public within the United Kingdom even fifty years after his death. The annual British Academy of Songwriters, Composers and Authors (BASCA) awards were established in his memory as the Ivor Novello Awards, or the "Ivors," which continue to recognize British achievements in songwriting and music recording. Beyond this very public connection, it is apparent that many British reviewers of *Gosford* were familiar with Novello and his songs (especially "Keep the Home Fires Burning," his first hit and a Great War anthem from 1914), as well as his film and stage career, and his homosexuality. In contrast, Novello was unknown to U.S. critics and likely audiences before the film, and American critics appeared unaware of his career, life, and sexuality, as were most viewers outside of Britain.[43]

By comparison, both songs selected for *Downton* have been in circulation within the United States and Britain for decades since their premiere, and were thus potentially more familiar with mainstream audiences on both sides of the Atlantic. For British audiences, "If You Were the Only Girl" remained in circulation through most of the century, appearing in live performances, recordings, and the BBC series *The Duchess of Duke Street* (1976–1977), where it served both to establish the First World War period and a nostalgic context, very much like its use in *Downton*.[44] "If You Were the Only Girl" was perhaps one of the most recorded English music hall songs in the United States, and proved popular during World War II when it reached a new generation of soldiers and sweethearts longing to escape the violent conflict. Postwar, it was a hit for Bing Crosby in 1947, and during the ensuring decades the song was rerecorded dozens of times by the likes of Doris Day, Perry Como, Dean Martin, and Barbra Streisand. The Academy Award-winning *The Bridge on the River Kwai*, (1957) another transatlantic production that combined a British director (David Lean), American financing (Columbia Pictures), and international casting (Alec Guiness and William Holden), featured the song performed in a POW camp entertainment: all of which re-enforced both the song's British origins and its wartime associations, exploited by *Downton Abbey*.[45]

"Look for the Silver Lining" quickly became established in the Great American Songbook, with some of the best known versions recorded and distributed internationally by major pop and jazz singers including Andy Williams, Tony Bennett, and Chet Baker; it was featured in the Jerome Kern tribute film *Till the Clouds Roll By* (Whorf, 1946) performed by Judy Garland. The song followed a similar path in Britain, beginning with the production of *Sally* that premiered on September 10, 1921, at the Winter Garden Theatre in London, featuring newcomer Dorothy Dickson, an American-born singer and actress who would become a West End star and entertainer.[46] No doubt, for British audiences immediately after the Great War the song's lyrics would have added resonance, for DeSylva's song uses the image of dark clouds with silver linings that appeared in Novello and Ford's "Keep the Home Fires Burning," one of the conflict's unofficial anthems ("There's a silver lining / Through the dark clouds shining" compared with "Look for the silver lining / When e'er a cloud appears in the blue"). Dickson recorded "Look for the Silver Lining" with costar George Straub, and it became known as her theme song in later years: likely she sang it often at the London Stagedoor Canteen, where she frequently performed for troops during the Second World War.[47] The song's wartime resonance solidified when *Sally* was revived at the Prince's Theatre in wartime London in 1942, and proved equally popular with West End audiences that included Allied soldiers on leave.

In summary, both *Gosford* and *Downton* use source music from their respective period settings to amplify key plot moments, dissolving the boundaries between diegetic and nondiegetic spaces in innovative ways. As in other aspects of the later series, it is likely that at least some of the impetus for creating contrapuntal soundtracks that engage with significant moments in the plot originated in the earlier production. Yet the creators of each chose different repertoires that reflect larger issues of marketing, production, distribution, and financing as previously discussed. While the *Gosford* songs were little known outside Britain, *Downton's* songs had an established history in both target markets for the series, reinforcing the necessity of the series to reach American viewers on a larger scale.

Conclusion: Class and Audience

Like its immediate predecessors, *Gosford Park* and *Downton Abbey* negotiate a hybridized identity: as British heritage films with American producers, international stars, and transatlantic appeal. Yet the nine years between the release of *Gosford* and the launch of *Downton* saw a global financial meltdown that reshaped *Downton*'s financing model and significantly impacted audiences as well.

For American viewing audiences, a large part of the appeal of the British heritage genre exists in "the cultural myth of 'Englishness,' of tradition, stability, and fair play" that "exists outside TV drama only in the historic imaginary."[48] Given the similar myth of classlessness in the American imagination, British heritage offers an opportunity to experience clearly delineated social classes, even as the tensions between the classes are overwhelmingly limited to the upper and middle classes as in *A Room with a View*, or at least confined within a single strata of society, as in the servant romance of *The Remains of the Day*.[49] The guilt-free nostalgia fueled the Austen craze, in which differing expressions of class relationships "correspond quite closely to the nationality of the filmmakers," according to Carol M. Dole. "The solidly British productions take the hardest look at class, while the mainstream American films tend on the surface to ridicule class snobbery but on a deeper level to ratify class divisions."[50]

By contrast, *Gosford* offered a far more critical view of class divisions, confronting much more directly the abusive, ultimately devastating nature of class rule. Unlike most Merchant Ivory films, and even the more class-critical *Persuasion*, the central tensions in *Gosford* occur between the titled class and the working and servant classes. These relationships are represented in the past through Sir William's affairs with the workers at his factories; in the present via his affair with Elsie (Emily Watson); and through Lady Sylvia's affair with Henry Denton, which is abruptly terminated when his real status is revealed.

While *Gosford* expands on previous heritage works by critiquing the rigidity of class structures, *Downton* tends to be less critical and even validating of the servant/master relationship. The "implausibly enlightened"[51] upper class is characterized by the "paternalistic benevolence" of Lord Robert and his clan, the impact of which "validates and sanitises class inequality by framing it in terms of mutual support and even love. The view it presents, of a world in which people work together for the good of the whole, is idyllic and reassuring," in Katherine Byrne's words.[52] As such, *Downton*'s class relationships, characters, and plots can be seen as an endorsement of the class divisions that make the managing, maintenance, and continuance of the great house possible, reinforced by the unquestioning loyalty of the "good" servants to the family (Mr. Carson, Mrs. Hughes, Anna) and the vilification of disloyal servants (O'Brien, Thomas).[53]

Instead of critiquing class divisions, the series offers what Chapman describes as "a broadly progressive attitude towards those who are positioned on the margins or periphery of society," including "those trapped by legal and social situations" such as Bates and Thomas, who is an outcast because he is gay.[54] Obviously the settings of *Downton* and *Gosford* demand an overwhelmingly white cast as well, thus offering viewers an escape to a racially homogeneous world of the imaginary past from the contentious class, political, nationalist, ethnic, and racial conflicts of the present.

Moreover, both *Gosford* and *Downton* appealed widely to audiences on either side of the 2008 financial crisis. *Gosford* appeared just as the "housing bubble" in the United States further accelerated after a period of extensive growth, at the beginning of a five-year expansion of historic proportions. At a moment when increased home values and McMansions represented to many Americans financial security and social status, the graciousness of *Gosford*'s well-ordered country estate and its unquestioned value must have had a special resonance.[55] Fast forward to 2010, after the housing bubble burst in 2006, home values declined nearly nationwide, and the subprime mortgage disaster infected the global economy: homeowners facing a loss of equity if not foreclosure may well have identified with the Lord Robert's struggle to keep hold of his beloved Downton Abbey through his own marriage as well as that of Lady Mary, despite differences in class and era. Moreover, as Jesseca Cornelson observes, *Downton*'s focus on masters and servants embody post-recession anxieties "about the shrinking middle class" as well as "an increased awareness of growing disparity between social classes," appealing to audiences "by offering a comforting nostalgia for an earlier time whose clear-cut and constant class distinctions are perhaps easier to understand" than those of the post-recession current day.[56]

These and other issues embodied in *Downton Abbey* have led some critics to characterize it as overly conservative.[57] As such, the series directly contradicts the ethos of *Gosford Park*, despite the many similarities between the two. Indeed, like all British heritage productions, *Gosford Park* and *Downton Abbey* provide as much, or more, insight into the contemporary conditions of their production as they do into the historical periods conjured by their settings and soundtracks.

NOTES

1. Mitchell Zuckoff, *Robert Altman: The Oral Biography* (New York: Alfred A. Knopf, 2009), 469.

2. For an extensive comparison of *Gosford Park* compared to *The Rules of the Game*, see Gayle Sherwood [Magee], "Song, Genre, and Transatlantic Dialogue in *Gosford Park*," *Journal of the Society for American Music* 2/4 (November 2008): 477–505.

3. Both treatments are preserved in the Robert Altman Archives, along with Fellowes's initial drafts of the screenplay. University of Michigan, Special Collections, Robert Altman Archives, *Gosford Park* series: hereafter Altman Archives.

4. This definition is offered by James Quinn and Jane Kingsley-Smith as a summary "of the characteristics attributed to the 1980s heritage film by Andrew Higson in his seminal definition of the category." Quinn and Kingsley-Smith, "Kenneth Branagh's *Henry V* (1989): Genre and Interpretation," in *British Historical Cinema: The History, Heritage and Costume Film*, ed. Claire Monk and Amy Sargent, British Popular Cinema (New York: Routledge, 2002), 167 and 173n7.

5. Robert Altman and David Thompson, *Altman on Altman* (London: Faber and Faber, 2006), 196–97.

6. Tino Balio, "The Art Film Market in the New Hollywood," in *Hollywood and Europe: Economics, Culture, National Identity: 1945–95*, ed. Geoffrey Nowell-Smith and Steven Ricci, UCLA Film and Television Archive Studies in History, Criticism and Theory (London: BFI, 1998), 64.

7. Linda Troost and Sayre Greenfield, "Introduction: Watching Ourselves Watching," in *Jane Austen in Hollywood*, ed. Linda Troost and Sayre Greenfield, 2d ed. (Lexington: University of Kentucky Press, 2001), 1.

8. Sarah Cardwell, "Production Contexts of Adaptations of *Persuasion*," in *British Television Drama*, ed. Jonathan Bignell and Stephen Lacey, 2d ed. (New York: Palgrave Macmillan, 2014), 89.

9. Zuckoff, 471.

10. *Ibid.*

11. *Ibid.*, 470–72.

12. *Ibid.*, 471.

13. Neame's quotation is found in Rebecca Eaton, *Making Masterpiece* (New York: Viking, 2013), 243, which also contains an account of Eaton's decision to program *Upstairs, Downstairs* instead of *Downton Abbey*, as well as her later change of heart (229–44).

14. As James Chapman notes, "American investment has increasingly become an economic necessity for the more expensive television dramas—and at a cost of £1 million per episode *Downton Abbey* is squarely in the upper cost bracket of British (and for that matter U.S.) television production." James Chapman, "*Downton Abbey*: Reinventing the British Costume Drama," *British Television Drama*, ed. Jonathan Bignell and Stephen Lacey, 2d ed. (New York: Palgrave Macmillan, 2014), 134.

15. Eaton, 248; see also Laura Jacobs, "Spotlight: Innocence Abroad," *Vanity Fair*, January 2011: online at http://www.vanityfair.com/news/2011/01/elizabeth-mcgovern-201101.

16. Quoted in Eaton, 232.

17. Henry Mance, "The *Downton Abbey* Man," *Financial Times*, 24 July 2015, 2.

18. As I have argued elsewhere, too much has been made of Altman's incorporation of improvisation in his films, and *Gosford Park* was no exception. For the most accurate description of the relationship between Fellowes's script, Altman's direction, and "improvisation," see the accounts by Balaban, Levy, and Fellowes in Zuckoff, 474–76. The most significant "improvisation" involved redefining the relationship between the characters of Mrs. Parks and Mrs. Croft, as well as their cathartic reunion at the end of the film (recounted by Levy and Fellowes in Zuckoff, 476). Other key lines appear to have been developed in rehearsal, such as the dialogue at the dinner table involving selling boots for the Sudanese army, or Lady Trentham's key phrase, "It seems to be much more than background music," which was substituted for Fellowes's written line "You're spoiling us, Mr. Novello. *Quel embarras de richesses.*" And one scene in the film resulted from an accident on set during filming (in which the footman George spills hot coffee on the lap of Henry Denton). While Fellowes was rewriting dialogue through the film's shooting according to ideas generated on- and off-set with Altman, the core of the film, especially the scenes in the "murder sequence," remained stable throughout Fellowes's many drafts which are preserved in the Altman Archives, *Gosford Park* series.

19. Zuckoff, 474–75.

20. For a discussion of homosexuality in *Downton*, see Lucy Brown, "Homosexual Lives: Representation and Reinterpretation in *Upstairs, Downstairs* and *Downton Abbey*," in *Upstairs and Downstairs: British Costume Drama Television from The Forsyte Saga to Downton Abbey*, ed. James Leggott and Julie Anne Taddeo (New York: Rowan & Littlefield, 2015), 263–73.

21. See, for example, Scene 88 in the deleted scenes on the *Gosford Park* DVD, in which Novello speaks candidly to the character of Weissman (Balaban) about Henry Denton (Philippe). Novello's other comments suggests that not only is he fully aware of their gay relationship, but he is experienced himself.

22. *Persuasion* uses employs Chopin's Prelude Op. 28, No. 21 in B-flat major, a suitably romantic albeit anachronistic choice, since he twenty-four preludes in Chopin's Op. 28 were completed and published in 1839, while Austen completed *Persuasion* in 1816, and the novel was published posthumously in 1818.

23. For a detailed discussion of the music in this scene, see Robynn J. Stilwell, "Sense & Sensibility: Form, Genre, and Function in the Film Score," *Acta Musicologica* 72/2 (2000): 230–33.

24. For a contrasting interpretation of this sequence, see Karen Beth Strovas and Scott M. Strovas, "'What Are We Going to Do with Uncle Arthur?' Music in the British Serialized Period Drama," in *Upstairs and Downstairs: British Costume Drama Television from The Forsyte Saga to Downton Abbey*, ed. James Leggott and Julie Anne Taddeo (New York: Rowan & Littlefield, 2015), 99–101.

25. Hrishikesh Hirway, *Song Exploder 37: John Lunn (Downton Abbey)*, Interview: online at https://soundcloud.com/hrishihirway/song-exploder-37-john-lunn, 3:37–3:42.

26. The soundtrack's composer, John Lunn, states that he was given the opening credits to the American television series *The West Wing* (NBC, 1999–2006) as a model "because, I suppose, there was some sort of political thing between upstairs and downstairs. It's like a small country, Downton Abbey, people lead and serve and people do. Musically, it wasn't a great direction." Indeed, it is difficult to find any significant musical similarity between the two themes. Melinda Newman, "*Downton Abbey* Composer John Lunn Talks Show's Success, Likely Tour: Exclusive," *Billboard*, 12 June 2015: online at http://www.billboard.com/articles/news/6598056/downton-abbey-composer-john-lunn-interview-music-cast-tour.

27. Chapman, 137, notes, "Like *Gosford Park*, *Downton Abbey* makes extensive use of Steadicam and a mobile camera to keep close to the actors and follow their movements." The roaming, dolly-like camera work during the dinner table conversations in *Downton Abbey* is particularly similar to such scenes in *Gosford Park*.

28. Lucy Elvis, "Topophilia: Or, How We Got Hooked on *Downton*," *Downton Abbey and Philosophy*, ed. Adam Barkman and Robert Arp (Chicago: Open Court, 2016), 131.

29. Robert Altman, Liner Notes to *Gosford Park: Original Motion Picture Soundtrack*, Decca 289 470 387-2.

30. Brian McFarlane, "Class of '32: Brian McFarlane Reviews Gosford Park and Interviews Its Oscar-Winning Screenwriter, Julian Fellowes," *Meanjin* 61/3 (September 2002): 152.

31. See Sherwood [Magee], "Song, Genre, and Transatlantic Dialogue in *Gosford Park*," 477–505.

32. For discussions of another use of source music, Puccini's "O Mio Babbino Caro" in 4: 2, see Strovas and Strovas, 106–07, and Katherine Byrne, "New Developments in Heritage: The Recent Dark Side of *Downton* 'Downer' *Abbey*," in *Upstairs and Downstairs: British Costume Drama Television from The Forsyte Saga to Downton Abbey*, ed. James Leggott and Julie Anne Taddeo (New York: Rowan & Littlefield, 2015), 177–89, particularly the music's connection to *A Room with a View* (183).

33. Strovas and Strovas, 104.

34. For opening date and theater, see Stephen Banfield, *Jerome Kern* (New Haven: Yale University Press, 2006), 18. For the original title *Maid o' Money*, see "Theatrical Notes," *New York Times*, 9 October 1919, 16, and "Another 'Civilian Clothes,'" *Washington Post*, 12 October 1919, 52. For notices of the show's Washington,

D.C., performances, see Frank L. Morse, "Theatrical Christmas Gifts at Box Office Rates" and "Plays and Photoplays on View This Week," *Washington Post*, 21 December 1919, 3–4. These notices postdate the show's opening in Worcester, suggesting that the tryouts started in Worcester and the show closed in Washington a few weeks later, as mentioned in a 1985 article in the *New York Times*: "*Zip!* opened in Worcester, Mass., moved on to Springfield and Providence, then closed in Washington, canceling bookings in Newark and New York." John S. Wilson, "City's Singing Up a Storm on Kern's Centennial," *New York Times*, 25 January 1985: online at http://www.nytimes.com/1985/01/25/arts/city-s-singing-up-a-storm-on-kern-s-centennial.html.

35. Steven Suskin, *Show Tunes: The Songs, Shows, and Careers of Broadway's Major Composers* (New York: Oxford University Press, 2010): 6.

36. The recording is available on YouTube at the time of this writing, at https://www.youtube.com/watch?v=eImvscBf8uU. The image of the recording label as well as other details are available online at https://www.discogs.com/Marion-Harris-Look-For-The-Silver-Lining-Im-Gonna-Do-It-If-I-Like-It/release/6556836.

37. *Musical Talk Podcast*, interview with Julian Fellowes, 8 September 2013: online at https://www.youtube.com/watch?v=uZ7wFJO1-dY.

38. For criticisms of anachronisms in *Downton Abbey*, see for example Ephraim Hardcastle, "Research Isn't His Strong Point for the Creator of *Downton Abbey*," *Daily Mail* (UK), 8 November 2011: online at http://www.dailymail.co.uk/news/article-2058807/Downton-Abbey-Research-isnt-strong-point-creator-Julian-Fellowes.html; and *NPR Morning Edition*, "I'm Just Sayin': There are Anachronisms in *Downton*," 13 February 2012: online at http://www.npr.org/2012/02/13/146652747/im-just-sayin-there-are-anachronisms-in-downton.

39. Altman Archives, *Gosford Park* series, Typed List by Julian Fellowes, "Titles and modes of address in 'Gosford Park.'"

40. *Ibid.*, faxed letter from Fellowes to Altman, 10 September 2000, and email from Fellowes to Balaban, 16 September 2000.

41. Zuckoff, 475.

42. *Ibid.*, 474.

43. See, for example, Marcus Berkmann, "*Gosford Park* [Review]," *Spectator* (UK), 2 February 2002: 43, which states, "Jeremy Northam is a little too heterosexual to be playing Ivor Novello." By comparison, Stephen Holden's review in the *New York Times* assumed readers would not know anything about Novello, let alone his sexuality, explaining that "Novello was a real-life movie star who also composed numerous English hit songs in a Noel Coward style." Holden, "Full of Baronial Splendor and Hatefulness," *New York Times*, 26 December 2001: online at http://www.nytimes.com/movie/review?res=9804EFD81531F935A15751C1A9679 C8B63.

44. For a discussion of *The Duchess of Duke Street* within the larger context of television costume dramas, see Katherine Byrne, *Edwardians on Screen* (New York: Palgrave Macmillan, 2015), 27–28 and passim.

45. For a brief discussion of this scene, in which the soldier playing "the only girl in the world" is in drag, within a larger context, see Robert Eberwein, *Armed Forces: Masculinity and Sexuality in the American War Film* (New Brunswick: Rutgers University Press, 2007), 93–95.

46. For the London production history of *Sally*, see Dan Dete, *The Complete Book of 1940s Broadway Musicals* (New York: Rowan & Littlefield, 2015), 432. For an overview of Dickson's life, see Robert McG. Thomas, "Dorothy Dickson, Musical Star of British Stage, Is Dead at 102," *New York Times*, 27 September 1995: online at http://www.nytimes.com/1995/09/27/obituaries/dorothy-dickson-musical-star-of-british-stage-is-dead-at-102.html.

47. According to Ross Laird, *Moanin' Low: A Discography of Female Popular Vocal Recordings, 1920–1933* (Westport, CT: Greenwood, 1996), 150, Dickson and Stroud's recordings were made in London on October 7, 1921, with the Winter Garden orchestra. A snippet of Dickson and Straub's recording of "Look for the Silver Lining" from 1921 is available online at http://www.guidetomusicaltheatre.com/shows_s/sally.htm.

48. Robin Nelson, "Costume Drama," *The Television Genre Book*, ed. Glen Creeber, 3d ed. (London: Palgrave/British Film Institute, 2015), 53.

49. Martin A. Hipsky, "Anglophil(m)ia: Why Does America Watch Merchant-Ivory Movies?" *Journal of Popular Film & Television* 22/3 (Fall 1994): 106 summarizes the appeal of "Merchant-Ivoryesque films" to U.S. audiences thusly: "class conflict takes the form of tension over relative levels of gentility. Once the less-genteel figures are vindicated, as by film's end they inevitably are, we can all breathe a sigh of satisfaction, forgetting how limited the scope of inter-class tension has been. In many ways, these historical films function to efface the very social history they purport to portray; they provide North American viewers with a kind of sanitized, guilt-free nostalgia. It is, after all, the historical landscape of our trans-Atlantic cousins there on the screen, and while we are aware of empire and class injustices hovering somewhere beyond the movies' immediate social landscape, they trouble us not, as they do not signify any dirty historical laundry of our own."

50. Carol M. Dole, "Austen, Class, and the American Market," in *Jane Austen in Hollywood*, ed. Linda Troost and Sayre Greenfield, 2d ed. (Lexington: University Press of Kentucky, 2001), 60.

51. Mance, "The *Downton Abbey* Man," *Financial Times*, 24 July 2015, 2.

52. Byrne, 75.

53. For a more detailed consideration of O'Brien and Thomas as representatives of class tension in *Downton*, see Byrne, 77–81.

54. Chapman, 140. Chapman notes as well that *Downton Abbey*'s class critique is less sharp than that of *Gosford Park*, likely because of Robert Altman's comparative "radicalism" on the subject (139).

55. Karl E. Case and Robert J. Shiller, "Is There a Bubble in the Housing Market?" *Brookings Papers on Economic Activity* 2003: 299 defined the in-progress housing bubble as "a situation in which excessive public expectations of future price increases cause prices to be temporarily elevated. During a housing price bubble, homebuyers think that a home that they would normally consider too expensive for them is now an acceptable purchase because they will be compensated by significant further price increases. They will not need to save as much as they otherwise might, because they expect the increased value of their home to do the saving for them."

56. Jesseca Cornelson, "Master, Servants, and the Effaced Middle Classes," r in *The Great Recession in Fiction, Film, and Television*, ed. Kirk Boyle and Daniel Mrozowski (Lanham, MD: Lexington Press, 2013), 163 and 166.

57. Byrne, 70, states that "the Abbey itself deliberately functions as a microcosm for the state, and it is difficult to ignore the implication that twenty-firstcentury Britain would be more successful if it were organized in the same hierarchal and patriarchal way."

WORKS CITED

Altman, Robert. Liner Notes to *Gosford Park: Original Motion Picture Soundtrack*. Decca 289 470 387–2.

Altman, Robert, and David Thompson. *Altman on Altman*. London: Faber & Faber, 2006.

Balio, Tino. "The Art Film Market in the New Hollywood." In *Hollywood and Europe: Economics, Culture, National Identity: 1945–95*, Geoffrey Nowell-Smith and Steven Ricci, eds. UCLA Film and Television Archive Studies in History, Criticism and Theory. London: BFI, 1998, 63–73.

Banfield, Stephen. *Jerome Kern*. New Haven: Yale University Press, 2006.

Brown, Lucy. "Homosexual Lives: Representation and Reinterpretation in *Upstairs, Downstairs* and *Downton Abbey*." In *Upstairs and Downstairs: British Costume Drama Television from The Forsyte Saga to Downton Abbey*. James Leggott and Julie Anne Taddeo, eds. New York: Rowman & Littlefield, 2015, 263–73.

Byrne, Katherine. *Edwardians on Screen*. New York: Palgrave Macmillan, 2015.

Byrne, Katherine. "New Developments in Heritage: The Recent Dark Side of *Downton* 'Downer' *Abbey*." In *Upstairs and Downstairs: British Costume Drama Television from The Forsyte Saga to Downton Abbey*. James Leggott and Julie Anne Taddeo, eds. New York: Rowman & Littlefield, 2015, 177–189.

Cardwell, Sarah. "Persuaded? The Impact of Changing Production Contexts on Three Adaptations of *Persuasion*." In *British Television Drama*. Jonathan Bignell and Stephen Lacey, eds. 2d ed. New York: Palgrave Macmillan, 2014, 84–97.

Case, Karl E., and Robert J. Shiller. "Is There a Bubble in the Housing Market?" *Brookings Papers on Economic Activity* 2003: 299–362.

Chapman, James. "*Downton Abbey*: Reinventing the British Costume Drama." In *British Television Drama*. Jonathan Bignell and Stephen Lacey, eds. 2d ed. New York: Palgrave Macmillan, 2014, 131–42.

Cornelson, Jesseca. "Master, Servants, and the Effaced Middle Classes." In *The Great Recession in Fiction, Film, and Television*. Kirk Boyle and Daniel Mrozowski, eds. Lanham, MD: Lexington Press, 2013, 163–88.

Dete, Dan. *The Complete Book of 1940s Broadway Musicals*. New York: Rowman & Littlefield, 2015.

Dole, Carol M. "Austen, Class, and the American Market." In *Jane Austen in Hollywood*. Linda Troost and Sayre Greenfield, eds. 2d ed. Lexington: University of Kentucky Press, 2001, 58–78.

Eaton, Rebecca. *Making Masterpiece*. New York: Viking, 2013.

Eberwein, Robert. *Armed Forces: Masculinity and Sexuality in the American War Film*. New Brunswick: Rutgers University Press, 2007.

Elvis, Lucy. "Topophilia: Or, How We Got Hooked on *Downton*." *Downton Abbey and Philosophy*. Adam Barkman and Robert Arp, eds. Chicago: Open Court, 2016, 129–38.

Hipsky, Martin A. "Anglophil(m)ia: Why does America Watch Merchant-Ivory Movies?" *Journal of Popular Film & Television* 22/3 (Fall 1994): 98–107.

Laird, Ross. *Moanin' Low: A Discography of Female Popular Vocal Recordings, 1920–1933*. Westport, CT: Greenwood, 1996.

Nelson, Robin. "Costume Drama." *The Television Genre Book*. Glen Creeber, ed. 3d ed. London: Palgrave/British Film Institute, 2015, 52–53.

Quinn, James, and Jane Kingsley-Smith. "Kenneth Branagh's *Henry V* (1989): Genre and Interpretation." In *British Historical Cinema: The History, Heritage and Costume Film*. Claire Monk and Amy Sargent, eds. British Popular Cinema. New York: Routledge, 2002, 163–75.

Sherwood [Magee], Gayle. "Song, Genre, and Transatlantic Dialogue in *Gosford Park*." *Journal of the Society for American Music* 2/4 (November 2008): 477–505.

Stilwell, Robynn J. "Sense & Sensibility. Form, Genre, and Function in the Film Score." *Acta Musicologica* 72/2 (2000): 219–40.

Strovas, Karen Beth, and Scott M. Strovas. "'What Are We Going to Do with Uncle Arthur?' Music in the

British Serialized Period Drama." In *Upstairs and Downstairs: British Costume Drama Television from The Forsyte Saga to Downton Abbey*. James Leggott and Julie Anne Taddeo, eds. New York: Rowan & Littlefield, 2015, 95–110.

Suskin, Steven. *Show Tunes: The Songs, Shows, and Careers of Broadway's Major Composers*. New York: Oxford University Press, 2010.

Troost, Linda, and Sayre Greenfield. "Introduction: Watching Ourselves Watching." In *Jane Austen in Hollywood*. Linda Troost and Sayre Greenfield, eds. 2d ed. Lexington: University of Kentucky Press, 2001, 1–12.

Zuckoff, Mitchell. *Robert Altman: The Oral Biography*. New York: Alfred A. Knopf, 2009.

Series Two of *Downton Abbey*
War! What Are We Good For?

ELIZABETH FITZGERALD

In American culture, there's great respect for an enterprising spirit. People are encouraged to follow their dreams and reach for the stars with utmost confidence in themselves. Of course, these sentiments are often met with financial or practical challenges. But beyond that, they assume a socially acceptable sense of purpose, even from a young age. It's a common question to ask small children what they want to be when they grow up. While the askers understand that people inevitably change their answers as interests mature, there's still an expectation that they should have something well respected and financially sound in mind.

As a result, people of any age often find themselves overwhelmed with the question's heavy implications. I see it in my classes of freshman college students, many of whom aren't sure what to major in or what career to pursue. Some have been out of school for years and are trying to find a new purpose. I watch as my parents' generation nears retirement and frets over what they'll do with their lives once their decades-long careers come to a close. In the same way, the characters on *Downton Abbey*, though vastly different from contemporary Americans in wealth, status, and historical period, can't figure out what to do with themselves. Instead of accepting this unknown, they desperately try to remedy it as quickly as possible. This theme becomes increasingly pronounced in later seasons of the show, but begins to take shape in the much-maligned second series.

Criticism of *Downton Abbey* often accuses the series of being escapism for viewers dreaming about life as aristocrats with glamorous clothes and breathtaking country estates.[1] This interpretation of the show pits the show's values against Americans' identifying Puritan work ethic. As Americans, we take great pride in our work and are even touchier about it when the media laments that our jobs are being outsourced, our students are behind in STEM fields,[2] and many businesses and banks are going under completely. As a result, when some critics encounter the frills and drama of *Downton Abbey*, they may feel a need to disassociate themselves from it in order to defend their belief that hard work, not inherited status and titles, is what brings the best rewards.

However, if critics look more closely at what goes on with the majority of the characters on the show they would notice that these characters from historical fiction actually share many contemporary Americans' anxieties. From Series Two onward, most of the characters in *Downton Abbey* agonize about how useful or how necessary they are. And as is the case with many Americans today, they can't help but measure their use, and also their personal value, by their work. The work we do is essential to how society perceives us: teachers are seen as having large amounts of time "off," and stay-at-home parents are often described in shorthand as "not working." Details aside, the heated nature of these debates confirms that in any society, some types of work will be considered more legitimate than others. Shifting values and trends deem what work is worthwhile and what isn't. It's a capricious standard at best, yet we can't stop measuring others and ourselves up to it.

In Series Two of *Downton Abbey*, set during World War I, most of the characters experience a crisis where they reevaluate what they do and strive to prove to themselves or others that they are necessary. Their often-unsuccessful search for purpose encompasses characters' jobs as well as their personal commitments to others, affecting "upstairs" and "downstairs" characters alike. The fear of uselessness is highlighted near the end of Series Two, when Cousin Isobel, the perpetual do-gooder, is trying to keep Downton functioning as a convalescent home. She asks Cora Grantham, "Well, that life of changing clothes and killing things and eating them, do you really want it again? Would you rather Downton was useful?" (2:6). Naturally, everyone wants Downton to be useful, but the conflict arises in the discrepancies between what qualifies as useful. Instead of ignoring this tension, *Downton* self-consciously brings all of its insecurities to the surface.

As early as 1:2, the servants' jobs are called into question. Matthew, having recently found out that he stands to inherit Downton, shuns the help of Molesley, his new butler. After not allowing Molesley to help him get dressed, he accidentally belittles him by saying, "surely you have better things to do" and adding that Molesley's job "seems a very silly occupation for a grown man" (Fellowes 102). Hearing this, Molesley appears to wilt. In a pragmatic sense, what Molesley is doing *is* unnecessary, as Matthew is capable of picking out and putting on his own clothes, but Matthew quickly realizes Molesley's need to feel that his job is worthwhile and permanent. In a later scene, Matthew purposely asks him for help. In this way, he is supporting Cora's answer to Cousin Isobel's question about making Downton useful, which is that they "provide employment" (2:6). Even though the Granthams may create jobs for servants, it is still unclear whether the servant help is necessary. In the case of moping Molesley, his role is only temporarily acknowledged. As the series progresses, viewers get many more opportunities to see him look pathetic and pointless. He remains out of place in nearly every season.

There's no doubt that Molesley is placed in an unusual situation, working for someone who doesn't want his services. Yet historically, questions as to the purpose of servants in the early twentieth century were not unusual. New technology, like electric lights, helped make maintaining a home easier in the sense that servants had a reprieve from individually lighting numerous candles and oil lamps and battling the soot they'd left behind. Also, many of the jobs servants used to do within a large country estate began to be outsourced to commercial shops in town. In the article "Troops of Servants: Labour and Planning in the Country House 1840–1914," Jill Franklin explains that public cleaners, dairies, and bakehouses became more common, and reduced the work of servants employed by a larger household (227–228).

Because the nature of service work didn't produce anything clearly measurable, servants' roles seemed even more mysterious. Today, scholars like Jane Miller observe that servants "have been left out of an analysis that measures, values, and rewards labor in terms of productivity" (70). In the eyes of political zealots and historians, servants "lacked the glamour and heroism of workers in heavy industry or even of farm laborers" (Miller 70). The second series of *Downton Abbey*, set from 1916 to 1918, takes place well after the publication of Karl Marx and Frederick Engels' *The Communist Manifesto* in 1848. While their revolutionary theories shaped the public's views of workers in industry, Marx and Engels' writings are not easily applied to the servant characters of *Downton Abbey*. Aside from the introduction of new inventions here and there, the servants at Downton Abbey are largely sheltered on an estate in the countryside, removed from the day-to-day effects of the industrial revolution on urban life, like the increase in factory work. Servants in a country manor didn't fit the archetype of "worker," and to some degree, the work they did seemed as frivolous as that of the people they served. The real struggles of servants at the time were not considered fashionable or cause-worthy. Even today, the scholarly historical interest in servants' living and working conditions focuses mainly on the seventeenth through the nineteenth centuries in England, stopping before the twentieth.

In *Downton Abbey*, the younger characters' desire to leave service emphasizes that they have trouble seeing their current work as valuable. In Series Two, Gwen, Ethel, and Thomas imagine more ambitious careers for themselves where they stand a chance of acquiring more status or even fame. They do not have the same respect for the job as Mrs. Hughes and Mr. Carson who were likely hired years earlier when service jobs in country estates were considered among the best options in the field, and there was a lot of competition for the positions (Franklin 212). The younger servants' attitudes reflect some of the major shifts happening in the service industry at the time. Servants lost some bargaining power as a group around World War I as their numbers decreased by a few hundred thousand (Hopkins 170). This decrease could be attributed to aristocrats hiring fewer servants as a measure to economize during the war, but fewer people looking for jobs in the service profession contributed as well (Hopkins 170).

The conflicts that sometimes erupt among the different servants on the series demonstrate how the economy, and the prestige of being a servant in an aristocratic house, had changed over time. Because many of the servants are caught in a more old-fashioned mindset, their opinions seem to contradict the need for reform Marx and Engels advocate. Writing fifty years before the series is set, Marx and Engels observe that the bourgeoisie had "pitilessly torn asunder the motley feudal ties that bound man to his 'natural superiors,' and [had] left remaining no other nexus between man and man than naked self-interest, than callus 'cash payment'" (12). Mrs. Hughes and Mr. Carson, however, demonstrate the near opposite of the broken ties Marx and Engels describe. They thrive off of the trust created between them and the people they serve not just because it is the way they earn a living but also because it is an essential part of their identity. As Nicolaus Mills observes, at Downton Abbey, there are a number of strong but often complicated ties between people both within and across classes. The servants who realize this and find a niche where they feel they are needed are the most content even to the point of making great sacrifices: Mrs. Hughes passes up an offer of marriage in order to continue her work at Downton; Mr. Carson is accused of constantly making work for himself every moment of his day.[3] Not only do these two seem unaware of the specter of communism, they'd be passively uninterested if it floated by.

In fact, their behavior seems more akin to Adam Smith's description of how civilization is established by the mutual agreements in division of labor. Smith argues, "man has almost constant occasion for the help of his brethren" (30–31). He describes a way of making progress by framing one's actions in relation to the needs of others; he advocates altruistic behavior, whether genuine or in appearance, as the best way to get ahead. At Downton Abbey, the servants' most valuable work involves a sense of trust between themselves and the people they serve. By proving that they have a unique and essential role in the household, the servants are able to continue on. Film critic Roger Ebert, in his assessment of the second series of *Downton Abbey*, agrees: "There is pride in doing one's job well, in being the epitome of a footman, a ladies' maid, a butler, a valet." Servants like Molesley who feel as though their roles are shifting and unsubstantial flit nervously from one desperate plan to another.

Molesley's anxiety about not being needed is not just a personal struggle but rather something that is representative of the service profession as a whole during World War I. When country estates like the fictional Downton Abbey were built, the size of their servants' quarters reflected how much power and money the lord and lady had. According to Franklin, "No one supposed that the work done in the house increased in proportion to the number of servants; on the contrary, the more there were the lighter their duties" (213). When Lord and Lady Grantham greet their guests by lining up their servants outside of the Abbey, most of the servants do not have a particular job to do at this moment. Their purpose in this instance is to look like pieces of fine china on display in a hutch. By showing a collection of Mrs. Hughes, Mr. Carson, O'Brien, Thomas, Bates, Anna, Gwen or Ethel, William or Mr. Lang, Lord and Lady Grantham can impress their guests with the knowledge that all these people are in their employment, along with a number of other servants like Mrs. Patmore and Daisy tucked away in the kitchen.

Much as Miller alludes to in her discussion of where servants fit in history, what is or isn't useful within the world of *Downton Abbey* is subjective, based on the background of the character mulling over this question. For instance, in terms of how Matthew appraises Molesley's help, it is unclear to him what Molesley is actually doing. It's no wonder that Matthew, a lawyer, is baffled by the servant/employer relationship. Illana Krausman Ben-Amos, in "Gifts and Favors: Informal Support in Early Modern England," describes how servants' contracts were typically "short," and "incomplete," which often led to confusion when the courts needed to get involved (310). Even if Matthew personally hadn't faced conflicts with servants' contracts, Molesley's lack of a defined role or job expectations on its own is enough to be unsettling. In Matthew's home, at least at first, there isn't a clear need for Molesley, nor respect for his livelihood. In fact, servants were often perceived as being caught in a sort of social and economic no-man's-land. According to Miller, the servants in an aristocratic house existed "on the fringes of middle-class and, indeed, of upper-class life" (70). Because Molesley is more aware of the social rules for the upper classes than Matthew is, he in some ways appears both superior and inferior to Matthew, which puts them both in an uncomfortable situation.

Molesley's prewar unease described earlier only sets the stage for a number of characters looking for more meaningful occupations in light of England's involvement in World War I. In behavior that models Adam Smith's theories, the characters set out with determination to find what people need and how they can fulfill it for them. Across England, men headed to war as part of the draft and voluntary enlistment. While they were away, many women found new roles for themselves as they ran spouses' and family members' businesses. There was a sense of common need for people to be industrious in order to help the country as a whole produce the food, tools, and weapons needed to keep fighting. With World War I as a key element of Series Two, the show focuses even more directly on characters trying to be useful and failing or experiencing tragic consequences because of their efforts. The question of whether Downton as a whole is useful hovers over the storyline. In 2:1, female activists show up at a fundraiser at Downton Abbey, handing out white feathers as a symbol of cowardice to humiliate any men who are not in uniform. The pressure to be useful, in this case to the war effort, is clearly not only a personal compulsion but something that is reinforced even by external forces.

For the male characters, the pressure to serve in the war is particularly connected to their identity as men. Even today, when there are more women working and acting as the main providers for their families, many men still have a strong sense of pride and purpose connected with their ability to financially support a family through their work. Their desire is not necessarily based on a need to create power for themselves, but rather may be connected to concepts of chivalry, which make them feel it is their responsibility to serve other members of their community whom they see as being in greater need. Wartime creates the need for soldiers, the perfect masculine job. In *From Chivalry to Terrorism: War and the Changing Nature of Masculinity*, Leo Braudy argues, "questions of heroism shade imperceptibly into questions of masculinity" (xii). War allows men to fulfill the archetype of hero by giving them a clear way to work not only for themselves but also for the good of their fellow soldiers and citizens.

In the case of *Downton Abbey*, World War I provides that strong sense of cause for the male characters. They are expected to be actively involved because of the influence of what Braudy calls "wartime masculinity ... a top-down and bottom-up effort to emphasize a code of masculine behavior more single-minded and more traditional than the wide array of circumstances and personal nature that influences the behavior of men in non-war situations" (xvi). Braudy's analysis resembles Miller's focus on groups whose work was not considered valuable in society. Servants did not seem to be useful on the home front during World War I, as they appeared to support a life of luxury as opposed to a life of productivity. If men's appropriate roles became even more narrowly defined during wartime, it would follow that being a male servant on a country estate during World War I was particularly frowned upon.

Because of this, the Dowager Countess' attempts to prevent some of her servants from going to war by making up ailments for them are incredibly damaging to their reputations. She pretends Molesley has trouble with his lungs and William has a bad skin condition (2:1). Even after the Dowager is called out on her plan, a nervous Molesley goes to Dr. Clarkson to reassert the fiction that he has problems with his lungs. Molesley evades the chance to serve in the war and fulfill a more classically masculine role than being a servant. Aside from having a natural fear of combat, he realizes becoming a soldier might result in the permanent loss of his peacetime career. Molesley feels compelled to advance his career as a servant in order to substantiate his role in the household. Like Carson and Mrs. Hughes, he still believes service work will be his path to success. Unlike their situations, however, Molesley's position seems in danger of being cut. Clearly, his definition of useful work is separate from most other characters' in Series Two and hasn't adapted to fit the wartime mentality. He pays for his decision by ending up further diminished in the eyes of the other characters, even if they do not know the fraud in his situation. He cannot attract Anna's interest, for instance, and his gifts to Lord Grantham are simply passed along to give credit to other people. He becomes hard to take seriously as he stays behind doing a job where he is often forgotten.

The idea of men working service jobs would eventually become more socially acceptable, as part what Braudy calls the "erosion of the traditional definition of masculinity" in the later twentieth century (xii). He notes the changes in profession for men, with a move from industry and agriculture to an expanding range of "white collar work and a service economy" (Braudy xii). In the later twentieth century, many men in countries like Britain and the U.S. did not have jobs that were considered to be manly in the sense of needing physical strength. While the definition of what it means to be masculine has since broadened to include men working in offices, or with computers, during World War I, the idea was more restrictive.

In response to these social pressures, most of the male characters in Series Two of *Downton Abbey* scramble to find a place for themselves. Their new ventures, in one way or another, end poorly, to say the least. William is eager to get to the front lines but once there, ends up mortally wounded. He risks his own life in order to protect both his country as a whole and more specifically, Matthew. On William's deathbed at Downton Abbey, he quickly marries Daisy. By helping provide for a girl who is otherwise destitute and lacking a family he fulfills truly chivalrous goals, but doesn't live to enjoy any of these successes.

Even Lord Grantham himself prepares to head to war, albeit as part of a misunderstanding. Although he isn't killed by his efforts, the magnanimous Lord Grantham has a fall from grace in Series Two that is largely based on his own sense that people both in Downton Abbey and in the larger country have no use for him. He's suddenly unsatisfied by his privileged life and a title that supposedly confirms his importance. He floats adrift and eventually becomes tempted not by some sultry minx, but rather a maid who, both emotionally and financially, radiates a strong need for him, as well as a deep concern for his well being. She is recently widowed and her son is smart enough but not wealthy enough to attend a good school. The temptation to be helpful proves to be an overwhelming aphrodisiac to both Lord Grantham and the maid.

In Series Two, Lord Grantham becomes an example of altruism being taken too far. Even before this series, Grantham is defined by his soft heart. Nicolaus Mills describes him as "[treating] those who work for him with a compassion that goes well beyond noblesse oblige." Even though Grantham's kindness isn't treated humorously in the show, it is so pronounced that it opens itself up as an easy target for late-night comedy. In Jimmy Fallon's parody called "Downton Sixbey," his version of Lord Grantham waits with the patience of a saint as Bates takes several minutes to drag himself (complete with an iron leg) across an entire room to hand deliver a letter ("Downton Sixbey Episode 1"). Fallon's version of Grantham doesn't seem too far off from the original character, who invites the grandparents of an illegitimate child over for dinner as a way to have them meet and acknowledge their grandchild and the baby's mother, another former maid at the Abbey. So it's not surprising that when Grantham loses out on an opportunity to be good-hearted and heroic by serving on active duty, he also loses his self-worth. This is compounded by his belief that even all the women in the Abbey have found jobs with busy schedules. His wife, cousin, and mother are busy running the convalescent home and seem to have little spare time. In 2:5 and 2:6, he passes Cora twice as she is rushing from place to place briefly telling him she won't be able to go to their friends' parties with him. As a result, he thinks of himself as "a foolish man who's lost his way" (2:7). Enter Jane, the picture of need as a widow trying to raise a son, providing Grantham with the opportunity to put on some figurative gleaming armor and come to her rescue. She represents the perfect opportunity for him to help her, and for her to return the favor. Their similarities come out in the scenes where they lock eyes, and she achingly says, "I wish you knew how much I want to help" (2:8). Her siren song promises to make them both feel useful again.

As Grantham observes with his wife Cora, the war provides the ladies of Downton Abbey an opportunity to find unique occupations. Because of the intense push for cooperation the war creates, Sibyl and Edith jump at the chance to find a place where they are needed. Sibyl begins work as a nurse, tending to wounded soldiers; Edith finds use for her driving skills on a neighboring farm. On the surface, both of these new jobs seem to be a chance for feminist progress. These women who initially were meant to oversee an estate and to find an appropriate person to marry suddenly have jobs that are better suited to their individual talents and interests. When one of the young women is complimented for doing a particular task, she is quick to make sure each sister is associated with a different type of work. Mary, after being complimented by Isobel for her care of Matthew, remarks, "It's nothing. Sibyl's the nurse in this family" (2:5). Similarly, after Branson offers to teach Sibyl about fixing an engine, she identifies that work as "Edith's territory" (2:6). By finding separate ways to help others, the sisters develop clearer identities. Before, Edith and Sibyl, as the younger daughters, had less attention on them while everyone was focused on whom Mary would marry. Through their new pursuits, though, Edith and Sibyl develop skills that make them stand out from others and help them fulfill more particular needs. For Edith, who seems to have few suitors, she suddenly feels in great demand, driving a tractor to fill in for a farm hand who is off to war.

Still, as with most characters on *Downton Abbey*, just when Edith appears to find a place where she is needed and wanted, she steps outside the bounds of ethics. She inappropriately reaches out to John Drake, a farmer, to feel even more desired. Interestingly, before Edith kisses the married farmer, they have a brief conversation that ties their attraction to one another with his ability to come up with work that only she can do. The farmer says wistfully to her, "I'll be forced to invent some tasks in order for you to come much more," to which Edith responds, "Then start inventing, please" (2:2). The happiness can't last long, though. Series Two establishes a trend of characters finding a perfect need to fulfill, then being punished for those very efforts later on. The same goes for Edith, who receives a note thanking her for her help and—worst of all for someone who is looking for a place in the world—telling her she is no longer *needed* on the farm (2:2).

Edith's sister, Sibyl, enjoys her new job as a nurse, and often speaks to how fulfilling it is. Like her father's and Edith's attempts to be helpful, Sibyl's altruistic work is not, at least to others, the act of heroism that she sees it to be. Sibyl, while growing closer to Branson, has her work dismissed by him as "bringing hot drinks to a lot of randy officers" (2:4). While Sibyl's work is seen by her family as revolutionary, Branson sees it as not going far enough. Even though Branson is supposed to be a symbol of political and social rebellion, he knocks down Sibyl's work. He overlooks the fact that she is stepping into an unfamiliar and somewhat intimidating world in her work as a nurse. Although she doesn't lose her job in the sense that Edith loses hers, Branson's words suggest that she is unnecessary. His description of her makes it seem like she is fetishistic entertainment for the soldiers rather than a true nurse. Like Matthew's snap at Molesley, Branson's words are said dismissively in a moment of frustration, but there is honesty in his reaction. His sentiment is clear: the work she is doing is a waste of time and he doesn't see it as enough of a reason for her to delay running off with him.

The Abbey's official inhabitants aren't the only ones looking for a sense of purpose.

Their fixation with finding something to do is contagious, and infects the meek, gentle Lavinia as well. Lavinia, after accepting that her fiancé Matthew may never walk again and can never be a lover to her, demands that he allow her to take care of him. While to some extent Lavinia's dedication is understandable, as she loves him and was engaged to him, she becomes somewhat obsessed with her new role. After Cora invites her back to the Abbey, Lavinia tells Matthew of the way she has found to be useful:

> LAVINIA: I love you. I'm going to look after you; that's all there is to it.
> MATTHEW: And if I refuse?
> LAVINIA: I'm sorry but I mean it. You won't frighten me away, whatever you do [2:6].[4]

During this conversation, she grabs his wheelchair and begins pushing him. The expression on his face makes Matthew look like he's just been kidnapped. Certainly, if anyone is frightened by this new situation, it's Matthew. The power dynamic in their relationship significantly changes when Lavinia insists she knows what is best for him, rather than trusting his own decisions. She becomes equally businesslike when considering her own happiness as she gives up the chance for a fulfilling marriage in order to have a job to do. By staying with Matthew, she will always know she is needed and can reassure herself that she is doing something good. In the larger plot of the show, Lavinia is, transparently, the weakest link in a love triangle with Matthew and Mary, and her death by influenza fits neatly with serial drama's ways of bringing lovers together. Symbolically, though, it is as if her whole existence depends on helping Matthew. Once he regains his ability to walk, she must depart from the story because she is no longer needed. In fact, as she's dying, she makes Matthew laugh by continuing to assert that she took better care of him when he was injured than Mary would have (2:8). There's obviously no competing with Lavinia's relentless care and attention. Unlike William, whose death helps prove he had a heroic purpose, Lavinia dies from losing her clear purpose.[5] Either way, try too hard to find a role for yourself, and you'll end up harming yourself or others, or so *Downton Abbey* seems to suggest.

The lengths Lavinia and other characters take to help others might be considered "pathological altruism" (Angier). According to doctors studying this phenomenon, when altruistic behavior is taken too far, it becomes "unhelpful, unproductive and even destructive" (Angier). As is shown on *Downton Abbey*, the result of such behavior is often some type of harm to the people involved in it or the person they are attempting to help. Barbara Oakley suggests that all this focus on serving others takes a lot of energy on all sides. "The laws of thermodynamics dictate that the transfer of energy will itself exact a tax, which means that the overall disorder churned up by the transaction will be slightly greater than the new orderliness created" (Angier). On *Downton Abbey*, in spite of all of the cooperation and compassion, more and more disorder is stirred up. This contributes to the plot but also shows something is the matter with the characters desperate to find a job for themselves to do. Many doctors speculate that people become hooked on altruistic behavior because they feel they are inadequate and unworthy of having their own needs and desires (Angier).

Like Lavinia, Mr. Lang shows a similar dependence on his work, but for different reasons. He suffers from shell-shock after his time at war, but continues to work with Carson's level of meticulousness. When he breaks down in the middle of serving dinner, O'Brien tries to comfort him by telling him he "shouldn't be working yet" (2:2). Mr. Lang responds poignantly, "I must work. I don't know what to do else. I have to work" (2:2).

Since his life is haunted by what he's seen and experienced, he is not going to find joy in doing much for his own sake. Rather, if he can focus on a particular task or fulfilling someone else's needs, he can let other voices and ideas guide him, rather than his own nightmarish thoughts.

The term "workaholic" is used to describe such contemporary behavior, and its obvious similarity to the word "alcoholic" suggests that work can be treated in the same way as a drug that promises at least the illusion of escape. Many people today still seek work as a refuge from whatever weighs on their minds. It gives them a sense of control they might not have otherwise. Lang's situation in particular helps generate the "compassion" in the series that Mills describes as the trademark of the show. Lang's confession brings out a gentle, caring side of O'Brien that she rarely reveals. The sense of compassion does not just appear within the show, but is formed in the viewers' attachment to the characters as well. Viewers know what it feels like to place so much stock in their work and to turn to it when other aspects of their lives feel out of order.

However, the struggles for usefulness are not always taken so solemnly on *Downton Abbey*. Cousin Isobel's desire to find a place for herself is easily manipulated by the Dowager Countess when she tests out different causes on her, waiting for her to take the bait and move out of Downton Abbey. Helping the convalescent soldier? Finding work for jobless women? Aiding refugees? The Dowager knows Isobel will feel her heart pulled toward one of these causes. She finally holds Isobel's attention when she conjures up images of refugees "flung across Europe far from their homelands and in so much need of *your* help" (2:6). The Dowager Countess' elaborations on why Isobel specifically would be so useful for this job are clearly fabrications, even to Isobel, who questions where the Dowager got this information. But in the world of *Downton Abbey*, it is more important for Isobel to have a cause than to find out if the Dowager Countess is weaving some elaborate yarn to get an annoying relative to hit the road.

In an equally entertaining but less altruistic way, in Series Two Thomas tries everything imaginable to prove to Carson and Lord Grantham that they completely depend on his services. Thomas, who was previously intolerable to most of his fellow workers, strives to make himself as helpful as possible downstairs after he realizes he has completely wasted his savings on a scam of selling rationed goods. Thomas fittingly claims to Carson, "I'll try to make myself useful" (2:8). To hold the attention of Lord Grantham, Thomas temporarily kidnaps the family dog in hopes of looking heroic when he "rescues" it later. But when his elaborate, selfish plans to appear selfless go awry, it is all the more entertaining for audiences. Thomas' behavior near the end of Series Two is again representative of Adam Smith's observation about how labor is exchanged in order to create a civilized society. Smith explains that caring emotions aren't necessary to create the patterns of exchange needed to drive an economy. "It is not from the benevolence of the butcher, the brewer, or the baker that we expect our dinner, but from their regard to their own interest" (Smith 30–31). While many characters on *Downton Abbey* are obsessed with working for the good of others, Thomas demonstrates is that it is only important that others *believe* we are working for their good and that they are having their needs met. The motivation can be pathologically selfless, as in the case of Lavinia, or simply disguised as being selfless, as is the case with Thomas.

Because most of the characters' attempts to be useful end unsuccessfully in the second series, viewers have an easier time sympathizing with them, especially at a time when many of their own jobs are in question. Fans of the series may personally be trying to prove their own usefulness or watching the comedy of their fellow employees trying to convince their superiors that they deserve to stay. Like O'Brien, they may grimly realize "we're all essential, till we get sacked" (3:1). Both in the context of the show and in today's work world, workers find themselves questioning the value and stability of their livelihoods. As a result of these musings, many of the characters treat themselves like consumer products and, consistent with Adam Smith's beliefs about fulfilling one another's needs, try to make sure they are always in demand. Regardless of where people fall in society, they share a similar fear that they'll no longer be needed. *Downton Abbey* is acutely aware of this fear and reflects on it both seriously and playfully.

Of course one could argue there are some notable exceptions to the idea that a search for usefulness is always punished in the second series. A prominent general publically thanks Edith, for instance, for her hard work tending to the soldiers.[6] Even Thomas somehow manages to receive a promotion from all his scheming. These little victories only show the extrinsic benefits of serving others can be very inconsistent. For workers who are already feeling insecure about their position, there is often little to encourage or reassure them. As in Thomas' case, sometimes those who are good at looking—rather than being—hard at work have their efforts most valued. This unfairness gets even more pronounced in Series Three, when workers can get away with only good looks in their favor. While Carson insists "hard work and diligence weigh more than beauty in the real world," the Dowager Countess gleefully quips, "If only that were true!" (3:3). When hoping for acknowledgment of their efforts, the characters discover the extremely unpredictable nature of their little service economy.

The characters' obsession with staying busy and staying needed raises questions about what actually forms their identity. In the end, are people more than what they are able to do for one another? This question is fresh in the minds of the aristocratic characters of *Downton Abbey*, who previously had meaning in their lives simply because of who they were, rather than what they did. As nobility, their place and purpose in life were defined for them. As true gentlemen and women, they were not expected to work. However, during Series Two, work presents itself as a means to differentiate the aristocratic characters from one another. It promises a sense of individuality and importance that exists beyond a network of family connections. In *Dignity at Work*, Randy Hodson argues that "meaningful work is essential for dignity" because human beings "want to see themselves as effective players who are getting somewhere in life as a result of their own efforts" (3, 44). While the characters in *Downton Abbey* are without a doubt privileged, their way of life prevents them from experiencing the pride of progressing because of their own actions. For the most part, instead of creating something new on their own, they are defending the ideas, wealth, estate, and belongings that others have gained for them. As a result, they struggle to function in a larger society that relies on more and more capitalist virtues.

If viewers question what importance the characters have in the world outside the Abbey, the series wisely brings these questions to the surface. With World War I as background to the second series' events, characters' previous roles no longer seem stable or satisfying. Their new sense of anxiety crosses boundaries of both class and level of morality, as their similar concerns but opposite approaches to coping with them create intriguing links across the episodes. Hank Stuever, in his description of why Series Two seems "disappointing," describes Downton Abbey as "a house full of fascinating people with not nearly enough to do." Rather than being a flaw in the writing, however, this lack of something to do develops into an important theme over the next four series.[7] The second series of *Downton Abbey* establishes this conflict by repeatedly undercutting characters' attempts to prove themselves. Viewers find themselves laughing and cringing at failings that relate so closely to their own fraught search for purpose.

Notes

1. One particularly spirited argument by Simon Schama of Columbia University describes *Downton Abbey* as "a servile soap opera that an American public desperate for something, anything, to take its mind off the perplexities of the present seems only too happy to down in great, grateful gulps." Likewise, Hank Stuever, from the Washington Post, believes that the show "is the very definition of escapism."

2. STEM: science, technology, engineering, and math.

3. With Mr. Carson and Mrs. Hughes, it's difficult to tell what came first: their love for one another or their love of their work.

4. In Series Three, viewers experience déjà vu when Edith's promises to Sir Anthony Strallan parallel Lavinia's to Matthew. Edith makes Sir Anthony squirm when she declares, "I don't love you *in spite* of your need to be looked after; I love you *because* of it. I want you to be my life's work" (3:2). If women in the later twentieth century are accused of marrying bad boys in order to treat them as projects and rehabilitate them, *Downton Abbey* suggests that between the World Wars, every woman longed for a disabled man to become her "life's work."

5. Ironically, in Series Three, Lavinia's desire to be helpful is posthumously fulfilled when the money Matthew inherits from her family helps save Downton Abbey.

6. The great need for volunteer help during the war years necessitates that all three Grantham sisters at some point provide care for wounded soldiers. Their roles are still distinct from one another in that Sybil has some medical training, while Mary and Edith help with humanitarian matters.

7. It takes thirteen long years for characters like Edith, Molesley, and Thomas to happily settle into vocations of magazine owner, teacher, and butler. While several characters successfully find purpose by the final episode of the entire series, the path to it begins messily in Series Two.

Works Cited

Angier, Natalie. "The Pathological Altruist Gives Till Someone Hurts." *The New York Times.* The New York Times, 3 Oct. 2011. Web. 25 June 2012.

Ben-Amos, Ilana Krausman. "Gifts and Favors: Informal Support in Early Modern England." *The Journal of Modern History* 72.2 (June 2000): 295–228. *JSTOR.* Web. 26 June 2012.

Braudy, Leo. *From Chivalry to Terrorism: War and the Changing Nature of Masculinity.* New York: Knopf, 2005. *ebrary.* Web. 23 June 2012.

"Downton Sixbey Episode 1." *Late Night with Jimmy Fallon.* NBC.COM. NBC Universal Media. Web. 3 July 2012.

Ebert, Roger. "Think of Me as the B, Carson." *Roger Ebert's Journal.* Chicago Sun-Times. suntimesonline.com 19 Jan. 2012. Web. 14 Aug. 2012.

Fellowes, Julian. *Downton Abbey: The Complete Scripts Season One.* New York: William Morris, 2012. Print.

Franklin, Jill. "Troops of Servants: Labour and Planning in the Country House 1840–1914." *Victorian Studies* 19.2 (1975): 211–239. *JSTOR.* Web. 26 June 2012.

Hodson, Randy. *Dignity at Work.* Cambridge: Cambridge University Press, 2001. *ebrary.* Web. 29 June 2012.

Hopkins, Eric. *Industrialization and Society: A Social History, 1830–1951.* London: Routledge, 2000. *ebrary.* Web. 26 June 2012.

Marx, Karl, and Frederick Engels. *The Communist Manifesto.* London, 1848. *ebrary.* Web. 17 May 2012.

Miller, Jane. "Doing For." *Raritan* 28.3 (2009): 66–78. *Humanities International Complete.* Web. 11 June 2012.

Mills, Nicolaus. "Why 'Downton Abbey' Is a Hit in America." *CNN Opinion.* CNN. 25 Feb. 2012. Web. 12 May 2012.

Schama, Simon. "No Downers in 'Downton.'" *The Daily Beast.* Newsweek/Daily Beast. 16 Jan. 2012. Web. 12 May 2012.

Smith, Adam. *Wealth of Nations.* London: 1776. *ebrary.* Web. 17 May 2012.

Stuever, Hank. "Stiff Upper Lips for 'Downton Abbey's' Disappointing Return." *The Washington Post.* washingtonpost.com. 5 Jan. 2012. Web. 14 Aug. 2012.

"There's always something"

Representing Race

Jennifer Poulos Nesbitt

In Series Five of *Downton Abbey*, Lady Mary Crawley justifies her decision to sleep with Lord Gillingham outside marriage with a veiled reference to Nancy Cunard: "Of course these days some women do [have sex before marriage]. I was talking to Lady Cunard's daughter last week and she was so graphic I almost fainted" (5:1). With this reference, *Downton* also proposes that rules for women's sexual behavior were changing ever so slightly[1]: Nancy Cunard's affairs in the 1920s were scandalous but not entirely destructive of her social status. We might see this moment as marking the difference between sexual mores—again, for women—in 1912 (Season One) and 1924 (Season Five). When Kemal Pamuk raped Mary in 1912, her reputation could be ruined no matter the context. There seems to be some wiggle room in 1924.

England's *Telegraph* heralded this change in morality in a 2014 article entitled "*Downton Abbey* Reveals its Raunchy Side" by Nancy Philipson, but one might suggestively replace *raunchy* with *racy*. Today, Nancy Cunard is known as an advocate for civil rights and an ardent promoter of African and African American artists and culture. She has also been criticized for "racial romanticism and her refusal to acknowledge her race and class privilege."[2] In 1924, when Mary Crawley refers to her, Cunard had not yet begun her relationship with Henry Crowder, an African American jazz musician, nor sent around the pamphlet version of *Black Man and White Ladyship* (1931) to her mother's friends for Christmas, nor produced the astounding anthology *Negro* (1934). Mary does not know the future, but the *Downton* audience could. Mary's reference to sexual knowledge is retroactively racialized even if the timing allows plausible deniability to the feisty historicists on *Downton*'s production team. The proximity of the reference—as "Lady Cunard's daughter" instead of Nancy Cunard—both deflects immediate identification ("Wait? Is that Nancy? Did the Cunards have another daughter?") and brackets racial content in a sexually charged remark. This strategy is emblematic of *Downton Abbey*'s treatment of race, a topic latent in many romantic relationships featuring aristocratic women and variously "othered" men but flattened in commentary about *Downton*.

In general, *Downton* is seen as focusing on race only in Season Four, when Gary Carr played African American Jack Ross, the first and only first and only "black character," described by Filipa Jodelka. His truncated romance with Lady Rose MacClare supplies evidence that *Downton Abbey* does address race, but this plot effectively restricts the category of race to a narrow plot arc in *Downton Abbey*. For example, as I will argue later, *Downton Abbey* portrays Rose's later marriage to a Jewish man as a difference in faith rather than race. Moving further back in the series, Sybil Crawley's marriage to Tom Branson, an Irishman, excites no racial slurs even though popular iconography and discourse racialized the Irish. Nor does anyone overtly castigate Mary for sex with a "*Turkish gentleman*" (1:3, emphasis added); she is threatened with social ruin for sexual activity alone. Despite their American Jewish heritage, *Downton Abbey* presents the Crawley daughters as English roses[3]—as is perhaps signified by their manifest surrogate in later seasons, Rose. When it comes to romance on *Downton Abbey*, there is indeed "always something" (6:6), as the Dowager says, but the series carefully manages the relationship of that "something" to race.

The methods *Downton* uses to deflect or interrupt conversations about race are modeled in the representation of the Jack Ross-Rose MacClare romance both within the series and in the reception of that plot in popular commentary. *Downton Abbey* positions race as an American, and specifically *African* American, problem imported temporarily to *Downton Abbey,* a site of Englishness, and commentators generally follow this lead, resulting in a curtailed discussion of the broader context for understanding race in the series. The discourse surrounding the Ross-MacClare plot illuminate the elision of racial content in romance plots both preceding and succeeding this deliberate address of race. To conclude, I argue that *Downton*'s presentation of birth control masks an underlying anxiety about English racial purity as a sign of national fitness. *Downton Abbey* capitalizes on the indeterminacy and flexibility of race as a category to maintain racial boundaries without rendering whiteness visible, and thus contestable, as an element of Englishness.

Observant *Downton* watchers might challenge this characterization: objections to racial intermingling do occur, and characters do exhibit racism. The Dowager refers to Kemal Pamuk as a "foreigner," but this remark precedes her knowledge of his sexual attack on Mary by nearly a year.[4] The nanny calls Miss Sybbie, the daughter of Lady Sybil and Irishman Tom Branson, a "wicked little cross-breed" (4:1) and an exiled Russian aristocrat denies Atticus Aldridge's claim to be Russian because he is Jewish. Lady Flintshire, Rose's mother, uses subterfuge to break off the match with Aldridge, trotting out stereotypes of misers and wanderers in the process (Season Five). Tom Branson refuses to acknowledge Jack Ross when Rose introduces them, and Mary, Rosamund, and Tony Gillingham all watch the proceedings with disapproval (4:4). Carson later asks Ross, "Have you never thought of visiting Africa?" (4:5). Such demonstrations of what might be called real racism toss a bone to historical accuracy, but the charge of racism only sticks to negatively portrayed characters like the Russian aristocrats, Lady Flintshire, Larry Merton, and occasionally the Dowager—who is excused her vagrant tongue because she is meant to represent the prejudices of a by-gone age.

These exceptions prove the rule: race is not an issue for the real English as embodied by the Crawley family and staff. They remain immune from mean-spirited prejudice and, with some tempering, aligned with present-day tolerance. As *Downton Abbey* producer and writer Julian Fellowes averred in an interview, the Crawleys' tolerance arises from their privilege "because they were more traveled, they were more sophisticated, they were more educated" (Itzkoff). He adds that "however much people were perfectly happy to have all sorts of people at their parties, there was a rule governing who you settled down with. I don't think we tried to whitewash that" (Itzkoff). Fellowes' statements gain credence in the scene in which Mary conspires to end the engagement between Rose and

Jack because Mary's objection to the match is not based on her beliefs but social practicality in an intolerant world. She claims that her father would object less to Ross' "color" than his profession (4:8).[5] *Downton* justifies Mary's attitude further by introducing the idea that Ross' mother also disapproves of the match out of fear of what others will do. Mary departs after expressing support for inter-racial marriage "in a better world" (4:8). Presumably this "better world" the Crawley family anticipates is now, when the enlightened celebrate diversity and promote tolerance of difference of all kinds, and Fellowes shields Mary—and by extension her family—from accusations of prejudice in preventing the marriage.

But *Downton*'s celebration of diversity and promotion of tolerance methodically minimizes race as a motivating factor in the drive toward a coupled-up, fertile finale. When commentator Mo Moulton calls Rose's relationship with Jack Ross "a flirtation" (Moulton, "Differences"), she understates the seriousness of a relationship that progresses to an engagement. Given the speed and efficiency with which this plot arcs, however, Moulton might be justified: *Downton* flirts with rather than seriously engages racism as an English problem. On *Downton*, racism is Americanized by transforming the stated historical model for the Jack Ross, Leslie Hutchinson ("Hutch"), a Grenadian and a subject of the British Empire. The switch in citizenship prevents the recognition that there are black British citizens resident in England. The Jack Ross-Rose MacClare romance, then, exemplifies at the level of plot what Mary Crawley's allusion to Nancy Cunard exemplifies in dialogue, a simultaneous address and suspension of race as integral to Englishness.

Such an elision is important to examine because *Downton Abbey* participates in the tradition of heritage film, a phenomenon associated with Thatcherite politics, as well as the genre of country house novels and poems.[6] Country house novels tend to feature inheritance and marriage plots that stand in for questions about appropriate national belonging: the house and its occupants norm the nation, its normative citizens, and national values.[7] Strategic intermarriage is a key element of incorporating and co-opting internal and external challenges to aristocratic power; the choices of the Crawley daughters indicate the parameters of strategic intermarriage for the next generation. In these marriages, race must be effaced in the matrices of identity politics *Downton Abbey* negotiates.

Substituting American for British citizenship on the program deliberately disconnects issues of racism from English society: on *Downton Abbey*, Jack must and can be interpreted in the context of black American entertainers in Europe, but this relocation of context forecloses insights into racist colonial ideologies underpinning English whiteness that an analysis of Leslie Hutchinson might offer. As Mo Moulton suggests, Ross "invites the viewer to imagine 1920s England as a homogeneously white place where racial diversity is linked mainly with modernization and Americanization" ("Race and Imperialism"). This strategy makes race an American problem, imported to Britain on a wave of interest in jazz, rather than a homegrown phenomenon. Jack Ross can thus tell Carson, in the flat American accent that precedes him into the servant's hall, "I'm no more African than you are. Well, not much. My people came over in the 1790s. We won't go into why or how" (4:5). This discreet allusion to American slavery invites a chivalrous response from Carson, who notes England's leadership "in the fight against slavery" (4:5). Carson conveniently forgets that abolition was necessary because England had profited from slave-trading and enslaved labor in its own colonies, including sugar plantations in the West Indies where Leslie Hutchinson was born.

The switch in national origin led to gaps in popular commentary as Ross' onscreen identity did not allow connections to his supposed historical origins in the British Empire. In American commentary, Jack Ross' descent from enslaved African people led commentators to name Nancy Cunard and Henry Crowder as historical models for Rose MacClare and Jack Ross. *Huffington Post* commentator Sonia Grant lamented *Downton's* pusillanimity on matters of race: "imagine, for instance, how melodramatic it would be if the characters Lady Rose MacClare and Jack Ross were based on actual individuals from a similar time and circumstance: Nancy Cunard and Henry Crowder." By contrast, English popular media ran stories about Leslie Hutchinson's scandalous life, offering superficial parallels between Hutchinson and Ross on the basis of musical talent and "sexual shenanigans" with white women and men (Wilson). But Rose's blithe protest connecting prejudice against Ross to "imperial nonsense about racial purity" (4:8) spurred little discussion.

Details of Leslie Hutchinson's story create a much more textured, and much less flattering, picture of racial politics and attitudes in England in the 1920s. For example, Hutch's marriage to "a black Anglo-Chinese girl Ella Byrd" (Thornton) from Beach, Georgia[8] links American use of indentured Chinese labor after emancipation to similar practices in the British West Indies. Moreover, Hutch may first have appeared in England at the British Empire Exhibition (1924–1925) as part of a West Indian Regiment Band (McKay 139).[9] The Hutchinsons purchased a house in Hampstead in 1928, where Ella, according to biographer Charlotte Breese, "lived quietly" in the deep shadows of Hutch's stardom for most of her life (69); Hutchinson's brother Ivan, who emigrated in 1926, also lived there (Breese 70). The notion that black people could be home-owning citizens with extended families in England is tacitly elided when Fellowes shifts Ross' citizenship, which limits the context in which the Crawley family can be understood as having a race.

As an effaced historical referent, Hutchinson's biography links *Downton Abbey* to black British history and British imperialism. The regiment band, for example, points to the role of military units from the colonies in the Great War. Peter Fryer, in his monumental study of the black British people *Staying Power*,[10] reports that the British West Indies Regiment lost 185 men to battle and a further 1,071 to disease, as well as 697 wounded (296); despite this service, black troops were prohibited from participating in victory celebrations (315). Black men, who faced extreme employment discrimination before the war, worked in industry and the merchant service as replacements for men who had joined the military (295–296). After the war, discrimination returned as demobilized white soldiers were favored for employment and the government secretly attempted to prevent black soldiers from learning they were eligible for unemployment payments (298–299). In 1919, there were riots due to unemployment, as well as racially motivated violence against black people fueled by prejudice, rumor and, as always, fears that white Englishwomen would suffer from insatiable black male lust (298–316). Similar fears governed reaction to France stationing black troops in the Rhineland after the war. Black troops were accused of raping German women and boys; in an article for the *Worker's Dreadnought*, Claude McKay refuted both the accuracy of the reporting and the virulent depiction of black men (316–321). All of these events occur in the span of years during which *Downton Abbey* is set. Fryer points out that "four years after the riots of 1919 [the riots] had been expunged from white memories" (316). This amnesia may account, in the 1920s, for the Crawley family's blindness to race as a contemporary and divisive *British* issue, but *Downton Abbey*'s producers have a broader historical knowledge and the power of artistic choice.[11]

Leslie Hutchinson's intimate connections with the aristocracy and royalty also make race an integral part of England's domestic and international relations. Julian Fellowes, in an interview with the *New York Times*, describes Hutchinson as "a tremendous cabaret star, a friend of Cole Porter's, and he had affairs with lots of people including Tallulah Bankhead." Later Fellowes remarks, "Lord and Lady Mountbatten were among Hutch's best friends. And he would have been seen at their dinner parties. If he had tried to marry their daughter, that would have been a different story" (Itzkoff). In Fellowes' presentation, Hutchinson confines his bohemianism to male and female American entertainers, while members of the aristocracy are Hutchinson's friends and invite him to approved social engagements. The story is, in fact, quite different: Hutchinson had affairs with men and women, including the two people named in the first quotation, and he did not romance the Mountbatten's daughter, but allegedly Edwina herself. According to articles published in England's *Daily Mail* and *Telegraph*, Edwina, married to royalty and later Vicereine of India, apparently "didn't mind who talked, or what they said" and publicly kissed and fondled Hutch on numerous occasions (Wilson). Hutchinson was known for his sexual prowess and his attentions to white women—a reputation that probably gained from racist assumptions about black people's sexual appetites.[12] In 1930 he fathered a child with a debutante; the child was put up for adoption because its mixed-race parentage was unacceptable among the upper classes (Thornton). Admittedly, the *Daily Mail* and the *Telegraph* are not the most reliable journalistic sources, and Edwina Mountbatten's biographer Janet Morgan declares that the stories linking Edwina and Hutchinson are "piffle" (227). Morgan contends that the rumors stem from "people who wanted to believe that their prejudices were being violated," but she confirms that Edwina had given Hutch an expensive cigarette case, "affectionately inscribed" (227). Moving among the accounts offered by Fellowes, Morgan, and the newspapers, it seems clear that somewhere between denial of any sexual relationship and flagrant copulation lies a fear that aristocratic women might engage in mutual, consensual relationships with black men—and black men with a claim to citizenship at that. Changing Jack Ross' nationality is a kind of whitewashing, as it redirects inquiry away from conflicts over the role of race in establishing Englishness in the 1920s and frames the issue as a product of foreign intervention.

In the series itself, *Downton Abbey* addresses the effects of racism circumspectly and speculatively. Although there are many vague statements about the dangers faced by an interracial couple, none of those events come to pass: there is no visual evidence of racial violence. The closest the series comes to manifesting broad social disapproval are the remarks of Rose's companions at the nightclub when she first meets Ross: "Things have come to a pretty pass when you have to be rescued by a black band leader," offers her Aunt Rosamund (4:4). When Rose meets Jack at a Thirsk tea-shop, Tom Branson catches a glimpse through the shop window, and later predicts "trouble"; a double-take on the part of an unidentified local man confirms his reaction as normal and reasonably protective in the social context (4:8). Rose and Jack's conversation in the shop similarly alludes to trouble without enacting it visually. When she touches his cheek, he recoils. When she accuses him of being "self-conscious," he responds, "A black singer with the daughter of a marquess in a north Yorkshire town. Why should we attract attention?" (4:8). But attract attention—outside the shop—is all they do: they have not been refused service (as Hutchinson and Robeson both were at times), nor have any patrons indicated disapproval. Nor does anyone find the relationship worth reporting to the earl, the countess, or the dowager. In London, Rose and Jack kiss under a bridge (4:7), which may signify that they are shielded from and wish to avoid public exposure. The wide camera angle on the scene, however, suggests that the couple is clearly visible: again, no protests or jeers ensue. This situation differs significantly from the private gatherings at which Edwina Mountbatten fondled Hutchinson, yet the world seems unconcerned.

Similarly, racist response to Rose's engagement is cast in the subjunctive, anticipating without exposing racism among *Downton*'s cast of characters. Jack asks Rose, "will Lord Grantham enjoy the *différence*? Or Lady Mary?" (4:7), an idea he repeats when Mary confronts him about the engagement: "I suppose you are here to say that Lord Flintshire would find the prospect of a black son-in-law preposterous. And your father would agree" (4:8). But the audience for the series never sees Lord Grantham's—let alone Lord Flintshire's—reaction, because both remain ignorant of the romance. Mary absolves herself when she claims to believe Jack loves Rose, though she does not think Rose's love could "survive what they'll do to you." Ending the engagement is a matter of protecting all concerned from the racism of unnamed others whose actions are described in vague terms. Mary tells Rose she would prefer her "not to lose control of [her] life" and Jack confirms, "I don't want to spoil her life" (4:8). Even Rose's enchanting race blindness focuses on rhetoric rather than action: "I won't listen to any imperialist nonsense about racial purity, and how he should be horse-whipped for daring to dream." To Rose, racism is words to which she must "listen," rather than acts of violence or discrimination; her notion of Jack being "horse-whipped" is steeped in class privilege that belies the sticks, bricks and incendiaries that featured in the 1919 riots. Finally, her idea that Jack is "daring to dream" reinforces the white superiority she claims to despise. The truncation of the romance prevents the possibility that Julian Fellowes might have to tell a historically accurate story of the social and economic response to mixed-race couples.

Despite its limitations, however, the Jack Ross plot allows *Downton* to cut race from the frame of other romantic entanglements and limit it, implicitly, to a romantic partner with observable variation in skin color. Thus, the introduction of a Jewish suitor for Rose involves a different kind of "*différence*": religion. Racial connotations of Jewishness are present, but the script focuses aggressively on religious difference. Isobel Crawley avers, "It's not like the Catholics, is it? She won't be expected to convert" (5:6). Atticus informs Lord Grantham, "We both know a difference in religion is a big thing" (5:7). Even Lord Sinderby's objections are couched in terms of a decision to "marry outside the faith" (5:7). As Moulton explains, the link between the Crawleys and the Aldridges "is class; religion is incidental. The Crawleys might well have accepted the Aldridges, leaders of the Jewish community, even while flinching from lower-class Jewish residents of the East end [*sic*]" ("Differences"). Indeed, the Dowager insulates herself from charges of prejudice when she describes attending the 1878 marriage of the Earl of Rosebery to Hannah Rothschild, a society marriage thoroughly covered in the illustrated newspapers of the time (Cowan 49–51). "In marrying a Rothschild," the dowager adds coyly, "there are certain compensations" (5:8). She has good reason to know, since Cora, whose father was Jewish, brought a fortune to Downton's needy coffers, and Lord Grantham chose her for that reason.

The idea of Jewish people as a racial group who must assert, and re-assert, their claim to Englishness also circulates in the series, but anti–Semitism is a characteristic of negatively portrayed characters. Ephraim Atticus Aldridge is the scion of a titled Jewish family (the Sinderbys) with roots in England since the reign of Richard III (1483–1485) (Rachel Aldridge) and multiple connections within the English aristocracy. Lord Sinderby explains that he has retained the family's Anglicized name because "the family felt they were English now, and they wanted to stay ... English" (5:7). Even so, Lord Grantham remarks that Lord Sinderby will overcome his neighbors' English "principles" with "the chance of good shooting or eating well" (5:8). Negative racial stereotyping comes from Carson—the downstairs version of the dowager—who calls the Aldridges "that sort" and Lady Flintshire. The subtle discrimination practiced and/or acknowledged by the Downton crowd contrasts with deep-seated xenophobic racism from aristocratic Russian refugees. One Russian aristocrat shouts that Atticus is "not Russian now," in the twentieth century, nor were his ancestors "Russian then," in the nineteenth century, because he is Jewish. Rose's confusion at this outburst highlights the conflicting categories and definition of national and ethnic belonging while also confirming the tacit assumption that racial difference is about skin color.

The Russian prince's virulent rejection of Atticus' Russian roots points to the intertwined, overlapping, and paradoxical relationship between class and race, a relationship that allows discourses of class to imply things about race, and vice versa. Class categories are racialized, as we will see with Tom Branson's Irishness, and racial categories have a class, as is the case with Atticus. Context and contingency determines how these overlapping categories emerge rhetorically in a given situation. The Russian count disparages Atticus' ethnic and religious origins, but there is an element of class prejudice as well, as many of the Jewish refugees from Russia were poor. The refugee characterizes Atticus' family as they were in Russia, whereas Rose, the Crawleys, and *Downton* viewers and characters respond to him as he is, the well-mannered member of a titled family. In the nineteenth century, the Jewish population of England was primarily urban and associated with stereotypical occupations including "the financier, the pedlar [*sic*] and old-clothesman, the sharp entrepreneur, the rather shady ancillary of the machinery of the law" (Cowen xi). One group, the financiers like the Rothschilds and the fictional Sinderbys, was also acculturating to Victorian England and rising in class status; the first Jewish peer was created in 1885. However, between 1881 and 1914, waves of pogroms increased England's Jewish population due to "a mass immigration impelled by a combination of Russian persecution and economic pressures" (Cowen xi). One wave of migration occurred in 1905, just seven years before the setting of *Downton*'s first season. Typical fears about new, economically needy, minority groups engendered legislation to control and limit immigration (Cowan xvi–xvii). Anti-Semitic beliefs were common in early twentieth-century England and Ireland and surfaced more virulently in response to particular events. Glassman has shown that even during the period when Jews were expelled from England, "anti–Jewish sentiments continued to be spread by the preacher, the playwright, the writer, and the storyteller" (9). There were complaints that the Second Anglo-Boer War (1899–1902) was fought to protect Jewish interests (Bar-Yosef and Valman 1–2), and in 1912 both the Marconi Scandal and the Indian Silver Affair created "a large anti–Semitic reaction" even though no wrongdoing was proven (Langham 80). Thus even though "the financiers" like the Sinderbys move in the upper echelons of society, they are still vulnerable to anti–Semitic attacks that endanger their class privilege. Jewish people in England were caught by dichotomies of familiarity and difference, the desired and reviled other: they were "infinitely wealthy and yet abjectly poor; refusing to assimilate yet assuming a false English identity; cosmopolitan and tribal; 'alien' and yet almost overly familiar; ideal colonizer and undesirable immigrant; white but not quite" (Bar-Yosef and Valman 3). In Rose's marriage to Atticus, his class status diffuses racial stigma associated with lower classes of people, and the series avoids confronting anti–Semitism in its most racialized manifestations to create a vision of a harmonious and tolerant English social world.

The treatment of race in the romances of Rose MacClare, which occur after the midpoint of the series, provide a blueprint for reanimating racial content in romances earlier in the series. Rose is "the embodiment of the 'English rose' ideal" (Moulton, "Differences"), but she also condenses the romantic experiments plotted through the Crawley daughters. Her relationships with Ross and Aldridge evoke Mary's early fascination with Kemal Pamuk. Like Edith, she has an affair with a married man, and she flirts with a working-class man at a tea-dance, evoking memories of Sybil's romance with Tom Branson. Branson's differences with the Crawley household—upstairs and down—are depicted as those of class and nationality rather than race. The only indication that his relationship with Sybil might be considered in light of race comes from an ignorant and cruel nanny, and she is promptly fired. *Downton* projects Branson's racial likeness to his English counterparts by emphasizing his nationalist politics—he supports an independent Irish nation rather than a racial group—and merging him seamlessly with the downstairs staff otherwise. No one, not even Carson, makes offensive remarks about his Irishness.[13]

Yet racialized depictions of the Irish were common in the nineteenth century and persisted through World War II (Moulton, *Ireland* 317–320). L. Perry Curtis' well-known study of nineteenth-century political cartoons captures the representation of the Irish "as 'white Negro' and simian Celt" in order to establish their inferiority to English people and justify the work of empire (Curtis 13). Many of these simian figures were directly associated with political activity on behalf of Irish Home Rule or independence, as words like "Anarchy" or "Land League" or "Fenianism" are etched onto the bodies or clothing of the brutish portraits (see Curtis 42–49). Vincent Cheng links these images and beliefs not only to English nineteenth-century habits of seeing race as "synonymous with religion … and with social class" (16), but also to *fin de siècle* fears of racial decline that were most prominent in just before the Great War (17–19). These historical attitudes may faintly percolate in *Downton*'s dialogue when the dowager countess refers to Tom's Branson's uncouth brother as "a drunken gorilla" (3:6). Lord Grantham contemplates the inheritance of political attitudes through genetic material and muses that that he will have "a Fenian grandchild" (2:8). Visually, however, there is no difference between Branson and other Downton residents.

By the time of the Anglo-Irish War, the pervasiveness and extremity of such racist discourses about the Irish had shifted somewhat. Moulton notes, "evidence from the time of the Anglo-Irish War suggests that English people used the language of race to talk about the Irish inconsistently and to various ends" (*Ireland* 293), but the notion of racializing did persist often under the guise of critiques of Catholicism's effect on the Irish mentality (Moulton, *Ireland* 295). Moreover, Irish nationalists countered English racism with their own stereotypes to make sovereignty claims: "The very notion that there was still a pure and distinct Celtic race living in Ireland was an essentialist construction that, ironically enough, was equally acceptable (in fact essential) to both the Irish Nationalist and to the Anglo-Saxon imperialist" (Cheng 50).[14] An example of the ironies this situation enables occurs during the Great War, when Irish men living in England joined the military through cultural organizations like the London Gaelic League or the Irish Republican Brotherhood that "limited their membership to people of Irish descent" (Moulton, *Ireland* 111); these groups simultaneously supplies troops to England's war effort and cached weapons and money for the Irish cause (Moulton, *Ireland* 20–21). In the wake of the Great War and the treaty ending the Anglo-Irish War (1921), "the Irish in England were kept out of party politics and militant movements to the greatest extent possible" (Moulton, *Ireland* 3) because of perceived divided loyalties. This context provides additional reasons for the Crawleys to view Branson's involvement with the Labour Party and Sarah Bunting as a threat (Season Five); he might be returning to his roots in more ways than one.

In this context, the words Sibyl uses when she accepts Tom's proposal of marriage—"I'm ready to travel and you're my ticket" (2:7)—meld romance with foreign geography. Sybil meshes the erotic and the exotic, and she is not the only one to eroticize the exotic. The arrival of Kemal Pamuk generates an outpouring of statements fetishizing a Turkish man who fails negative Oriental spectacularly. Anna remarks that "he doesn't look like any Englishman I've ever met. Worse luck. I think he's beautiful," and Lord Grantham refers to "the gorgeous Turk" as "quite a treat for the ladies" (1:3). The objectifying remarks classify Pamuk as not-English, but the housemaid Gwen claims, "He doesn't look Turkish at all." In the interstices, in Pamuk's "infinite peculiarity," lies "a living tableau of queerness" (Said 103) with the capability of inciting desire across a spectrum of English character (Schmidt).[15] Julian Fellowes dismisses claims that he exoticized Pamuk by claiming a specific historical referent,[16] but his reliance on truth in fact does not eliminate cultural context for the Pamuk plot. In fact, Edward Said would claim it should incite our curiosity: "no matter how deep the specific exception, no matter how much a single Oriental can escape the fences placed around him, he is *first* an Oriental, *second* a human being, and *last* again an Oriental" (102). By particularizing Pamuk as a historical reality, Fellowes moves him into second category; the series itself discursively moves him into the third.

Like the Irish nationalists, Kemal Pamuk uses British assumptions to his advantage. When Pamuk plans his seduction of Mary, he informs Thomas that he "may need some help with the geography of the house" (1: (1:2). The seduction resembles a military campaign, and the enemy negotiates and conquers foreign terrain that symbolizes England. Peter Schmidt claims that Pamuk's careful mimicry makes him

> a dangerous rival to the British Empire, the Ottoman Turkish empire…. He's both more English than the English when it comes to certain skills, including horsemanship and the ability to captivate English maidenhood, and yet in other ways he's portrayed as an uncivilized rake, a barbarian, a man far handsomer, skilled, and ruthless than any of his English rivals.

Pamuk not only out–Englishes the English, but he challenges her with a lineage equal to, if not more selective than, the Granthams. Mary assents with a sniff when Pamuk suggests her family would object to him as a suitor; Pamuk then matches her disdain by indicating his family's distaste for a foreign match.[17] Kemal Pamuk may have an avatar in Mustafa Kemal Ataturk, with whom he partly shares a name, the so-called father of the Turks. Ataturk, who led Turkey in the early twentieth century, worked to modernize and democratize the Ottoman state. In photographs, Ataturk wears Western dress with aplomb, as does Pamuk, thus implying an ability to mimic Western ways.[18] Bar-Yosef and Valman note similar fears about acculturating Jewish English people: in both cases the ease with which supposedly different races can assume the accouterments and behaviors of Englishness produce anxiety about the stability of personal and national boundaries.

Schmidt, one of the few scholars to think through the implications of Pamuk's presence, wonders why "A Turk who's present for part of just a single episode thus plays a huge role in *Downton Abbey*'s eventual outcome." It is suggestive that Pamuk distracts Lady Mary from her putative job as Lord Grantham's eldest daughter: to reproduce a suitable male heir. At this point, Patrick Crawley, Downton's heir and Mary's fiancé, has been killed aboard the *Titanic* and she has rejected the new heir, Matthew Crawley. Adrift but aiming for marriage, Mary cultivates the harmless and gentlemanly Sir Evelyn Napier but is blown off course when "the gorgeous Turk," as Lord Grantham calls him, arrives. Pamuk subsequently rapes Mary and launches the romantic machinations that govern *Downton Abbey*'s plots through Season Three.[19] Media conversations about this plot circulate around whether and how Mary and Kemal had sex,[20] and whether or not intercourse was forced or consensual, but little to nothing is said about the interracial, inter-imperial, aspects of the coupling.

The cross-racial desires and fantasies swirling around the figure of Pamuk take refuge in pointed dialogue during the episode in which he appears. At dinner, Mary asks his opinion about whether "the housemaid [should] be kept enslaved" or encouraged to leave the confines of domestic service, and her choice of verb suggests that he, a product of Ottoman society, would be familiar with the enslavement and seclusion of women. Later, offended when Pamuk kisses her, she does not report his behavior so that he will not be "cast out into the darkness" by her father. Literally, she means the night, but the turn of phrase suggests that Mary is familiar with the swarthy heroes of Gothic literature and has racialized the geography of the world beyond Downton. Thomas, as usual, takes a more ironic approach, remarking to Daisy that he does not "think Mr. Pamuk bothered with cocoa much"—an allusion to Pamuk's preference for white women instead of the darker-skinned women with whom he is expected to couple. Thomas' remark also reverses itself to color Pamuk "cocoa" when his skin tone is indistinguishable from that of the English gentlemen surrounding him.

Thus a series that purports to be tremendously interested in chronicling the ways in which women's choices expanded in early twentieth-century England is also remarkably anxious to eliminate considerations of racial mixing from their sexual choices and to define race narrowly as observable (versus metaphorical) blackness. In parading race as an issue in Season Four with Jack Ross, *Downton Abbey* deflects attention from all the ways it reconstructs other romances to avoid or bracket race so that discourses cannot contest, and thus identify, whiteness as constitutive of English racial identity in *Downton Abbey*'s microcosm of English society. Such fears and anxieties permeate discussions of women's romantic and reproductive choices (or fate) during this period, whether voiced as fears that French colonial troops will abuse German women or that vulnerable Irish immigrants will become pregnant (Moulton, *Ireland* 280–292). Thus, the representation of birth control—the cervical cap—on *Downton Abbey*, captures the unresolved tensions in the series' desire to maintain white racial purity as a central feature of Englishness.

Key discussions of birth control use among the downstairs staff occur in counterpoint to discussions about national fitness at the upstairs breakfast table. The relationship between sexual choice and racial health is therefore narratively disconnected but aesthetically juxtaposed to forge a connection without rendering explicit the racist or racial motivations intrinsic to the promotion of birth control. Initially, birth control features in Lady Mary's projected affair with Viscount Gillingham and her desire to enjoy sex for pleasure and avoid the painful consequences of a pregnancy that would damage her reputation or force her to marry Gillingham. Mary's comments about extra-marital sex, quoted at the beginning of this essay, precede a request that Anna purchase her a cervical cap[21]—also known as the Prorace cap[22]—which she has seen illustrated in Marie Stopes' book *Married Love*. Mary's desire for the cap to control her fertility demonstrates her liberation, and participates in broader narratives about birth control's importance to women's liberation, sexual knowledge, and right to sexual pleasure. According to Jane Carey, this narrative of pleasure, promulgated by feminist historians, suppresses the disturbing "eugenic, and thus necessarily racial, dimensions of the birth control movements" (734)—whose pleasure, she would ask, is really promoted by using birth control?

The word *race* is rampant in eugenics discourse, but since the race in question is white and "most birth control rhetoric was directed at the working classes, it has not necessarily been read as racial" (Carey 735). In theory—aside from the issues raised by illegitimacy—Mary's pregnancies would be welcomed by eugenicists because births among the healthy, wealthy and wise (or "fit") help improve the quality of the race. "Negative" eugenics, on the other hand, attempts to suppress birth rates among those "unfit" due to poverty, poor health, or mental deficiency. The emergence of eugenics alongside social Darwinism, phrenology, and Mantegazza's Racial Trees (see Cheng 28) in the nineteenth century necessarily links the promotion of healthy whiteness to the repression of groups lower on the evolutionary ladder. An emphasis on racial health focuses on the improvement of the upper class white gene pool—Stopes wrote of "the creators of splendid babies" (qtd. in Carey 738)—and there is broad, unstated agreement about what constitutes an undesirable trait.

Downton Abbey does not frame Mary's interest in birth control in this manner, but "negative" eugenics and its attendant concerns about racial fitness subtly and discretely run through Season 5, Episode 6, when Rose's relationship with Atticus heats up. At breakfast upstairs, conversation is diverse, but contains the following explanation for Lord Grantham's plans to improve the cottages on his estate: "You can't get an A1 population out of C3 homes" (5:6). In the wake of the Great War, the British government promoted better housing stock—"Homes Fit for Heroes"—in order to improve the health of the lower classes. Eugenics sought similar ends; in speeches, Marie Stopes spoke of limiting birth in "'C3,' or poor and 'degenerate,' populations" and promoting births among A1 families (Cohen 102). Without comment, the conversation moves on to the news of Hitler's rise in Germany—as with the allusion to Nancy Cunard, the Crawley family does not know in the 1920s what the 1930s will bring, but the connections between eugenic projects in England and Germany's attempt to exterminate a race are well known the viewing public. Juxtaposed with these conversations are scenes in which Mr. Bates finds Mary's cervical cap, which Anna has hidden in their cottage. He accuses Anna of deliberately preventing a pregnancy with this "cunning piece of equipment" because she suspects Bates is a murderer, a category of "degenerate" whose damaged DNA eugenicists sought to eliminate from the gene pool. Bates' accusations are open to other interpretations: emotional ones, as a sign of a troubled marriage, or practical ones, as Anna might not wish to raise a murderer's child alone after her husband hangs. But sutured with the interspersed scenes, Bates' accusations implicitly refer to eugenic arguments about his fitness as a father as well. *Downton Abbey* does not make these connections explicit, but the editing of scenes suggests an underlying argument about women's reproductive choices and England's racial fitness in the twentieth (and thus twenty-first) century.

With this sinister insight, we are far from the manifold pleasures of watching *Downton Abbey*, and perhaps a diversion is in order. The comedy group Funny or Die scooped the arguments presented here in 2013, in "Downton Diddy," a sketch featuring P. Diddy (Sean Combs) as Lord Wilcot, the real first black character on the series. "Downton Diddy," digitally inserts Combs into scenes from *Downton Abbey*, where the characters appear to react to his remarks. He advises the actors to "just go on like I'm not here"—

an apt tag line for the approach *Downton Abbey* takes to the representation of black Britain. The mendaciousness with which *Downton Abbey* claims to address race offers insight into the ways *Downton* pursues a reputation as a supporter and chronicler of social change within carefully structured limits. Lady Mary's reference to Nancy Cunard as "Lady Cunard's daughter" is thus a touchstone for both the racial anxieties and desires encoded in *Downton*'s plots and for the aesthetics of effacement by which those anxieties and desires are managed. One might excuse these aesthetic choices as manifestations of good breeding. The deliberation with which *Downton Abbey* steers around confrontations with historically accurate depictions of racism and racialized discourse while simultaneously promoting the centrality of whiteness to Englishness suggests that is precisely the point.

Notes

1. At this time, extra-marital sex was considered normal for men, but a woman's fidelity was important to paternity, and thus policed much more carefully. However, it is also true that the aristocracy tolerated adultery for both men and women, partly as an outgrowth of marriages forged more as alliances than romances, and partly because divorce was a greater scandal than adultery. Thus, affairs and flirtations became a tacitly permitted outlet for unsatisfied desires—even for women. According to K.D. Reynolds, "The cardinal rule was that the legitimacy of the first son (and preferably the second as well) must not be in doubt.... After that, fidelity in marriage was no longer a primary *social* requirement: instead discretion became the watchword" (10). At house parties of the type Downton hosts, the mistress of the house may have allocated rooms to enable such discreet behavior among her guests.

2. Winkiel summarizes the critiques (527–528, n5–6), and Peter Kalliney has delved into the role of literary culture in creating some of the contradictions apparent in Cunard's work and reputation (38–74).

3. *The Chronicles of Downton Abbey* very carefully explains that Cora, Lady Grantham, is not Jewish, nor does she follow Jewish traditions: "while Martha's husband was Jewish, she herself is not, and their children were raised as Episcopalians" (Fellowes and Sturgis 102).

4. The Dowager continues, "No Englishman would ever think of dying in someone else's house, especially someone they didn't even know." The rape occurs in 1:3 set in March 1913. Following intercourse, Kemal Pamuk dies in Mary's bed, but the scandal regarding the manner and location of Pamuk's death does not emerge until 1:6 set in May 1914 (Wikipedia). In the immediate aftermath, the Dowager makes quaintly xenophobic remarks about the odd behaviors of foreigners, but she has no knowledge of the sexual element until a year later.

5. Lord Grantham's treatment of opera singer Dame Nellie Melba, in events featured earlier in season four, lends credence to Mary's claim (4:3). He has also pronounced Jack Ross as "a very decent fellow" (4:6)—but he does not know, and apparently never learns, of the relationship between Jack and Rose.

6. For *Downton*'s connection to heritage film, see Byrne. For connections to the country house genre, see Gill; Kelsall; and Nesbitt, *Narrative Settlements*.

7. *Downton Abbey* connects nation and house directly as the shooting location for the series, Highclere Castle, shares an architect with the Palace of Westminster, home to British Parliament. A further indication of the importance of the country house to the preservation of whiteness as a marker of Englishness comes from Robert Knox's nineteenth century analysis of race, *The Races of Men: A Philosophical Inquiry into the Influence of Race over the Destinies of Nations*. In the 1862 version of this text, Knox uses racist caricature to demonstrate the inferiority of the Irish and other races (52). By contrast, he illustrates the Anglo-Saxon race with a picture of a manor house with the caption, "An Anglo-Saxon house; it always, if possible, stands detached" (56). The substitution of the house for an Anglo-Saxon person resonates with the black-and-white series logo and the frequent shots of Highclere/Downton in splendid isolation. Robert Young and Ramchandran Sethuraman have discussed Knox's work at greater length; Young conducts an analysis of the racial rhetoric of the text (72–80) and Sethuraman points out the paradox of denying hybridity while using a hyphenated racial designation (Anglo-Saxon) (257).

8. Hutchinson's biographer Charlotte Breese could not locate either a marriage certificate for the couple or a birth certificate for Ella, as is notoriously the case for black families in the nineteenth-century rural South. Breese reports, however, that "there was a large white family called Byrd, many of whose black slaves, following the convention of the time, took on the name Byrd; there were also some Chinese families" (23).

9. Charlotte Breese puts his arrival in London in 1927, though he landed in Paris in 1924.

10. All future references in this paragraph are to Fryer's *Staying Power*. Page numbers as noted.

11. In 2012, popular media reported that Fellowes was interested in featuring an Indian character, and more generally in efforts "to open it [the series] up ethnically a bit" (Hall). Rather than address race via a character who represents Britain's imperial history, the series chose to develop Ross.

12. In an incident that illustrates the interchangeability of black entertainers seen as sexual predators, Lady Mountbatten sued *The People* in 1932 for implying she had a relationship "with a coloured man" presumed to be American singer Paul Robeson, a suit she won when both she and Robeson denied any acquaintance and the paper could not provide evidence (Thornton). Morgan rejects the idea that where there is smoke there must be fire, rejecting the idea that "if Robeson was not her paramour, some other black man must have been" (227). According to Wilson, after the libel trial, Hutchinson was less favored by the powerful. By the 40s, "he was struggling to make ends meet … while Edwina was by then Vicereine of India." Edwina was later linked with Jawaharlal Nehru.

13. The Crawley family does not use racialized epithets either, instead confining their disapproval to his revolutionary politics. It is also possible that an American audience is less attuned to racist stereotypes of Irish people. As Ignatiev recounts in *How the Irish Became White*, Irish immigrants to the United States abandoned abolitionist sentiments that remained common in Ireland in order to claim their allegiance and rights as Americans free from the influence of a foreign power. "To the extent color consciousness existed among newly arrived immigrants from Ireland," Ignatiev writes, "it was one among several ways they had of identifying themselves. To become white they had to learn to subordinate county, religious, or national animosities, not to mention any natural sympathies they may have felt for their fellow creatures, to a new solidarity based on color—a bond which, if must be remembered, was contradicted by their experience in Ireland" where people of the same color subjected them to brutal social, political and economic oppression (96).

14. Luke Gibbons offers compelling testimony to this joint enterprise by juxtaposing, on opposing pages, two 1885 caricatures, one featuring an Irish vampire bat and a British vampire bat as comments on the relationships between England and Ireland (82–83).

15. Schmidt points out that Pamuk ignites this desire in the maids, Mary and Thomas, who is seen "succumbing to an urge to paw Pamuk." Schmidt concludes that this plot reflects a continuing concern about "the fate of British character and the British empire itself" that displaces blame for the chaos instilled by sexual desire onto a "fear of 'Oriental' sexuality."

16. Fellowes bases his claim of historical accuracy on documents shielded from public view by aristocratic privilege: "the family secret was unearthed after the friend read the diary of a great aunt who owned a stately home" (Buckland). Fellowes confirms his status as a trusted class insider by alluding to proof but maintaining his personal loyalty with a promise that he "will never reveal" the source of "the secret" (Buckland).

17. The full line is as follows: "I don't think our union [marriage] would please your family [Mary sniffs] … or mine."

18. Coincidentally, Charlotte Breese claims that Leslie Hutchinson also knew Ataturk: Mustafa Kemal "was a 'hot jazz' fan and keen to update his country on the latest Western trends, he ordered his Paris agent to summon it to perform in Turkey. Being bisexual, he may also have been motivated by a weakness for Leslie" (30–31). The later portion of the quotation is pure speculation, but Breese also claims, in an incident that echoes the fear of the Orient, that as the band played "eleven of Ataturk's political rivals were hanged in the main square in Ankara" (31).

19. Schmidt suggests that Mary's lassitude and dissatisfaction with her own situation after the Pamuk affair might have to do with the realization that her sequestered, controlled life resembles the fate of "women in harems … at the mercy of male power, imprisoned in hidden spaces, surrounded by luxury yet also full of a kind of otiose melancholy." Such a reading lends more piquancy and resonance to Lady Sibyl's first rebellious move: the adoption of harem pants.

20. Examples include Jane Austen's World (https://janeaustensworld.wordpress.com/2012/03/04/questions-about-pamuk-downton-abbey/), Positively Smitten (http://positively-smitten.com/2013/02/24/an-analysis-of-downton-abbey-the-rape-of-mary-crawley/), and the French Exit (http://thefrenchexit.blogspot.com/2012/02/downtown-abbey-was-mary-date-raped-and.html).

21. The notion that Anna could simply purchase a cap in a pharmacy and then leave Mary to use it without some training seems improbable. Deborah Cohen reports that "the real challenge lay in teaching patients how to use their birth control appliances….The cervical cap … requires a user who is both familiar with her anatomy and willing to touch herself, as the cap must be placed deep in the vagina" (105).

22. A picture of Prorace cap—which has the words "Prorace" written across the dome—in the collection of Science Museum in London is accompanied by this caption: "The trademarked 'Prorace' is related to Stopes' belief in eugenics. This widely held theory in the early 1900s argued selective breeding could remove 'undesirables' from society" ("Prorace").

WORKS CITED

Bar-Yosef, Eitan, and Nadia Valman, eds. Introduction. *"The Jew" in Late-Victorian and Edwardian Culture: Between the East End and East Africa*. Houndsmills: Palgrave Macmillan, 2009. Print.

Breese, Charlotte. *Hutch*. London: Bloomsbury, 1999. Print.

Buckland, Lucy. *"Downton Creator Reveals Plot of Turkish Diplomat Who Blackmailed His Way into Lady Mary's Bed and Then Died Is True."* 11 October 2011. *The Daily Mail*. Web. 2 June 2016.

Carey, Jane. "The Racial Imperatives of Sex: Birth Control and Eugenics in Britain, the United States and Australia in the Interwar Years." *Women's History Review* 21.5 (2012): 733–752. *Taylor and Francis Online.* Web. 29 May 2016.

Cheng, Vincent. *Joyce, Race, and Empire.* Cambridge: Cambridge University Press, 1995. Print.

Cohen, Deborah. "Private Lives in Public Spaces: Marie Stopes, the Mothers' Clinics and the Practice of Contraception." *History Workshop* 35 (1993): 95–116. JSTOR. Web. 29 May 2016.

Cowen, Anne, and Roger. *Victorian Jews through British Eyes.* Oxford: Oxford University Press, 1986. Print.

Curtis, L. Perry. *Apes and Angels: The Irishman in Victorian Caricature.* Newton Abbot: David & Charles, 1971. Print.

Downton Abbey, Seasons 1–6. By Julian Fellowes. Carnival Films–PBS. 2010–2016.

"Downton Diddy." Feat. P. Diddy. *Funny or Die.* 31 May 2013. https://www.youtube.com/watch?v=eUihFufZfrM.

Fellowes, Jessica, and Matthew Sturgis. *The Chronicles of Downton Abbey.* New York: St. Martin's, 2012. Print.

Fryer, Peter. *Staying Power: Black People in Britain since 1504.* Atlantic Highlands: Humanities, 1984. Print.

Gibbons, Luke. *Gaelic Gothic: Race, Colonization, and Irish Culture.* Galway: Arlen, 2004. Print.

Gill, Richard. *Happy Rural Seat: The English Country House and the Literary Imagination.* New Haven: Yale University Press, 1972. Print.

Glassman, Bernard. *Anti-Semitic Stereotypes without Jews: Images of the Jews in England, 1290–1700.* Detroit: Wayne State University Press, 1975. Print.

Grant, Sonia. "*Downton Abbey* in Black and White." *Huffington Post.* 23 September 2013. Web. 20 April 2016.

Hall, James. "*Downton* Creator Considers Multicultural Abbey." 5 November 2012. *Telegraph.* Web. 30 May 2016.

Ignatiev, Noel. *How the Irish Became White.* New York: Routledge, 1995. Print.

Itzkoff, Dave. "Julian Fellowes on Viewer Criticism and *Downton Abbey*'s Future." 23 February 2014. *New York Times.* Web. 20 May 2016.

Jodelka, Filipa. "The Trouble with *Downton Abbey*'s New Black Character." *The Guardian* 1 May 2013. Web.

Kalliney, Peter. *Commonwealth of Letters: British Literary Culture and the Emergence of Postcolonial Aesthetics.* Oxford: Oxford University Press, 2013. Print.

Kelsall, M.M. *The Great Good Place: The Country House and English Literature.* New York: Columbia University Press, 1993. Print.

Knox, Robert. *The Races of Men.* London: Henry Renshaw, 1862. *Empire Online.* E-book. 11 August 2016. http://www.empire.amdigital.co.uk.ezaccess.libraries.psu.edu/Documents/Details/The Races of Men A Philosophical Enquiry by Robert Knox MD.

Langham, Raphael. *The Jews in Britain: A Chronology.* Houndsmills: Palgrave, 2005. Print.

McKay, George. *Circular Breathing: The Cultural Politics of Jazz in Britain.* Durham: Duke University Press, 2005. Print.

Morgan, Janet. *Edwina Mountbatten: A Life of Her Own.* London: HarperCollins, 1991.

Moulton, Mo. *Ireland and the Irish in Interwar England.* Cambridge: Cambridge University Press, 2014. Print.

_____. "Watching *Downton Abbey* with an Historian: Differences without Distinction." 15 February 2015. *The Toast.* Web. 5 May 2016.

_____. "Watching *Downton Abbey* with an Historian: Race and Imperialism." 5 February 2014. *The Toast.* Web. 5 May 2016.

Nesbitt, Jennifer. "The Absent Presence of Virginia Woolf: Queering *Downton Abbey*." *Journal of Popular Culture* 49.2 (2016): 250–270. Print.

_____. *Narrative Settlements: Geographies of British Women's Fiction between the Wars.* Toronto: University of Toronto Press, 2005. Print.

Philipson, Alice. "*Downton Abbey* Reveals its Raunchy Side." *Telegraph* 21 September 2014. Web.

"'Prorace' Cervical Cap, England, 1915–1925." n.d. *Brought to Life: Exploring the History of Medicine.* Web. 3 June 2016.

"Rachel Aldridge." n.d. *Downton Abbey Wiki.* Web. 1 June 2016.

Reynolds, K.D. *Aristocratic Women and Political Society in Victorian Britain.* Oxford: Clarendon, 1998. Print.

Said, Edward. *Orientalism.* New York: Vintage, 1979. Print.

Schmidt, Peter. "What Should I Do with the Dead Turk in the Bedroom? Class, Sex, and Otherness in *Downton Abbey*." 27 January 2012. *Peter Schmidt@English Literature, Swarthmore Xpress.* Web. 15 May 2016.

Sethuraman, Ramchandran. "Evidence-cum-Witness: Subaltern History, Violence, and the (De)formtion of Nation in Michelle Cliff's *No Telephone to Heaven*." *MFS: Modern Fiction Studies* 43.1 (Spring 1997): 249–287. *Project MUSE.* Web. 8 Aug. 2016.

Thornton, Michael. "The Royal Gigolo: Edwina Mountbatten Sued over Claims of an Affair with Black Singer Paul Robeson." *MailOnline.* 14 November 2008. Web. 19 May 2016.

Wikipedia. "List of *Downton Abbey* Episodes." 26 April 2016. *Wikipedia.* Web. 3 May 2016.

Wilson, Christopher. "The Scandalous Truth about *Downton Abbey*'s Royal Gigolo 'Jack Ross.'" 14 October 2013. *Telegraph.* Web. 19 May 2016.

Winkiel, Laura. "Nancy Cunard's Negro and the Transnational Politics of Race." *Modernism/Modernity* 13.3 (2006): 507–530. *Project MUSE.* Web. 19 April 2016.

Young, Robert C.J. *Colonial Desire: Hybridity in Theory, Culture and Race.* London: Routledge, 1995.

Downton Abbey, the Jazz Age and Adaptation to Change

ELLEN HERNANDEZ

Why is *Downton Abbey*, a television show about an aristocratic British family, their estate, and their servants, set a century ago, so popular with American audiences? It is precisely that depiction of aristocratic life that so attracts us and turns us off. It is both alien and subtly familiar in a way that fascinates us, draws us in, and, also, at turns either humbles or vindicates our lives as we see our societal status reflected in a particular group of characters. To British fans, it may be a window into the world of a noble class that still exists in their society and with whom they continue to live. Some of the Queen's subjects are still employed in the homes of the aristocracy or had parents or grandparents who were. Yet, to our American sensibilities, having fought to free ourselves from the yoke of royal authority, the laws and strictures of the Downton way of life may seem ridiculous upon first viewing. We do not have a hierarchy of families with ties to a monarchy and legal obligations, as such, to their community and land. Likewise, people who are employed in service jobs in the United States are not shackled to those careers and that social status for life if they can gain an education and strive for a more lucrative career. Furthermore, the lawyers, doctors, bankers, and business owners are not an underclass tolerated among the higher social ranks but are rather some of the more financially comfortable members of our communities.

On the other hand, we might see among the characters those whose way of life is too close for comfort. Those of us who enjoy the power and privilege of wealth might notice with chagrin that the Crawleys possess an attitude of entitlement that we share, an expectation that our days and our lives will go as planned and others will cooperate in making sure that that happens. Seeing that attitude mirrored for us in its stark self-centeredness and seeming callousness can be either illuminating or mortifying. Similarly, in the restricted lives of the servants, their endless efforts, their long-suffering, and their wistful dreams of a better future, others of us might find inspiration to rise above our current circumstances.

While the first three seasons of *Downton Abbey* portray life on an English country estate during the Edwardian era and the impact of World War I on that lifestyle, it is with Series Four that viewers are shown the influence of American society on the British in the 1920s, the *Jazz Age*. No doubt, American culture had a sharp influence on them in the late nineteenth and early twentieth centuries, particularly with the infusion of Amer-

76

ican heiresses and the fortunes they brought into marriages to those of noble rank. Yet, the impact of American music, dance, fashion, and other cultural features during the latter period cannot be minimized. As one society adapted to the attendant social and economic advances, the other could not help but experience the same need to adapt. Adaptation to change became the reality of aristocratic life.

British Class Structure

The structure of society within and around *Downton Abbey* is reflective of the time it depicts, which was a view of society that evolved from the fifth century through the early twentieth in England. The Crawleys live in and are responsible for an English manor house and estate. The house, land, and accompanying title are passed down to each successive male heir (a practice known as *male primogeniture*). This view originated in the Middle Ages (around 476 CE) and was the dominant view of English society through the Victorian Era (1800s) and into the Edwardian Era (early 1900s), which was the period of *Downton Abbey*'s first through third series. This idea, known as the *Great Chain of Being*, divided society into a hierarchy of ranks, degrees, and orders from the peasant laborer up to the duke, with the king as the highest-ranking human being. Every subject was thought to have a God-given place in which deference to those above and the right to command those below naturally followed from one's location in the hierarchy. During the Medieval Era, the king gave out parcels of land to Lords in exchange for loyalty and military aid, with each Lord giving out smaller parcels to lesser lords in turn on down to the peasants, who worked the land in exchange for protection (Valades).

In the manorial system of land tenure, originally conceived in Western Europe and brought to England from France through the Norman Conquest (in 1066), the *manor* was controlled by a lord, who lived in a manor house and controlled a large area of land along with its workers. Every noble had at least one, on which the king's court relied for food. The manor house, from which business was conducted, was residential property, and it was surrounded by arable land for farm tenancy (McDonald).

The Edwardian era (during the reign of King Edward VII), near the end of which we first meet the Crawley family, is the period between the reign of Queen Victoria and the modern age of the House of Windsor. It encompasses a time from about 1901 through 1910 when the rich lived lives of leisure and were not ashamed to display their wealth, a time of sharp class inequality. The aristocracy still maintained both titles and land, and they resided in the Manor House, the center of the rural community, surrounded by the labor of servants (*Edwardian Life*).

World War I signaled the end of the "long Edwardian summer." The Great War shattered individual lives and created seismic political and economic change on both sides of the Atlantic. Where the "robber barons" of the U.S. had produced heiresses like *Downton Abbey*'s Cora, whose marriages in Europe saved the aristocratic estates, in the war's aftermath, upper class families had to bid farewell to their pre-war way of life, as stated by Robert, Earl of Grantham, "We've dreamed a dream, my dear, but now it's over. The world was in a dream before the war, but now it's woken up and said goodbye to it. And so must we."

Let us backtrack for a moment to understand the intricacies of the relationships between family members and how the issue of inheritance impacted them. When Series

One opens in April 1912, with the news of the sinking of the *Titanic*, family patriarch Robert Crawley, the Earl of Grantham, is steward to Downton Abbey, a fictional Yorkshire country estate. His wife is American heiress, Cora Levinson, whose inheritance was infused into the estate to prevent it from going bankrupt more than twenty years earlier.

They have three daughters—Mary, Edith, and Sybil, the youngest, who is just on the verge of adulthood and "coming out" in aristocratic society (making her eligible for marriage, as are her older sisters). The eldest, Mary, was engaged to a cousin who died along with his father on the *Titanic*, thus making her eligible for courtship with new suitors. Since Robert has no male heirs, the estate and fortune will go to the next-in-line, distant cousin Matthew Crawley, a solicitor from Manchester with only some experience in aristocratic society. He and his mother, Isobel, a former nurse and the widow of a doctor, relocate their residence to Crawley House in the village near Downton, not too far from the Dower house where Robert's mother Violet, the Dowager Countess of Grantham, lives.

Action also revolves around the parallel and intersecting lives of *Downton Abbey*'s servants. They are led by the butler, Mr. Carson, and the head housekeeper, Mrs. Hughes. There are footmen, valets, lady's maids, housemaids, cooks, and kitchen maids. There are also other servants milling about the property, seen from time to time, particularly, Tom Branson, the chauffeur. There are additionally servants to the Dowager Countess, and to Matthew and his mother, though they initially eschew the need for them.

The central dilemma is not only that Matthew will inherit the estate and title but that the bulk of Cora's money has been "entailed" by Robert's father, meaning that it is attached to the estate and Matthew will inherit it as well, leaving Robert and his family virtually destitute and the survivors to be turned out upon his death. The eventual union between Matthew and Mary serves to keep Cora's inheritance within the family.

By the beginning of Series Four, a few events have occurred that affect or are affected by the issue of inheritance. First, youngest daughter Sybil has both defied convention by marrying the chauffeur, Tom, and also died during childbirth. After her death, Tom agrees to stay on and raise his daughter, also named Sybil, or "Sybbie," at Downton, working with Matthew to plan improvements to the estate that will make it more self-sustaining. Second, Matthew has subsequently died in a car accident following the birth of his and Mary's son, George, who becomes next-in-line to inherit the estate and title. Finally, Matthew has left a will naming Mary as *his* sole heir. This means that she is half owner of the estate because, prior to his death, Matthew had invested in it (to save it from Robert's bungled management). As part owner, she is entitled to make decisions about its management.

The union of Matthew and Mary and the infusion of Matthew's money saved the Downton estate, but his death by 1921 creates repercussions in the form of taxes, or "death duties," which becomes a focal point for the entirety of Series Four, revealing its significance in 1920s English society.

For his part, Robert wants to step back in and take over the sole running of Downton, and he wants to shield Mary from the world. He also wants to scrap Matthew's and Tom's intended plans. Eventually, though, Mary decides to take on a larger role, defying the conventions of the time. Why is it such a source of conflict that Mary might participate in running the estate? Unlike Robert's and Cora's relationship, in which their roles as Master and Mistress of the Manor are well-defined and Cora does not balk at her lack of involvement in estate matters, Mary's and Matthew's relationship in Series Three is more egalitarian. Matthew, probably because of his upper-middle-class upbringing, respects Mary's intelligence and experience, and consults her in matters of his role as presumptive heir and, eventually, co-manager of Downton's affairs. Although he is aware of how to conduct himself among aristocrats (and would have been able to take his rightful place among the House of Lords of Parliament had he lived), he is also liberal and is sympathetic to the issues of the disenfranchised. As a result of their more modern relationship, before the birth of their son, he writes a letter indicating his intention to change his will and make Mary his sole heir. This is so unusual an action that, when confronted with the information, Robert rejects giving his daughter Mary this much power in the running of the estate until the rest of the family convinces him that it's right to honor Matthew's intentions.

Economic Changes in 1920s England

Death Duties, or inheritance taxes, were the final nail in the coffin on many of England's country houses. Since 1900, in fact, some 1,200 such houses have been demolished in England and even more in Scotland (Worsley). The houses had lost income during the agricultural depression of the 1870s, spurring the influx of American heiresses to save them from financial ruin. Also, various reforms reduced the political power of the ruling class, and that, coupled with falling land prices and incomes in the early 1900s, caused many in the upper classes to give up their country house lifestyles. By 1909, a bill differentiated between earned income and income from investments, making the income tax more punitive for the landed gentry. A plan under Prime Minister Lloyd George in 1910 for a "super-tax" of the wealthy was defeated in the House of Lords, many of whom were the very landowners who would be affected, and so the Parliament Act of 1911 took their veto power away.

The idea of a Death Tax (or Legacy Duty), a tax payable on money bequeathed from a personal estate, had been introduced in England all the way back in 1796. By 1815, the percentage taken from the estate had been increased, and the only heir exempt from it was the spouse (*Legacy Duty*). Various laws were passed in the 1800s to reduce loopholes to avoiding payment. By 1940, the rate of 8 percent on estates valued at over one million pounds gradually increased to 50–65 percent to finance World War II and went even higher in the 1940s. This was often the deciding factor for families in selling off their estates.

So, we find that following Matthew's death, the inheritance taxes, based on the value of the estate, were so high and the cash flow so low, that the family could not afford to pay them and were in real danger of losing Downton. In light of this, and because of Robert being generally unsupportive of change to the way of conducting business, Matthew and Tom's plans for improvement of the estate through agricultural diversification, self-sustaining modernization, and gentry/farmer collaboration to increase its income were abandoned following Matthew's untimely demise.

Initially, Mary has no interest in being involved with the business of the estate and is resigned to allow her father to take over. Laws in the nineteenth century allowed for a dowager (the widow of a peer, or noble, such as Violet) to inherit one third of her spouse's estate, but inheritance was not guaranteed (Vic). Yet, at the time of his death, Matthew has not yet ascended to the rank of nobility that would provide that inheritance for Mary. Widows of World War I were given a small "pension" intended to confine them to the household and leading to remarriage (for practicality's sake) (Smith 60–61). Although Matthew served in the war, he did not die in the war, so Mary is not entitled to such a pension either. By 1922, the Law of Property Act passed in Parliament to allow husbands and wives to inherit property from one another equally. Matthew's final letter to Mary, formalized through witnesses and found later among his books when packing up his office, states his intention to write a will making Mary his sole heiress. Between this and her vested interest in George's future, Mary decides to become actively involved in the business of the estate. She shows that she wants to continue Matthew's legacy by supporting his ideas for change. Moving forward, Mary and Tom work collaboratively to plan a solution to the problem of paying the taxes.

More than the family, the servants must adapt to economic changes in the early 1920s. With Matthew's death, Mr. Molesley loses his post as valet, and he has to take a series of less-skilled jobs as a street paver, delivery person, and then footman (while a good job in service, it is a demotion from his previous positions as butler and valet). Following World War I and during the 1920s, increases in inheritance taxes (from 8 percent in 1894 to 40 percent by 1919) necessitated a sharp decline in the size of an estate's staff. In addition, high unemployment in England (nearly 12 percent in 1921) typically engendered loyalty from people who worked in service and farming because they needed to retain their jobs (Pettinger).

Economic misjudgment was core to some of these changes. Since there was a tendency for subsequent generations such as Robert and Cora's to waste and use up the finances, a somewhat Darwinian redistribution of wealth took place regardless of the imposed taxes (Will). Robert doesn't invest the capital gained from his marriage to Cora, and by the 1920s he is refusing to diversify his investments. His main income is from rents from tenant farmers, like the Drewes. During the 1920s, 20 percent of arable land in England stopped producing food as estates were sold off in parcels. This created shortages of food and drove up prices. The show also depicts Robert's resistance to modernization: no mechanization of farming, no new crops or livestock, and no new lines of business.

Fortunately, Tom persuades Matthew and later Mary to invest in the estate, and they generally ignore Robert's ideas. Robert's business management is terrible. At one point, he contemplates investing with American Charles Ponzi (yes, that Ponzi). He loses almost their entire fortune in an investment in a Canadian railroad deal that falls through. This plot point might well have been taken from the actual financial error by Jacob (Jac) Wendell, Jr., whose daughter, Catherine, later married the 6th Earl of Carnarvon, Lord of Highclere Castle, where *Downton Abbey* was filmed (Fiona 12). Robert wants to sell off land and pay the taxes in one lump sum. In real life, in 1926, Highclere had to sell its art collection with works by da Vinci and Gainsborough in order to stay afloat.

The stricture of the British social system circumscribed one's roles and responsibilities and impeded upward mobility. This is the general prejudice we see with Tom's new friend/love interest, Sarah Bunting, and the comments she makes against the Crawleys. Tom, on the other hand, sees it as more complex than the stereotypes she holds. While the restrictions removed the freedom to figure out one's individual place in the world, any Brits might have considered this freedom a burden, necessitating constant choices dictating actions and an unease among those of different social strata. We see the pull of this freedom, though, in the minor characters of Ivy and Jimmy, and even to some extent in Lady Edith, and this pull is ultimately what draws Ivy to the decision to leave for America.

Cultural Changes in 1920s England

Bobs and spit curls, low-waisted silhouettes, Ragtime and the Charleston made their way from America to England in the more liberal post-war period of the 1920s, the *Jazz Age*, a time of social and political turbulence but cultural expansiveness. Robert's niece, Rose, and other younger characters are drawn to the glamorous nightclubs, with their flappers and jazz music. At the time, this type of music represented a stark contrast with what had been popular before, and this new breed of young woman was seen as brash and disdainful of social and sexual norms. Having their origin in the U.S. and being exported to Europe along with American jazz music, their behavior both here and abroad was considered outlandish. The question we are left to ponder is: What impact did the introduction of these new elements have on the carefully crafted aristocratic culture?

We are introduced to Lady Rose MacClare in Series Three, when her family visits the Crawleys and the Crawleys then visit her parents' Scottish Highlands home. Her father, Marquess Hugh "Shrimpie" MacClare is Robert's cousin. His wife Susan is a dour woman who finds no joy in her life as wife and mother. Rose is a young girl with a desire to break free from the somber environment of her home, and she leaps at the chance to stay with her Crawley cousins when her parents take a post in India.

Rose is revealed to be a wild young girl, partying and drinking in London and meeting with a much-older married man. Rose is a free spirit, a rule-breaker, and a thrill-seeker. She is lovely and knows how she is expected to behave, but she wants to break out of the strictures of her position as daughter of a Marquess and cousin of an Earl. We could attribute her troubling behavior to adolescence, since she is just on the cusp of eighteen. But her family dysfunction, with her parents' loveless marriage, may also be the source of her attention-seeking.

In early episodes, we see Rose listening to music and reading popular magazines, wanting to go out dancing—generally having fun. To us, this might seem natural for a teenager, but for a young aristocratic woman of that time, it was quite apart from acceptable custom and etiquette. Our first inkling of Rose's adventurousness is when she coerces maid Anna into getting permission to accompany her to a tea dance in nearby York and runs into some trouble when two men instigate what becomes a brawl over her. When she arrives, we see her asking for liquor and flirting with potential dance partners. While dancing, she lies to her partner about working at Downton Abbey. Later, when he shows up at the back door, she dons a maid's outfit to continue the charade. Although she turns him down gently, she does have the audacity to kiss him before he goes.

She later meets up with Sir John Bullock at the Lotus Club in London and is rescued from an embarrassing social situation by Jack Ross, an African American jazz singer and bandleader. Bullock, who has been drinking heavily, is too aggressive with her on the dance floor, and, when she resists, he hurriedly retreats, leaving her stranded. Jack, who has been performing, has witnessed the scene, and he dashes off the stage to sweep her into his arms and continue dancing. When Jack comes to her aid at the Lotus Club, he makes an impression on her. He is refined and kind, perhaps kinder than any American the Crawleys have encountered, certainly kinder and more refined than Cora's mother Martha and brother Harold.

However, when Rose develops a relationship with Jack, it cannot end well if the writers are to portray attitudes of that time. She is infatuated with Jack, who returns her feelings, and she plots ways to see him without her family finding out. She arranges for Jack and his band to be the surprise entertainment at a birthday party for Robert at Downton, much to everyone's dismay above and below stairs. Late at night, after the party, Mary spies Rose and Jack in a compromising embrace in the servants' hall when they think they are alone. After they have been seeing each other for a bit, they develop strong feelings for one another, and Rose is intent on marrying him. Later, in a conversation with Mary, Jack reveals that he will not marry Rose because the difficulties of an interracial marriage would be too stressful for her. Rose blames Mary for interfering, but the truth is that Jack is being honorable.

Rose's impetuousness and rebelliousness are intertwined with popular music, culture, and fashion of the time. How did American Jazz music become popular in England after World War I? What impact did it have on the culture? Let's back up a bit to what was happening in the U.S. during the early twentieth century and examine a real-life "Jack Ross" and his scandalous relationship with an aristocratic woman.

American Jazz originated in New Orleans at the end of the 1800s, though the term "jazz" was not used until the end of World War I. Initially, this music form combined elements of Ragtime and the blues as well as some marching band music. It differs from the related musical forms by its improvisational nature, using the written music as merely a frame of reference for the performance. Artists such as Jelly Roll Morton developed early jazz music by making it more complex, and brought what was then called the *New Orleans sound* or *Hot Jazz* to the rest of the nation in the early twentieth century (Alexander). The first real stars—Louis Armstrong, King Oliver, and Kid Ory—emerged in the 1920s, thus ushering in what is known as the *Jazz Age*. However, many jazz artists were forced to leave New Orleans when racial prejudice and violence against African Americans and Creoles increased there.

Jazz musicians fled "up the river" to Kansas City and Chicago and relocated to New York City. Even though Kansas City was completely segregated, African American jazz musicians were highly sought after by dance halls, clubs, and restaurants frequented by whites (American Jazz Culture). Jazz music continued to flourish there through the 1930s, with artists such as Benny Moten, Walter Page, and Count Basie. Through them, bands grew from the standard ensemble of three instruments—trumpet, clarinet, and trombone—expanded to include saxophone and drums.

The distinctive *riff*—a repeated phrase or pattern overlaid by an improvised melody—was the distinguishing characteristic of Kansas City jazz, increasing its popularity and moving it toward what became the *big band* sound of the 1930s. The jazz that became popular further north along the Mississippi in Chicago's South Side, by contrast, was more precise, less wild. It became popular among white audiences although they had to go to African American dance halls and clubs to hear it. Eventually, jazz came to be recorded and broadcast on the radio, with some patrons preferring the more refined versions. Chicago jazz was popular throughout the 1920s, but it lost its blues-based sound and shifted more to what is known as *swing* music of the 1930s when Chicago gangsters and their clubs were done away with.

New York's early jazz music was influenced by Ragtime, which had been popular there since the turn of the century with musicians like Scott Joplin. People were drawn to the exciting and unpredictable music of New Orleans jazz played by groups like the Original Dixieland Jazz Band, and New York musicians tried to imitate it. The city's diverse backgrounds made jazz music appeal to all levels and groups in society there, with Louis Armstrong creating a whole new style of jazz inventiveness. George Gershwin's famous 1920s composition *Rhapsody in Blue* and the Harlem Renaissance also made jazz respectable and increased its popularity.

What some sociologists refer to as *bottom culture* (the culture of a minority group) grew to prominence, temporarily elevating the status of African Americans as their music became both desirable and profitable. However, the 1920s also saw an increase of activity by the Ku Klux Klan and other white supremacist groups. The takeover of New Orleans' politics by whites and the increased bigotry and violence actually spurred African Americans to protest their unfair treatment. In fact, jazz music's popularity may be credited for influencing them to fight for equal rights.

How did this popular American music make its way across the ocean and become as popular in Europe, or even more so? U.S. Prohibition in the 1920s prompted thousands of Americans to flee to Europe, in particular to Paris, to drink, dance, see and listen to the variety of entertainment. Artists Dalí, Picasso, and Cassatt, and the dancer Isadora Duncan were living in Paris, as were the literati expatriates Fitzgerald, Hemingway, Ezra Pound, Hart Crane, Gertrude Stein, and many others. They were joined by musicians Aaron Copeland and Cole Porter, and a host of writers, artists, and entertainers, intent on expanding and developing their art in the flashiest, most decadent era in French history (Greenberg).

African American musicians were arriving in Paris in droves and were more accepted by Parisians than they had been in America. Singer/dancer Josephine Baker became a household name in Paris. Her distinctive style influenced changes in fashion and her short hair became the defining image we have when we think of women of the Jazz Age: the *Bak-air Fixe* (pronounced *bock-air feeks*) (Trueman). In Paris, Americans could drink freely and women could hold hands on city streets without worrying about how it looked. Women could go out without a male to escort them, stay out at all-night parties, drive cars, and smoke in public.

In this post-war Europe, a new generation introduced a new culture with a new way of looking at things. They wanted change and freedom, and particularly for African Americans, this was something they could not quite attain in the U.S., no matter how popular jazz music had become. In Paris, a poor black Southern girl like Josephine Baker could make money, make the front page, become an international sensation, and be greeted by roaring applause in music boxes like Bricktop.

The Jazz Age blossomed in London in the 1920s, too. A group of young, idle aristocrats and bohemian artists embraced a life of partying and revelry. This group, referred to as *bright young things*, would have outrageous parties involving scavenger hunts or bathing parties, heavy drug use, reckless driving, and illicit sex. All of this was widely reported in the newspapers, with the titillating stories of excess causing much disapproval from conservatives.

Part of the rise in popularity of jazz music was due to the fact that it was dance music. *The Charleston*, named after Charleston, South Carolina, became a popular jazz dance craze in the 20s. First introduced through the song of the same name, it appeared in 1920s musicals like *The Ziegfeld Follies* and *Runnin' Wild*. Other dances included *The*

Shimmy and *The Black Bottom*. Some of these, like jazz music itself, most likely originated from African American dance forms.

The Victorian apparel and hairstyles of the early twentieth century were no longer appropriate to this form of dance. The post–World War I fashion industry began to target a society that revolved around this particular kind of music. The new focus on fashion is illustrated by a sharp increase in fashion magazines in the 1920s, with three major ones—*Vogue, The Queen,* and *Harper's Bazaar*—emerging during this era (Jazz). The clothes were popular among all ages because they fit many body types and could be easily mass produced.

The impact of jazz on fashion evolved in stages, just as jazz music did. The earliest stage introduced dropped waist dresses and Coco Chanel's long strands of glass beads and pearls, allowing more upper and lower body freedom for dancing. Later came chest binding and short bob haircuts, loose shift dresses with no waist and shorter skirts approaching knee length. Finally, ladies' fashions incorporated sleeveless gauzy or mesh, low-V-neck dresses with loosely fitted bodices and short, flared skirts. These were embroidered with gold sequins and worn with matching gold shoes and handbags and a long string of pearls (Peacock 58).

While changes to dress length and hairstyles are seen among the women of Downton, Rose's dress and appearance mimic the *flappers* of that time. Flappers' clothes were often much shorter than what had been seen in public, tending to expose legs and even knees. In addition, progressive women of that era wore stockings rolled just above the knees and went to male barbers for haircuts. They even wore such skimpy beachwear in public that they were sometimes arrested for indecent exposure (Trueman).

The term *flapper* could have one of several origins. Some believe it referred to a young bird flapping its wings. It is also Northern England's word for a teenage girl because of her flapping pigtails. It might also originate from a much older word for a young prostitute (Swartz). Originally meant to refer to a lively or spirited young girl who had not yet had her debut, or *coming out*, it emerged as a term for an impetuous, immature woman, then evolved to mean an independent, pleasure-seeking young woman, and for a while referred to adult women voters who might "flip" and vote differently from men. In fact, 1929, the year after all British women were granted the right to vote, was referred to as the *flapper election* because of the high female voter turnout (*The Women's Timeline*).

Not surprisingly, there were critics, from politicians, to educators, to writers, including Dorothy Parker in her poem "Flappers: A Hate Song":

> The playful flapper here we see,
> The fairest of the fair.
> She's not what Grandma used to be,—
> You might say au contraire.
>
> Her girlish ways make a stir,
> Her manners cause a scene,
> But there is no more harm in her
> Than in a submarine.
>
> She nightly knocks for many a goal
> The usual dancing men.
> Her speed is great, but her control
> Is something else again.

All spotlights focus on her pranks.
All tongues her prowess herald.
For which she well may render thanks
To God or Scott Fitzgerald.

Her golden rule is plain enough—
Just get them young and treat them rough.

Social Changes in 1920s England

At the same time, the Women's Civil Rights Movement influenced and was influenced by jazz as this form of music was viewed as a form of rebellion against set standards of society. So, into the world of *Downton Abbey* shimmies jazz music, flapper dresses, and an African American musician leaving the characters above and below stairs to confront the issue of race and the changing world.

Returning to the character of Jack Ross, we might ask whether the character of Jack Ross and his interaction with British nobility realistic of the time. The Jack Ross character is very likely based on the real British cabaret star of the 1920s and 1930s, Leslie "Hutch" Hutchinson. He was born in Grenada in 1900, became a child piano prodigy, and was featured in the BBC documentary *High Society's Favourite Gigolo*. Hutch was one of the biggest cabaret stars in the world at that time and later a popular war-time entertainer (Hemley).

His parents saved to send him to law school in New York at age sixteen, but he ditched school and went straight to Harlem to play music with Fats Waller and Duke Ellington, eventually performing with the Henry "Broadway" Jones ensemble (Chadbourne). He married and had the first of his seven children, all with different mothers, and often played for white millionaires such as the Vanderbilts, people who became his patrons when his father cut off his allowance. The Ku Klux Klan objected to the reception of this West Indian man into white homes, so he left for Paris in 1924.

He played regularly at Joe Zelli's, one of the "hipper" clubs there, and had affairs with composer Cole Porter and film stars Tallulah Bankhead, Merle Oberon, and Ivor Novello (Thornton, 2008). (Side note: Novello was a character in Julian Fellowes' screenplay for *Gosford Park*). Of course, as was the rule at the time, he could not appear on stage with white women, and his name would not appear in *Variety*, no matter how successful he otherwise was Wilson, 2013). Hutch popularized the Porter songs "Let's Do It," "Night and Day," "It's De-Lovely," "Begin the Beguine," "I've Got You Under My Skin," and "Anything Goes."

Lady Edwina Mountbatten, wife of Lord Louis "Dickie" Mountbatten, who was the uncle of Prince Phillip and great-grandson of Queen Victoria, encouraged Hutch to come to England in 1927, where he became popular. Lady Edwina was a famous heiress, and she and her husband shared an open marriage since both were bisexual; their affairs creating scandal for the royal family. In fact, when news of Edwina's affair with a black singer was reported in the paper *The People*, incorrectly identifying her lover as actor/singer Paul Robeson; King George V insisted she sue the newspaper for libel to save the royals' reputation.

By 1928, Hutch had won recording contracts and was a highly paid headliner at top London nightclubs. He bought a Rolls-Royce, a grand house in Hampstead, patronized London's best tailors, spoke five or six languages, and was on friendly terms with the

Prince of Wales (Edward VIII). In spite of his popularity and his service during World War II entertaining the troops, he still experienced racial prejudice. When he entertained at lavish Mayfair parties, his fee was large, but he was often obliged to go in by the servant's entrance.

In 1930, his affair with an English debutante, Elizabeth Corbett, resulted in pregnancy. Elizabeth's father was so angry that he tried to pursue Hutch through the courts. To avoid scandal, she was married off to an unsuspecting army officer. But, the baby was obviously biracial when born and was immediately given away for adoption.

The price Hutch paid for his ongoing affair with Lady Edwina was to never appear at a Royal Command Performance; to be dropped from BBC radio shows; to no longer be booked at certain theatres; and to never be recognized for his service entertaining the forces. He fell out of favor and died overweight, alcoholic, and in debt.

So, when we see Jack Ross and hear him sing "April Showers" in the first scene at The Lotus Club, it should not come as a surprise. Jazz music became popular among Europeans in the 1920s, and so did the fashion and other cultural influences that came along with it. Black musicians were socializing with whites, particular wealthy whites who served as their patrons. When Rose arranges for Jack Ross and his band to perform at Robert's birthday party, set in 1922, it is not farfetched from the reality of the time. However, the culture shock for the aristocratic Crawleys is apparent.

At the heart of the matter is not merely the issue of race but also of class. Jack and his band must eat below stairs with the servants while the opera singer Dame Nellie Melba dines with the family in a later episode. Although Carson, Robert, and Violet all initially think it inappropriate that even Dame Nellie join the guests in the dining room because she is a performer, Cora intercedes and plans are changed.

In another instance of class conflict, one storyline involves Mr. Carson's former performing partner, Charles Grigg, who finds himself destitute and ill, in a workhouse in nearby Ripon. Through the graciousness and generosity of Isobel, he is able to be made well and to move on to Belfast. This is not only an opportunity for Isobel to help someone and to come out of her grief over Matthew, but also an opportunity for Mr. Carson to have closure to that troubled relationship. This turn of events illustrates the ongoing use of workhouses as a staple of English society even in the twentieth century. The workhouse was a place where those on the welfare of the state were made to live and work, typically in terrible conditions doing hard labor. This was intentional to deter all except the truly destitute from applying for aid. The workhouse did not provide free medical care nor did it offer education for children and was, in essence, a prison for the poor.

Although he does not experience it as dire circumstances, the prejudice Tom feels as a former employee of the family eventually leads him to make some ill-advised decisions. Regardless of Tom's role as a member of the family and estate manager, he cannot help feeling out of place in Downton. We see his discomfort at the soiree and opera performance. We also see him considering his daughter Sybbie's future, as her little cousin George will inherit the estate and title while she will inherit nothing. This is reflected in Nanny West's contrasting attitude toward both children.

When he meets a local school teacher, Sarah Bunting, with whom he shares some liberal political views, we are reminded that he is truly of a different class, no matter the lifestyle he has adopted, and eventually he will have to address this internal conflict. As we watch Tom's struggles with his identity, and we see him contemplating romance, as well as watching Rose's rebellious personality, we think back to the character of Sybil and what she would have to say about all of this. She would likely support Rose's desire to break from traditions but advise her to be dignified in her actions, and she would gently remind Tom to take pride in his heritage while making use of his newfound privilege to promote positive change. She would herself, of course, have carried on the struggle for equal treatment among people from all walks of life.

Political Changes in 1920s England

Downton Abbey's women face their complex circumstances with courage, and they march forward into a new era that offers advancement although continues a climate of oppression. An examination of Progressive Reform and the suffrage movements both in the U.S. and the UK helps us understand how the expectations for women like Mary, Edith, and Rose had changed from Cora's time and how these changes affected the female servants as well.

What was happening in England in 1922 was a gradual decay of the coalition government. The collaboration of parties during the war no longer worked during peacetime. In the last few months of that year, months of internal dissension erupted and it collapsed. The new Labour Party had been created in 1918, arising to represent the interests of common workers. The Liberal Party split into two groups, and the Conservative Party was somewhat split but won a majority of the vote, propelling Andrew Bonar Law to seize the position of Prime Minister from the National Liberals' David Lloyd George. Yet, during this election, women did not have a role or a say in the government.

Consider how strange it was that a mistress of an estate such as Cora could employ scores of male gardeners, laborers, and servants who could vote, but she could not. The suffrage movement had begun in earnest with the 1897 founding of the National Union of Women's Suffrage and the 1903 formation of the Women's Social and Political Union, even going so far as to use violent protest, but they had not achieved their ultimate goal of voting rights by the time we first meet the Crawleys. The Labour Representative Committee of Parliament angered women by insisting that they just could not understand how Parliament worked. Suffragists were arrested and used prison hunger strikes as a means of garnering attention. Preliminary voting rights were granted to some women, but the right to vote was not fully granted to all women in England until 1928 with the Representation of the People Act (Searle 791).

Changes to Courtship and Marriage Practices in 1920s England

The 1920s brought significant changes for young women in courtship practices, marriage, and family life. Where women of the previous generation were completely focused on attaining a suitable match, young women of this era were more independent. They left their rural homes for city life. A young woman's flapper lifestyle would characterize her as brash, wild, and a bit naughty. In fact, a number of derogatory slang terms developed in the 1920s to describe these new women including *gold digger* and *red-hot mama*. This is when the terms *nooky* and *French kissing* developed for what people did on dates.

Not surprisingly, courtship became more informal in the 1920s. There were generally no longer chaperones and there was more freedom. Men and women instituted the rules of their relationship without other parties interceding, and no formal commitment need be made to each other. Couples went "out" instead of the man visiting the woman in her home. The most popular pastimes on dates were dancing and seeing movies. For example, we see Ivy and Jimmy go out dancing and to the movies together. Dancing had been a group activity before that time. Cars also enabled couples to have more privacy and intimacy (Kristen).

During Series Four, we see the changes in social mores played out in the development of a relationship of mutual support and admiration between Miss Baxter and Mr. Molesley. When Molesley becomes a footman, he advises her not to allow Thomas (the underbutler) to bully her. Emboldened by his kindness toward her, she observes that he is lucky to come from a village where everyone knows him and his family has a good reputation. She talks about his strength, his good character, and his resilience. In turn, he gives her courage to stand up for herself. In reality, female servants (i.e., maids) were not allowed to fraternize with men or risked "sacking" (DeLacy).

Series Four ends with the servants enjoying a day off at Brighton Beach. Mrs. Hughes and Mr. Carson, old friends who have known heartbreak and loneliness, have developed a close relationship that blooms in the last scene into something more romantic. We see them walking hand in hand into the water at the beach in the last episode, with Mrs. Hughes observing, "We still have a little living to do."

For her part, three different men pursue Lady Mary, at least two of who are strong candidates, but she repeatedly tells them that she is not ready to move on from Matthew. Tony Foyle (Lord Anthony Gillingham) is a childhood friend. His father has died, and he has come into his inheritance of estate and title. In April 1922, Tony sees Mary for the first time in many years when the Crawleys host a weekend party at Downton. Although he is on the cusp of becoming engaged to another heiress with whom he gets along well enough, in just a few days at Downton he declares his love for Mary. He asks her to agree to marry him when she is ready to move on. By the summer of 1922, Mary is also pursued by Charles Blake, who arrives for a brief stay at Downton with his friend, Evelyn Napier, a former suitor from Series One who rejected Mary then due to her flirtations and haughtiness. Now he has a renewed interest in her because she is mature and her haughtiness has been tempered. Blake and Napier are working on a report for the government on economic and agricultural changes in country estates and their effect on the nation's food production. Blake exhibits a seemingly negative view of the aristocracy and views her as aloof, but they begin to view one another differently when he helps her family save the new pigs they have purchased. Mary's opinion is also later altered when she learns that he is a distant cousin to Sir Severus Blake and the presumptive heir to his baronetcy on one of the largest estates in Ulster. The time she spends alone with these men is illustrative of the changing courtship practices of the time.

In addition, Mary's sister Edith is pursued by a married man, Michael Gregson. Theirs is the most egalitarian of relationships and possibly demonstrates the deepest love and commitment. By now, Edith has become a mature, independent woman who pursues a career of her own. She is trying to establish her identity as a single woman, apart from her family. Hers and Michael's relationship is potentially scandalous for her and for her family because of his marriage and his status as a writer and newspaper editor as opposed to someone of her class. He is unlike newspaper mogul Richard Carlisle, to whom Mary was once engaged. Carlisle was of the upper class, having bought his way into a title and being referred to as "Sir." The Crawleys didn't like his personality, but they accepted the match since Mary was "getting on in years" and was not yet settled. In contrast, Edith's family is not thrilled with her choice of Gregson, unaware of his marriage and plan to get a divorce, because he is an ordinary commoner who they consider beneath her status.

The public nature of their relationship is problematic. We see them together at a party with his literary friends (including Virginia Woolf). They kiss at a London restaurant (the Criterion) after she remarks that she can't believe she is out at a restaurant with a man, that five or ten years before they would not have, and that Cora told the girls never to eat at a public restaurant unless at a hotel they were staying at. A woman like Edith would previously have had a man come to her home at her parents' invitation and would be supervised; in fact, people of their class would have been more likely to dine in one another's homes rather than out at restaurants in an earlier era. This shows that Edith has become more modern.

Their private relationship proves problematic as well. When Edith's Aunt Rosamund confronts her about a sleepover at Michael's apartment in London, she warns Edith that her actions could affect her name and reputation and that of her family. Michael disappears while in Germany seeking a divorce from his mentally ill wife. We later learn that he got into a scuffle with some "Brown Shirts," ruffians who were a precursor to the Nazis and the SS, because he didn't like the ideas they espoused (and we learn in a subsequent series that he has been killed). Edith's resulting pregnancy is, of course, a potential source of scandal for the family. Edith is left to deal with the pregnancy on her own though she is also left with power of attorney over Michael's affairs. At first, she considers terminating the pregnancy, going to a building called Temple Gardens and ringing the bell for "Thompson"—a doctor. Then, she and her aunt plan for her to secretly have the baby and give it up for adoption in Switzerland. By the end of the season, she has had second thoughts and returns to take the baby back. She asks Mr. Drewe to care for the child, Marigold, saying that she is the daughter of a deceased friend of whom her family did not approve, and he agrees to do so.

For women of that time, pregnancy outside of marriage put them in a terrible conflict, as we see with Ethel, the former Downton maid who was reduced to poverty and prostitution trying to live as a single parent in Series Two. In the early twentieth century, it would not have been a commonly accepted practice for women to engage in sex before they were married. If they agreed to do so, it was more than likely that it was with their future husbands. Neither was divorce common in at that time. The only legal basis for it was adultery. Because of the disgrace associated with extra-marital sex, a person who had been granted a divorce would find social acceptance tricky ("Marriage and Divorce").

For women who engaged in sex with the men they dated, contraception was not readily available. Disapproval and legal punishment surrounded its distribution and use. For example, in the U.S. in 1914, nurse and activist Margaret Sanger was charged with a crime in New York just for disseminating contraceptive information. In the UK in 1921, scientist Marie Stopes, who believed in restricting family size, especially for the poor, opened the first birth-control clinic in Holloway, in north London ("Home and Family"). Her work drove away some of the disdain associated with birth control. Abortion was also uncommon and difficult to obtain, having been formally outlawed in the UK in 1861 (*Abortion Rights*). It was not legalized on a limited basis until the late 1930s in England and not fully until 1967.

During the time when Edith becomes pregnant, it would have been difficult to obtain an abortion, even for a wealthy woman. Because it was prohibited, clinics advertised it in newspapers and lady's magazines as a cure for "*menstrual blockages*" or "*female complaints.*" Abortions could be allowed by law if "done in good faith for the purpose only of preserving the life of the mother"—but that would not have been applicable in Edith's case. In 1922, both performing and receiving an abortion were serious offenses garnering life in prison if convicted. Of course, that would be if Edith even *lived* through the procedure—an unlikely outcome since abortion's illegal status meant no one was making sure an actual doctor performed the procedure or that it was being done safely. From 1923 to 1933, an estimated 15 percent of maternal deaths in the UK came from illegal abortion. Before its legalization in 1967, a woman who became pregnant from consensual, premarital sex, like Edith, would have had very little recourse other than ridicule or risking her life and freedom with a dangerous procedure (Lloyd).

Despite these social and cultural changes for women, in the final episode of Series Four, we still see a depiction of a formal presentation at court for young, aristocratic women. What did it mean to be presented, make one's debut, or "come out" at court? When a woman of the nobility turned eighteen, she could be presented at court before the Sovereign. She had to be sponsored by a woman who had herself been presented; a young woman who was not of the aristocracy could make a monetary "gift" to a sponsor, and this is what Cora's family would have done for her that brought her to the attention of Robert and his family decades before.

Why was "coming out" important? This was the mechanism by which a young woman from an aristocratic family or one who aspired to marry into one would make her formal entrance into noble society and would be, in a sense, "advertised" as being eligible to be courted. The ostensible purpose was for her to make her entrance into adult social circles as a young woman instead of a child, but the true purpose was to begin the process of securing a good marriage to someone of her same class.

Conclusion

Whether *Downton Abbey* is considered an example of historical fiction or just a glorified soap opera, its popularity suggests that it appeals to an international audience on some level. Where that appeal is not based on the familiarity of one's societal structure and history, it might be otherwise related to those ways in which we feel a connection. Nowhere is that more apparent than in the shared cultural changes of the Jazz Age, and their impact on economics, politics, and social reforms.

WORKS CITED

Alexander, Scott. "The History of Jazz Before 1930." *The Red Hot Jazz Archive.* http://www.redhotjazz.com/.

"American Jazz Culture in the 1920s." University of Minnesota at Duluth. http://www.d.umn.edu/cla/faculty/tbacig/studproj/is3099/jazzcult/20sjazz/.

Chadbourne, Eugene. "Artist Biography: Hutch." Allmusic.com.

DeLacey, Martha. "The REAL Story of Britain's Servant Class (and It Wasn't Exactly Downton Abbey): New BBC Series Reveals What It Was Really Like Downstairs." *The Daily Mail Online.* http://www.dailymail.co.uk/femail/article-2207935/Downton-Abbey-servants-New-BBC-series-Servants-The-True-Story-Life-Below-Stairs.html. 24 September 2012.

"Edwardian Life." *Manor House.* http://www.pbs.org/manorhouse/edwardianlife/introduction.html. 2012.

Greenberg, Arnie. "Paris Jazz Age: New Generation Explodes in Paris (1920s)." *Bonjour Paris.* http://bonjourparis.com/story/paris-jazz-age-new-generation-1920s/. 6 June 2009.

Hemley, Matthew. "Wartime Entertainer Hutch Remembered in Channel 4 Documentary." *The Stage News.* 23 July 2008.

Herbert, Fiona. *Lady Catherine, the Earl, and the Real Downton Abbey.* New York: Broadway Books, 2013.

"History of Abortion Law in the U.K." *Abortion Rights.* http://www.abortionrights.org.uk/history-of-abortion-law-in-the-uk/.

"Home and Family." *Exploring 20th Century London.* http://www.20thcenturylondon.org.uk/theme/home-family.

"Jazz: Dictator of Fashion." UM Duluth.

Kristen, et al. "Dating, Mating, and Relating: Dating and Courtship in Modern Society." 7 May 2014. http://jrscience.wcp.muohio.edu/reflections/finalarticles/datingmatingandrelating.d.html.

"Legacy Duty: Succession Duty and Estate Duty Records." *National Archives.* Series Reference IR Division 5. http://discovery.nationalarchives.gov.uk/details/r/C1029.

Lloyd, Sarah Anne. "*Downton Abbey* Season 4: What If Lady Edith Gets an Abortion?" *Wetpaint.* http://www.wetpaint.com/season-4-lady-edith-abortion-801443/. 3 February 2014.

"Marriage and Divorce." *Exploring 20th Century London.* http://www.20thcenturylondon.org.uk/theme/home-family.

McDonald, James. "Castles and Manor Houses." *Castles and Manor Houses, Inc.* www.castlesandmanorhouses.com. 1 October 2010.

Peacock, John. *Fashion Source Book: 1920s.* London: Thames and Hudson, 1997.

Pettinger, Tejvan. "UK Economy in the 1920s." *Economics Help.* http://www.economicshelp.org/blog/5948/economics/uk-economy-in-the-1920s/. 16 October 2012.

Searle, G.R., *A New England? Peace and War, 1886–1918.* New York: Oxford University Press, 2004.

Smith, Angela. "Historical Context." *Discourses Surrounding British Widows of the First World War.* London: Bloomsbury Academic, 2013.

Swartz, Dennis K. "Flappers and the Roaring 20s." *The Dandy.* http://www.thedandy.org/home/flappers-and-the-roaring-20-s.

Thornton, Michael. "The Royal Gigolo…." *The Daily Mail.* 14 November 2008.

Trueman, C.N. "The Jazz Age." *History Learning Site.* www.historylearningsite.co.uk. 22 May 2015.

Will, George. "*Downton Abbey* reveals the progressive dream." *The Press of Atlantic City.* 13 February 2014.

Wilson, Christopher. "The Scandalous Truth about Downton Abbey's Royal Gigolo 'Jack Ross.'" *The Telegraph.* 14 October 2013.

"The Women's Timeline." *Manchester Metropolitan University.* http://www.mmu.ac.uk/equality-and-diversity/doc/gender-equality-timeline.pdf.

Valades, Didacus. "Great Chain of Being." *Rhetorica Christiana.* 1579.

Vic. "Dowagers and Widows in 19th C. England." *Jane Austen's World.* Blog. www.wordpress.com. 14 September 2011.

Worsley, Giles. "Country houses: the lost legacy." *The Telegraph*, 15 June 2002.

"Not family friendly"
Downton Abbey *and the Specter of Male Same-Sex Kissing*

ANTHONY GUY PATRICIA

Proem

If incredibly high ratings and heaps of gushing praise are any indication, early twenty-first century popular television success, thy name is *Downton Abbey*. But despite attracting millions of fans across the globe and having received its share of acclaim, it simply cannot go unnoticed that, in the United States specifically and, perhaps, not surprisingly, some viewers of *Downton Abbey* have been so haunted by the specter of male homoeroticism in the first series that they felt compelled to express their displeasure with this aspect of the program in major online public outlets, such as the extensive, interactive product review forum at Amazon.com. That being the case, the first purpose of this essay is to present a detailed description of the moments in Series One of *Downton Abbey* that, for a minority in the audience, are problematic precisely because of their depiction of explicit male, same-sex intimacy. The second objective is to direct critical attention to these negative responses, responses that exhibit an exceptionally righteous form of what Byrne Fone aptly characterizes as the "last acceptable prejudice" in the Western world that, in turn, still widely circulates within the sphere of popular culture: that being homophobia, or the irrational fear of homosexuals and homosexuality (*Homophobia: A History* 3). And the final idea is to consider the extended implications of how this "controversy" over the male same-sex intimacy in the first series of *Downton Abbey* reflects larger societal and cultural trends connected with the depiction of non-normative male erotic realities in the medium of television that can now be quantified and brought into the relief of analytical discussion in a meaningful way that will prove enlightening to observers of popular culture and producers of cultural studies of all kinds.

In Which the Love-That-Dares-Not-Speak-Its-Name Not Only Speaks Its Name, but Dares-to-Show-Its-Face, in the Very First Episode of Downton Abbey

To set the stage, so to speak, for the larger concerns of this essay, it is necessary to know the details of the single, but nevertheless crucial, dramatic scene in *Downton Abbey* that has been the source of the indignant disapprobation alluded to in the proem above. It takes place near the end of 1:1, in a richly upholstered guest bedroom of Downton Abbey, the enormous castle in which The Right Honorable Robert Crawley, the Earl of Grantham, and his family live. The ambience and surroundings of the room are at once elegant, tasteful, and masculine. The time is night; candles flicker and the ornate gas lamps shine brightly in the otherwise dim space. An intense-looking young man dressed semi-formally in a starched, white, long-sleeved shirt with a smart, matching bow tie; a black- and green-striped vest with gold-plated buttons; and black, form-fitting trousers that emphasize his muscularity, steps into the frame of the shot from the viewer's right side. He places a heavy glass, containing a swallow or two of brandy, on a table that is set flush against a wall. His short black hair is perfectly, if not severely, combed so that it rests flat against his head. This character is Thomas Barrow, First Footman to the Craw-ley family, who has been assigned by Carson, the Butler of the household, to attend to the needs of the Duke of Crowborough, an esteemed visitor to Downton Abbey. "I don't *believe* that," he tells the Duke, his expression a study in considered pensiveness (Fellowes 65). And so the drama between the footman and the duke begins. This particular conflict will unfold in just under three minutes of running time; its repercussions, however, will have a more lasting effect on both Thomas and audiences of *Downton Abbey.*

"Well," the Duke responds to Thomas, "believe what you like" (65). At this point, the camera shifts just enough so that the Duke himself can be seen on the other side of the room. His Grace is standing with his back to a fireplace that has a healthy fire burning inside of it. "He won't break the entail," he continues explaining to Thomas while tying the sash of his silk robe, leaving just enough of a space in the material to expose some of the dark hair that adorns his chest (65). "The unknown cousin gets everything," he says with a sardonic laugh, "and Mary's inheritance will be the same as it always was" (65). Thomas does not quite know what to make of the information the Duke is conveying to him about his employer. "So, what now?" the footman asks, unable to keep the con-sternation from his voice (65). The Duke pours himself a drink before answering. Then he says, "Well you … you know how I'm fixed. I have to have an heiress, if it means going to New York to find one" (65). Having thus detailed the nature of his immediate circum-stances and what they may well compel him to do in terms of securing a financially ben-eficial heterosexual marriage for himself in the not-too distant future, the Duke sits down on the edge of the bed and waits for Thomas' reaction.

Thomas, with the beginnings of a cheeky, almost seductive, smile on his face, walks over and kneels before the Duke. "What about me?" he asks, cocking his head upward to look at the other man while he begins to remove the Duke's black leather slippers (65). The Duke looks down on the footman and tells him, "You … you will wish me well" (66). Thomas counters by reminding the Duke that he said he would secure Thomas employ-ment somewhere other than at Downton Abbey if that was what Thomas wanted. The Duke seems to be sincerely mystified about whether Thomas really wants to leave his current position with the Crawleys or not. Thomas insists that he is sick and tired of being a footman and that he would rather be a valet, the Duke's personal valet, in fact. "Thomas, I don't need a valet," the Duke tells him sharply (66). After placing the Duke's slippers out of the way, Thomas returns to the bed and sits down next to His Grace. Boldly, he places his right hand on the side of the Duke's head and strokes the other man's hair. Shortly thereafter, Thomas grasps the Duke's neck and says softly, "I want to be with you" (66). Then he leans toward and kisses the Duke on the lips. The Duke responds immediately by kissing Thomas back. There can be no question that the few moments in which their mouths are so joined here certainly indicate the passion and desire they have for one another.

However, the Duke soon brings the intimacy between him and Thomas to an end by breaking off the kiss and pulling the footman's hand away from his neck. But Thomas, his ardor piqued, seizes the opportunity to grasp the Duke's hand between both of his own and to place a series of delicate kisses upon it. "I just can't see it working, can you?" the Duke asks Thomas in a soft voice (66). He adds as Thomas continues to kiss his hand, "I mean, we don't seem to have the basis of a servant-master relationship, do we?" (66). Thomas tells the Duke, "You came here to be with me," to which the Duke, a little too quickly, says, "Among other reasons" (66, 67). It seems that he pauses just long enough to steel himself emotionally for whatever may happen, then informs Thomas, who is still kissing his hand, that "one swallow doesn't make a summer" (67). That is when Thomas stops what he is doing and raises his head so that he is looking directly into the Duke's eyes with his own. He lets go of the Duke's hand as his mouth drops open in confusion followed very quickly by stunned shock. Then he stands, stalks away from the bed, and seeks out his unfinished drink. "Aren't you forgetting something?" Thomas says acidly from across the room, seconds before gulping down the rest of his brandy (67). "What?" The Duke asks; then, after a moment, he lets out an incredulous laugh and says, "Are you threatening me? Because of a youthful dalliance? A few weeks of madness in a London season? You wouldn't hold that against me, surely" (67). Thomas coldly assures His Grace, "I would if I have to" (67). And so it seems that the two men have reached a stalemate of sorts.

Even though, in fairness, it does seem to pain him to hurt Thomas so, at least a little, the Duke nevertheless continues with his attempt to out-maneuver the other man. He rises to his feet and deliberately makes his way to a table that stands at the end of the bed, saying, "And who'll believe a greedy footman over the words of a Duke. If you're not careful you'll end up behind bars" (67). Thomas retorts, "I've got proof" (67). The Duke nods solemnly then pulls a packet of letters out of the center drawer of the table he is standing next to. "You mean these?" he says, showing the packet to Thomas (67). Thomas is stunned that the Duke has somehow managed to acquire the letters, which most certainly contain enough information to incriminate the Duke on account of his homosexual relationship with Thomas. However, the footman recovers quickly enough and lunges at the Duke. The Duke has just enough time to toss the letters into the fireplace where the fire speedily consumes them as he and Thomas grapple with one another. When it is clear to him that there is no way he will be able to salvage the letters that would keep the Duke within his power, a defeated Thomas stops struggling with him and calls him a bastard. His Grace tells the footman, "Don't be a bad loser. Go to bed" (67). But to this command he adds the sly suggestion, "Unless you want to stay" (67). With what little dignity he has left in the face of his humiliation and rejection, Thomas violently pushes himself away from the Duke, grabs his long-tailed overcoat, and leaves the guest bedroom. The scene closes seconds later with Thomas alone, panting and very near tears in the dark, shadowy hallway of the castle outside the room, his love affair with the Duke clearly at an end he never envisioned nor wanted.

Just like Thomas, sophisticated and aware viewers of *Downton Abbey* may well wish to pause at this point to catch their cumulative breath and to consider the sheer, technical excellence of the drama that has culminated with the Crawley family's First Footman and the Duke of Crowborough parting ways, presumably once and for all, in the wholly disturbing manner they did. Throughout 1:1, creator and principal writer Julian Fellowes has expertly laid the groundwork for just such a satisfying, and genuinely surprising, denouement in the Thomas/ Duke story arc. Fairly early on in the episode, Thomas is seen purposefully making his way through the village of Downton on a break from his duties authorized by Carson. Thomas' co-worker and only friend—and Lady's Maid to Cora Crawley, the Countess of Grantham—Miss O'Brien asks, "Where have you been?" when he returns to Downton Abbey proper, and he tells her where he was and adds, "Sending a telegram, if you must know" (37). Significantly, Thomas does not reveal to O'Brien to whom he sent his communication. As such, these seem like throwaway moments in the grand scheme of the overall narrative; but, most certainly, they are not.

In due course, the Duke of Crowborough arrives at Downton Abbey, ostensibly to secure the hand of Lady Mary Crawley in marriage. As he is being escorted into the castle itself, the Duke confesses to one and all that his personal servant was taken ill just prior to the Duke's journey from London, so he needs someone to look after him during his stay at the estate. The Duke avers when Carson asserts that he personally will see to His Grace: "Oh no, I wouldn't dream of being such a nuisance. Surely a footman," he says with a disarming smile as he turns toward the assembled household staff; when his bright gaze falls on Thomas, he stops short as, clearly, a thought crosses his mind. "I remember this man. Didn't you serve me when I dined with Lady Grantham in London" (50)? Thomas responds with "I did, Your Grace" (50). The Duke is pleased by being so informed of the correctness of his supposition. "Ah, there we are. We shall do very well together, won't we…?" (50). With all due respect, and with no show of offense taken at the Duke's having forgotten his name, the footman reminds the Duke that he is called Thomas. Thus it is established that Thomas and the Duke do have a previous relationship with each other, albeit one that seems to have been purely professional rather than sexual and/or romantic given that Thomas served the Duke when the Duke had meals with the Crawley family while they were away from Downton Abbey and in London.

Moments afterward, the Duke is seen in the company of Lady Mary Crawley, who is clearly smitten with His Grace. Rather oddly, the Duke asks Lady Mary to show him the secret passages and the attics of Downton Abbey. Though a bit nonplussed by this request, Lady Mary is game for the adventure. Before long, the mischievous pair end up on the top floor of the castle where the servants' quarters are located. The Duke, claiming he is doing an ethnographic study of the genus footman, starts entering the individual rooms. It is clear that he has ulterior motives for doing so, but he does not, of course, share those with Lady Mary. After dinner, His Grace expresses his desire to speak to Lady Mary's father, the Earl of Grantham, in order to ask for his permission to marry the young woman he thinks is eminently eligible because of what she stands to inherit upon the Earl's death given that his Lordship's heir presumptive was drowned in the sinking of the RMS *Titanic* on the night of April 14, 1912, several months earlier. But when the Earl makes it plain to the Duke that Lady Mary's inheritance will not be altered for the better because of his immediate heir's demise, the Duke backpedals and claims that he never intended to marry Lady Mary in the first place; the only reason he came to Downton, he insists, was to express his condolences for the Earl's familial loss in person. Being no fool, of course, the Earl sends the Duke packing. But since it is so late in the evening, there are no more trains between Downton and London until the next day. It is during this brief interim that the Duke and Thomas have the dramatic confrontation detailed above in which they share the passionate kiss only moments before their relationship comes to its definitive end.

The artful mechanics underlying the Thomas/Duke story arc in 1:1 of *Downton Abbey* can now be understood in full. Throughout its evolution, Fellowes has skillfully adhered to the narrative principle of "show rather than tell." He does not, in other words, provide viewers with long, boring scenes of exposition that reveal the backstory that, in turn, inform the present actions and interactions of both Thomas and the Duke and the other characters in their respective and collective orbits. Instead, all of the scenes involving Thomas and the Duke compel the current dramatic action while simultaneously conveying only the necessary details about their past that audiences need to fill in the blanks about their relationship for themselves. Everything, furthermore, falls neatly, perfectly, in fact, into place when Thomas and the Duke square off with one another, as it were, in the Duke's bedroom.

Thomas' sending of the telegram to an unknown recipient earlier in the episode, as opposed to being little more than a throwaway moment, turns out to have been quite significant since the message went from Thomas to the Duke, and it had to have contained some intimation that Lady Mary, the eldest daughter of Thomas' employer, was a good marriage prospect for the Duke—who himself was facing some kind of financial difficulty that placed him in the position of needing an heiress like her in order to secure his material future. That their association went beyond the professional to encompass both the physical and the affective is made clear by the gestures of intimacy the two men share as well as the Duke's comment about spending a "few weeks of madness" with Thomas during a recent London season. That the Duke's foray with Lady Mary into the secret passages and the attics of the castle was a subterfuge that enabled him to retrieve the love letters he sent to Thomas that would be sufficient evidence to incriminate him and, quite likely, subject him to prosecution for willfully engaging in the crime of sodomy with his social inferior, is made plain when the Duke slyly shows the documents to Thomas seconds before throwing them into the fire. And, given that the Duke was willing to take Lady Mary as his bride so that he would come into the possession of her money, in tandem with the fact that Thomas, seemingly, was just as willing to continue his relationship with the Duke even though he may have been married to Lady Mary, transforms this pair of characters into greedy, albeit entirely human, opportunists lacking in basic integrity.

There are many reasons why Fellowes won an Oscar in 2002 for the screenplay of the film *Gosford Park*, including the care and detail he put into the crafting of characters, the sheer intricacy of his plotting, and the subtle and sophisticated precision of his dialogue. Without question, these attributes are all on display in *Downton Abbey*, too. Thomas and the Duke's story arc provides but one example of many in the first series of Fellowes' creative skill in this regard. But, unable to see the forest through the trees, a few, specifically American, audience members of *Downton Abbey* were capable of appreciating such technical excellence because they could not countenance the series' open, honest, and accurate depiction of male, same-sex intimacy. Given their across-the-board specificity—the fact that the mere specter of male same-sex kissing makes *Downton Abbey* "not family friendly"—this essay now turns its critical energy toward producing a rhetorical and contextual analysis of those negative responses to the series.

On Sociomental Community Bonds and Expressions of Homophobia in the Brave New Electronic World of Amazon's Customer Product Reviews of Downton Abbey

In *Connecting: How We Form Social Bonds and Communities in the Internet Age*, Mary Chayko defines sociomental bonds as those "that exist primarily in a mental realm, a space that is not created solely in the imagination of one individual but requires two or more minds—a 'meeting of the minds'—to make possible" (1). She adds that such bonds "between people who cannot or do not meet face-to-face—have never been more prevalent, more central to people's lives, and more critical to an understanding of the times and of the social order" than in the technologically-infused epoch of the early twenty-first century (2). It is in this sociomental realm that online or internet communities consisting of disparate groups of people the world over have formed during the last fifteen to twenty years. One of the first of these kinds of communities to come into being was that associated with "Earth's Biggest Bookstore," otherwise known as Amazon.com. As Robert Spector explains in his historical study of this phenomenally successful business, *Amazon.com: Get Big Fast*, from the beginning the e-retail behemoth "promoted the idea of creating a *community* of customers. The company fostered this comfy-clubby feeling by encouraging readers to write and submit book reviews," which would be posted at Amazon.com for consumers to consult at will as they shopped in this brave new world of electronic commerce (78, emphasis in the original). Spector notes that such "'audience participation' gave readers the feeling that they were making a contribution to the thoroughness of the Web site's information" (78). With this knowledge in mind, it can be understood that Amazon's community of customers that Spector mentions is a sociomental community in the exact same sense that Chayko uses to describe such communities in her sociological-grounded work.

Insofar as the Web site is a popular cultural and social force to be reckoned with in the world today, it is entirely significant that it is among the reviews of Series One of *Downton Abbey* that Amazon.com's sociomental community of customers have posted to the site that pointed critiques of the drama's representation of male homoeroticism are to be found. As of the initial drafting of this essay in the early summer of 2012, the DVD and Blu-ray editions of *Downton Abbey* have a combined 583 customer reviews at Amazon.com's U.S. portal, distributed as follows: 465 at five stars, 54 at four stars, 24 at three stars, 18 at two stars, and 22 at one star. These ratings seem to confirm the notion that, as mentioned earlier, the overall reaction to the program has been a primarily positive one. That said, further investigation of the 22 one star customer reviews reveals that fourteen of them were awarded to *Downton Abbey* because of technical issues, such as damaged or missing discs and playback aspect ratio problems that those buyers were, quite understandably, unhappy with; or because of what can be described as aesthetic objections involving, for instance, the absence of adequate period detail, or the lack of believability in the characters and their stories, that other consumers found to be not to their liking. Fair enough. But the remaining eight one star customer reviews, however, evidence nothing but the most virulent form of homophobia, and all of them are of a piece with one another.

It is worth looking at these homophobic reviews of *Downton Abbey* in some detail from a critical rhetorical perspective. To begin, an Amazon.com customer with the name of Florida Homeschooler titled his/her review "BEWARE!"; this is an imperative that appears in all capitals and includes an exclamation point for emphasis. With this title, Florida Homeschooler seeks to warn Amazon's sociomental community of customers that there is something they should be cautious of, if not downright afraid of, as regards *Downton Abbey*. Where netiquette is concerned, this reviewer's use of all capitals is a violation of decorum. As David Crystal explains in *Language and the Internet*, the "lower-case default mentality" of electronic linguistics "means that any use of capitalization is a strongly marked form of communication. Messages wholly in capitals are considered to be 'shouting,' and usually avoided" (92). Obviously, Florida Homeschooler failed to adhere to this doctrine of avoidance in his/her determination to make certain that his/her views were known to others. He/She seems to have felt that there was no other alternative but to engage in the electronic equivalent of screaming at the top of his/her lungs in order to gain the attention of others in the virtual world. Florida Homeschooler continues by praising the acting, costumes, and scenery of *Downton Abbey*, but this praise is followed by the immediate qualification that the series "is not your typical sweet period piece." The logical fallacy at the heart of this statement is the implication that all period pieces are, or are supposed to be, sweet. Another problem with this assertion is the fact that Florida Homeschooler does not define what he/she means by "sweet"; no criteria are presented in support of the use of such a term. It can be argued, therefore, that the resulting indeterminacy of this bland adjective renders the entire point he/she is trying to make moot.

Florida Homeschooler proceeds by using a pair of exclamatory remarks that follow one upon another, albeit without total capitalization this time, to counsel those in his/her audience to not watch *Downton Abbey* with their children. Why? His/Her sole reason for this proscription seems to be the fact that the series features two men who kiss each other, and that this kiss occurs even before the first hour of the drama has run its course. He/She thus seeks to protect his/her and others' children from something he/she deems to be completely threatening to their emotional, psychological and, it can be surmised, spiritual or religious, well being. Guarding them is, without question, something responsible parents are supposed to do for their kids as they are rearing them. But the bigger problem, in this case, is *what* this individual is trying to shield these young people from: two human beings, both of whom just happen to be male, kissing as human beings have done since time immemorial. Florida Homeschooler thus conflates the ontological categories of men and kissing and transforms them into something bad, something wrong, something ugly … something mothers and fathers should not, for any reason, let their children see with their innocent eyes because they could be, somehow, hurt or damaged for having witnessed such a thing. The extended, although cleverly unwritten, implication here is that boys who see this representation of two men kissing will grow up into men who want to kiss other men like Thomas and the Duke do in *Downton Abbey*. In itself this is a classic move on Florida Homeschooler's part, one designed to inspire fear in his/her readers about the potential results of allowing impressionable children to view the scene he/she considers to be problematic in *Downton Abbey*; by not specifying these possibilities in any way, Florida Homeschooler succeeds at encouraging others to imagine the worst for themselves, which, to him/her and those who think and see the world as myopically as he/she does, can only be a child who grows up to be anything other than heterosexual.

Unhappy as he/she is about the male same-sex kissing, Florida Homeschooler does not fail to chastise the over 500 of his/her fellow Amazon reviewers that have expressed such unqualified admiration for *Downton Abbey* without alerting others to the program's featuring of homosexuality. "Could someone have at least warned us?" he/she complains about this blatant disregard for his/her family's apparently delicate sensibilities where human nature is concerned. Linda B. from Portland, Oregon, seems to provide just the kind of warning about *Downton Abbey* that Florida Homeschooler felt was absent from Amazon when he/she posted his/her comments to the site. Linda B. titled her review "R-rated scenes," and in it she writes, "I ordered this DVD because I love period films but I was not prepared for the homosexual scenes (two men making love). It was extremely offensive and I did not finish watching the DVD." Short and to-the-point, surely these statements would have provided Florida Homeschooler with the information he/she felt entitled to be in possession of before watching *Downton Abbey* and being confronted with material he/she considered to be inappropriate for, specifically, heterosexual family viewing. Yet, Linda B.'s review is not without its own problems. For example, in parentheses she uses the phrase "two men making love" in reference to Thomas and the Duke, which is totally inaccurate. As detailed above, the only thing that Thomas and the Duke do is kiss a couple of times on the lips followed by Thomas tenderly kissing the Duke's hand. Since Linda B. is obviously using the expression "make love" as a euphemism for "have sex," she is in the wrong to consider Thomas and the Duke's kissing in the scene as the equivalent of engaging in out-and-out sexual relations. Linda B.'s comment, factually incorrect as it is, exposes the faulty logic at its core: whenever gay men are involved, their entire association must be about no more than sex; it cannot be about love, or affection, or anything else, for that matter.

Another issue with Linda B.'s remarks is that she, like Florida Homeschooler, feels that she should have been "prepared for the homosexual scenes" in *Downton Abbey* in some way, although what form this preparation was supposed to have taken she leaves unspecified. This is quite ironic considering the fact that, when *Downton Abbey* was screened on PBS, each episode was preceded by the corporation's standard parental TV-PG warning that the content of the program may not be suitable for all persons and age groups. Perhaps she wishes that the DVD set of *Downton Abbey* that she purchased and claims she did not finish watching because she was so offended by it had come with a label warning her of its explicit homosexual content; labels similar to those that are affixed to CDs or that accompany motion picture advertising and packaging that warn consumers—notably parents, of potentially objectionable material. And therein lies a rather grand irony; no one seems to find it necessary to warn the gay and lesbian community that the mass media productions they have chosen to view might feature displays of heterosexual affection that they could find offensive. Gay, lesbian, bisexual, transgender, queer, questioning, intersex, and allied groups are just supposed to accept the fact that this is the way things are in the world of heterosexist, one-size-fits-all entertainment; their sensibilities be damned. Hence the double standard that Florida Homeschooler and Linda B. seem to advocate in this regard is quite telling in its hypocrisy.

Meanwhile, B. Evans, from somewhere in the USA, makes the same errors of fact and of logic in his/her review of *Downton Abbey* as those made by Linda B. titling his/her piece "Not acceptable," he/she writes, "We were really interested in and enjoying this show with our whole family until a very seedy and needless scene of two men who began kissing on a bed and speaking of their previous encounters." Evans continues: "We felt that we had been subjected to seeing sexual imagery that we would rather not have seen and it was upsetting for us all." Thomas and the Duke do indeed mention their preexisting relationship with each other, but they do not discuss the erotic side of their "encounters" at all if, as seems more than likely, Evans implies that they do by her use of this specific term in this context. Furthermore, like Linda B., Evans automatically equates Thomas and the Duke's kissing with their having sex, as his/her employment of the phrase "sexual imagery" in this review makes quite clear. From Evans' perspective, once again, when they involve gay men, circumstances can only be of a sexual nature. There are no possible alternatives. Evans seems to have no conception of the fact that homosexuals, just like their heterosexual counterparts, kiss one another all the time and for all sorts of reasons that have nothing to do with sex. To him/her, the very notion of two men kissing each other like Thomas and the Duke do in the scene in *Downton Abbey* he/she singles out for comment in his/her review, is "seedy and needless." For Evans, this pair of derogatory adjectives implies, much more forcefully even than the statements posted by Florida Homeschooler and Linda B., that there is something unsavory and pointless about the idea of two males kissing one another, whether in a television series like *Downton Abbey* or in real life. It is difficult not to wonder if Evans would be so condemnatory if the situation involved a man and a woman, and the only conclusion to be reached on that point is a negative one. The very idea of, specifically, two men kissing is, for Evans and family, so distressing that programs featuring such representations must be switched off and reviewed, notifying others of their failings and posted to one of the most heavily-trafficked Web sites in the world. Evans, it seems, would wholeheartedly agree with Sue's Reviews from Lake Forest, California's assertion in her "Gay Kissing Scene" piece on *Downton Abbey*, that not "everyone wants to witness homosexual kissing. It's really too bad that the makers of this story felt the need to do that. Warning to those who, like me, do not want to watch nor support that kind of movie." Indeed, the creators and writers of programs that dare to include homosexual kissing should be ashamed of themselves and their productions should be shunned, at least according to Sue's Reviews. But Sue's Reviews, not unlike B. Evans, Linda B., and Florida Homeschooler, does not even stop to consider the possibility that not everyone wants to witness heterosexual kissing, either, and in so doing, makes plain her homophobia for all to recognize.

Along strikingly similar lines, in his review of *Downton Abbey* entitled "Guys kissing," DonP from Arkansas notes bluntly, "Turned it off as soon as two guys started kissing on screen. Disgusting," while Max, from an undisclosed location on America's East Coast, explains in his post, "Great potential but disappointingly not family-friendly," and that "[b]eing an avid fan of period films old and new, I was greatly looking forward to this production. Such fabulous actors, scenery, costumes, and more. However (SPOILER) the graphic portrayal of a same-sex relationship in the first episode makes it definitely not suitable for our family's entertainment preferences. Really a shame." Meanwhile, L.M. Jordan is even more patently offensive in his piece called "Unpleasantly surprised," in which he writes, "I recently saw on broadcast TV part of a first season episode and thought this mini-series had promise…. So, I bought a copy. However, within the first 30 minutes of the first episode a sodomite 'love' scene compelled me to stop the player, apologize to my wife and trash season one. Ruined." He goes on to complain that it is "getting more and more difficult to find modern productions which have not been altered to include sodomite characters and themes. I'm sorry I wasted my money on this filth." Lastly, following in the footsteps of Florida Homeschooler, Meghan Allred from Virginia chooses to use all capitals to head her commentary on *Downton Abbey* with "NOT FAMILY FRIENDLY," although, contra Florida Homeschooler, she does not include an exclamation point at the end of her title. Nevertheless, Allred proceeds to reveal that she "rented this for family movie night because we like period pieces. It started off good enough, but then took a turn for the worse when two guys started kissing. I'm furious that my children saw a glimpse of such a scene before I could turn off the TV. Did not watch any more of the movie. Extremely disappointed." Extremely disappointed indeed. And thus Allred once more rehearses an all-too- familiar theme about what she, and others like her, considers to be the cardinal sin of *Downton Abbey*: its unflinching representation of a gay male character and corresponding homoerotic acts like kissing.

Downton Abbey *and the Anti-Gay Rhetoric of Disgust, Sodomy and Save the Children*

In an essay entitled "Creating Community in Cyberspace: Criteria for a Discourse Technology Project," Stephen P. Steinberg, like Mary Chayko earlier, considers the idea of virtual communities. He notes that technology—such as the Internet—can be used to enable, augment, and to increase the "opportunities for effective public discourse," but only if technology, as a tool, is deployed in specific ways that contribute to a measurable outcome (237–238). He goes on to insist that "a shared situation is not enough, by itself, to create a community ... a true community must also have *real work to do together* in responding to that situation" (239, emphasis in the original). For Steinberg, who is following the ideas of his colleague Thomas Bender, this "real work to do together" involves the coming together of individuals with "conflicts to resolve" in a way that encompasses a "combination of assertion of interest, respect for difference, and commitment to civic responsibility" ("The Thinning of American Political Culture" 33). Many of the "existing online communities," according to Steinberg, "address the notion of *real work to do together* only partially, if at all" (240). Amazon.com, with its product review forum, falls into this category of online community from Steinberg's point of view. He concedes that this Web site does provide the means for "visitors to glean a form of collective wisdom from the aggregated responses," but he also points out the fact that the program's reviewers are "not compelled to contribute toward some sort of discernible end (i.e., there is no *real work* to do, merely talk for talk's sake)," and thus this type of medium fails, again in his words, to foster "the kind of productive, engaged public discourse that is central to building and strengthening diverse, inclusive communities" (241). There can be no question but that product reviewers such as Florida Homeschooler, Linda B., B. Evans, Sue, DonP, Max, L.M. Jordan, and Meghan Allred do not seek to contribute to the creation of a community with the kind of altruistic aims Steinberg identifies; they would much rather perpetuate bigotry, divisiveness, and incivility in their quest to maintain the hegemony of the heterosexist status quo.

Of course it must be noted that, in the Western world of the early twenty-first century, people like Florida Homeschooler, Linda B., B. Evans, Sue, DonP, Max, L.M. Jordan, and Meghan Allred are certainly entitled to express their views in just about any manner they see fit, within the confines of the law. But when such persons elect to post their assessments in a freely-accessible arena like the product review forum of Amazon.com, those ideas automatically become the subject of critique because they are instantiations of *public*, rather than private, opinion. They are also, not incidentally, particular exempla of a larger, ongoing discourse having to do with gay rights and gay visibility in conflict with strenuous moral, religious, or personal objections to homosexuals and homosexuality. Taken as a whole, the responses to *Downton Abbey* detailed above can be seen to form a coherent, anti-gay rhetorical narrative of the type that has been in circulation since the nineteenth century when, as Michel Foucault so eloquently and bluntly revealed in the first volume of his *The History of Sexuality*, the homosexual had become "a species" (43). It was a species that, once identified and labeled, those at every level of the hegemonic heterosexist regime sought to control, if not to eradicate outright, through any and all of the considerably potent means at their disposal in the psychological, mental, medical, social, familial, religious, legal, educational, moral, ethical, and philosophical realms.

As has been demonstrated above, the opening gambit of the anti-gay reactionary screed associated with *Downton Abbey* is the vehement assertion of the notion that any type of representation of male homosexuals or male homoeroticism—no matter how benign or in keeping with the dictates of character and plot within the larger structure of an overarching story that necessarily propels fictional drama—are unsuitable subjects for television programming. Furthermore, the specific imperatives, adjectives, and metaphors the cohort of reviewers under discussion use to describe the single kiss and the other intimacies the characters of Thomas and the Duke of Crowborough share, which include such gems as "beware," "seedy," "needless," "R-rated," "offensive," "unwatchable," "sodomitical," "filthy," "disgusting," "disappointing," "not family friendly," and "took a turn for the worse," only serve to reinforce the general ethos of ugliness they perceive to be the defining feature of *Downton Abbey*. To put it more baldly, this collection of descriptors epitomizes a veritable rhetoric of disgust. On this point, Martha C. Nussbaum adds that, for some time now, "our society, like many others, has confronted same-sex orientations and acts with a politics of disgust, as many people react to the uncomfortable presence of gays and lesbians with a deep aversion akin to that inspired by bodily wastes, slimy insects, and spoiled food—and then," in turn, "cite that very reaction to justify a range of legal restrictions, from sodomy laws to bans on same-sex marriage" (*From Disgust to Humanity: Sexual Orientation and Constitutional Law* xiii). Though they are careful not to say so explicitly, there can be little doubt that Florida Homeschooler, Linda B., B. Evans, Sue, DonP, Max, L.M. Jordan, and Meghan Allred would seek to impose the force of law in the exact manner Nussbaum discusses in her work—by using their outraged disgust to guide and form public policy—in order to prevent the creators, writers, and producers of programs like *Downton Abbey* from ever including representations of male homosexuals in an open, honest, and historically accurate manner, complete with the affectionate homoeroticism that is depicted as occurring between Thomas and the Duke explored above. That brand of potential censorship is entirely disturbing because it would only serve to perpetuate the vicious cycle of blatant hatred and intolerance that the gay community at large has endured for far too long.

L.M. Jordan's double invocation of the word "sodomite," the first followed by the term love encased in scare quotes, lends an unmistakably biblical cast to the body of public criticism leveled at *Downton Abbey* because of its forthright inclusion of the homosexual character Thomas, and the corresponding scene with obvious homoerotic content involving Thomas and the Duke kissing. For Jordon, sodomite is such a potent rhetorical signifier that he feels no need to explain its connotations. However, deconstructing it for the purposes of this essay begins with remembering the basic elements of the Sodom and Gomorrah story from Genesis. In Christian mythology, the ancient Middle Eastern cities of Sodom and Gomorrah were destroyed by God because a preponderance of the male residents of both unrepentantly engaged in the filthy sin of sodomy—simplistically thought equivalent to the act of anal sex—with members of their own gender. But it must be understood that Jordan's use of this trope flies in the face of decades of religious and secular scholarship that thoroughly debunks the anti-gay, sodomitical interpretation of Genesis 19. For example, Jennifer Wright Knust, in her recent monograph *Unprotected Texts: The Bible's Surprising Contradictions about Sex and Desire*, explains that, although "popularly invoked to prove God's hatred of homosexuality, among biblical scholars today this story [about Sodom and Gomorrah] is thought to teach something else entirely: the importance of showing hospitality to strangers" (168–169). She continues with "Lot willingly presented the angels [that visited him with specific intentions] with food and shelter, the men of Sodom demanded to 'know' the strangers in their midst, going so far as seeking to rape them. As such, the Sodomites violated ancient cultural customs in the worst way, attempting to harm the strangers in their midst rather than extending them protection, food, and shelter" (169). In other words, the Sodom and Gomorrah myth has nothing to do with the kinds of consensual, same-sex, intimate relationships between men (and women, for that matter) that have manifested so prolifically in more recent times. Thus Jordan's conflation of biblical sodomy and the story of Thomas and the Duke of Crowborough in *Downton Abbey* proves to be no more than a rhetorical fallacy of the most damaging sort, not to mention anachronistic in the extreme.

The last, and perhaps most significant, facet of the anti-gay rhetorical narrative associated with a specific faction of the public's reception of *Downton Abbey* is its unmistakable "save the children" philosophy. Recall that the Amazon reviewer Florida Homeschooler cautioned his/her readers against watching the series with their children because it has one scene in which two men—Thomas and the Duke—kiss each other on the mouth; that B. Evans claimed his/her entire family which, presumably, includes a number of kids, was upset by the visual representation of that kind of male homoeroticism in 1:1; that Meghan Allred was made downright furious that her children even caught a glimpse of the intimacy Thomas and the Duke shared with one another on the bed before she could switch the program off; and that more than one poster, like Max for example, insistently described the drama as "disappointingly not family-friendly" for no other reason than because of the innocent same-sex smooch it presented as a central part of its overall storyline encompassing the whole of the Crawley family, their servants, and their associates.

In their specificity, these remarks about children in need of protection from homosexuals and homoeroticism, and the lack of so-called family friendliness, echo those made in the late 1970s when, according to Fred Fejes, Americans began to argue publicly and bitterly about the issue of gay rights. Fejes explains that this argument finds its origins on the "morning of January 18, 1977, the county commissioners of Dade County, Florida, met to debate and then vote on a law banning discrimination on the basis of sexual preference" (*Gay Rights and Moral Panic: The Origins of America's Debate on Homosexuality* 2). As the language here implies, the statute under consideration would have made it illegal in a large part of Southern Florida for those in positions of authority in both the public and private sectors to discriminate against anyone on the basis of their sexual orientation. Leading the charge against the passage of this law was the entertainer and

Florida orange juice national spokesperson, Anita Bryant. According to Fejes, at the time, Bryant "was an embodiment of the traditional American wholesomeness and values that had been so greatly challenged by the cultural and social upheavals of the 1960s and 1970s" (2). Appearing before the Dade County Commission, Bryant claimed that "approval of the law would endanger her children by exposing them to homosexuality. The law would 'violate my rights and all the rights [of] all the decent and morally upstanding citizens, regardless of their race, or religion' to provide their children with a morally healthy environment" (2). Following Bryant, another speaker had similar words for the commissioners: "'I have children in private school. Both of these schools accept anyone regardless of race, color, or creed. But I do not want these children [to] have a homosexual figure that they may learn to admire and decide too they will become homosexual'" (82). Bryant and her supporters did not want gay people to be seen or heard from then, just like Florida Homeschooler, B. Evans, Meghan Allred, and Max do not want gay people to be seen or heard from over thirty-five years later, and for the same exact reasons: so that their children cannot possibly be influenced to countenance either homosexuality or gay people; so that their children will neither be "recruited" by homosexuals and turn gay as a result, regardless of their innate natures; and, most troubling of all perhaps, so that their children will remain forever ignorant of the fact that gay people exist in the world, that gay people deserve respect, and that gay people feel and experience love like any other human being that has ever walked the face of the earth.

As Fejes details, Bryant and the many others who, aligned with her, were against approval of the 1977 gay rights law in Dade County, Florida, were not successful in persuading the commissioners to agree with their views; "by [a] five to three" vote "the ordinance passed" that January (82). But, in response, Bryant's group almost immediately formed the hysterically-named Save Our Children organization, with Bryant as its public face and voice, that did manage to effect the overwhelming repeal of the gay rights ordinance less than six months later. The repeal was a devastating blow to the gay community in Southern Florida and all throughout the rest of America, too. In contrast, the small cadre of anti-gay viewers of *Downton Abbey* under discussion in this essay have utterly failed to achieve a similar substantive impact on the program, its producers, or its broadcasters. Thomas, as gay as ever, remains very much a central character in the drama and, though he was not presented as kissing another male in Series Two, he was beyond devastated when the blinded, World War I soldier he was nursing at the Downton Village Wounded Veterans' Hospital committed suicide because the young man could no longer cope with the all-too likely permanency of his disability (2:2). Indeed, Thomas' breaking down into tears after finding out about the death of the handsome, young Lieutenant Edward Courtenay, was, for many, one of the most emotionally devastating moments in the entirety of *Downton Abbey*'s second series. Furthermore, Julian Fellowes, in remarks given to Jim Halterman, an entertainment reporter at the gay pop culture Web site Afterelton.com (now known as Backlot.com), indicated that Thomas' character would be even more fully developed and fleshed out in the show's third series, which aired in the UK starting in September 2012, and in the U.S. starting in January 2013 ("PBS at TCAs: 'Emotional' Thomas on 'Downton Abbey,' Cheyenne Jackson as Annie? 'Knots Landing' Redux?"). This did indeed turn out to be the case, and it was done in fine *Downton Abbey*/Julian Fellowes form.

In 3:1, Thomas had a falling out with O'Brien, his partner in crime at Downton, because Thomas would not support the idea of O'Brien's nephew, Alfred Nugent, who had only recently joined the Crawley family's downstairs staff as a footman, becoming a valet within an exceptionally short period of time. Thomas' reasoning, though selfish, was understandable. He had to work for years before he earned a promotion from footman to valet and he simply could not countenance the idea that Alfred might be able to do the same after just a few weeks. But, when Alfred is given a trial run as valet to Matthew Crawley, Thomas takes drastic action; pretending to give him a tip of the trade leads Alfred to ruin a pair of Matthew's dress pants—and to be demoted back to footman as a result. For this stunt, O'Brien vows to take revenge against Thomas. These initial circumstances set up a story arc that runs through the entirety of Series Three and that also proves germane to any discussion of *Downton Abbey*'s representation of male homo-eroticism.

Knowing him as well as she does, O'Brien has little trouble convincing Thomas that the handsome Jimmy Kent, another new footman at Downton, is in love with him but is too afraid to approach Thomas romantically on his own. Late one night in 3:7, after much private wrestling with his own tormented thoughts, the completely besotted Thomas steels into Jimmy's room while Jimmy is sleeping and kisses him. At the same moment Thomas is kissing Jimmy, Alfred knocks, opens the door, and sees what is going on. Thomas is stunned and confused, while both Alfred and Jimmy are, not surprisingly, outraged by what Thomas has done. It does not take long before Thomas realizes he has been completely and utterly duped by O'Brien. However, that matters little given that his fate—inclusive of his career at Downton and his life as a free man in England, a country that imprisoned homosexuals like Thomas for crimes against humanity and nature in 1920—quite literally hangs in the balance. Using Amazon.com as a barometer, this male same-sex kiss did not generate the same amount of hysterical, reactionary responses as the example in Series One discussed above. Indeed, Series Three has an astonishing 5,524 total reviews and a solid five star rating. The negative pieces focus on two broad areas of concern: (1) that the Instant Videos broadcast via Amazon's streaming video service, and the DVDs/Blu-rays sold in the U.S. by the company, may be missing scenes that, as they understood things, were included in all of the UK versions of the series; this is especially problematic since the electronic and physical packaging claims that U.S. consumers/viewers are screening or receiving copies of the, presumably, uncut "Original UK Edition," and (2) the shocking plot developments involving two beloved upstairs characters, Lady Sybil and Matthew Crawley, both of whom die in the course of the series; the former as a result of complications during pregnancy, the latter due to a car accident. It seems, in fact, that the likes of Florida Homeschooler, Linda B., B. Evans, Sue's Reviews, DonP, Max, L.M. Jordan, and Meghan Allred were true to their individual and collective words—they did not elect to watch any more *Downton Abbey* episodes after having been subjected to what they considered to be horrific visions of Thomas and the Duke of Crowborough kissing in Series One.

It is not the case, however, that the homosexuality in Series Three of *Downton Abbey* escaped the notice of anti-gay detractors. But of the 5,524 Amazon reviews mentioned above, only three—a minuscule number in ratio terms—evidence negative reactions to this aspect of the drama. RAS, in a piece entitled "misleading historicity," opines that he/she thinks "it very unlikely in a Grand House like Downton Abbey to find so much drama regarding the aspects of some scenes involving homosexuality. Almost all of the servant class were vowed into celibacy and also would rarely include a husband and wife team." RAS hastens to add that this is just his/her "opinion as to what I wish to view .... is that still allowed??????????? This was not meant to offend anyone, as I judge no one to their choice of life, nor discriminate against anyone. I wouldn't have liked torrid love scenes with the Crowley's [*sic*] either. Just felt it took away the grandeur of looking into a era almost all but gone." Setting aside its rather glaring grammatical, mechanical, and orthographic deficiencies, RAS seems to believe that homosexuals and homosexuality did not exist during the era brought to life by *Downton Abbey* and, thus, do not warrant depiction in any way, shape, or form. And while the rhetorical question about whether or not personal opinions regarding the type of programming one wishes to watch are allowed is valid, when such inquiries are placed in a public forum like Amazon.com, they are fair game for critique from any quarter. Also, as with nearly all of the reviewers who chose to comment negatively on the intimacies that took place between Thomas and the Duke of Crowborough in Series One, RAS deliberately conflates Thomas' kissing of Jimmy in Series Three with a "torrid love scene." Such an assessment reveals a profound ignorance about what a "torrid love scene" between fictional characters really is, as well as RAS' hypocrisy as regards his/her insistence that his/her remarks are not meant to offend anyone or cast judgment on what he/she quaintly refers to as anyone's "choice of life," a.k.a., their sexual preferences. RAS' myopia prevents him/her from understanding that gay men like Thomas do what they do (i.e., fall in love with other men) because they are born that way, not because they willfully elect to engage in behaviors that are outside of the common and the heteronormative.

Meanwhile, Christopher Borchardt, in a review tellingly called "Agenda pushing," notes that "[u]p until this season the show was going good and not going crazy pushing propaganda (almost all PBS supported shows do). But in season 3 we were subjected to multiple episodes (at the end of the season) which seemed to focus almost wholly on pushing the homosexual agenda." Borchardt goes on to complain that even in a "WW1 era series, each episode attacked conservative and moral values. We were not surprised that a PBS supported show did this, but disappointed that again we can not [*sic*] even enjoy a 'classical' drama without social indoctrination." The irony here is, of course, the fact that Borchardt seems entirely unaware that, embedded within his claim that both *Downton Abbey* and PBS are "pushing the homosexual agenda" through the narrative of Thomas and Jimmy, lies his own heterosexist pogrom that seeks to demean, if not to eradicate entirely, anything involving the open and honest depiction of the realities of male homosexuality across times and cultures. For Borchardt, "conservative and moral values" are not, apparently, a form of "social indoctrination" that he finds as pernicious as the "homosexual agenda," something that, it should be noted, he fails to define in any kind of a substantive way.

By far, however, the most vituperative commentary on the Thomas and Jimmy story arc in Series Three of *Downton Abbey* comes from a reviewer who posts at Amazon under the name Therehere. Not surprisingly, perhaps, Therehere's piece, entitled "Episode 6 is the worst," is Biblically-inflected, which goes a long way toward explaining its vehemence. He/She proclaims at the outset that he/she is finished with watching *Downton* because of its frank treatment of homoeroticism: this aspect of the program "ended my like for the show." He/She then accuses the writers of taking scripture out of context in order to present a confusing notion of what sin is and what sin is not—with homosexuality falling squarely within the designation of sin in Therehere's view. To make this point as forcefully as possible, Therehere trots out the old chestnut of a passage from Leviticus that, supposedly, condemns intimate same-sex relations between males: "If a man also lie with mankind, as he lieth with a woman, both of them have committed an abomination: they shall surely be put to death; their blood shall be upon them" (*KJV* 20:13). As numerous authorities, both secular and ecumenical, have painstakingly sought to make clear in the last two or three decades, interpreting these lines in such a repressive manner only exposes the interpreter as woefully uninformed and conveniently selective.

One of the more recent scholarly considerations of Leviticus 20:13 was published by the well-regarded philosophy professor John Corvino. In *What's Wrong with Homosexuality?*, Corvino argues that, while the passage may indeed refer to sex amongst males, it does not mention either lesbianism or "other forms of romantic interaction between men besides anal intercourse" (32). This is a significant caesura that those who would wield Leviticus 20:13 as a weapon against gays fail to acknowledge. Even so, Corvino allows that "[o]ne might naturally take 'as with a woman' to refer to *any* romantic or sexual activity" (32). However, he insists immediately afterward that "reading it that way supplies information that is not explicitly in the text. It requires interpretation and thus introduces human fallibility" into the equation (32). This particular prohibition, therefore, cannot be the inerrant word of God that fundamentalists and literalists would have their followers and others believe. Corvino is also savvy enough to remark on the lack of logic—and the hypocrisy—in the widespread thinking that Christians are exempt from Leviticus' dietary, marriage, slavery, and other assorted laws because of the existence of the New Testament which, it is claimed, overrides the Old Testament, while simultaneously holding only homosexuals accountable to 20:13 (33–35). For Corvino, this is a manifestation of the "often flawed rules of fallible human beings, rules that are intricately bound to the authors' cultural circumstances" and not those of twenty-first-century Western man (35–36). In other words, Leviticus 20:13 does not apply to people of the current epoch who are attracted to members of their own gender and should not be used to denigrate them. Corvino's insights therefore provide a powerful rebuttal to the likes of Therehere who continue to inflict their ugly brand of abuse on fictional characters like *Downton Abbey*'s Thomas and, by extension, his real-life counterparts.

Beyond the realm of "off-the-cuff" response, the Thomas and Jimmy story in Series Three of *Downton* did engender equally significant concerns associated with representations of homosexuals and homoeroticism and the thorny problem of historical accuracy. Though time and space constraints prevent a full treatment of these issues from being presented in this essay, they do warrant at least some comment. Given the rigid moral and behavioral limitations placed on those employed at estates like Downton Abbey in the first quarter of the twentieth century, many viewers found the idea that Thomas would, first, steal into Jimmy's bedroom during the middle of the night without being invited to do so, and second, that he would go so far as to kiss the other young man while he was sleeping, to be completely implausible. As cultural critic June Thomas puts it in her analysis of this plotline, "Servants in great houses were generally expected to live celibate lives. As we saw in Season 1, below stairs the men's quarters are separated from the women's rooms by a locked door, whose key Mrs. Hughes keeps guarded on a heavy metal key ring" ("*Downton Abbey*, Season 3; Is the treatment of Thomas an anachronistic 21st-century fantasy?" n.p.). If men and women were expected to remain chaste, the same quite likely applied to male-male, and female-female couples, too, even if their quarters were not segregated. But, the demands of this particular story called for Thomas to do exactly as he did, and whether his actions accorded with history or not. What mitigates any disparity as regards historical accuracy is the fact that Fellowes takes the time to make sure that Thomas' reasoning is clear throughout the unfolding of this drama. On this point, June Thomas rightly notes that Rob James-Collier "did a great job of conveying Thomas' struggle. After years of loneliness and contempt, love seemed to be calling from across the hall. He knew the risks—a beating, dismissal, jail—but he gave in to his romantic side and kissed the man he had been told was mooning over him. There was," she adds furthermore, "no suggestion of Thomas forcing himself on Jimmy, who is physically strong and an independent thinker; he was simply making the first move" (n.p.). Considering the society that Thomas is part of did not allow for people to be homosexual in an open and above board manner as is commonplace 100 years later, it seems rather true to life that Thomas read the signs about Jimmy as best he could and took the only chance he knew how to take to find some kind of happiness in his life. From this perspective, the Thomas and Jimmy story has a great deal more plausibility than its detractors have claimed. Even so, armchair historians also had serious problems with the idea that Lord Grantham would be willing to keep a known homosexual, who had transgressed in the manner Thomas had done, in his employ—especially as his personal valet. Once again, June Thomas offers crucial insight on this matter. "Would Robert have been content to employ a 'body servant' whom he knew to harbor homosexual urges" she asks? "If the man did his job well and observed all the appropriate proprieties, as Thomas Barrow apparently did, Lord Grantham would put up with a great deal," she insists ("Treatment of Thomas" n.p.). In other words, Thomas being dismissed from his position at Downton for the offense he committed would be far more anachronistic than his being kept on staff as is dramatized so superbly in Series Three. The questions of historical accuracy that have been raised are thus effectively rendered moot.

Conclusions: Downton Abbey *and Gay Visibility in American Television*

In the long history of television in America, gay male characters with fully-realized personalities and the stories to match have, until very recently, been few and far between. As Rodger Streitmatter explains in *From "Perverts" to "Fab Five": The Media's Changing Depiction of Gay Men and Lesbians*, although homosexuals had been featured on news programs and in documentaries—almost always framed in reactionary and/or sensationalistic ways—since the mid to late 1960s, the first bona fide recurring gay character did not appear on a mainstream series until the fall of 1977 (37). His name was Jodie Dallas, played by a very young Billy Crystal, and he was a major figure on ABC's over-the-top daytime drama spoof cum sitcom, *Soap* (1977–1981). Revolutionary as he was, though, Jodie polarized as much as he delighted audiences. Streitmatter writes that, at the time, some were concerned that, with Jodie, *Soap* was "sending the message that gay men are effeminate and narcissistic twits who use their limp wrists and mincing mannerisms to propel themselves into the spotlight," while others "praised both the character and the series as shining such a rose-colored light on gay men" that could only be beneficial in the long term (37). But when the *Soap* bible, crafted by Susan Harris, who would go on to bring *The Golden Girls* to life on NBC in 1985, created the circumstances in which Jodie became the boyfriend of another man, "the two men were not allowed to have any physical contact with each other" on camera, unlike, not at all surprisingly, their heterosexual counterparts (42). Gay characters like Jodie could be both seen and heard from, but only as long as their representation did not encompass homoerotic intimacy of any kind.

After *Soap* was canceled by ABC in 1981 because of declining ratings, seventeen years would have to pass before gay male characters would return to mainstream American television in any kind of a significant way. NBC's smart and sophisticated comedy, *Will & Grace* (1998–2006) which premiered in September of 1998, brought not one, but two openly gay men as starring characters into the collective consciousness of U.S. viewers every week for eight seasons and almost two-hundred episodes. These were Will Truman (Eric McCormack) and Jack MacFarland (Sean Hayes), two close friends living their event-filled lives alongside their respective, female BFF's Grace (Debra Messing) and Karen (Megan Mullally), in New York City. Although *Will & Grace* often came under fire for its lack of homoerotic content during its tenure, as one of the most popular sitcoms in history to feature likeable gay male characters in starring roles, the positive influence of the show on attitudes toward homosexuals and homosexuality cannot be underestimated. On this point, it warrants noting that no less a figure than Joe Biden, Vice-President of the United States, recently claimed that *Will & Grace* "did more to educate the American public than almost anything anybody has ever done" in regards to the simple fact that gay people are human beings worthy of the utmost respect, nuanced and accurate representation, and fully equal treatment under the law (qtd. in Yellin, "Biden Says He Is 'Absolutely Comfortable' with Same-Sex Marriage"). The power of television, the medium of the masses, to change the hearts and minds of those who might not otherwise be reached, is not to be taken lightly, as Biden's comments on the effects of *Will & Grace* make clear.

Unlike all previous eras combined, the early twenty-first century has—following in the path blazed by programs like *Soap* and *Will & Grace*—witnessed nothing less than a veritable explosion in gay male characters appearing on American television shows of all kinds and on almost all channels spanning the network and cable spectrum. A short list of these important fictional figures would include: *Glee*'s Kurt Hummel (Chris Colfer) and Blaine Anderson (Darren Criss) on FOX, *Brothers & Sisters*' Kevin Walker (Matthew Rhys) and Scotty Wandell (Luke Macfarlane) on ABC, *As the World Turns*' Luke Snyder (Van Hansis) and Noah Mayer (Jake Silberman) on CBS, *Days of Our Lives*' Will Horton (Chandler Massey) and Sonny Kiriakis (Freddie Smith) on NBC, and *Queer as Folk*'s Brian Kinney (Gale Harold) and Justin Taylor (Randy Harrison) on Showtime, to name but ten of the many worthy of mention in this context. The larger point to be made, of course, is that *Downton Abbey*'s Thomas is a reflection of the continuing trend toward openness and inclusion of gay characters on television. The reactionary comments of anti-gay product reviewers at Amazon.com notwithstanding, he is a welcome and necessary addition to this growing pantheon. Put in slightly different terms, *Downton Abbey* would not be *Downton Abbey* without Thomas in all of his conflicted, gay, and homoerotic glory; and Fellowes and his team of collaborators deserve nothing but praise for choosing not to diminish Thomas' character in any way because of the intolerance of a tiny minority of close-minded and provincial American viewers. And may Thomas' queer tenure on *Downton Abbey* continue for a long time to come.

Postscript: Thomas Barrow's Happy Ending

Since this essay was originally written, *Downton Abbey*'s phenomenally successful television run has come to an end after a total of six series and fifty-two episodes. Despite the wishes of some viewers, the character of Thomas Barrow remained a mainstay throughout; he was at times heroic, almost always self-serving, on occasion downright villainous, and he was always interesting to watch regardless of the predicaments in which he found himself. But, after Series Three and his ill-fated, unrequited relationship with Jimmy Kent, Thomas' involvements with other men never ventured out of the realm of the platonic. Indeed, after Jimmy, the only other male character Thomas showed any interest in was Andrew "Andy" Parker, a footman hired on at Downton following Lady Rose's marriage to Atticus Aldridge.

As this story arc unfolded, complete with Thomas' touchingly sincere attempt to teach the illiterate Andy how to read, the under-butler took great pains to insist to one and all that he only wanted to be friends with Andy, nothing more. Given his past behavior, these repeated pronouncements were greeted with skepticism on the part of Thomas' coworkers and *Downton Abbey*'s audiences alike. Nevertheless, Thomas' unhappiness—which clearly derives from the fact that the Crawleys and Mr. Carson decide that his services are no longer needed at Downton rather than any angst over an unattainable object of desire—leads him to attempt suicide by slitting his wrists. Thankfully, Thomas is found before his self-inflicted wounds harm him fatally and he survives. And, in due course, he is asked to return and become Butler of Downton Abbey when Mr. Carson's illness (Parkinson's disease; though it was not called as such in 1925) prevents him from continuing in that role for the Crawley family. So Thomas, like all of the other characters in the series, gets a happy ending.

At this time, there are—not surprisingly considering its popularity—tens of thousands of product reviews of the six *Downton Abbey* series at Amazon.com. What has changed since this essay was first composed is the fact that the reviews which disparage the series for its inclusion and treatment of male homosexuality and Thomas' character simply for being gay are nowhere near as prominent as they were some four years ago. In fact, quickly scanning the reviews yields only two—one each for Series Four and Series Five—have the same negative tone and content as those discussed above. For instance, the Series Four reviewer writes: "If you are offended by homosexual behavior on the screen, then you will not like *Downton Abbey*. Too bad, I had high hopes of liking it" (Kent Parsons), while the Series Five reviewer explains: "I was an avid fan but this season is very disappointing. It's gone to trashy and annoying. They would long ago have dumped the queer and that school teacher is not bringing anything good to the party. I think this will be the last season, because it went from classy to trashy" (mysay). Once again, discounting the fact that it closely mirrors heterosexual behavior, "homosexual behavior" is depicted as something ugly, disgusting, and unworthy of depiction on television; and the "queer"—with the term used in its pejorative sense—must be "dumped" because he is too "trashy" for delicate heterosexist sensibilities. As already noted, however, such homophobic commentary reflects the opinions of a definitely minuscule minority. And that in itself is a development worth noting within the larger discourse of tolerance and acceptance where representations of homosexuality in popular culture are concerned.

ACKNOWLEDGMENTS

This piece, a true labor of love, began its life—in much shorter form—as an essay I presented in the TV: Drama Series paper session at the 24th Annual Meeting of the Far West Popular Culture Association and American Culture Association in Las Vegas,

Nevada, 24–26 February 2012. I am deeply indebted to Dr. Felicia Campbell, the Executive Director of the FWPCA/ACA, as well as to the Department of English at the University of Nevada, Las Vegas, for supporting my work on *Downton Abbey*.

WORKS CITED

Allred, Meghan. "NOT FAMILY FRIENDLY." Rev. of *Downton Abbey*. Series One. Amazon.com. 26 May. 2012. Accessed 19 Aug. 2012. Web.

B., Linda. "R-rated scenes." Rev. of *Downton Abbey*. Series One. Amazon.com. 16 Apr. 2011. Accessed 19 Aug. 2012. Web.

Bender, Thomas. "The Thinning of American Political Culture." In *Public Discourse in America: Conversation and Community in the Twenty-First Century*. Eds. Judith Rodin and Stephen P. Steinberg. Philadelphia: University of Pennsylvania Press, 2003. 27–34. Print.

Borchardt, Christopher. "Agenda Pushing." Rev. of *Downton Abbey*. Series Three. Amazon.com. 18 Apr. 2013. Accessed 12 Jun. 2013. Web.

Chayko, Mary. *Connecting: How We Form Social Bonds and Communities in the Internet Age*. Albany: State University of New York Press, 2002. Print.

Corvino, John. *What's Wrong with Homosexuality?* Oxford: Oxford University Press, 2013. Print.

Crystal, David. *Language and the Internet*, 2d ed. Cambridge: Cambridge University Press, 2006. Print.

DonP. "Guys kissing." Rev. of *Downton Abbey*. Series One. Amazon.com. 6 Aug. 2011. Accessed 19 Aug. 2012. Web.

Downton Abbey. Series One. Episode One. Dir. Brian Percival, Ben Bolt, Brian Kelly. Writ. Julian Fellowes, Shelagh Stephenson, Tina Pepler. Perf. Hugh Bonneville, Elizabeth McGovern, Maggie Smith, Jim Carter, Phyllis Logan, Michelle Dockery, Dan Stevens. PBS, Masterpiece Classic, Carnival Films, 2011. DVD.

Downton Abbey. Series Three. Episode Seven. Dir. David Evans. Writ. Julian Fellowes. Perf. Hugh Bonneville, Elizabeth McGovern, Maggie Smith, Jim Carter, Phyllis Logan, Michelle Dockery, Dan Stevens, Rob James-Collier, Matt Milne, Ed Speleers. PBS, Masterpiece Classic, Carnival Films, 2013. DVD.

Evans, B. "Not acceptable." Rev. of *Downton Abbey*. Series One. Amazon.com. 3 Feb. 2011. Accessed 19 Aug. 2012. Web.

Fellowes, Julian. *Downton Abbey: The Complete Scripts, Season One*. New York: William Morrow, 2012. Print.

Fejes, Fred. *Gay Rights and Moral Panic: The Origins of America's Debate on Homosexuality*. New York: Palgrave Macmillan, 2008. Print.

Fone, Byrne. *Homophobia: A History*. New York: Metropolitan Books, 2000. Print.

Foucault, Michel. *The History of Sexuality: Volume I: An Introduction*. Trans. Robert Hurley. New York: Vintage/Random House, 1990. Print.

Halterman, Jim. "PBS at TCAs: 'Emotional' Thomas on 'Downton Abbey,' Cheyenne Jackson as Annie? 'Knots Landing' Redux?" AfterElton.com. 24 July 2012. Accessed 19 Aug. 2012. Web.

Homeschooler, Florida. "BEWARE!" Rev. of *Downton Abbey*. Series One. Amazon.com. 19 Dec. 2011. Accessed 19 Aug. 2012. Web.

Jordan, L.M. "Unpleasantly surprised." Rev. of *Downton Abbey*. Series One. Amazon.com. 20 Mar. 2012. Accessed 19 Aug. 2012. Web.

King James Version Bible. Leviticus 20:13. BibleGateway.com. Web. 12 Jun. 2013.

Knust, Jennifer Wright. *Unprotected Texts: The Bible's Surprising Contradictions About Sex and Desire*. New York: HarperOne, 2011. Print.

Max. "Great potential but disappointingly not family-friendly." Rev. of *Downton Abbey*. Series One. Amazon.com. 11 Jan. 2011. Accessed 19 Aug. 2012. Web.

mysay. "To trashy and annoying. they would Long ago have dumped the queer...." Rev. of *Downton Abbey*. Series Five. 2 Feb. 2015. Accessed 13 May 2016. Web.

Nussbaum, Martha C. *From Disgust to Humanity: Sexual Orientation and Constitutional Law*. Oxford: Oxford University Press, 2010. Print.

Parsons, Kent. "1.0 out of 5 stars Very disappointing." Rev. of *Downton Abbey*. Series Four. Amazon.com. 31 Mar. 2015. Accessed 13 May 2016. Web.

RAS. "misleading historicity." Rev. of *Downton Abbey*. Series Three. Amazon.com. 24 Mar. 2013. Accessed 12 Jun. 2013. Web.

Spector, Robert. *Amazon.com: Get Big Fast*. New York: HarperBusiness, 2000. Print.

Steinberg, Stephen P. "Creating Community in Cyberspace: Criteria for a Discourse Technology Project." In *Public Discourse in America: Conversation and Community in the Twenty-First Century*. Eds. Judith Rodin and Stephen P. Steinberg. Philadelphia: University of Pennsylvania Press, 2003. 237–248. Print.

Streitmatter, Rodger. *From "Perverts" to "Fab Five": The Media's Changing Depiction of Gay Men and Lesbians*. New York: Routledge, 2009. Print.

Sue's Reviews. "Not acceptable." Rev. of *Downton Abbey*. Series One. Amazon.com. 7 Apr. 2011. Accessed 19 Aug. 2012. Web.

Therehere. "Episode 6 is the worst." Rev. of *Downton Abbey*. Series Three. Amazon.com. 18 Feb. 2013. Accessed 12 Jun. 2013. Web.

Thomas, June. "*Downton Abbey*, Season 3; Is the Treatment of Thomas an Anachronistic 21st-Century Fantasy?" Slate.com. 11 Feb. 2013. Accessed 12 Jun. 2013. Web.

Yellin, Jessica. "Biden Says He Is 'Absolutely Comfortable' with Same-Sex Marriage." CNN.com. 6 May. 2012. Accessed 19 Aug. 2012. Web.

Wearing the Trousers

"Female" Voices in "Male" Spaces

Joy E. Morrow

Downton Abbey became a global phenomenon in its six seasons. Downton Abbey itself is a manor house, and the general plot of the show is the chronicling of the lives of the residents of the house, both upstairs and down. The premise of the show is that Downton and its residents serve as a microcosm to illustrate the shaping and changing of English culture in the opening years of the twentieth century. As Katherine Byrne says in her article on the filmmakers adapting the Edwardian period, "Set between 1912 and the 1920s, with lavish costumes and careful period detail and making a visual fetish of the stately home (a shot of which lovingly appears between every scene in the first Season)" (312). The visual grandeur surrounding the "Season" romanticizes the period and draws the audience into the world of that time, causing the viewer to become more engrossed in the setting, allowing them to better engage with a time not their own. This period was one of radical change, mostly brought about by new technologies which were affecting the ways people lived their day to day lives. Shifts in the economy were opening up new opportunities for people in all circumstances of life, from members of the lowest classes to people of the upper crust. Ideological value shifts also brought significant political changes in the culture.

Most of these cultural changes were brought about by significant historical events, the readiest example being World War I, each one culturally galvanizing and wide-scale in their ramifications, effecting the broader global community. *Downton Abbey* with its diverse, almost to the point of becoming tokenistic, ensemble cast of residents serves as an illustration of the sweeping changes for England as a whole, demonstrating various ethnicities, classes, and genders in a distinct way to represent the whole of those groups at the time. However, it is important to remember that *Downton Abbey* is not a perfect historical documentary; but rather, a period drama, a work of fiction. As Alun Munslow put it,

> Given that all history is as "aesthetic, subjective and ironically constructed creation," essentially a story about the past, it is also necessary to accept that the evaluation of one as more authentic or true than another is a problematic concept.... After all, all history is "personal, impressionistic and expressive undertaking that always exceeds the empirical" [qtd. in Byrne 313].

Though the show was widely, and understandably, acclaimed for its accuracy, particularly in costume, mannerisms, and set design, history would, at times, take a backseat to the drama. In fiction this is understandable, since dramatic plot is what creates the tensions that procreate character growth and engaging narratives. *Downton* is not beloved because of its historical points; the show is beloved because of how easy it was for the viewer to get invested in its characters.

The Edwardian period brought an increase of cultural and economic capital and power for the women of England; however, this increase in power for the ladies of Downton does not seem to come with the radical paradigm shift that came to other women at the time. The lives of the downstairs women of Downton are radically affected by this increase in power, but the lives of the upstairs ladies seem to be affected primarily by circumstances rather than by a new possession of power. An examination of the actions and treatment of the female members of the family shows them to be the ones in control of Downton. Though the lords are respected, the ladies are the ones deferred to and, at times, feared. They hold sexual, social, and institutional power, despite history portraying these fields as "male" occupied spaces in a primarily "male" dominated system.

The female members of the upstairs family consist of the following: Cora, Lady Grantham; her three daughters—Mary, Edith, and Sybil—Lord Grantham's niece, Rose; Isobel Crawley; and the Dowager Countess, Violet Crawley. Cora is an American heiress who was married to Lord Grantham for a title in exchange for funds to keep the estate afloat. In a review article discussing the show by Peter Lawler, Cora is described in the following manner: "[She] reminds [the viewer] constantly that being an American isn't all about the money ... she's armed with a secure personal identity that can be at home anywhere. This also means, of course, that she will love her husband and children no matter where and no matter what" (28–29).

Cora's loving devotion to her husband resulted in four children, three living. Mary, the eldest, is seen as cold and calculating, but is praised for her strength and ability to make hard decisions. Michelle Dockery, the actress who plays Mary in the series, explains that her character "feels she should have been born a boy and then everything would have been so much easier. She fights against her femininity in a way" (qtd. in Fellowes 202). Mary's overarching story throughout the show illustrates her struggles of finding her place as a daughter in a son's position. Edith is the middle child in every sense of the stereotype. Laura Carmichael, who plays Edith, talks of how her character "suffers the heartbreak of not being the favourite daughter and not getting the opportunities that the others have" (qtd. in Fellowes 208). Edith's access to female power and her character arc are initiated by female competition, particularly with Mary. Her development as a character comes from channeling the female power she is instilled with on her own terms. Sybil and Cousin Rose are two sides of the same coin in terms of character arc and development representing the young up-and-coming, modern woman of the period, attempting to break away from the perceived conservatism of the Victorians. They are more likely to express their power by more overtly breaking the prescribed social mold. Isobel Crawley is a more nontraditional member of the family. She is the mother of the estate's heir by default. She comes into the family as the busy middle-class woman from Manchester with a bustling driving-force for taking action and making changes to match. Finally, there is Violet Crawley, the Dowager Countess, independent and willing to do whatever it takes to get what she wants, feared as a force with which to be reckoned. As the eldest relative, she is meant to represent ties to the old world and the thought processes of it, to provide a more solid point of reference for the changes of the period. She of all the women expresses her power most directly; in many ways, she serves as the leader of all these upstairs women, who all, predominately serve as the driving force of Downton. Their force keeps the viewer drawn into the world created by the show's setting. As is stated in Caroline Bainbridge's "Feminine Enunciation in Women's Cinema," "The space of cinematic fantasy allows [the viewer] to begin to construct a mode of representation for aspects of the feminine that are traditionally buried within discursive constructs" (134). The positioning of these female characters as works of fiction occupying a real temporal space gives them the function of not just characters but also as bridges between the audience and the period, creating a greater sense of understanding for the viewer. This diverse collection of women creates a dynamic that easily lends itself to theoretical analysis.

Downton Abbey has become a fascinating subject for feminist theorists. Partially this is due to the period in which the show is set; the Edwardian period was a time of rapid change for women in terms of presence in the workplace and social presence. Partially this fascination also comes from the way the female characters are written. Some viewers perceive the women of Downton as ultra-modern figures rising above the societal norms and restrictions under which they were born. This perception comes from a cultural outsider looking in. Any historical drama has to deal with audience appropriation of the period; in the case of *Downton Abbey*, postmodern perceptions of the Edwardian period contribute significantly to viewer expectations of how *Downtown Abbey* as a show would handle the period and the actions of the characters. These characters are expected to occupy two temporal spaces; lensing these characters is key.

The Marxist work of Luce Irigaray is known for equalizing the sexes without removing all differentiation between them. As one analysis of Irigaray's work states, "To transform this reality, Irigaray considers that it is imperative to promote the formulation of civil regulations for women, not equal but equivalent to those of men's, that is, human rights related to the specific necessities and conditions of each one of the sexes" (García 67). Her theories establish the equal worth of both men and women within the different roles in society, which has caused her to be considered a favorite of feminist critics.

> Feminist critics in general find Irigaray's critique of phallocentric "identity" powerful and frequently persuasive. When woman is reduced to the same as or less than man, equality is clearly impossible. Debate as to the value of Irigaray's analyses of identity, equality, sameness, and difference centers for the most part on her visionary recreations of an undefinable, nonunitary female identity based on difference [Holmlund 289].

The question becomes one of the power dynamics between the two sexes. Irigaray opens her essay "Women on the Market" with the following statement: "The society we know, our own culture, is based upon the exchange of women. Without the exchange of women, we are told, we would fall back into anarchy" (170). This idea is one postmodern women in the West are culturally told to snub, because of its surface-level implications. Viewers of the show may expect to pity the women, especially the younger ones, who are married off for the sake of a name and then cheer when those characters defy social custom and marry for love. However, the treatment of the upstairs female characters reflects the theories presented in Irigaray's text. The women of Downton are not interested in breaking away from their gender and becoming more like men; the opposite is the case, these women, for the most part, embrace their femininity and their roles within that gender. Irigaray's text illustrates how a commodity on a market has power over the buyer, not vice versa. In this sense, she takes the recognized vulgar Marxist economic model of buyer, producer, and product, and brings it into more socially-charged paradigms. With women taking on the role of both producer and product in Irigaray's model, there is a stronger power dynamic that plays out over the men as buyers. By giving the appearance of remaining under male authority as a whole, the women are able to hold power over the individual men in their lives because these women know that the men believe themselves incapable without them.

In some specific cases, the upstairs women treat their gender as a role to play more than an actual state of being. Often there are exchanges about how a woman should behave over how women should be. Predominately, these exchanges come as quips from the Dowager Countess, such as telling the girls that "vulgarity is no substitute for wit" and about how their behaviors are tied to their social positions. Cora has similar talks with the girls, particularly on the subjects of marriage and their careers. This perception of gender as a performative act in context is reminiscent of Judith Butler's theories on gender:"[I]f gender is instituted through acts which are internally discontinuous, then the *appearance of substance* is precisely that, a constructed identity, a performative accomplishment" (901). In context of the show, it is important to note that the performance of gender has more to do with class than it does with biological gender. The question is not what makes one a woman, but rather, what makes one a lady in the manor-house world. This insistence that the center of being comes from economic class over gender illustrates the central paradigm of the world of the show. Power is based in class over gender which allows the viewer to understand why the upstairs women of Downton Abbey may be more liberal in their actions than is initially expected.

The Edwardian period was a time of perceived "sexual" liberation for women in comparison to the socio-cultural expectations of the Victorian era. The world changed after World War I, and with the twenties came the flappers and jazz. Dance halls were becoming a more prominent place of socializing for the genders; these places used primarily for mingling and flirtations. Adrian Tinniswood's *The Long Week-end* discusses the new type of woman that could exist in these dance halls. "The shameless abandon with which the new free woman danced, allowing her partner a near-sexual closeness of embrace, her immodest dress and coiffure and her profane looseness of language" were what made these social gatherings so desirable to the youth of the time (Graves and Hodge 42). Cousin Rose exemplifies this sexualized attitude of women in Series Four and Five. Mary calls her an all-out flapper, though Rose denies the title, her denial of the role probably stemming from a desire to not lose her class status and its advantages. Rose is the more sexually aware of the upstairs women, while being the most unaware simultaneously. Rose presents herself as young and carefree, wanting to be the modern woman, believing this title and its scandalizing implications would allow her to break away from her controlling mother, who serves as her arc's primary antagonist. She recognizes pleasure over power; however, as her arc continues, she learns control. She begins to channel her female power primarily through her marriage, following the examples of the women to whom she had been exposed while in residence at Downton. Despite this more traditional expression of power, Rose maintains her own rebellious individuality when she marries. Her husband is Jewish, and neither side of the family approves of the other. Rose asserts her own power as a person to bring the families together, endearing herself to her in-laws and gaining control over her domineering mother. She merges the roaring of the twenties with the elegance of Downton and becomes a woman with one foot in the old ways and the one in the new. This ability to sustain such duality gives Rose more power in comparison to other female characters who choose one or the other. She has further capital, giving her more of a commodity in her marriage and making her a better producer, because she possessed a willingness to drive and to shift the role she was expected to perform, allowing her to embrace a modern identity.

But this sexual awareness, although portrayed as new to the culture, is not a new attitude to the women of Downton. The upstairs women illustrate their sexual empowerment from one of their earliest moments on screen in the first episode. While the three sisters descend the staircase for the funeral of Mary's unofficial betrothed, Mary comments how she would have only married the man if nothing better had come along. Though chastised by her two sisters for her insensitivity, Mary's attitude seems sure, even though her execution is not. Later in Series One, she breaks the established courtship rules, willingly joining suitors unchaperoned, eventually taking one of the house visitors, an emissary from Turkey, to her bed. This decision shows the younger Mary's inexperience when it comes to her sexual power; her brief affair has repercussions throughout the entire run of the show, while Mary gains nothing material from the dalliance. The Turk and Mary made it clear that their affair will not end in marriage; he is not going to give her any political favors; she is not going to use her position to give him any social favors amongst the English. It was just supposed to be one night of sex, until he dies in Mary's bed, which threatens to bring a scandal down on the family that would ruin the prospects of all three daughters. Mary turns to Cora for help, and it is Cora, Mary, and their friend and housemaid, Anna, who create the cover-up. The perpetuated drama of this incident runs over the course of the first five series and illustrates the consequences of Mary's inexperience; however, she grows. In Series Five, Mary has a second extra-marital affair, and this time she is ready for all the consequences. Instead of appealing to other members of her family, as during her first affair, Mary handles the threat of exposure on her own. Throughout the earlier series, when Mary is threatened several times with blackmail over her first affair, each time she is saved by either family or fortune. Furthermore, in Series Five, Mary takes a lover and ends the relationship with him when she is not satisfied, even though he is expecting them to marry. At the beginning of Series Six, the show's final season, a woman arrives to blackmail Mary about her second affair. This time, Mary does not hide behind anyone or anything. She tells the woman to go ahead and expose her. Though she knows that scandal is coming, Mary also knows that she will rise above it. As a result, her father officially gives her the title of manager of the estate, because Mary shows how capable she has become at handling her power and asserting it over others. Mary was already established as a strong character who can be cutthroat when it came to getting what she wants. The shift in attitude from her first extra-marital affair to her second illustrates how she has matured and handled herself as a character. She recognizes her power and position to the point that she overtly exercises this power over a man of her class outside the family, and she is the one to whom authority is submitted. Of all the female characters, Mary will take on the attitudes and actions of a man, treating her gender as happenstance, something that needs to be worked with. She does not act ashamed of being a woman; she simply does not let being a woman dictate what social space she occupies and what social rules she follows.

Sybil, the youngest daughter, also uses her romantic ventures as a means of illustrating her disregard for prescribed social systems. Sybil is considered to be the sweetest of the sisters and the most innocent. Out of the three main sisters, she is the only one who does not have an extra-marital affair. Instead she just runs off with the chauffer in an attempted elopement. Even with being the one with the most agreeable and kind temperament, Sybil is also the most overtly revolutionary. She does not want the old ways to carry into the new era, and she uses her marriage as a way to escape from her manor-house life. She tells Tom, her husband to be, that she wants out, and he is her ticket. She takes this ticket, discovering that in many ways it is a one-way trip. Her parents are absent from her wedding, and she learns to accustom herself to living without the material and social resources of Downton. Along with injuring her relationship with her father, Sybil loses friendships, when she leaves her class. As Foucault says in *Discipline and Punishment*, "Disciplinary power has as its correlative an individuality" (156). Even though she is happy and does not regret her choices, Sybil is made to feel a level of punishment for her decisions that she cannot express to those around her, even her sisters. By asserting her own power to such an extreme degree, Sybil marginalizes herself. Though she abides by the traditional sexual practices of the time, Sybil's marriage is the more controversial, and she uses it as a way of asserting her own power over her own person. However, in Series Three, in spite of everything she did to break away from her class and the role it entailed, Sybil decides to return to her pre-independent paradigm in order to protect her husband, when he is exiled from his home-country due to his involvement with the Irish uprising against the English. She submits to the social order established in her family and tries to encourage her husband to do the same. At the same time, however, there is a change in her attitude toward her family. She knows her role of wife and mother-to-be provides her more liberties than she had as simply daughter. She also asserts her will over her family's wishes, specifically her father's. Sybil's husband wants their baby christened Catholic, and her father thinks the baby should be christened through the Church of England. In order to ensure that her father comes around, Sybil appeals to her mother's and Mary's influence. The conservative Dowager Countess even plays the role in persuading her son to her granddaughter's point of view. The fact that the women band together to reconcile the issues between these two men illustrates how the affairs of the house and family are settled through the primary influences of the women in the family throughout.

Unlike her two sisters, Edith's romantic liaisons exist primarily outside her family home. However, at first, she attempts to fit in the mold set by her familial expectations; also her priority seems to be to out-do Mary rather than be her own person. Edith's determination to play the role of "lady" as established by those around her keeps her from attaining the power that is within that mold. She treats the concept of female power as something that comes with accomplishing certain stages of life, rather than something created and executed no matter where a woman is within those stages. Edith feels least favored of the three daughters because out of the three, she is the least in touch with whom she is as an individual. Edith recognizes on a level that her sisters are more advanced than herself, so she tries to mimic their actions in order to gain the sense of self that they have and maybe rise above them to the point of being considered the most prominent, i.e., the most empowered, sister, particularly over Mary. Edith falls in love with Mary's first betrothed, tries to seduce Mary's second intended, and finally tries to settle with a neighbor, Sir Anthony Strallan, a member of the local gentry. He is several years her senior and in poor health, which elicits significant criticism from her family. However, Edith's attitude persuades them to accept him as her suitor, which provides a glimpse into the power that Edith holds over those around her. These moments are the ones that allow Edith to exemplify who she is as an individual; therefore, they are her most empowered moments. Her own gratification is enough to persuade those around her of her decisions, to a point. In the situation of her first potential marriage, the Dowager Countess persuades Edith to let Strallen go when he leaves her at the altar. The Dowager Countess' power overrides Edith's need to rise immediately to equal capital of her married sisters. The fact that Edith allows for this interference, once again illustrates how out of touch she is with her own sense of power. As the show's narrative progresses, Edith grows to not be so easily dominated by the other women in her life.

Edith is brought to her lowest when she is left at the altar; she resigns herself to being a spinster and considers herself a failure because she is unable to attain what she feels is the cultural capital she is expected to have. As she interfered at the wedding, the Dowager Countess interferes again, telling Edith to go find something to do.

> [D]aughters [in that period] were expected to take up business careers, or at least do *something*. Some, of course, regarded their business life as an interval between school and marriage, and this naturally debarred them from jobs in which continuity of work was of more advantage to employers than cheap labour. Doing *something* often meant pretending to take up music or art [Graves and Hodge 45].

"Pretending to take up music or art" is probably what the Dowager Countess had in mind when she told Edith to find something to do. However, Edith begins a career, which introduces her to her next two lovers, both away from her home and class. She brings men into Downton, rather than meeting them there, and it is her power as her own woman that gets them accepted into her family. Edith's storyline illustrates how the sexual power of these women is not their primary power, as one might expect; instead, their sexual power comes from who they are as a people and the power they have gained as individuals elsewhere.

Sexual escapades are not limited to the young women of Downton; the older women get to express their sexual power as well. However, their escapades are not marked by trying to grow as individuals; rather, it illustrates how superior these women are and how confident they are in their own persons. The Dowager Countess when she was younger had an attempted affair with a Russian prince. Her story parallels those of some of the younger women, illustrating the cyclic nature of this personal growth and power in these upper-class women. Cora has an opportunity to have an affair, during a rough patch in her marriage with Lord Grantham. Although she is tempted, Cora refuses because she does not wish to lose the position she holds as wife and mother within the house and the influence she has over it. An affair would have compromised the power she held and would have hindered her accessing it, after the fact. An affair would cause her to lose her power that she accesses through her marriage.

Marriage for a manor house member at the time involved a lot of strategy. The right amount of money needed to be on the table, as well as the right name. However, the manners and demeanors of the women were vital to the match. Marriage for the Edwardian upper class was a showcase of means and heritage. A strong marriage could give society all the information needed for it to place the couple. Marriage served as a catalyst for capital, and since a woman predominantly exercised her power and her identity as wife and mother, the capital created from a good marriage is of vital importance to the characters of Downton, especially in earlier seasons before the idea of the "working woman" became more culturally common. For instance, in Series One, Cora and Mary have the following exchange:

MARY: How many times am I to be ordered to marry the man sitting next to me at dinner?
CORA: As many times as it takes.

Getting the younger girls suitably married is one of the central priorities for Cora and the Dowager Countess, since that is the equivalent to the girls leaving the nest and completely seizing their own individual power. Another discussion that comes every time a marriage is on the horizon is the discussion of what the bride-to-be is going to do with her house. Her house is her kingdom and it is how her social peers and members of the community identify her. In Edwardian England, the house served as a physical representation of wealth, which is what draws attention both in the period and to contemporary audiences to the manor-house world. As Simon Nowell-Smith states, "In so far as any group in a community imposes a popular image of its domestic life on an age, for Edwardian England that group was the very rich … any account of Edwardian domestic life must give to the rich more attention" (141). Women played key roles in the house; in many ways they ran the social-scene of not only the house, but the village as well. Decisions on staff and houseguests came primarily from the female members, and, as the show illustrates constantly, the dining room can serve as a political and social battleground. The extravagance of these social gatherings was one of the most notable points of the Edwardian upper class as is clarified in *Upstairs, Downstairs*, "Extravagance, comfort and luxury in all things, including dining, epitomized the mood of Edwardian high society. In fact, the success of her dinner parties was so important to the reputation of the Edwardian hostess that often chefs could command wages ten times higher than those of butlers" (Warwick 90). A woman's role in the social scene is one of the most visible ones that she holds.

The Dowager Countess serves as the family matriarch and the front for the rest of the Crawley women. The Countess' wit has become a staple and one of the most beloved parts of the show; she says what she wants, knowing that she will normally evade all consequences of doing so. It is important to remember that the Dowager Countess, by representing the preceding generation, represents the Victorians. In popular cultures, the Victorians are normally perceived as people constantly under self-imposed and cultural repression, as uptight and stiff-necked people. However, the Dowager Countess illustrates adaptability. Even though she does not like the new technology that accompanies the new era, she uses it. Despite being against the new social order developing, she learns to operate and thrive underneath that emerging order. With her own rhetoric, she places herself above the men in her life. Like Mary, the Dowager Countess illustrates the theories of Irigaray. Unlike Mary, most of the power that the Dowager Countess practices over the immediate house of Downton Abbey and over her husband is told to the viewers in the dialogue, since there are no flashbacks in any of the seasons. The Dowager Countess constantly reaffirms that she is never wrong and, most interestingly, how she ran Downton for years. The later statement would imply that the Dowager Countess, like Mary, was the one running the estate, most likely indirectly, while she and her husband were in residence. If the treatment of her by her son and the servants who were employed at the same time the Dowager Countess lived in the house is any indication, the previous Earl of Grantham would have submitted to the authority of his wife, and she in turn would not be overt in this authority so that her womanliness would not be brought into question by those with which she shared a social circle.

When necessary, the Countess is not afraid of using her position to override the men in her life. In Series Two, when told that the local doctor would not approve a transfer of a wounded local boy who worked at the abbey and who saved the life of the heir, the Dowager storms out of the hospital straight to the phone at the house to call one of her acquaintances in office, and she gets that boy home. She tells Edith that the circumstance was a lesson for her, when one gives lower classes power; it goes to their heads causing them to forget to whom they can say no. Despite her gender, the Countess is accustomed to giving orders and having those orders obeyed. The Dowager is not the only family member who pushes what people might perceive are her boundaries in terms of power. When the initial heir dies unexpectedly, Cora and the Dowager do everything they can to fight for Mary to inherit at least part of the money from the estate if not the whole thing. The Lords Grantham entail away the estate to male heirs only. The Dowager's husband also tied Cora's independent fortune to the estate, so her daughters cannot inherit that as well. When the issue of finding an heir arises, the two Ladies Grantham take it upon themselves to give Mary a chance to take the place as heir, though her father does not want to break up the estate, even for his daughters. While he chooses to ally himself with the estate, the title, and the heritage, the women ally with each other and their offspring. They choose the course of action that will keep them, and their up-and-coming daughters, assured of their positions. This conflict that runs the course of Series One illustrates the initiative of the women of the family over the men.

In more day-to-day life, most of the social power of the women of Downton is exemplified at the village hospital. The hospital is primarily funded by the family, so the family has significant input in its running. Up until the final season, the Dowager Countess sits as chair of the hospital board. One of the main story arcs of Series Six centers on the hospital, and the central conflict of that arc comes from Cora and the Dowager Countess. The changes in the culture finally overtake the Countess, and she is forced to hand her social power in the community to Cora, who is more willing to adapt quickly to the changes of the world. Despite this major arc excluding her from centrality, throughout the majority of the show, Isobel Crawley takes a prominent role in the hospital. Isobel was married to a doctor and is not one to sit around and do nothing. At the suggestion of the main family, Isobel gets involved with the hospital, and she starts being a force of change in the community. She spearheads dozens of social projects. She works with refugees, immigrants, prostitutes, and wounded soldiers. Her business defines her as a character, and she is the only one who stands up consistently to the Dowager Countess. While the Dowager Countess adapts to change, Isobel embraces it. Even though she is an idealist, she does not allow herself to be bossed around by anyone who disagrees with her.

Isobel has one more cause that she is involved with during the show, but the show focuses more on Sybil's involvement than Isobel's, that cause being women's rights. Sybil, as the more radical female member of the family, uses the suffrage movement as an outlet for her to help bring about the changes she believes are best for the culture. Suffrage had been on the horizon of the English culture for several decades preceding the show's selected time period. On the English suffrage movement, Ellen DuBois contextualizes the changes that accompanied the cause: "In the years after 1884, new political prospects began to appear for women eager for an expanded public role…. Women in England were beginning to be a force in local politics and even hold municipal office in growing numbers" (64). Women getting the vote opened the doors on a wider cultural scale. The treatment of the suffrage movement illustrates female empowerment in Downton, but in a way that the viewer may not expect. Besides Sybil, and to a significantly lesser extent Isobel, the women of Downton do not seem to care about the suffrage movement at all, certainly not to the point of feeling the need to get involved in the cause. This lack of interest is partially due to the fact that the women of Downton do not feel limited by their gender to the point that they feel the need for more overt power in the culture. This lack of interest also further illustrates the value of class over gender. The suffrage movement in the early 1900s for Britain was not about giving just women the vote; it was about gaining universal suffrage across the nation, since access to a voice in government was limited by class as well as gender. This shift in power would have serious repercussions for an already fading, grandiose upper class, which would be a high-priority concern for the women of Downton. Isobel and Sybil's involvement falls directly in line with their characters, since they are the greatest proponents of disrupting the lifestyle of the Edwardian upper-crust, the ones most discontent with the status quo. They are willing to give up some of their own power-capital for what they perceive to be the greater good. In contrast, the other women of Downton Abbey are more comfortable playing their power games behind the scenes. This discretion allows them the ability to hide behind their gender when necessary while maintaining control. The more accessible the power of the upper crust becomes, the less significant the power that these women hold becomes. In this sense, the majority of the women of Downton Abbey find the coming social changes threatening, until they learn how to practice their power amongst these changes.

The Edwardian period brought about new work opportunities previously inaccessible for women. After World War I there was an increase in women not only needing to work, but choosing to work. The three daughters of Downton fall into the latter category. While several women of lower classes were already making the shift from predominately female domestic service to more traditionally male corporate work, thanks to the invention of the typewriter, the majority of this workplace change came about because of the Great War.

Britain was no longer at its imperial peak, and World War I devastated psyches in ways for which the British culture was not prepared. The displacement of men by the war opened up more opportunities for women to work in ways and fields from which they were previously excluded. In many ways the war demanded that women enter the workforce. Downton Abbey is not excluded from this; the women each play a role in the war effort as an exemplar and usually a leader as well. Sybil leads the family effort by promptly leaving the home to train to be a nurse. In preparation for her nursing course, Sybil descends downstairs to get lessons from the staff in basic domestic skills. Mr. Carson does not approve, thinking Sybil's behavior improper, but rather than "troubling his lordship" with Sybil's escapades, he goes to Cora, and she greenlights Sybil's decision without a discussion with Lord Grantham. Edith also descends outside the traditional boundaries of her class and gender. With the war taking more and more of England's men, causing the available workforce to diminish, women were having to rise up and fill the void; this increase of female presence in the workplace is represented by statistics such as the following: "By 1911 [the proportion of female clerks had risen] to 32 in every 100. For middle-class girls, several forms of superior training were leading to superior jobs ... by 1901 there were 212 women doctors, 140 women dentists, and even two women accountants" (Nowell-Smith 187).

Edith takes initiative, having the chauffer teach her to drive, telling her family that she wants to learn, since soon there will be no more young men to drive them around. She then volunteers to go to a local farm to help the farmer by driving his tractor, since the local farm boys were at the front. Like Sybil, she descends downstairs from her class without the permission of the male members of her family. The other ladies of the home help in more traditional manners by throwing fundraisers and entertaining the soldiers. During the course of the war, which serves as the backdrop for Series Two, it seems that the women are doing more for the effort than the men left at home. Lord Grantham mopes around feeling useless, while his female family members turn Downton into a hospital, though they are eager to have their home back to normal with the end of the war, particularly the Dowager Countess and Cora.

Mary as the first-born takes on the responsibility in many ways of a son, especially after the death of her husband. When Mary initially marries the heir of the estate, she is not formally running the estate, but she gives constant advice to her husband, which he often heeds. Mary's treatment of the role of wife is one of the show's primary illustrations of Irigaray's theories. Mary serves as a commodity for her husband, not only as the vessel for bearing the next heir of the estate, but she has he cultural capital that transfers to her husband upon marriage. Her husband is a distant relative, who is also a distinct member of the middle class. For better or worse for the estate, he is a fish out of water. Mary, as a well-trained member of the Edwardian upper class, thanks to her mother and grandmother, serves as a mentor to her husband. As a producer of not only the next generation but also of cultural capital, Mary holds even more power over her husband, the future Earl and co-owner of the estate. When it looks like the family will be expulsed from the estate, Mary is the one that gives her husband the solution to save it. Throughout the first half of Series Three, Mary is the one primarily attempting to find the financial means to save the estate, alongside the ever-present Dowager Countess. After the death of her husband, Mary is pulled out of her grief by managing the estate formally with the title. She takes the running of the estate into her own hands, from the managing of the livestock to the development of the land and future plans related to its management. By the end of the final season, Mary has more control of the estate than her father, the Earl of Grantham, and more economic capital and prestige than her second husband.

Of all the women upstairs, Edith's career is the one with the most modern trajectory. In Series Three, she is invited to write a weekly column for a magazine, and when the editor, who falls in with her, dies and leaves her his magazine, she becomes a proper woman of business. Edith as an unmarried woman uses the magazine as an outlet for the expression of her own power. Instead of her production coming from her offspring or her house, Edith's production comes from her work. She creates value in her work and a place for her to express her own identity. The magazine requires her to live in London, away from the estate. This removal takes Edith away from the competition with Mary and forces Edith to develop as an individual. This separation from what Edith's initial motivation of competition forces Edith to actually draw power from herself instead of having that sense power be dictated by circumstance. Having authority in London is different than at Downton. Edith encounters difficulties due to her gender previously unknown to her at Downton. This antagonism is by no means insurmountable; she learns to work her gender to her advantage. Her success allows her to take her place properly amongst the power-wielding upstairs women of Downton. When men refuse to work for her, Edith hires women, allowing for more female voices to occupy the workforce. She dispenses the empowered nature of the women of Downton to women of lower class. Not only that, Edith and the women that she hires dispense messages of female empowerment to their readers through their ladies' magazine. The power paradigm shifts in a way that reflects the more overt cultural empowerment coming to all women of Britain in that period. Her experiences at Downton allow her to gain credence over male speculation; Edith's success causes her successes to feel sweeter to the viewer.

Often people will only associate female empowerment with breaking out of a particular system, and this taints people's perspectives on history. Although maybe not as overtly as it is portrayed in the show, female voices had the ability to circumvent the barriers around male-occupied spaces, and not just the spaces within the home. This exercise of authority was more available to women of a higher social order because they did not have to be concerned with more immediate needs for survival. The social system imposed on women in the Edwardian period was not ideal, but those women learned to thrive under it in many ways. Gendered spaces are arbitrary; they are only affective as long as they are enforced. Since the gendered roles are subordinate to the class roles in *Downton Abbey*, the women of the higher class can and do wield more power than the viewer might initially expect. This usage of female empowerment in the context of a historical drama allows the viewer to appreciate the strength of the characters all the more because they maintain the balancing act of appearing to operate within the prescribed social system, while creating operable spaces for themselves outside it.

Works Cited

Bainbridge, Caroline. "Feminine Enunciation In Women's Cinema." *Paragraph* 25.3 (2002): 129–141. *Academic Search Premier*. Web. 19 Apr. 2016.

Byrne, Katherine. "Adapting Heritage: Class And Conservatism In Downton Abbey." *Rethinking History* 18.3 (2014): 311–327. *Academic Search Premier*. Web. 19 Apr. 2016

Butler, Judith. "Performative Acts and Gender Constitution" *Literary Theory: An Anthology*. Eds. Julie Rivkin and Michael Ryan. Oxford: Blackwell, 2004. 900–911. Print.

Downton Abbey. Crea. Julian Fellowes. Per. Hugh Bonneville, Maggie Smith, and Michelle Dockery. Carnival Film and Television, 2010–2015. Film.

DuBois, Ellen Carol. *Harriet Stanton Blatch and the Winning of Woman Suffrage*. New Haven: Yale University Press, 1997. Print.

Fellowes, Jessica. *The World of Downton Abbey*. New York: St. Martin's Press, 2011. Print.

Foucault, Michel. *Discipline and Punish*. Trans. Alan Sheridan. New York: Vintage Books, 1995. Print.

García Oramas, Maria. "A Gendered Education Towards The Fulfillment of Democracy." *Paragraph* 25.3 (2002): 66–77. *Academic Search Premier*. Web. 19 Apr. 2016.

Graves, Robert, and Alan Hodge. *The Long Week-end: A Social History of Great Britain 1918–1939*. New York: W.W. Norton, 1963. Print.

Holmlund, Christine. "The Lesbian, The Mother, The Heterosexual Lover: Irigaray's Recodings of Difference." *Feminist Studies* 17.2 (1991): 283–293. *Academic Search Premier*. Web. 19 Apr. 2016.

Irigaray, Luce. *This Sex Which Is Not One*. Trans. Catherine Porter and Carolyn Burke. Ithaca: Cornell University Press, 1985. Print.

Lawler, Peter. "Downton Abbey's Astute Nostalgia." *Intercollegiate Review* (2014): 28–29. *Academic Search Premier*. Web. 19 Apr. 2016.

Nowell-Smith, Simon. *Edwardian England 1901–1914*. London: Oxford University Press, 1964. Print.

Warwick, Sarah. *Upstairs & Downstairs: The Illustrated Guide to the Real World of Downton Abbey*. London: Carlton Books, 2011. Print.

Feminist Tendencies

Jennifer Harrison

A maid becomes destitute as a result of an unplanned pregnancy.... The eldest daughter of an earl becomes a victim of abuse at the hands of her fiancé.... Women are rebuked for speaking out of turn.... Each of these story lines reflect Edwardian social justice, questionable though it may be to the twenty-first-century viewer, these situations are at the forefront of the experiences of the well-to-do Crawley family and their staff in England between 1912 and 1921. The early twentieth-century Edwardian setting jabs at social mores, via sparks of feminist leanings, including participation in suffragist rallies; female character's attempts to select their own careers and their own suitors; women's refusal to allow their parents, in particular, their fathers, to influence their decisions.

What is it about *Downton Abbey* that has created such a loyal following of eager viewers? Yes, it is a soap opera, but it is a soap opera that, from the first scene of Series One, effectively reels in the viewer. Why? Do Edwardian values enthrall or anger twenty-first-century viewers? The stories of the Crawleys and their staff reflect both villains and heroines; evasion of morals does not differentiate by class. Edwardian society imposed stringent expectations on English women, expectations which were inclusive of class lines at times, and *Downton Abbey* portrays the efforts of the women of Downton, both upstairs and downstairs, to secure their presence in society. Lady Mary, in Series One, notes, "Women like me don't have a life.... But we're stuck in a waiting room, until we marry" (1: 4). Similar echoes of class status woes appear in Series Three, when Sybil tells her sister Mary, in reference to her husband, former Downton chauffeur Tom Branson, "Somehow none of this seems to matter when we're in Dublin. Class and all that just seems to fade away ... but here he feels so patronized, and he hates it" (3:1).

The women are integral to the series; they scheme and exert control over situations, and yet, they run into brick walls, at various points, in terms of society's expectations. *Downton Abbey* depicts the double standard of sexuality; while the male characters are free to have affairs as they choose, rarely with consequences, the women are constrained by society's whisperings when an affair becomes public. Class status also impacts those consequences, as the results are different for maid Ethel Parks, who loses her job after her affair with Charles Bryant is revealed; Sybil Crawley's affair with chauffeur Tom Branson resulted in family uproar, while Edith Crawley's revelation about her sister Mary's night with attaché Kamel Pamuk, a man who coerced her into having sex and then

127

mysteriously died in her bed, aroused censure. And, yet, throughout much of the after-math of the encounter with Pamuk, Mary blames herself for the incident; her life, in many ways, follows a vicious cycle, becoming the victim, again, of an authoritative man via her engagement to newspaper magnate Richard Carlisle. Does *Downton Abbey* provide a disservice to viewers by not exploring further Mary's powerlessness in early twentieth-century England?

The central emphasis in *Downton Abbey* appears to be the dreaded entail, and more specifically, on the quest to find a suitable husband, a quest accurate in terms of historic representation, albeit with scattered interruptions here and there with feminist tendencies, particularly with the character of Sybil Crawley, suffragist and independent thinker extra-ordinaire, or Edith Crawley's war work efforts driving a tractor or postwar role as a jour-nalist on women's issues, or even the nursing roles of mothers Cora and Isobel Crawley and the efforts of "Nurse Sybil" during the war. As such, this essay seeks to consider the rampant sexism in *Downton Abbey*, as well as the reflection of historical purview in the depictions of class status and challenges to social mores.

Downton Abbey may represent a time period nearly a century removed from modern twenty-first-century sensibilities; however, the series has captivated "Abbey-ites," with its presentation of patriarchy, and the intensifying struggle against it during and after World War I. While the Crawley sisters may have financial resources with which the majority of viewers may not be able to relate, they experience struggles not dissimilar to those of their viewers. Time period fades away in these circumstances, and the characters, love them or otherwise, become human. The two worlds which, while on the surface should not mix, become intertwined in not-so-surprising ways during the Great War and the immediate postwar period. *Downton Abbey* not only explores the potential for blurred lines, but also the mannerisms and strong wills of the female characters, both upstairs and downstairs.

Is feminism rampant in *Downton Abbey*? This essay will not go so far as to imply a blatant display of feminism during Series One, Two, and Three; however, *Downton Abbey* demonstrates subtle feminist tendencies, for example, when similar experiences, with differing consequences, befall Lady Mary Crawley and maid Ethel; regardless of their different social standings, the censure is still the same—a potential for public scandal. Youngest daughter Sybil Crawley espouses political views as she attends a suffragette rally and takes a political stance on women's rights before the war, and then joins the war effort as a nurse, all while committing class transgression when she falls for, and marries, chauffeur Thom Branson. Middle daughter Lady Edith, while perhaps stereo-typically representative of the middle child caught between the adored oldest sister and the baby of the family, is not surprisingly, bitter, but, she, too, attempts to become involved in public service, driving a tractor during the war, and then working at home when Downtown Abbey is transformed into a convalescent center for ailing officers.[1]

Viewers are treated to the evolution of Lady Mary Crawley from a cold-hearted, ambitious eldest daughter who felt she had to prove she could be as successful as a male heir, to one who, while never wavering from expressing her opinion, recognizes the value of sympathy and compassion; it is quite possible that the greatest metamorphosis occurs with her character. The scandal with Turkish diplomat Kemal Pamuk raises questions about sexual impropriety, but also the nature of societal understanding of sexual assault. Mary's secret becomes less and less secretive as more individuals become aware of what happened one fateful night in 1912. Eve Kosofsky Sedgwick, in *The Epistemology of the*

Closet, acknowledges, "Knowledge, after all, is not itself power, although it is the magnetic field of power. Ignorance and opacity collude or compete with knowledge in mobilizing the flows of energy, desire, goods, meanings, persons" (4). Watching the unfolding of events such as Pamuk's supposed deflowering of Lady Mary; the destitution that results from the liaison between housemaid Ethel and Major Brooks, who refused to acknowledge his illegitimate son; the browbeating and physical handling Lady Mary experiences at the hands of her Series Two fiancé, Richard Carlisle; and even the sexism surrounding divorce with the experiences of Mr. Bates, indicate why the feminist movement took England and America by storm by the mid-twentieth century. Did these characters accept their circumstances? For a while, it seemed each might, but then, perhaps too late for a few, they fought to preserve their reputations.

Class status, as much as gender, impact the lives of those living in, or visiting, Downton. As a March 2011 *Daily Mail* editorial notes, "The class system which lies behind all these historical fantasies was, in reality, a deplorable thing. It deemed one person better than another simply because of their differences in wealth. It decreed that one woman, born to privilege, should never have to cook, or wash her clothes, or look after her own children..., and another woman, because she was poor should be forced to do all these things for her mistress" (Wilson 18). Rachel Cooke argues, "The whole set-up feels ersatz, a mere vehicle for gawping at silverware and hunting jackets.... The script oozes nostalgic approval for the days when people not only knew the difference between an earl and duke, but cared about it, too" (48). Julian Fellowes has defended his presentation of class status as plausible; the Oscar-winning writer, who recently earned his own peerage, notes, "1912 is not that long ago. There were cars, trains, electricity, and telephones. I hope that viewers, while they may not identify with the era, might understand that these are 'modern' people, and therefore enjoy examining their relationships." Fellowes further acknowledges potential societal misperceptions in reference to class status: "Different classes could be friendly. The television cliché that domestic staff were maltreated is unrealistic. There was plenty of work for those downstairs, so no one ever had to stay. But it was a time when everyone knew the rules. Any friendship was governed by the master, who unlike the servant, could dictate the degree of intimacy" (Dunwoodie 42). As such, are both Wilson and Cooke wrong? Not at all, but it is in this aspect that Fellowes provides a disturbing, yes, but somewhat plausible outlook on class status, or at least as much as will be depicted in a television melodrama. It is quite likely that the presentation of life downstairs in *Downtown Abbey* radically underestimates the number of servants and household staff to run a household like Downton, as well as the level of cleanliness in the lower portion of the estate. In reference to the near camaraderie depicted between downstairs staff and upstairs occupants, author Fellowes describes the "tendency to assess everyone from their background":

> Experience tells you this is tosh. We are talking about hundreds of thousands of people. Some were horrid, some were charming, some were both. The idea that there is any norm is ridiculous. I just don't believe in generalisations. Why would not an aristocratic young woman such as Lady Sybil help her servant if she were a nice woman? Some of the assumptions are so simplistic. You could not be dressed and undressed and washed by someone you detested. It wouldn't be agreeable. That relationship is strange to us—the ladies' maid helping you into your underwear. We have difficulty imagining that that level of intimacy would be restful [Grice].

Further, in his introduction to the 2001 UK edition of George Orwell's *The Road to Wigan Pier*, Richard Hoggart writes, "Each decade we shiftily declare we have buried class, and each decade the coffin stays empty" (iv). Classism, like sexism, abounds in *Downton Abbey*, and yes, while Fellowes may take dramatic license, there is no doubt that, as the twentieth century entered its second decade, the profession of domestic service had begun to change, decreasing in numbers, but, perhaps, slowly increasing in resonance.

Interestingly enough, eighteenth-century economist Adam Smith commented on the profession of domestic service that this type of employment solidified the class system. In *The Wealth of Nations*, Smith noted, "A man grows rich by employing a multitude of manufacturers: he grows poor, by maintaining a multitude of menial servants" (Valenze 155). While the Crawley family never considers any of their servants as menial, outside of Downton, society deemed them as such.

Is there a sense of responsibility demonstrated on the part of the privileged Crawleys towards those who work for them? How does this co-exist with the rampant sexism and classism of the early twentieth century? Carson, the butler who is responsible for the male staff—food, wine, and the dining room—has been at Downton since he was a young man (after his days as an actor), and he is particularly fond of Lady Mary, occasionally bestowing fatherly advice upon her. Mrs. Hughes, as housekeeper, is responsible for the female staff and the maintenance of the home, and while she is a bit prickly to decipher, she is fiercely loyal to the Crawley family. Anna, head housemaid, is responsible for Mary, and the two, despite their mistress / servant relationship, share advice, albeit within the polite confines of class expectations, with Anna deferring to Mary as "m'Lady." Series Three includes a discussion of how to refer to Anna; servants, including female servants, were referred to by their last names after marriage. Anna maintained her status as "Anna" because there would be confusion if both she and her husband, John Bates, were referred to by their surname; servants in the same household were not permitted, typically, to marry, although Anna and John Bates are an exception. Upon John's return from prison in Series Three, they were provided a cottage on the estate. Mr. Bates, the valet to the Earl of Grantham, is a war comrade of Robert Crawley's, and Crawley, in spite of a few hiccups here and there, trusts Bates with his life. Miss O'Brien, the maid to the Countess Grantham (Cora Crawley), is also loyal to a fault, although her loyalty is often misguided as she attempts to steer Cora in a particular decision-making direction; her near obsession with Cora is tested when she suspects that Cora, newly pregnant with a fourth child, may be considering a new maid. Like much of *Downton Abbey*, these events are not forgotten, reappearing in Series Three with the mention of "Her Ladyship's Soap" during a discussion between John Bates and O'Brien.

Cora, or rather, Cora's money, is a prominent piece of Series One, a lurker in Series Two, and an unfortunate loss in Series Three; in fact, it could be a character all on its own. When Countess Cora married Robert, Earl of Grantham, she combined her American family money with the landed estate at Downton Abbey. Since wealthy families were encouraged, née expected, to produce a male heir, it was obvious that, at some point, since the Crawleys had three daughters, this would produce a potential problem for the future of Downton Abbey. The entail for Downton specified that the property would need to transfer to a male heir (sexism, here we come!), and there was nothing, apparently, the Crawleys could do to procure the future of Downton for their daughters without marrying off one, preferably the eldest Mary, to a suitable mate. Thus begins Series One of *Downton Abbey*.

Much distress is attributed to the entail during Series One and Two, and money itself becomes a character in Series Three. The Earl remarks to Mary, "My fortune is the work of others, who laboured to build a great dynasty. Do I have the right to destroy their work? Or impoverish that dynasty? I am a custodian, my dear, not an owner" (1:4). Earlier, he had similarly remarked to his mother, the Dowager Countess, "I have given my life to Downton. I was born here and I hope to die here. I claim no career beyond the nurture of this house and the estate. It is my third parent and my fourth child" (1:1). Comments such as these reflect, on one hand, the Earl's love for Downton, and his recognition of his "duty" to the community that Downton serves and protects, including the staff that works and lives at Downton. This loyalty, however, is greatly tested throughout Series One, when the possibility looms that the Crawleys would lose Downton if a suitable partner is not located for Mary; the marriage quest consumes much of the plot for Series One. In continuation of the same conversation between Mary and her father, the Earl notes, "If I could take Mama's money out of the estate, Downton would have to be sold to pay for it. Is that what you want?" Mary responds, "I'd never marry any man that I was told to. I'm stubborn. I wish I wasn't, but I am" (1:4). With this statement, viewers are not only treated to Mary Crawley's fortitude, but a realization that the stage has been set for an uphill battle.

What the Earl does not know at this point is that Mary's life has already been incredibly altered, not only due to the quest to find a suitable match, whether that match would be her third cousin, once removed, Matthew Crawley, or another suitable peer, but also because his daughter's dalliance with Turkish diplomat Pamuk would bring potentially startling consequences, as more and more individuals become aware of the potential for disgrace to the family. And, of course, since this is a made-for-television production, the majority of the individuals who discover Mary's potential disgrace are only too eager to use this against her. It is through the remainder of Series One and Series Two that viewers are treated to the humanization of Mary Crawley as she struggles with the inner turmoil created by her liaison with Pamuk.

From the arrival of Turkish diplomat Pamuk, it was clear that there was a lustful connection between he and Mary Crawley; neither was shy in demonstrating an attraction for the other during the hunting excursion for example, although Mary was careful to maintain the pretext of propriety during the hunt. The theme of the afternoon, a hunting excursion, was a crafty interlude from author Julian Fellowes, particularly since, at times, it seems that the hunt was less for foul or game, and more for each other. Pamuk, at one point during an exchange with Mary, notes, "Sometimes we must endure a little pain in order to achieve satisfaction" (1:3). Ah, Mr. Fellowes, if that is not foreshadowing, what is? In the interlude before dinner, it is revealed that Thomas has misread signals from Pamuk, while helping him dress for dinner; Pamuk is enraged, and, in exchange for not reporting Thomas, secures his assistance navigating the house that evening, namely to Mary Crawley's room, with the thinly-veiled insinuation that he desires to sleep with Mary Crawley. When Pamuk arrives at Mary's room, she initially tries to resist him, but succumbs to Pamuk's charm. To the twenty-first-century viewer, their liaison is somewhat questionable, as it appeared to be more the beginning of a sexual assault, as opposed to romantic, consensual lovemaking. Pamuk tells Mary when she protests that she will be pure for her husband, "Don't worry. You can still be a virgin for your husband" (1:3), thus implying one form of sexual activity, and it appears that Mary relents, but not without hesitation.[2]

Does Lady Mary allow herself to be seduced? On one hand, that step seems out of character for the normally controlled, strong-willed, and quick-witted Mary, a woman painfully aware of the role she plays in the future of Downton, while on the other, she has a fiery side that alludes to the possibility that she would be a willing candidate for a consensual tête-à-tête. Whether what actually occurred between them was consensual is debatable, but part of Mary's reaction after what occurs next could be connected more to shame from a sexual assault than the loss of sexual propriety, and what others will think. When Pamuk dies in her bed, her mother and housemaid Anna become complicit by assisting with the transfer of Pamuk's body to his chambers; with this transfer, the three women set the stage for the discovery of Pamuk's body the next morning by his footman, Thomas. James Fenton in *The New York Review of Books* contends, in reference to Pamuk's death, "The young and the beautiful are not expected to conk out in this way [in reference to sex], to take, as it were, the Nelson Rockefeller option. But soap opera scripts require that they do—that they hang from such periodical cliffs and that they sometimes fall from them."

This story line impacts the remainder of Series One, and parallels the entail story line, also involving Mary and the future of Downton. Both story lines reveal an implicit sexism, but also indicate that character defamation and ill-will cross class lines, and may even originate in one's own family. Irin Carmon, *Salon* staff writer, noted, "the first Series of the show so often sets up a challenge to the aristocratic order, as the characters chafe against their roles, only to finally find fundamental honor in them." This strife and ultimate discovery of honor characterizes much of Series Two, which finds Downton in flux with the arrival of World War I. It is the same strife and honor that embodies character development in *Downton Abbey*. Carina Chocano, writing in reference to class, and the Earl in particular, in the *New York Times*, argues, "It's not just that the earl takes his role as steward of the British class system seriously; it's that he's positively messianic in his flock tending…. In fact, save for an uncharacteristic, but not at all inconsistent, indiscretion toward the end of the second series, the earl's behavior is a model of self-effacing forbearance." His daughter, Lady Mary Crawley, is at times cruel and self-absorbed, particularly in her treatment of younger sister Edith throughout Series One and parts of Series Two and Three. That cruelty is addressed after Sybil's death in Series Three, when Mary comments, "She was the only person in the world who always thought you and I were such nice people." When Edith ponders if their relationship will improve, Mary notes that they will always be at odds, "But since this is the last time the three of will be together in this life, let's love each other now, as sisters should" (3:5). This reveals Mary's empathetic and insightful side, much more evident after the crises revolving around her reputation and her future in Series One and Two, and again, after the death of her sister Sybil in Series Three.

Lady Mary's future is uncertain for much of Series One and Two, particularly in reference to the nefarious code, the entail, that indicates that she is not a suitable heir to Downton. With the apparent deaths of Robert's cousin James and his son Patrick on the *Titanic*, Mary has lost her fiancé, and the security of Downton's future is unstable. Ironically, while the entail may be a relic of the past, and the Crawleys seem intent upon adhering to this legality, Robert Crawley representative of many members of the British elite who, at the end of the nineteenth century, after not finding a suitable British woman, had married a wealthy American, in this case, a Jewish American daughter of a dry goods business owner from Cincinnati, Ohio. However, this sort of forward thinking does not necessarily apply over twenty years later in reference to the future of Downton Abbey.

So, how does Lady Mary cope with the pressure of the entail, referred to in parlance as the "great matter"? Viewers observed the results of her dalliance with Pamuk, and Mary's retreat, for a period of time, into sullenness. In a conversation with Matthew not long after Pamuk's death, she indicates, "Sometimes I rather envy you, having somewhere to go every morning." When Matthew inquires if her life were "satisfactory," she very nearly whines, "Women like me don't have a life. We choose clothes and pay calls and work for charity and do the season. But we're stuck in a waiting room, until we marry." When Matthew protests, "I've made you angry," her retort is, "My life makes me angry. Not you" (1:4). It is the "stuck in a waiting room" misery that defines much of the remainder of Series One for Mary, and even Series Two, as she realizes that she made a mistake in letting Matthew slip away. Similarly, the resulting tension as both try to fight their attraction characterizes the remaining episodes of Series One and Two. Does Mary let her guilt over her interaction with Pamuk get in the way, or is it her inability to see past class barriers that clouds her judgment? Is it really possible that a character present for one episode (Pamuk) could have nearly the same impact as the harbinger of the doom, the entail?

The parallel crises of the futures of Downton Abbey and Lady Mary are not the only intriguing examples of the intersection between sexism and classism. Intermixed are occasional examples of feminist tendencies. At one point, Cora, Sybil, and Edith indirectly discuss women's rights; when Sybil makes an offhand comment that the Dowager Countess could wait for them for dinner to begin; Cora notes, "So women's rights begin at home? I see. Well, I'm all for that" (1:4). The camera angle also includes chauffeur Branson's smile at the discussion, perhaps an important foreshadowing; nonetheless, while this is not an overt display of feminism, it is a nod to activist intent. It was exactly this conversation that prompts Branson's boldness in approaching Sybil: "I'm quite political.... I've brought a few pamphlets I thought might interest you, about the vote." Sybil's response, "Thank you.... But please don't mention it to my father. Or my grandmother. One whiff of reform, and she hears the rattle of the guillotine," may have been uttered more out of shyness than embarrassment at being discovered for her forthright perspectives by a member of the household staff. Branson's response, "I'm a socialist, not a revolutionary. And I won't always be a chauffeur," not only acknowledges his recognition of his place in the household hierarchy, but also foreshadows political views presented throughout the remaining episodes, echoing a request from Branson to borrow books on the subjects of history and politics from Lord Crawley's library (1:4).

Additional feminist tendencies are apparent in May 1914 when Sybil and Isobel Crawley encounter a protest/rally for freedom. Chauffeur Branson rescues both women when the protester's agitation escalates; interestingly enough, Sybil would have escaped from this situation unscathed had it not been for the mistaken communication from John Bates to Lord Crawley that Sybil had attended the rally. Her father was horrified that their Irish "radical" driver had taken Sybil to the rally; the latter prompted a household discussion of Sybil's political tendencies. Lady Mary and her grandmother, the Dowager Countess, speak about Sybil's actions; when Mary indicates that Sybil has her own opinions (how forward of her!), the Countess counters that once Sybil marries, "then her husband will tell her what her opinions are." Just when it seems that the sexism of the era may have stumbled somewhat, viewers are reminded of the standards of the early twentieth century. Even Matthew and Mary discuss Lady Sybil's political proclivities; Mary reports that "she's [Sybil] discovered politics, which of course makes Papa see red"

(1:6). Matthew, never one to miss a moment during the early days of their apparent courtship, teases Mary that if she really likes to argue, they should see more of each other. Touché!

The debate over the extent of Sybil's political intentions continues, although once again viewers are reminded of the intersection between classism and sexism in Downton Abbey. Not long after the rally, Gwen, Sybil's maid and a young woman who desired to work in the world of business as a secretary, speaks with Sybil regarding the search for a secretarial position. When Sybil attempts to reassure her, Gwen replies with the frustration evident on her face, "Forgive me, m'lady, but you don't get it. You're brought up to think it's all within your grasp, that if you want something enough it'll come to you. But we're not like that. We don't think our dreams are bound to come true, because they almost never do." Ever compassionate Sybil sympathizes as much as her standing allows, "Then that's why we'll stick together. Your dream is my dream now" (1:6).

This previous situation may also be an interesting twist on feminism as well. Sara Ahmed argues, "To be recognized as a feminist is to be assigned to a difficult category and a category of difficulty. You are 'already read' as 'not easy to get along with' when you name yourself a feminist. You have to show that you are not difficult through displaying signs of good will and happiness." This is tested again in Series Three when Edith is offered a position as a journalist with a newspaper in London, writing a weekly column on issues impacting women. Her father objects, which eventually leads to a dinner table conversation between the Dowager Countess, Isobel Crawley, and Lord Grantham. When Lord Grantham, ever the concerned father, notes, "Mama, talk to them. Say something sensible," Isobel interjects, "Yes, let's hear how a woman's place is in the home." The Dowager Countess, in a surprise move, comments, "I don't think ... eventually in the home, but I see no harm in her having some fun before she gets there.... And, another thing, Edith isn't getting any younger. Perhaps she isn't cut out for domestic life" (3:7). Leave it to the Dowager Countess for a priceless zinger; on one hand, she encourages Edith's "feminism," while on the other, she berates her lack of a suitor.

Series Three offers an interesting twist on classism when, after the death of Sybil, Branson is offered the position of Downton estate manager. Early twentieth-century British society, firmly rooted in class standings, yet Branson is able to cross the tiers not once, but twice, moving from downstairs to upstairs, uncomfortable though it may be, with his marriage to Sybil, and then again, in the wake of her death, as he remains with baby Sybil in the Downton household, and, with the encouragement of Matthew, and deeply contested support, at least initially, from father-in-law Crawley, takes on the estate management role.

If nothing else, change is a constant theme in *Downton Abbey*. In a 19 February 2013 interview published in the *New York Times*, show creator Julian Fellowes notes,

> We started the show in 1912, which was just before the Great War. When you get to the '20s, you get into a very much accelerated rate of change. But it wasn't completely clear how much the world had changed. There were new inventions of course, but at the same time, a lot of people, both rich and poor, were living in a pretty similar way to the way they'd lived before the war....underneath the surface, in fact, the economic realities were making it clearer and clearer that actually, the world for most people had changed substantially.... Was it the modern world or was it all the same? [Itzkoff].

As such, fortitude and strength of character are key components of life at Downton, but at times, both are in short supply. At the end of 1:6, Matthew proposes to Mary, and while she does not refuse, she tells him she would like to think about it, hence the necessity of fortitude—on the part of both. While the family was away for the season, rumors began to circulate about Lady Mary, and, in particular, rumors which appear to originate with a letter written by Edith to the Turkish ambassador. Nearly simultaneously, Matthew tells Mary he will be leaving Downton, essentially that he will not wait forever. Yet again, the ominous cloud of the entail looms, as Mary cries on Carson's shoulder. However, both events—Mary's reputation and the entail, namely, the two key themes of Series One and Two of *Downton Abbey*—are overshadowed by England's declaration of war against Germany.

While the war will bring significant change to Downton, the beginning of England's involvement in the war does not seem to change the status quo very much, at least between the sisters. Mary had been in London with her Aunt Rosamond, and it seems that Edith was, quite literally, chomping at the bit to share the latest news with Mary, knowing that the news of Matthew's engagement to Lavinia Swire will upset her. Mary, refusing to play the victim, shares her own news later—that of her apparent interest in newspaper mogul Richard Carlisle, a character strikingly similar to Rupert Murdoch. Carlisle represents the nouveau riche, a label which will leave him somewhat embittered as he tries to emulate the standards of the Crawleys and those like them, yet another interesting twist on the classism theme—that of the potential misgivings of a member of the upper class who did not earn his money and/or reputation via generations of inheritance.

While Mary is attempting to reconcile her feelings, another character is making hers quite well known. Vera Bates, the estranged wife of valet John Bates, casts a shadow on the downstairs world of Downton, and interestingly enough, that shadow will stretch upstairs by the end of Series Two. Lady Mary, in an effort to prevent Vera from revealing the Pamuk situation, informs Carlisle of what happened with the Turkish diplomat. Carlisle seems initially sympathetic, and willing to help Mary, but in exchange for his support (and for, ultimately, saving Mary's reputation), she must marry him, noting, "When you are my wife, you are entitled to be in my debt" (2:4). In spite of Vera's attempts at blackmail, Carlisle has purchased the exclusive rights to Mary's story, thereby, for all intents and purposes, owning her future. Comments such as those related to indebtedness are echoed with physicality when Carlisle pushes Mary up against the wall after bringing Lavinia to see her fiancé, Matthew during his convalescence at Downton; with an arm restraining her, he threatens to tell the world about her entanglement with Kemal Pamuk, reminding Mary that she has provided valuable information that he may use against her in the future. "You have given me the power to destroy you, and don't think I won't use it…. Don't ever cross me, do you understand? Never. Absolutely never" (2:6). Again, the rampant sexism of early twentieth-century England reappears, this time in the form of physical restraint.

Coincidentally, though, it may be Carlisle who needs Mary more than she needs him; even though his wealth is as significant as that of the Crawley family, he lacks the social graces, something which Mary knows all too well. As Alexander Chee notes in a *Salon* article, "Much in the way her mother's money solved her father's problems, she believes her father's rank will provide the social acceptance Sir Richard covets, neatly reversed symmetry." This is the second time Mary has allowed herself to be controlled by a man; coincidentally this control is in direct reaction to the first. Mary's options, heretofore, are vanquished; as long as she remains with Carlisle, her future is secure. If she "crosses him," that future becomes immediately uncertain. Has she traded a life that is potentially insecure for one in which the secret is safe, or does leaving the secret in the hands of one who could, quite frankly, "ruin her," resolve a potential crisis regarding Mary's reputation?

When Robert inquires of Mary if she remained with Carlisle because of the threat of exposure, he woefully notes, "You're not the first Crawley to make a mistake." Mary laments, "In Mama's phrase, I am 'damaged goods' now. Richard is, after all, prepared to marry me in spite of it. He is in a position to give me a life." Her father gently retorts, "And that's worth it? Even though he already sets your teeth on edge. What about Matthew? How does he view the late Mr. Pamuk?" (2:9). Robert's demeanor reflects not only the concern of a loving father, but acknowledgment of a shared impropriety, knowledge to which only he is privy. He suggests that Mary end her engagement and visit her aunt in America while the scandal abates, acknowledging that Downton will already be victim to newsmongers with the Bates verdict. Mary is concerned that Carlisle will share her tale with the rest of England, while her father, in a rare move that reveals more fatherly instinct than concern for public image, notes, "I don't want my daughter to be married to a man who threatens her with ruin. I want a good man for you, a brave man. Find a cowboy in the Middle West, and bring him back to shake us up a bit" (2:9). For what seems to be a continuing theme in the postwar Downton household, concern for appearances is secondary to a daughter's welfare. Interestingly enough, Mary, like her mother Cora earlier, opts for an approach that focuses on the appearance of propriety, not exactly a feminist or even rebellious stance; her father took the more audacious course of action with a "let's take our chances with the public" response. While Mary may be the character who grows the most in *Downton Abbey*, she is also the character who vacillates between rebelliousness and demureness more than any other.

At the same time, Mary also has to end a relationship with the man who had secured her future; that conversation further reveals an intense anger from Carlisle, greater than that depicted in previous scenes, leading the viewer to think that Mary may have dodged a bullet, at least in terms of life partners. She is forced to acknowledge her gratitude to Carlisle, who, in turn reminds her that he kept her "filthy scandal" out of the papers, as well as that of Bates. In response to Carlisle's threats to expose her, her retort, "And you wonder why we wouldn't make each other happy?" hearkens to the fearless Mary, the one who took her chances with scandal (prior to the arrival of Vera Bates). In the melee that ensues with the arrival of Matthew, Lord Crawley enters the drawing room, and orders the men to stop fighting. Carlisle, again demonstrating his temper, snarls, "How smooth you are. What a model of manners and elegance. I wonder if you will be quite so serene when the papers are full of your eldest daughter's exploits" (2:9).

Carlisle's departure is full of classic Mary, demure, in accord with societal expectations, on one hand, rebellious on the other. Mary approaches Carlisle, "I suppose you feel I've used you, and I'm sorry if I have…." Carlisle, "I'm warning you, I'll feel no guilt in exposing you. My job is to sell newspapers." Mary, in a placatory tone, "I just didn't want our final words to be angry ones." Carlisle's retort is classic Carlisle, "I loved you, you know, more than you knew, and much, much more than you loved me." Mary's response returns to demure Mary, "And I hope the next woman you love deserves you more than I did" (2:9). Was this a calculated response? After all, Mary had been waiting for Carlisle before he left. She may just have saved herself from possible ruin by putting herself down to Carlisle. This was hardly a move of feminist tendency, but perhaps a risk worth taking.

In the time between Robert learning of Mary's transgressions before the war, and the departure of Carlisle from the Crawleys' lives, Matthew and Mary share a conversation that foreshadows the conclusion of the Series Two Christmas Special. When Matthew asks if she loved Pamuk, Mary's response is that of the fallen Jezebel, even labeling herself as such: "It was lust. What does it matter? I'm Tess of the D'Urbevilles to your Angel Claire. I have fallen. I am impure." When Matthew tells her to "brave the storm," she acknowledges that she cares what others think of her, and praises Sybil for being the "strong one." Matthew urges her to end her relationship with Carlisle; one month of scandal is better than a "lifetime of misery." The parting comment from Matthew at the end of this scene, "I never would—I never could—despise you" (2:9) sets the stage for the final moments of the Christmas special when Matthew asks Mary to be his wife.

What is most interesting about the exploration of sexual impropriety, bribery, and societal standards in Series Two is reflected in the interconnectedness of class and gender, and the inconstancy of human actions between fearlessness and modesty, some of which reflected both classist and feminist tendencies. Does *Downton Abbey* provide a disservice to viewers in terms of the depiction of the sexual double standard, or is this one of the more accurate time period portrayals in *Downton*? In Series One, Mary violated society's standards of sexual propriety with her encounter with Kemal Pamuk, in itself a potential violation of more than her chastity. While Mary has to reduce herself to male control, perhaps for the second time, in her engagement to Richard Carlisle, her experiences are paralleled, and perhaps intensified, in the paternity crisis facing housemaid Ethel Parks. With the transformation of Downton into a convalescence center comes the arrival of Major Charles Bryant; his affair with Ethel results not only in the termination of her job upon discovery of the affair, but her pregnancy and Bryant's disavowal of his newborn son.

One disturbing element, perhaps more so than the depiction of societal double standards, is *Downton Abbey*'s depiction of Ethel as a bit of a flirt. Upon arrival at Downton, she announced that she did not intend to stay long as a housemaid; this was merely a stepping stone for her. Unfortunately for Ethel, truer words were never spoken (at least for the first part of the previous statement). Did Fellowes intentionally create a coquettish character to depict the double standard, yet again, in early twentieth-century English society, or is the character of Ethel meant to imply that, by being flirtatious, Ethel's behavior precipitates her downfall? Surely, twenty-first-century viewers know better than to equate flirtations with downfall, but did Fellowes mean to imply that early twentieth-century society did not? To make matters worse, Ethel could not have chosen more of a rogue with whom to start an illicit relationship; Major Bryant refuses to acknowledge his son, even though he and Ethel had been caught in the act by Mrs. Hughes. Even that discovery was treated with a bit of a jest, as Mrs. Hughes remarks in a huff, "I may not be a woman of the world, but I don't live in a sack!" (2:3). Even though Mrs. Hughes fires Ethel for her inappropriate behavior, Major Bryant, of course, receives no repercussions, other than the ire of Mrs. Hughes, but for a man of his title and financial status, that is inconsequential.

Viewers are treated to Mrs. Hughes' concern for Ethel when she reveals her pregnancy, and after the birth of her son, Mrs. Hughes becomes, quite literally, her only ally. Society has turned its back on the woman who bore a child out of wedlock. The cynic in me would argue that if the situation were different, and Mary had become pregnant as a result of her encounter with Pamuk, she would have been sent to America while the furor subsided, and then returned later to only whispers of her infidelity. Class status, in the case of Ethel, intensified what was already a challenging situation, to the point that Mrs. Hughes even suggests that Ethel move to the city, where no one would know her, and claim that, with the death of Major Bryant towards the end of the war, she was a war widow. Mary's response is classic Mary: "The truth is, Ethel made her choice and now she's stuck with it. Aren't we all stuck with the choices we've made?" (2: 6). It seems the double standard has reappeared. On one hand, Mary is fretting about her own choices, while on the other, vilifying a young woman who took a similar step (albeit, perhaps on a more consensual basis than Mary's encounter with Pamuk). It was difficult to determine if her reaction was one of relief (that the same did not occur with her), or frustration over the trajectory of her own life in the years since Pamuk.

Societal double standards notwithstanding, *Downton Abbey* presents the intersection of classist and feminist tendencies, and the inequities of wealth and birthright are token characteristics with the central theme of the estate's future. In spite of criticism that *Downton Abbey* overlooks reality, including in its depiction of class and gender, the series is, as Emily Nussbaum wrote in the 23 January 2012 edition of *The New Yorker*, "situated precisely on the Venn diagram where "prestige" meets "guilty pleasure." This author could not agree more.

NOTES

1. The convalescent center at Downton was for officers, and would not be sullied with soldiers from the ranks; an exception, however, will be made for footman William in Series Two.

2. It is important to note that, in *Downton Abbey: The Complete Scripts, Season One* (2012), series creator Julian Fellowes notes,

> In the edit, the Powers made a cut we all came to regret. After commenting that Mary "could still be a virgin for your husband," which stayed in, Kemal was supposed to say: "A little imagination, a phial of blood hidden beneath the pillow, you wouldn't be the first." But this was excised. Despite arguing fairly passionately, I could not convince them the lines were needed. I explained that, without them, it was anyone's guess what Kemal was doing to Mary that would leave her virginity intact. But they were confident that no one would make any untoward connection. "Nobody will think that," they said. But everyone thought it…. All of which meant they assumed that Pamuk must have done something unspeakable which we won't name here [162].

WORKS CITED

Ahmed, Sara. "Feminist Killjoys (And Other Willful Subjects)." *The Scholar and Feminist Online* 8.3 (Summer 2010). Web. http://barnard.edu/sfonline/polyphonic/print_ahmed.htm. 28 September 2012.

Anderson, John. "To the Manor Born." *America* 206.8 (202): 33. *MasterFILE Premier*. Web. 28 September 2012.

Carmon, Irin. "Why Liberals Love 'Downton Abbey.'" Salon.com, 7 January 2012. Web. http://www.salon.com/2012/01/07/why_liberals_love_downton_abbey. 15 July 2012.

Chee, Alexander. "Parvenucracy: 'Downton Abbey'" Salon.com, 30 July 2012. Web. http://www.salon.com/2012/07/30/parvenucracy_downton_abbey_salpart/. 13 August 2012.

Chocano, Carina. "The Upside-Down Appeal of 'Downton Abbey'" *The New York Times Reprints* 17 February 2012. Web. http://www.nytimes.com/2012/02/19/magazine/downton-abbey.html?pagewanted=all&_r=0. 28 September 2012.

Cooke, Rachel. "Heirs and Graces." *New Statesman.* 139.5022 (11 October 2010): 48–49. *Master File Premier.* Web. 15 July 2012.

Dunwoodie, Eileen. "Highclere Castle on Screen." *Britain* 79.2 (2011): 36–43. *MasterFILE Premier.* Web. 1 August 2012.

Fenton, James. "The Abbey That Jumped the Shark." *The New York Review of Books*, 8 March 2012. Web. http://www.nybooks.com/articles/archives/2012/mar/08/abbey-jumped-shark/?pagination=false. 1 August 2012.

Grice, Elizabeth. "Julian Fellowes: My Pride, Their Prejudice." *Telegraph*, 12 November 2010. Web. http://www.telegraph.co.uk/culture/tvandradio/8One256Three0/Julian-Fellowes-My-Pride-their-prejudice.html. 1 August 2012.

Hoggart, Richard. Introduction. *The Road to Wigan Pier* by George Orwell. 1937. London: Penguin UK, 2001. Print.

Itzkoff, Dave. "More Season 3 Conversation with 'Downton Abbey' Creator Julian Fellowes." *The New York Times ArtsBeat*, 19 February 2013. Web. http://artsbeat.blogs.nytimes.com/2013/02/19/more-season-3-conversation. 9 March 2013.

Jordan, Ellen. *The Women's Movement and Women's Employment in Nineteenth Century Britain*. London: Routledge, 1999. Digital file. *eBook Collection (EBSCOhost)*.

Nussbaum, Emily. "Horsey Set: The Upscale Temptations of 'Luck' and 'Downton Abbey.'" *The New Yorker*. 23 January 2012. Web. http://www.newyorker.com/arts/critics/television/2012/01/23/120123crte_television_nussbaum. 28 September 2012.

Rice, Lynette. "Return to Downton Abbey." *Entertainment Weekly* 1188 (2012): 40. *MasterFILE Premier*. Web. 1 July 2012.

Rose, Sonya O. *Limited Livelihoods: Gender and Class in Nineteenth-Century England*. London: Routledge, 2003. Digital file. *eBook Collection (EBSCOhost)*.

Sedgwick, Eve K. *Epistemology of the Closet*, 2d ed. Berkeley: University of California Press, 2008. Print.

Simonton, Deborah. *A History of European Women's Work: 1700 to the Present*. London: Routledge, 1998. Digital file. *eBook Collection (EBSCOhost)*.

Valenze, Deborah. *The First Industrial Woman*. New York: Oxford University Press, 1995. Print. 155.

Wilson, A.N. "The Downton Delusion." *Daily Mail* 12 March 2011: 18. *Regional Business News*. Web. 1 August 2012.

"Damaged" First, Romance Later

The Patterning of Courtship
on Lady Mary Crawley

RACHEL L. CARAZO

Downton Abbey begins with Lady Mary Crawley's brief romance with Mr. Kemal Pamuk, a Turkish visitor whose philosophy of love and courtship opposes everything that Britain, just after the reign of Edward VII (1901–1910), represents. Nevertheless, when Pamuk comments to Mary that "[s]ometimes we must endure a little pain in order to achieve satisfaction," he is setting the standard to which all other romances in *Downton Abbey*, including those of Lady Edith Crawley, Lady Sybil Crawley, Isobel Crawley, Lady Rose MacClare, Anna Bates, Daisy Mason, Thomas Barrow, Mrs. Hughes (Carson), adhere.[1] When measured against British social mores, Mary becomes a "damaged" good, a state that she must reenact in her subsequent romances. Yet Mary is not alone in being "damaged" first and finding love later. Her romance with Pamuk remains a prototype for others, and the result, whether happy or problematic, also depends on the social perception of "damaged" goods, making Mary more than just a principal character but also an archetype for romance in the series.

Edwardian Progress and the Heroic Archetype

In order to understand how Lady Mary Crawley's romantic archetype fits into the historical periods represented in the series, which, tantalizingly, are only a hundred years removed from the modern world,[2] a brief overview of the philosophies during this time is essential. *Downton Abbey* begins with a major event, the sinking of the *Titanic* in April 1912, which establishes the drama just after the reign of Edward VII, the son of Queen Victoria (1837–1901). Edward's influence, which began in 1880 while he was still the Prince of Wales, was substantial, and by the time of his death and the ascension of King George V in 1910, *La Belle Époque* in which his reign was situated had lasting effects on aristocratic houses, such as those belonging to the fictitious Crawley family.[3]

Edwardian Britain functioned with a sense of optimism, which World War I muted, and experienced important social changes, many of which are visible in the series.[4] For example, women like Edith Crawley began to own and run their own publications, even hiring female editors when biased men refused to work for them.[5] Seemingly simple changes for hair and clothes also mattered; Sybil models dressy pants for her family (2:4)[6] and Mary chooses to shorten her hair at the end of Series Five.[7]

Nevertheless, these Edwardian social changes were both local and international. In Britain, "the years between 1900 and 1914 were ushering in many reforms and the beginnings of a welfare state: the needs of the ordinary person were no longer going to be ignored."[8] With this concern for the individual, even a poorer individual, was also the hope for a lasting world peace. While Edward lived, Britain allied with France and Russia in the Triple Entente, and women began to enter the workforce, leading to the 1910s when "young women [like Lady Edith Crawley] from well-to-do backgrounds thought of attending college and striking out on their own."[9]

Yet Edward VII gave Britain a mixed image of being a rebel, in which adultery committed by the upper classes could be acceptable,[10] adhering to standards of purity and propriety. Edward inspired a "cult of youth" that began to affect change in the strict social strata of the kingdom.[11] In a period known as Khaki Fever, women began to chase soldiers and freely flaunt their sexuality while society began to deem unmarried women with children, whose fathers were long-term partners, as war widows.[12]

However, the purity image was also vital to the period. Unmarried women were expected to be virgins, which is the main stress for Lady Mary Crawley after she has sex with Mr. Pamuk.[13] When Ethel, a servant at Downton, becomes pregnant from her visits with a soldier, she has to leave service and struggle to make a life on her own, often facing scorn from her supposed social betters (2:3).[14] In addition, divorce was considered a scandal, and women could not obtain a divorce from their husbands unless the men abused or abandoned them.[15] With these social concerns at the forefront, it is clear how young women, such as the three daughters of the Earl of Grantham, could find navigating romance and their passions so difficult.

Lady Mary Crawley, as a prototype for romantic relationships in the series, fits somewhere in the middle of these two social situations from the periods in which she lives. Unlike the middle class women whose purity constraints were slowly beginning to ease by the start of World War I,[16] Mary's birth in an aristocratic household pressures her to remain pure until marriage. In addition, her damaged relationship with Kemal Pamuk, at first denies the optimism associated with unconstrained sexual relations, epitomized by Edward VII's example "of the untamable bachelor, the bon viveur," during the Edwardian and World War I periods, but it nevertheless, in its essence, strives to create happiness.[17] Mary's subsequent relationships with Matthew Crawley and Henry Talbot, which are ultimately successful in producing a marriage, still follow the same patterns of constraint before freedom.

The Damaged Phase: Mary Crawley and Kemal Pamuk

Even though Mary was quietly engaged to her cousin Patrick, the heir to the estate, she did not love him, and his death on the *Titanic* freed her of the imposition. Patrick's death also made Matthew Crawley, a young lawyer from Manchester and Mary's later love interest, the heir to the Earldom of Grantham. Yet Mary's fling with the Turkish Kemal Pamuk, which results in her becoming a damaged good, begins the first of her romances upon which other courtships are modeled.

The fact that Kemal is Turkish and represents an outside culture remains critical to preparing an archetypal relationship for Mary and other characters, and even a type of anti-hero role for Mary, since her romantic and personal choices often oppose accepted social mores for women. According to an assessment of Edwardian Britain, "Edward's privileged lifestyle was shared by many in a society where the gap between the rich and the poor had widened considerably. Never before had British society's lifestyles been so stratified."[18] Yet when a foreigner comes to Downton and creates a ripple in their stratified world, the results are profound. In fact, despite the divisions between upstairs and downstairs in the house, Mary's archetype becomes available for the rich *and* the poor. Consequently, the damaged phase not only epitomizes Downton romances, but it also socially equalizes them.

With these trends in mind, Mary's life-changing first meeting with Kemal Pamuk indicates that her decisions will challenge social expectations.

> *Mary looks up and her jaw drops. Riding towards her is one of the handsomest, sexiest men she has ever seen in her life. He stands in his stirrups and doffs his silk hat.*
> KEMAL: Lady Mary Crawley, I presume?
> MARY: You presume right.
> KEMAL: Sorry to be so dishevelled. We've been on a train since dawn and we had to change in a shed.
> MARY: You don't look dishevelled to me.[19]

Immediately, Mary is physically attracted to Kemal, and her evaluation of him, which exceeds her expectations, also primes her for their sexual encounter.

Mary's daring appears immediately after their introduction. As they ride together, she and Kemal decide not to follow the others over the bridge, an easier path that represents the social acceptability of Evelyn Napier, Mary's intended suitor. Instead, Mary and Kemal have their horses jump over the water.

> MARY: I hope the day is living up to your expectations.
> KEMAL: It is exceeding them in every way.
> *The look he gives her is unmistakable.*
> MARY: Where's Mr. Napier?
> KEMAL: He's gone over the bridge. Look.
> *He points to a group including Napier on the road.*
> KEMAL: And what about you? Will you follow him? Or come over the jump with me?
> MARY: Oh, I was never much one for going round by the road.
> KEMAL: You believe in living dangerously, then?
> MARY: Of course. What did the Frenchman say? *L'audace, toujours l'audace.*
> *He smiles at this. They are kindred spirits.*
> KEMAL: Stay by me and we'll take it together.[20]

Now that they have recognized their mutual attraction, Kemal must still determine how far he can progress with his pursuit of Mary. He flirts with her after dinner, and he decides, with the help of Thomas, after blackmailing him, to visit Mary in her bedroom.

When Kemal first arrives, Mary is shocked, and she declares: "Do you have any idea what you're asking? I'd be ruined if they even knew we'd had this conversation."[21] However, despite these protests, Kemal charms her and succeeds with the pursuit. Mary feels damaged, but the judgment is worse when other characters learn what has happened, for Kemal's death during intercourse prompts Mary to include her maid, Anna, and her mother, Cora, since she cannot carry his body back to his bedroom by herself. At first, Cora balks:

CORA: I couldn't. It's not possible.
MARY: If you don't, we will figure in a scandal of such magnitude it will never be forgotten until long after we're both dead.
CORA: But I—
MARY: I'll be ruined, Mama. Ruined and notorious, a laughing stock, a social pariah. Is that what you want for your eldest daughter? Is it what you want for the family?"[22]

After this plea, Cora agrees to help. Yet once these two women know the truth, Mary's status as a damaged good develops into her greatest concern. This state also becomes the most enduring archetype for romances in the rest of the series.

Damaged as a State of Being

There are two main ways that characters can be considered damaged in the series. These are physical states, in which a body part or a social status recognized by other members of society causes a difficulty in the romance, or an emotional state of feeling damaged and unworthy for the relationship. Sometimes the two damaged states are interwoven and interrelated. However, separating them also demonstrates just how pervasive the *damaged first* phase relates to characters in the series.

The character with the most visibly damaged body part is Mr. Bates, who walks with a limp due to a war injury. This impediment causes drama in the Crawley household as the family and servants alike judge him. Mr. Carson comments to the Earl of Grantham: "I am not entirely sure he will prove equal to the task but your lordship will be the judge of that."[23] Carson, as the head butler, reserves the right to judge the aptitude of everyone under his supervision. Yet other characters, like Thomas Barrow and Miss O'Brien, are not kind about Mr. Bates' physical infirmity. Thomas even complains to Mr. Carson, "Not lazy, exactly. But he just can't carry. He can hardly manage his lordship's cases."[24] However, despite the machinations led by Thomas and Miss O'Brien, Anna shows Bates kindness and this sentiment eventually turns into love, a huge accomplishment in an era when servant romances were only condoned by "a very enlightened employer."[25] Anna even defends Bates during the earliest discussions of his lameness by the family:

ANNA: Perhaps she misunderstood.
MARY: No. it was quite plain. O'Brien told her Bates can't do the job properly. Why was he taken on?
ANNA: He was Lord Grantham's batman when he was fighting the Boers.
MARY: I know that, but even so.
SYBIL: I think it's romantic.
MARY: I don't. How can a valet do his work if he's lame?
ANNA: He's not very lame.[26]

Anna is always considerate to Bates and she clearly favors him. However, Bates does not at first consider himself worthy of her, and he believes (wrongly) that trying to repair his leg with a painful device will mend his damaged state.[27]

Both Matthew Crawley, Mary's first husband, and Henry Talbot, her second husband, are damaged in a social sense. Matthew may be the heir of the earldom and the estate, but he is a mere lawyer from Manchester, as Mary reminds her family:

MARY: He isn't one of us.
SYBIL: But Cousin Freddie's studying for the bar, and so is Vivian MacDonald.

MARY: At Lincoln's Inn. Not sitting at a dirty little desk in Ripon. Besides, his father was a *doctor*.

SYBIL: There's nothing wrong with doctors. We all need doctors.

MARY: We all need crossing sweepers and draymen, too. It doesn't mean we have to dine with them.[28]

Later, Mary's second husband-to-be encounters similar concerns. Henry has no stable income, especially once his car racing days are over. While Mary at first considers herself too damaged by her fling with Mr. Pamuk to marry Matthew,[29] she begins her relationship with Henry with the intention of it not lasting due to his hobbies and social inutility.[30] Even the seemingly middle-class Charles Blake, another of Mary's love interests, encounters her bias about money before she realizes that his family is wealthy.[31] Thus, even when some characters do not actually marry, they still begin in a damaged state, where there is some physical or psychological impediment.

Tom Branson's love of Lady Sybil Crawley definitely passes through a damaged phase due to his social station. Branson is the chauffeur at Downton and his dreams of marrying Sybil always seem far from actualization. She protests often, but Branson intuits the truth and presses her toward action.

BRANSON (CONT'D): The truth is, I'll stay at Downton until you want to run away with me.

SYBIL: Don't be ridiculous.

BRANSON: You're too scared to admit it, but you're in love with me.[32]

He is right; Sybil does love him, but she has internalized the biases of her family so well that it is difficult for her to break free of them. A conversation that Sybil has with Mary demonstrates this fact.

MARY: We are talking about…?

SYBIL: Branson. Yes.

MARY: The chauffeur, Branson.

SYBIL: Oh, how disappointing of you.

MARY: I'm just trying to get it straight in my head. You and the chauffeur.

SYBIL: Oh Mary, you know I don't care about all of that.

MARY: Oh darling, darling, don't be such a baby. This isn't Fairyland. What did you think? You'd marry the chauffeur and we'd all come to tea?

SYBIL: Don't be silly. I told you, I don't even think I like him.[33]

This exchange is especially indicative of Sybil's woes. She claims to be above Mary's petty concerns, but she is nevertheless faltering in her willingness to declare her love for Branson. Social expectations are therefore affecting her, even if she refuses to admit it.

Lady Rose MacClare's engagement with Atticus Aldridge encounters two "damaged" attributes: religion and contrived infidelity. Rose is not bothered by the fact that Atticus is Jewish, but many other characters, especially her mother, Susan, the Marchioness of Flintshire, are bothered by it. Yet the real test of their love occurs when Rose's mother pays a woman to pretend to seduce Atticus and another operative to photograph this woman standing in Atticus' hotel room.[34] Rose, whose own damaged state comes from her parents' discord and scandalizing divorce, for "divorce equalled shame and rejection in their world,"[35] briefly considers ending the engagement after these pictures surface.[36]

Thomas Barrow, whose character will remain unique throughout, is damaged because of his sexuality. Even though people in modern times are more accepting of homosexuality, the laws of Edwardian and World War I Britain criminalized the practice. Thus, in regard to romance in the series, Thomas might be labeled as damaged due to this social consideration even though this research does not judge him negatively.

Thomas' damaged phase appears early and also relates to Mr. Pamuk, making his damaged state a possible archetype for same-sex romances as Mary's is for heterosexual relationships. When Kemal discovers Thomas' preferences, he leads him on, enticing Thomas to touch him on the cheek. When Kemal angers, this discussion follows:

> THOMAS: I'm sorry, sir. I thought—
> KEMAL: That will teach you not to believe what the English say about foreigners.
> *He is standing very still, staring at the servant.*
> KEMAL (CONT'D): I ought to report you.
> THOMAS: I think you must have mistaken—
> KEMAL: I mistook nothing. But I will make you an offer.[37]

Kemal then uses his power over Thomas to sneak into Mary's bedroom, beginning the entire process of being her damaged before finding love.

During an earlier visit of Philip, the Duke of Crowborough, Thomas loses his letters, which he could have used as evidence of their romance. Crowborough tricks Mary into leading him into Thomas' bedroom in the servants' quarters. Yet Thomas confronts Crowborough when the duke refuses him, not realizing at first that he has lost his evidence:

> CROWBOROUGH (CONT'D): Because of a youthful dalliance? A few weeks of madness in a London Season? You wouldn't hold that against me, surely?
> THOMAS: I would if I have to.
> CROWBOROUGH: Who'd believe a greedy footman against the word of a duke? If you're not very careful, you'll end up behind bars.[38]

The format of this discussion, when a man learns Thomas' secret and refuses either to form a relationship with him or continue an existing one, sets the standard for Thomas' damaged phase with other characters, including James "Jimmy" Kent and Andy, heterosexual servants to whom Thomas is attracted. Thomas deals with these refusals in different ways, but the result remains the same. His sexual preferences are considered damaged and it does not matter if his affections are returned, for he usually keeps his true feelings hidden just beneath the surface.

Isobel Crawley, although married and widowed before the main action of the show, endures a damaged phase with her romance with Lord Merton. First, Isobel has reservations about remarrying, a psychological burden which appears during Dr. Clarkson's brief interest in her and in the preliminary stages of her courtship with Merton. On the other hand, Merton's physical burdens are his diagnosis with anemia and his two sons from his previous marriage. Neither of his sons likes Isobel, and his son Larry Grey especially does his best to scare her away. During one dinner scene, Larry causes discord:

> LARRY: You mean to marry Mrs. Crawley here. She seems very nice, and I wish you both every happiness.
> ISOBEL: Thank you.
> LARRY: But that doesn't prevent me from seeing the wide disparity in class and background may prove your undoing.
> ROBERT: What did you say?
> LARRY: Only that Mrs. Crawley, a decent, middle-class woman with neither birth nor fortune, is expecting to fill our mother's shoes as one of the leaders of the county.[39]

After this insulting speech, Isobel cancels her engagement with Merton, believing that she should be able to enter a family that can at least treat her politely even if they do not like her.[40]

Finally, Mary passes through a damaged stage where she has two suitors, Tony Gillingham and Charles Blake, the latter of which, at the end of Series Four, hints at a struggle between the men over her when he asks, "So now…. Let battle commence?"[41] Nevertheless, when Mary chooses to have an experimental relationship with Gillingham in Series Five, she creates a situation in which her damaged state returns in the social sense, since another maid later tries to blackmail her in Series Six, but also in the physical sense for Gillingham. Lady Mabel Lane Fox had been engaged to Gillingham until he fell desperately in love with Mary; he, therefore, becomes damaged and separated from his rightful bride by having premarital sex with Mary. Yet Lane Fox, who has just as much of a social presence as Mary, forgives Gillingham for his wandering and marries him in the end, moving Mary toward the last of her romances.

Damaged as a State of Mind

Mary Crawley's misgivings about her damaged state in the earlier seasons, which at first keep her from marrying Matthew, show how being damaged is also a state of mind. Mary falls in love with Matthew, after a time during which they dislike each other; but even after he proposes, she fears telling him the truth.

> MARY: I'd have to tell him.
> CORA: Oh…. Is it absolutely necessary?
> MARY: If I didn't, I'd feel as if I'd caught him with a lie.[42]

These hesitations lead Matthew temporarily toward Lavinia, a kind woman who has no similar inner conflict and whose engagement with Matthew only ends with her tragic death from the Spanish flu. Mary also fears the revelation of her secret by Sir Richard Carlisle, to whom she is briefly engaged, until his overbearing manner and Mary's courage about telling the truth to Matthew allow her and Matthew to marry each other.[43] However, Mary's psychological conflict does not end after her first marriage. The horrors of Matthew's death in a car accident at the end of Series Three return during her courtship with Henry Talbot, a race car driver. In Series Six, when Talbot's friend and main racing rival, Charlie Rogers, dies in a fiery crash during a race, Mary's worst fears reappear, returning her to the damaged mental state that never really left her.

Lady Sybil's early hesitation to declare her love for Branson also reflects a damaged psychological state. Sybil clearly loves him, but the reservations of her family and the strict, Edwardian social order surface during their courtship. When Branson finally reveals his feelings for her, frustrations are apparent.

> BRANSON: I know I shouldn't say it, but I can't keep it in any longer.
> SYBIL: I wish you would.
> BRANSON: I've told myself and told myself you're too far above me, but things are changing. When the war's over, the world won't be the same place as it was when it started.[44]

Branson, being very political, believes that the members of the aristocracy are stymying progress. For him, Sybil's social status is her greatest shortcoming, while his status inspires the same reservations for her.

Yet even after Branson becomes a part of the family, he is not immune to similar psychological concerns; after Sybil's death, Branson dedicates himself to Downton and to his daughter. However, when he meets Miss Sarah Bunting, a woman passionate about her political and reformist beliefs, Branson feels attracted to her. Bunting, though, does not get along with everyone at Downton, especially the Earl of Grantham, Robert Crawley, and this discord finally persuades Branson to discontinue his friendship with her.

> BRANSON: I'd like things to change, but I don't think in black and white terms any more.
> MISS BUNTING: While I do?
> BRANSON: Look, I'm not going to pretend I haven't enjoyed knowing you. In fact, I'm relieved to know I'm not the only Socialist left on this earth. But maybe we should call it a day before one of us gets hurt.[45]

Branson has radical views, and these beliefs still weigh on him sometimes as he ages; however, he learns how to manage them, and even though he never forgets who his is, these psychological factors are the same issues that affected his courtship with Sybil.

Lady Edith Crawley also passes through several damaged phases since she fears becoming a spinster, which "equalled another kind of social reject" in this highly stratified society.[46] Her attitude about love tends to be pessimistic, and the role that Mary often plays in making Edith's romances more difficult situates Edith in a seemingly endless cycle of damaged pursuits. First, many of the men that Edith considers attractive prefer Mary. This slight occurs with Pamuk, their cousin Patrick, Philip, the Duke of Crowborough, and especially Matthew, after Edith takes Matthew on a tour of several local churches, hoping that the outing will kindle his affections.[47] However, Edith eventually deals with her own personal issues in three particular courtships.

Sir Anthony Strallan is an older neighbor, whose affections for Edith grow as they spend more time together. Strallan, though, is much older than Edith, and this perceived, damaged state makes the Crawley family counsel her against the marriage. However, for a long time, the Crawleys accept Edith's bid for this marriage to occur since he makes Edith happy. Edith explains simply: "We seemed to have a lot to talk about."[48] Edith goes all the way to the altar, but Strallan has second thoughts, due to the Crawleys' constant concerns, and he leaves her single.

After Strallan, Edith meets Harry Gregson, and the romance that follows is damaged in the social sense because the pair has premarital sex, resulting in a pregnancy that Edith must hide from her family. Edith places her daughter, Marigold, under the care of the Drewes, the tenants of Yew Tree Farm; but the disgust that Mrs. Drewe feels at Edith's continual presence at her house culminates in the Drewes leaving their tenancy and Edith taking Marigold to Downton as her ward.

Edith receives word that Gregson has been killed in Germany, destroying her hopes of being happy, sending her into depression. By chance, her re-acquaintance with Bertie Pelham in London begins to develop into a serious affection, but she does not initially tell Bertie about Marigold, and this mixture of being damaged physically and psychologically weighs heavily upon her. When Bertie *does* learn about Marigold, it comes from Mary, rekindling the emotional rift between the sisters that has always haunted Edith and pushed her into a more damaged state. Bertie, who is about to become the Marquess of Hexham, ends their engagement and leaves Edith in the same emotionally damaged state where she began.

With the servants, both Mr. Bates and Anna follow each other in successive, damaged states. Bates' first wife, Vera, dies under mysterious circumstances. It becomes obvious that she killed herself and implicated Bates, but the police incarcerate him and send him to trial. Anna supports Bates through the ordeal, but it emotionally exhausts them.

A similar problem with the law occurs when Gillingham's servant, Mr. Green, rapes

Anna during a party, when the family and staff are all upstairs. At this point, Anna and Bates are married, but Anna feels so damaged by the experience that she isolates herself from Bates. Yet Bates does not forsake her; he states, "I promise you this—nothing bad is going to happen to you again."[49] In addition, someone murders Mr. Green, and Anna becomes the main suspect. Anna thus follows Bates' storyline; she spends time in jail and endures multiple interrogations, adding to her strain of being unable to conceive a child.

The courtship between Mr. Carson and Mrs. Hughes is fairly benign since they have known each other for a long time. Before they marry, Mrs. Hughes seems content with her life in service, for she turns down a proposal from an old friend, Joe Burns, and she shares her feelings about it with Carson:

> MRS. HUGHES: In many ways I *wanted* to accept. But I'm not that farm girl anymore. I was flattered, of course, but I've changed, Mr. Carson.
> CARSON: Life's altered you, as it's altered me. And what would be the point of living if we didn't let life change us?[50]

However, their ages place them in a psychological state that makes Mr. Carson, at first, fear that his suit will not be accepted and that makes Mrs. Hughes believe that if Carson wants a full marriage, her aging body will not attract him.[51] Their wedding plans also encounter emotional dissonance when Carson insists on having the wedding and reception at Downton while Mrs. Hughes wants a simpler, more intimate setting. Later, once they are married, Carson's continual disappointment with the meals that Mrs. Hughes cooks cause problems, straining their hopes, especially those of Mrs. Hughes, for long-term happiness.[52]

Daisy's misguided courtships reveal her damaged states as well. William Mason, another servant, initially loves Daisy, but Daisy is in love with Thomas, who, knowing the trouble that it will cause, encourages Daisy's affections for him to spite William.[53] Daisy's initial disgust at the idea of caring for William arises during her interactions with Mrs. Patmore.

> MRS. PATMORE: Put that in the larder before you go, and never mind your flirting.
> DAISY: I wasn't flirting. Not with *him*.
> *She finds the idea outlandish, which puzzles the cook.*
> MRS. PATMORE: William's not a bad lad.
> DAISY: He's nice enough. But he isn't like Thomas.
> MRS. PATMORE: No. He is *not*.[54]

Daisy only realizes that she loves William while he courts another girl, stalling their relationship, which ends in a brief marriage after he returns from war, terminally ill.[55] However, Daisy's misguided love for men only when they choose to love someone else is, once again, apparent to Ms. Patmore, who points this out to Daisy in Series Six, when Daisy's psychological issues prevent her from loving Andy. As Thomas departs for his new job, Daisy does, though, begin to reflect on her preferences.

> DAISY: Strange, to think I was soft on him once.
> MRS. PATMORE: Well, you were never much of a judge in that department.[56]

In addition to these misperceptions, Daisy's psychological issues are not limited to romances. At William's death, she becomes heir to William's father, and the pair begin a friendship that lasts throughout the series.

Lastly, and most dramatically, Thomas has a definite, psychologically damaged phase.

Being attracted to men in a world where same-sex relationships are taboo weighs upon his mental wellbeing. Thomas' repeated failures at relationships, coupled with the reality that he will soon lose his job at Downton due to the downsizing of aristocratic households, results in a suicide attempt. His recovery, and the hiding of what happened from the bulk of the servants by Anna, Mrs. Hughes (Carson), Miss Baxter, and Andy, give Thomas time to consider his life and why he has made such choices. Anna especially incites this self-evaluation when she recommends: "Why not use the time to try and understand what brought you so low?"[57] Thus, from this damaged phase, Thomas attempts to recover a life for himself that will not destroy him.

The Romantic Phase

The reality is that not every courtship that occurs in the series survives into the romantic phase. Branson and Miss Bunting no longer see each other; Edith never consummates her affection for Strallan and loses Gregson after a brief intimacy. However, most of the *Downton* relationships reach a point where the partners *are* happy and the toils that they endured during their damaged phases vanish far behind them.

Mary does marry Matthew in the early part of the series, even with the apparent blessing of Lavinia's spirit through a planchette board.[58] They spend a few happy years together and have a son, George, who can inherit the estate and the earldom. Mary also overcomes her fear of an automotive death for Henry Talbot, who assists in this decision by giving up racing and opening a car shop with Branson. At the end of Series Six, Mary, not wanting to steal Edith's happy moment, announces quietly that she and Talbot will be having a child together.

Branson does marry Sybil, and their time together, until her tragic death, is quite happy. Branson spends several years with the Crawley family, keeping his daughter, Sybil, close them. However, he briefly moves to the United States, giving himself time to understand his main goals in life. Eventually, he returns with young Sybil, reconnecting with *his* family and his position as a caretaker of Downton. He has no foreseeable romantic relationships, but he is extremely happy. His partnership in the automotive shop with Henry Talbot also predicts that he will be productive and amenable to the right relationship should the moment arise, leaving behind his past fears about society and status that he once shared with Lady Sybil.

Edith finally finds an enduring love. Mary helps her begin a reconciliation with Bertie, and with the courage that she lacked before, Edith tells her future mother-in-law the truth about Marigold. In return, Mrs. Pelham renegotiates her image with the Crawley family and her son:

> MRS. PELHAM: I'm afraid, that is a reflection on me.
> ROBERT: Oh, no, not at all.
> EDITH: I hope you won't regret it.
> MRS. PELHAM: Should I turn down a daughter-in-law who, in addition to having birth and brains, is entirely and unimpeachably honest?
> CORA: I have been waiting for someone to work that out.[59]

With this honesty with herself and others, Edith forgets her anger and reconciles with Mary, leading her to a position as Marchioness and the security in love about which she had always dreamed but never seemed to be able to reach.

Anna and Mr. Bates succeed in finding love and family. Their movement from their damaged states begins slowly due to their trials with the law, but the key moment, which allows Bates to have a positive view of himself, occurs when Mrs. Hughes learns about the apparatus on Bates' leg and encourages him to throw it into the water.

MRS. HUGHES: Do you think we ought to say a few words?
BATES: What? Good riddance?
MRS. HUGHES: That and your promise.
BATES: Very well. I promise I will never again try to cure myself. I will spend my life happily as the butt of others' jokes and I will never mind them.
MRS. HUGHES: We all carry scars, Mr. Bates, inside or out, and we must all put up with them as best we can. You're no different to the rest of us. Remember that.
BATES: I will try to. That I do promise.[60]

Once Mr. Bates is cleared of murder charges, as is Anna, their focus settles on starting a family. Mary, who sees herself in Anna's struggle to get pregnant, for Mary had trouble conceiving a child with Matthew until she visited a London doctor, brings Anna to the same facility. At the end of the series, Anna gives birth in Mary's bedroom, and the future of the Bates family, as well as that of the Crawley family, seems optimistic.

Rose and Atticus, whose storyline moves off-screen for a time after their marriage, are nevertheless happy after their personal trials. They live for a time in the United States, and they have a daughter. Before the close of the series, they visit Downton and joyfully celebrate the good fortune of their family.

Even Isobel's damaged relationship with Lord Merton changes when he is diagnosed with pernicious anemia. Isobel perceives this terminal illness as an acute reminder of her lost time with him, and she rekindles their relationship. Yet Larry Grey is not quite finished with his intervention in the relationship. When the selfish interests of Larry and his new wife try to force Merton to remain with them, both the Dowager Countess, Violet Crawley, and Isobel intervene. Isobel and Merton marry, expecting the worst, but Dr. Clarkson's bid to get a second opinion discovers that the anemia is not terminal. Thus, Isobel and Merton get their happy ending after great physical and emotional struggles.

Mrs. Hughes and Mr. Carson manage to overcome their uncertainties. Carson expects a full marriage, and he loves Mrs. Hughes despite her age. Carson also allows the wedding to occur at the schoolhouse, just as Mrs. Hughes wanted. In addition, Mrs. Hughes and Mrs. Patmore resolve the dinner issue; Mrs. Hughes fakes a hand injury and forces Carson to cook dinner. He then learns how difficult it is and how the world does not fall apart if a dish is over or undercooked.

Most problematic is Thomas' happy ending. Since homosexual relationships are still not condoned by post–Edwardian and post-war society, Thomas cannot marry like the other characters. Even the open-mindedness of the show's creators cannot alter the biases of history. Yet the writers are keenly aware, as are the viewers, that Thomas does have another love, an affection that has been threatened and damaged during the entire series; Thomas loves his participation at Downton, and he dreams of rising to the highest position, that of butler. When Mr. Carson becomes ill and too physically unstable to continue his leading role, Thomas is appointed to replace him.

Thomas, who is working at another house, eagerly accepts Robert Crawley's offer, and his dreams are finally realized. In fact, his departure from Downton is not celebrated even though, in some situations, he serves as the antagonist to the other characters. Mrs. Patmore comments, "I don't know if you're a good thing or a bad thing, Mr. Barrow, but we've all been together a long time."[61] This acceptance of Thomas and all facets of his character is very important to his future. Even though Thomas' ending remains problematic within the context, because the contemporary viewing audience is more accepting of same-sex relationships, it is clear that the Crawley family shows some enlightenment despite the constraints of the time period. Members of the staff and household are aware of Thomas' sexuality, but these feelings, in the end, do not prohibit him from gaining the very status that he has always wanted. Thomas does not have a human partner, but he still has a happy ending because he remains integral to Downton with the hope that society will become more tolerant, just as his Downton family has become over time.

In addition, Thomas *does* have more friends at the end of the series than he did at the beginning, countering the notion that his damaged phase produced no human bonds. Thomas becomes friends with Andy after he teaches Andy to read; Thomas feels gratitude and respect toward Anna, Miss Baxter, and Mrs. Hughes, who helped him recover after his suicide attempt; Thomas also feels a sense of self-maturation, of which he is proud, when he comments, "I arrived here as a boy, I leave as a man."[62] Thomas, therefore, remains a challenge to the archetype provided by Mary. He reimagines it in a manner that makes him a possible archetype for future homosexual characters while still adhering to the necessity to progress through the damaged/romantic phases.

From the positive and negative romantic experiences of the characters in the *Downton Abbey* series, it is clear that every relationship not already established by marriage follows the archetype established by Lady Mary Crawley and Kemal Pamuk. Relationships begin with a damaged phase, whether physical, emotional, or both, and progress to the romantic phase, during which the characters receive their happy endings. Even though some aspects of the archetype are problematic, especially for Thomas, the progression of the damaged/romantic stages leaves the possibility for adaptation depending on the nature of the character's personality difference with Mary's. Overall, the conclusion of the *Downton* series is happy, and even if sadness lingers for certain characters, the words of Kemal Pamuk still echo across their storylines; "[s]ometimes we must endure a little pain in order to achieve satisfaction," and this notion promises that even though the series has ended, the opportunity for certain pains to transform from the damaged into the romantic remains a real probability.[63]

NOTES

1. Julian Fellowes, *Downton Abbey: The Complete Scripts—Season One* (New York: William Morrow, 2012), 158.
2. Jacky Hyams, *The Real Life Downton Abbey* (London: John Blake, 2011), x.
3. "Edwardian Britain," *Information Britain*, accessed April 25, 2016, http://www.information-britain.co.uk/historydetails/article/24/.
4. *Ibid.*
5. *Downton Abbey: Series Six*, 2016.
6. *Downton Abbey: Series One*, 2011.
7. *Downton Abbey: Series Five*, 2015.
8. Hyams, *Real Life*, xiii.
9. "The Edwardian Era," *Edwardian Promenade*, accessed April 25, 2016, http://www.edwardianpromenade.com/the-edwardian-era/
10. Frances Osborne, "Sex in the *Downton Abbey* Era," *The Huffington Post*, accessed April 25, 2016, http://www.huffingtonpost.com/frances-osborne/sex_b_1597879.html.
11. "The Edwardian Era."
12. Osborne, "Sex in the *Downton*," 2–3.
13. *Ibid.*, 1.
14. *Downton Abbey: Series Two*, 2012.
15. Osborne, "Sex in the *Downton*," 1.

16. *Ibid.*, 2.
17. "Edwardian Britain," 2.
18. *Ibid.*, 3.
19. Fellowes, *Scripts—Series One*, 149–150.
20. *Ibid.*, 151.
21. *Ibid.*, 161.
22. *Ibid.*, 165.
23. *Ibid.*, 23.
24. *Ibid.*, 39.
25. Hyams, *Real Life*, xi.
26. Fellowes, *Scripts—Series One*, 38.
27. *Ibid.*, 145.
28. *Ibid.*, 103.
29. *Downton Abbey: Series Two.*
30. *Downton Abbey: Series Six.*
31. *Downton Abbey: Series Four.*
32. Julian Fellowes, *Downton Abbey: The Complete Scripts—Series Two* (New York: William Morrow, 2013), 203.
33. Fellowes, *Scripts—Series Two*, 228.
34. *Downton Abbey: Series Five.*
35. Hyams, *Real Life*, xii.
36. *Downton Abbey: Series Five.*
37. Fellowes, *Scripts—Series One*, 156.
38. *Ibid.*, 67.
39. *Downton Abbey: Series Five.*
40. *Ibid.*
41. *Downton Abbey: Series Four.*
42. Fellowes, *Scripts—Series One*, 337.
43. *Downton Abbey: Series Two.*
44. Fellowes, *Scripts—Series Two*, 65.
45. *Downton Abbey: Series Five.*
46. Hyams, *Real Life*, xii.
47. Fellowes, *Scripts—Series One*, 146.
48. *Ibid.*, 278.
49. *Downton Abbey: Series Four.*
50. Fellowes, *Scripts—Series One*, 238.
51. *Downton Abbey: Series Six.*
52. *Ibid.*
53. Fellowes, *Scripts—Series One*, 202.
54. *Ibid.*, 129.
55. *Downton Abbey: Series Two.*
56. *Downton Abbey: Series Six.*
57. *Ibid.*
58. Fellowes, *Scripts—Series Two*, 579.
59. *Downton Abbey: Series Six.*
60. Fellowes, *Scripts—Series One*, 184.
61. *Downton Abbey: Series Six.*
62. *Ibid.*
63. Fellowes, *Scripts—Series One*, 158.

Works Cited

Downtown Abbey: Series 1. Creator Julian Fellowes. Perf. Hugh Bonneville, Maggie Smith, Michelle Dockery. PBS, 2011. Film.
Downtown Abbey: Series 2. Creator Julian Fellowes. Perf. Hugh Bonneville, Maggie Smith, Michelle Dockery. PBS, 2012. Film.
Downtown Abbey: Series 3. Creator Julian Fellowes. Perf. Hugh Bonneville, Maggie Smith, Michelle Dockery. PBS, 2013. Film.
Downtown Abbey: Series 4. Creator Julian Fellowes. Perf. Hugh Bonneville, Maggie Smith, Michelle Dockery. PBS, 2014. Film.
Downtown Abbey: Series 5. Creator Julian Fellowes. Perf. Hugh Bonneville, Maggie Smith, Michelle Dockery. PBS, 2015. Film.

Downtown Abbey: Series 6. Creator Julian Fellowes. Perf. Hugh Bonneville, Maggie Smith, Michelle Dockery. PBS, 2016. Film.

"Edwardian Britain." *Information Britain.* 2012. Web. 25 April 2016. http://www.information-britain.co.uk/historydetails/article/24/.

"The Edwardian Era." *Edwardian Promenade.* 2016. Web. 25 April 2016. http://www.edwardianpromenade.com/the-edwardian-era/.

Fellowes, Julian. *Downton Abbey: The Complete Scripts—Series One.* New York: William Morrow, 2012. Print.

Fellowes, Julian. *Downton Abbey: The Complete Scripts—Series Two.* New York: William Morrow, 2013. Print.

Hyams, Jacky. *The Real Life Downton Abbey.* London: John Blake, 2011. Print.

Osborne, Frances. "Sex in the *Downton Abbey* Era." *Huffington Post.* 14 June 2016. Web. 25 April 2016. http://www.huffingtonpost.com/frances-osborne/sex_b_1597879.html.

Lady Sybil Must Die

Class and Gender Constraints

MARY RUTH MAROTTE

For fans of *Downton Abbey,* the death of Lady Sybil Crawley Branson was akin to the shot heard round the world. A favorite of viewers far and wide, Lady Sybil, the beautiful and youngest Crawley, was the one on whom many had pinned their hopes to enact change in the arenas of class and gender. Sybil shows herself in Series One to be poised to champion various causes, and her disposition—empathetic and determined—seems to strike the right note with all those with whom she interacts. Her loveliness belies a tough motivation that many underestimate. Sybil's death is interesting to consider, both for the symbolic meaning of the loss of this particular character—a character who seems to fuse so many worlds and worldviews—and for the way that her character is killed off, in childbirth. Sybil's awakening in Series One and Two as to how her body has not been her own but rather a manipulated and commodified object inspires in her a rejection of the social mores and codes of her era. This rejection ultimately lays the groundwork for the bond she forges with Tom Branson, the Irish Socialist who becomes her husband. Their relationship inaugurates a reconsideration of narratives of nobility, even inspiring Sybil's grandmother, the Dowager Countess, to reexamine what it means to be "aristocratic." The chain of events that lead to Sybil's untimely death just after she gives birth to her daughter evidences the palpable threat Sybil poses in the ways that she has destabilized what many consider the natural order.

Unlike so many around her who are bound to a system that constrains and constricts them, Sybil has no allegiance to a system that privileges few at the expense of many. In short, she is a socialist even before her interactions with Branson, before she really understands the meaning of the term. Sybil's intuition guides her, and this intuition endorses a system in which everyone should be allowed to express themselves as they see fit and move towards opportunities that will allow them room to grow and to develop a sense of individuality. Certainly, though, this perspective is not one that is shared by many within the walls of Downton Abbey, a place where there is a clear delineation between how one lives "upstairs" and how one lives "downstairs." Of course, many of the characters' most profound relationships are those that transgress the boundaries of upstairs/downstairs. The relationships between Carson and Mary, O'Brien and Cora, and Mr. Bates and Lord Grantham are all rich and complicated, with the characters interacting in significant ways, confiding in one another, seeking solace in one another, and exposing vulnerabilities that remain concealed even to family members.

While these relationships are significant, none is explicitly romantic or poses any real threat to the social order quite like the union of Lady Sybil Crawley and Tom Branson. Lady Sybil, with her burgeoning ideas about social justice and her distaste for class distinction, is an arbiter of change in the series. Her decision to marry Branson, the chauffeur, is one that wreaks havoc on the household. Such a bold decision not only repudiates deeply entrenched social mores and codes but also revises society's notions as to the appropriate use of the female body. Michel Foucault argues in *Discipline and Punish*, that "the body is directly involved in a political field; power relations have an immediate hold upon it; they invest it, mark it, train it, torture it, force it to carry out tasks, to perform ceremonies, to emit signs" (549). Like nearly every woman with whom she shares company, Lady Sybil's body has been disciplined thus in the society she inhabits. Like most young women of her day born into aristocratic society, she experiences viscerally the juxtaposition of extreme privilege and profound limitation. A lady's maid tends to her every need and helps her in and out of her clothes. She lives in stately Downtown Abby, dines on the finest food, drinks the finest wine, and lives a life that differs drastically from the life of a parlor maid. Nevertheless, Sybil shares many of the restrictions and concerns of the women who live and toil downstairs. After all, she exists in an environment that does not encourage any attempts to assert her own opinions and desires; and many, like her father Lord Grantham, find a lady speaking her mind to be falling outside the parameters of acceptable notions of femininity. What's more, she cannot cast a vote of her own. All told, what Sybil must work against in her pursuit of social change—both in terms of class and gender—is considerable. As Susan Bordo observes, "Our bodies ... are constituted by culture," and Bordo explores in her work, more specifically, how women's bodies have been inscripted and coded throughout the centuries and the damaging results therein (52).

Cultural inscription of this kind is evident in *Downton Abbey* and finds interesting resonance in the clothing that Sybil and the other women wear. Custom and tradition collapse into clothing in 1:1 when the women must wear black in mourning their cousin, Patrick, heir to Downton, who they believe to have gone down with the *Titanic*. Lady Mary Crawley, the daughter who has been engaged to Patrick, complains of the mourning wear, about the dismal black. While she will comply with the dictates of custom and tradition, she is impatient with her mourning wear not only because of its style and color but because she must wear it out of a show of dedication to the memory of a fiancé whom she did not choose. For the match, we learn, was made only to preserve the family's fortune and to secure the future of Downton Abbey. That Mary must wear clothing that assigns her a false sentiment is unbearable to her and becomes an early indication of the way that clothing works to control a woman's emotional and physical response. Bordo confirms that in the history of fashion, "the social manipulation of the female body emerges as an absolutely central strategy in the maintenance of power relations between the sexes over the last hundred years" (91). Societal impositions on women's clothing, it seems, not only limit their sartorial freedom but extend also into the realm of cultivation of independence and free-will.

These strict parameters exist and work upon the female characters quite handily; for example, for her father's sake, and to save Downton, Mary will marry Matthew, a love-match ultimately but one that started out as anything but. And American heiress

Cora Crawley has, by law, given her entire inheritance toward the maintenance of Downton Abbey, only to see it mismanaged by her husband, as we come to find out in Series Three. Even Lady Edith seems to internalize her lack of beauty so much that she has become ugly in behavior, thwarting others' attempts at happiness because her looks have kept her in the shadows of affection of both of her parents. All of these women are compromised by a society that deems them valuable only for the ways in which they can help further the very patriarchal system that keeps them oppressed. Interesting, then, is Sybil, the youngest of the three Crawley daughters, who seems to dodge society's gaze in significant ways. Sybil, who is both beautiful and kind, emerges in Series One very much a woman aware of the compromised position of her aristocratic body and cognizant of the inequities of her social milieu, and we witness Sybil making calculated moves to resist class and gender restraints. For example, after she has a political discussion on women's voting rights with Preston in 1:4, she demonstrates the independent spirit of her mind by showing up for dinner in harem pants rather than the more appropriate evening gown, to the great horror of her grandmother. Sybil's choice of clothing has been thought-out and intentional; in fact, she has directed the seamstress to design this particular outfit, one that she knows will defy custom and tradition. In wearing these pants, she effectively deconstructs the "clothes" of femininity and any meaning tied to the term, breaking down what she would consider an artificial construct. In donning the harem pants, she reinscribes femininity with power and claims power through mimicry and play by refashioning men's trousers that are cut and styled for women. Her statement is that trousers should be and can be comfortable for women, for women are as capable as men. Though she says little as she enters the room, the camera's panning of the legs of the pants and Sybil's beaming, confident smile speak volumes.

In this moment, Sybil lays claim to a path that will lead her towards transgressive ideas and actions. What is worth noting about Sybil is the ease and confidence with which she enacts her radicalism. Though shocked and uncomfortable at her sartorial choice, her family allows her to continue what they perceive to be childish pranks. But while they are desperately attempting to cling to the last vestiges of an aristocratic way of life that is falling apart, they fail to realize that Sybil's motives and actions are furthering the demise of this life they hold so dear. Through such subversive play, Sybil is able to make dramatic and important statements about class and gender oppression.

Sybil shows a fascination with the burgeoning feminist movement early on in the show's run by listening to Branson's socialist ideology, reading pamphlets about the women's movement, and attending a rally in which liberal candidates speak about various issues—all of which elicits in her sizable guilt about how her position upstairs compromises the lives of those who live downstairs (1:4). While Mary grumbles against early attempts marry her off to the most suitable husband, she ultimately accepts and even embraces her destiny and inheritance of a tradition of hunting, lounging, luxurious living, and constrained and prescribed living. In fact, Mary most keenly resembles her father in her dedication to all the aforementioned traditions. Sybil's resistance, then, through action against the aristocratic "norm" symbolizes the breakdown of several key assumptions about a woman's place in aristocratic society. Indeed, she is the only "upstairs" inhabitant who spends any time "downstairs" understanding those below her as individuals rather than extensions of the people they serve. Sybil recognizes that the maids, footmen, butlers, and kitchen staff are, in fact, oppressed, perhaps because she recognizes the extent of her own oppression in a society that seeks to limit the freedom of women's bodies, whether aristocratic or common. Indeed, while many are shocked and dismayed that Gwen, the parlor maid, has been taking correspondence courses in typewriting to try for secretarial work (as if she could possibly find a better position than as a maid at Downton Abbey!), Sybil is neither shocked nor dismayed but rather bent on assisting Gwen in her pursuit. In fact, she says to Gwen: "Your dream is my dream now. And I'll make it come true" (1:6).

It is fitting, then, that in Sybil's quest to find Gwen employment as a secretary, she must give Gwen her own clothes so that Gwen may present herself as something other than a parlor maid. Sybil realizes perceptively that the overwhelming majority of these young women face a world that frustrates their attempts to carve out a new identity for themselves outside the constraints of class and gender, and understand the power that clothing both has to constrain, or alternately, to revise, societal understanding of class and gender. It is soon after her success in landing Gwen employment (and the coveted social mobility in a society that attempts to squash any notion that such movement is possible, especially for women) that she herself decides to trade in her glamorous frocks for the working habit of a nurse, and in doing so, attempts to revise her own cultural and societal script. In leaving Downton, she makes both a literal and metaphorical move away from the expectations of imposed aristocratic femininity towards establishing her own individuality.

Sybil's choice to become a nurse, then, is one that not only takes her out of the restricted space of Downton Abbey but is also one in which she is able to wear a uniform that authorizes her as more than decorative bauble. Her nurse's habit becomes a costume that forges her new identity. Unlike the mourning black the women must wear in the first episode, clothing that assigns them emotions they may or may not feel, the nursing habit becomes the first step in Sybil claiming a voice for herself outside of the powerful and watchful gaze of Downton Abbey. When she puts on the uniform, she is able to simultaneously erase the signs of her aristocratic birth and demonstrate her effectiveness and usefulness in a society that formerly only commodified her good looks. It is at this point that she begins to feel and to be productive and useful. It is important, then, that she resists returning to Downton, for when she returns home for dinner, she must transform back into a veritable backdrop piece of beauty and elegance, performing the proper turns and phrasings of nobility, a performance she appears to find more and more awkward and unnatural the more she sees of the significant loss and trauma of the war. It is through her transformation into a nurse that she is more clearly able to see the social construction of both class and gender roles, and in understanding the inherent limitations, finds herself wanting out and wanting more. In performing this role, she is able to turn towards more ways to agitate and resist.

The evidence of a breakdown of the aristocratic way of life is never so evident as it is when we see wounded soldiers occupying the stately drawing rooms of Downton Abbey, with Edith even becoming a capable nurse and attendant, finally realizing her own usefulness. It is in Series Two that this transformation takes place, when Sybil and Isobel Crawley work together to persuade Lord and Lady Grantham to turn Downton into a convalescent home for wounded soldiers home from the war. Of course, Sybil's decision to become a nurse is one nurtured by her cousin, Isobel Crawley, a woman quite the anomaly, a character propelled from the middle class to aristocratic heights when her son, Matthew, is named heir to Downton Abbey. In her role as a nurse herself, she has lived more freely (more freely in the sense that she has had to earn an income) than her upper-class female counterparts, enjoying the very sense of usefulness that Sybil desires. Though her ideas always prove helpful and good, her desire to be "of use" is met with eye-rolling derision and scorn by women and men alike, an unfair reaction to a woman who in 1:2 saves a young farmer's life by suggesting a treatment learned and put to use in her days as a nurse. While Sybil advocates social equality and feminine productivity in the bloom of youth and beauty, Isobel attempts similar feats in late middle-age, and it is hard to discern which woman meets with greater condescension. While Sybil's class-crossing love affair with Branson frustrates Lord Grantham's idea of aristocratic propriety, Isobel's mere presence in a room inspires ire. Isobel demonstrates time and again a keen understanding of how she and others might serve their country, the sort of woman Horace Walpole would have likened to a "hyena in petticoats" because she does not "know her place." In Series Three, Isobel even begins to assist and educate women who have turned to prostitution. These attempts to advocate, too, are met with derision, as is her attempt to help Ethel, a former Downton maid who has been punished by the patriarchal establishment in more ways than one: for giving into desire, for having a child out-of-wedlock, for turning to prostitution to feed her child. Isobel, unlike everyone around her but Sybil, it seems, is determined to rewrite various notions about women's bodies. All around her, though, we hear castigations of women like Ethel. And it is Isobel who offers to help her, to recuperate her in her role as a maid, much to the horror of everyone around her. Both those upstairs and downstairs seem to agree that she is beyond recuperation for the ways that she has strayed beyond the parameters of acceptable femininity.

Certainly Isobel, in her activity and busyness, challenges how femininity has been framed in the aristocratic realm. Cora Crawley's quiet passivity, after all, is in stark contrast to Isobel's frank activity. But even as Cora resists Isobel's attempts to assume a position of control, it is Cora who is the most changed by Isobel's presence and ideas. When Downton becomes the convalescent home, it is Cora who becomes decidedly more active once Isobel enters the picture, but it is at the expense of her husband's self-esteem that she does so. Certainly Lord Grantham has a crisis of masculinity during the war, when he is not assigned to active duty but is asked to remain as a sort of figurehead at home to keep up the spirits of the ladies. His feelings of emasculation are furthered when his wife seems to find fulfillment in duties that do not directly involve him. Subsequently, he strays from his marriage, and Cora must return to a state of passivity—indeed a consumptive state—for Lord Grantham to recuperate his sense of purpose. Even though Cora is the one suffering from consumption, she apologizes for her inattentive behavior and promises him that she will rededicate herself to him and the family. Her punishment—with illness—for her attempts to move outside of the realm of acceptable femininity demonstrates just how disciplined her body is within this strict hierarchical society. As Judith Lowder Newton observes, in "Power and the Ideology of 'Woman's Sphere,'" genteel women held a certain power at this period of time, but it is a power particular to their influence, to consider the ways that they should observe good sense and good taste for the betterment of the society as a whole. But, concludes Newton, to venture outside of that sphere, as Cora does in her growing interest in wartime issues, is going to be perceived as to the detriment of society: "Having influence, in fact, having the ability to persuade others to do or to be something that was in their own interest, was made contingent upon the renunciation of such self-advancing forms of power as control or self-definition" (882). In order for Lord Grantham to maintain his position of supremacy, his wife must serve as the looking glass that reflects him as twice his normal size.

While Isobel remains at the periphery, in a sort of liminal state, not firmly entrenched in either the middle class or the aristocratic class, Cora's position as aristocratic lady is more limited. Women like Isobel, therefore, are the ones who must pave the way for women like Sybil to even imagine a life of usefulness, and certainly Sybil must move away from the prescriptions of aristocratic femininity in order not to fall into the same trap as her mother. There are, after all, substantial roadblocks in her journey away from the crippling dictates of gender and class. It is crucial, then, how the uniform of the nurse functions as a shield of sorts against the social coding to which Sybil seems particularly vulnerable. When the war ends and her nursing skills are no longer needed, Sybil must return to her former position, and in donning the clothes of the past, her vulnerability reemerges. It is in this vulnerable state, arguably, that she turns to Branson, the chauffeur.

A union with Branson becomes a way for Sybil to continue to slough off her past and define herself authoritatively. Branson is not of noble blood, but his intentions with regard to the Irish political rebellion are noble, and he never stoops to obsequious behavior in his solicitations of Sybil's affections. Pierre Bourdieu's theories of social placement are useful in analyzing both Sybil's and Branson's characters and the bond they share. Bourdieu argues that any individual is known and knows his place in the world through a certain sort of regulatory behaviors that are not necessarily a codified set of rules but rather a logic governed by the group to which they belong. Through conditioning over and over time, these rules become 'embodied' in one's mental and physical structure (Bourdieu and Wacquant 126–127). Bourdieu's theories of capital are also interesting in an analysis of Branson and Sybil's attraction to him. According to Bourdieu, the most powerful form of capital is symbolic, as it confers the power to name or identify others, to represent common sense and to create official versions of the social world. He realizes early on Sybil is sympathetic to the causes he holds dear, and he engages her by offering up a way that she might assert her voice—by giving her pamphlets on the women's vote. He has cultivated a revolutionary ideology that might erase, or at the very least mitigate, the oppressive limitations of class and seems equally concerned with gender oppression. In his ideology and actions he is the very opposite of the docile body that Carson, the butler of Downton inhabits, one that has internalized his class positioning, a body that Foucault would argue is "bound up … with its economic use" (549). Though Branson's class positioning and his nationality as an Irishman in England doubly subjugate him, he refuses to acknowledge any limitation: "I'm a socialist, not a revolutionary. And I won't always be a chauffeur" (1:4). He continuously serves as a destabilizing force in the house. And while the downstairs contingent thwarts Branson's plan to dump a mixture of oil, cow manure, and sour milk on the visiting British Army General, he constantly keeps those upstairs and downstairs alike fumbling for a semblance of control over his unpredictable movements. He is, in fact, a body that resists the very discipline and control of which Foucault speaks and thus emerges the perfect revolutionary figure because he proves less vulnerable to manipulation. Branson, importantly, is not the only character in the series who questions the privileges that those upstairs enjoy. Originally introduced as the footman of Downton Abbey, Thomas' perceived "evil nature" is associated mostly with his contempt for his employers, but his contempt emerges from an understandable frustration at being continuously overlooked for more prestigious appointments. Characters portrayed as good-hearted and kind are those most dedicated to their assigned roles in society—Carson and Mr. Bates being two examples of downstairs workers who allow their bodies to be subjected to the control of others. While Thomas and Branson share a desire to write themselves into the noble narrative, recognizing how those subservient to the aristocracy are perpetrating their own subjugation by internalizing ideas of themselves as somehow lesser or powerless, Thomas differs from Branson inasmuch as his highest aspiration before the war is to move up to the position of Lord Grantham's valet, the highest station he envisions within a rigid class system. Branson remains the lone revolutionary who oftentimes looks as if he will lose his mind with the downstairs contingent as they bow with effusive politeness to those he views as their oppressors.

Unlike some of the other love matches on the show, ones that stay true to the dictates of class, at least with regard to the established social order—between Mary and Matthew, and between Anna and Mr. Bates, for example—Sybil's and Branson's relationship seems less about romantic love than about a reaction to the imposed rules and regulations of a social order that with the war seem bound to change. What's more, their relationship is not given the same leisurely development onscreen as the other couples.' Separated by nationality and class, the star-crossed quality of such a relationship would seem to offer the necessary tension and drama that would supersede even that of Mary and Matthew. But this union is more pragmatic than passionate, more about revolution than love. Though World War I is the backdrop of the show, especially in Series Two, Branson is our reminder that there has been ideological oppression served up by the English for centuries. His reference to the Easter Rising of 1916 and his cousin's unjust execution, and his fearless voicing of frustrations with the political reality of his day ignite Sybil's simmering rage, for she sees in Preston a way out. While Mary bemoans her fate by telling Matthew that she has no life, that her future has been written for her, Sybil's realization of this is accompanied by action against the inevitability of such a life. Furthermore, she feels a complicity in Preston's subjugation and desires absolution of culpability in a system that appoints certain people as chauffeurs and others as landed aristocrats. Certainly Sybil transgresses boundaries of class by acknowledging him as a possible love interest, but she also transgresses boundaries of gender by asserting her voice in defending her choice of a mate to her father and grandmother. She is loud, angry, and resistant in her pursuit of some sort of approval for her union with Branson, wanting her father and grandmother to acknowledge the union as legitimate and thus deconstruct the discourse of aristocracy. This series certainly has elements of the traditional soap opera, so the viewer would expect that the relationship between Sybil and Branson would be fraught with romantic tension. Interestingly, though, this relationship is fueled not by the couple's passion for one another, but their passion for reform. Any idea that this match is about romance should be quelled when Sybil remarks to Branson that he is her ticket out of a life she finds purposeless and stifling. Branson has a similar interest in marrying Sybil— to reaffirm his strong notion that nobility is socially-constructed, not any essential truth. He desires to insert his Irish revolutionary spirit into Sybil's English aristocratic family line. It is political—together they will revise a system they deem faulty and oppressive. If their union is less about romance than revolution, it becomes clearer why this relationship is more of a threat to notions of nobility and aristocracy—this union is all about explosive potential for change. Preston continuously verbalizes that he is worthy of Sybil's affection and is completely unapologetic in his pursuit of her as his wife. For, to him, barriers of class are not in any way essential, but rather constructions of the mind implemented by the dominant class for effective discipline and control of the commoners, a way of maintaining the upstairs/downstairs dynamic.

When they are given their family's (reluctant) blessing in 2:6, the ensuing conversation between Lord Grantham and the Dowager Countess speaks to the social construction of aristocracy. As the episode draws to a close, the Dowager Countess searches for a way to come to terms with a marriage that seems inevitable, referring to some remote "Bransons" down the line who might be tied to the aristocracy. This bit of dialogue is offered mostly for comedic effect, but this conversation evidences how craftily the discourse of nobility is constructed, how language is used to embolden some and deny others. What is evident also in this exchange is how immoveable the aristocracy will be in the face of inevitable change. Instead of accepting Branson as the Irish Socialist with whom their daughter has fallen in love, they attempt to connect him somehow to themselves, thus denying his history and struggle.

During Sybil's pregnancy the viewer is able to see the limitations placed on the female body, especially an aristocratic body that has been "contaminated" by her association with Branson, a man who encourages her attempts to mobilize efforts to thwart British control of Ireland, a man who encourages her to use her voice for change. Nevertheless, we do not glimpse fully the extent of these limitations until the childbirth episode when her body becomes the sight of male contestation of power. Lord Grantham greets the news of Sybil's pregnancy with a powerfully negative response; he feels that his noble line will now be compromised by Branson's lineage. With the birth of Sybil's and Branson's child, there will no longer be a consistent narrative of nobility—the child she carries signifies the birth of a new narrative, and we see this poignantly after Sybil's death, with Branson asserting his control over the direction that the new young Sybil's life will take. With the union of Sybil and Branson, we witness the emergence of meritocracy and begin to see fissures in a system that marginalizes so many and ennobles so few. The relationship, then, portends the breakdown of the upstairs/downstairs binary. Though Lord Grantham finally gives his blessing, there is little doubt that he still disapproves of the marriage, as we learn that he has not attended the wedding nor does he want to meet the child who is to come from this union. Nevertheless, his wife and daughters subvert his desires and bring Sybil back to Downton for the duration of her pregnancy, a pregnancy that ends in her death.

Sybil's birthing experience and subsequent death evidence the degree to which her voice is silenced by those who assume control over her body, a body she has strived to maintain control over. Certainly the time spent at Downton has had quite an effect on Branson. Matthew's overtures of friendship and solidarity have weakened Branson's resistance, literally and figuratively speaking, and Branson becomes temporarily convinced that this family has allowed him into their sphere. Sybil, too, is glad to be home and in the company of the family she loves. Away from their political responsibilities abroad, their resistance weakens, it seems, and they become vulnerable again to those who earlier in the series have had control over their decisions and movements. When Sybil goes into labor, her body is literally wrenched from her and her husband's control and a sinister and oppressive force in the form of the "specialist" invades the birthing room.

The contentiousness with which Dr. Clarkson and Sir Philip Tapsell, the specialist brought in by Lord Grantham, bicker over the appropriate course of action when Sybil exhibits strange symptoms speaks to the distance that they have put between the woman and her experience of childbirth. Faith is not instilled in the viewer when Sir Philip says, bragging about a particularly difficult delivery, that he told the woman: "I'll get the baby out of you one way or another" (3:4). That the country doctor, Clarkson, actually diagnoses eclampsia speaks not to his skill as a doctor necessarily but to his willingness to take all of his knowledge of Sybil as a patient and a person into account in his diagnosis. He sees her not merely as a pregnant patient—one of many in the faceless throng of women to treat—but as Sybil, the woman he has known since she was a child. This knowledge of her allows him to recognize the misdiagnosis of the "specialist," a man who believes that he has control over the birthing room just as he has control over the typical woman of the age. After all, the way he sees it, Sybil is a healthy young woman who has shown no signs of a high-risk pregnancy, so there is no cause for concern. But Sybil, as if making a statement about the individuality of a woman's response to pregnancy and childbirth, defies easy categorization, which proves deadly. The focus of this episode is on the men who have wrestled the decisions away from the woman experiencing childbirth, and this is done ostensibly to emphasize the lack of control women had over their bodies. Though she has fought to maintain control of her body and her life, ultimately it is Lord Grantham and Sir Philip who determine her fate. They jockey for position, seemingly more concerned with losing credibility than they are about saving Sybil's life. Lord Grantham's power has waned significantly during the war, and he seizes this opportunity as one in which he can reclaim a sense of control. After all, there is evidence aplenty that his masculinity is in jeopardy, first in his inability to serve in the war and in his mismanagement of the finances at Downton Abbey. Through control of Sybil's body he seeks to reestablish his place at the helm of the house. What happens, though, is that he and the specialist are wrong—and the repercussions of their arrogance mean death for Sybil.

Sybil must die, of course. Sybil, the stealth reformer who joins her life to a cause, who intuitively resists categorization and classification, who seeks to alter the discourse of nobility, and who joins herself to Branson as gesture of protest against this discourse. The overwhelming response to Sybil's death—both on-screen and off, though, suggests the power that she had as a revolutionary and reformer. And with the birth of her daughter, another Sybil, we witness the power that she had in her quiet optimism, an optimism that seeks not only to disrupt but to breakdown the binary of upstairs/downstairs forever.

Works Cited

Bordo, Susan. "Unbearable Weight: Feminism, Western Culture, and the Body." *Feminist Literary Theory and Criticism*. Eds. Sandra Gilbert and Susan Gubar. New York: Norton, 2007.

Bourdieu, Pierre, and Loïc J.D. Wacquant. An Invitation to Reflexive Sociology. Chicago: University of Chicago Press, 1992.

Foucault, Michel. *Discipline and Punish*. New York: Vintage, 1995.

Newton, Judith Lowder. "Power and the Ideology of 'Woman's Sphere.'" *Feminisms*. Eds. Robin R. Warhol and Diane Price Herndl. New Brunswick: Rutgers University Press, 1997.

"We are allies, my dear"

Defining British and American National Identity

Melissa Wehler

In one of the first scenes from *Downton Abbey*, the viewer is introduced to the two matriarchs of the Crawley family, the Right Honorable Violet Crawley, Dowager Countess of Grantham, and the Right Honorable Lady Cora Crawley, Countess of Grantham, who despite their difference of opinions and positions are forming an alliance to save Cora's entail from an unknown cousin and heir-apparent. Cora greets the agreed upon cease-fire as a hopeful sign for the future of their relationship: Cora asks, "Are we to be friends, then?" to which Violet answers, "We are allies, my dear, which can be a good deal more effective" (1:1). Violet's use of the word "allies" in her diplomatic dealings with her American daughter-in-law foreshadow the inevitable onslaught of World War I where the relatively nascent alliance between Great Britain and the United States would face its most serious test. Violet's alliance with Cora, based on mutual personal interests, demonstrates the not only the alliance between the two countesses but also the increasing alliance between Great Britain and the United States in the years before the Great War and forefronts issues about defining national identities in an increasingly globally-defined world.

Set amidst the historical, cultural, and political upheaval of World War I, *Downton Abbey* showcases individual and national struggles to define and redefine British and American national identities in the early twentieth century. While the entire cast of characters represents the struggle with the changing social landscape, the dueling Countesses of Grantham offer viewers an interesting microcosm of the "special" relationship between America and Britain. The relationship between Violet and Cora, drawn along historical, social, and political lines, offers the most concrete vision for the imminent future of British and American relations and identities, and in doing so, offers American and British viewers alike a unique perspective on nationalist identities both past and present. In examining the historically defined dynamic between these two powerful, female protagonists, we can better understand how and why this British television series has found its own powerful allies in the American viewing public.

Making Friends: Downton Abbey
and the Anglo-American "Special" Relationship

Beginning in April 1912, the *Downton Abbey* series is historically situated in the years known as the First or Great Rapprochement.[1] Rapprochement, a word meaning "a coming or bringing together," generally refers to the relationship between two nations while The Great Rapprochement specifically refers to a period of social, diplomatic, and political unity between Great Britain and the United States that began in the late nineteenth century.[2] While there were many factors influencing the rapprochement of these two nations including their common language, history, and culture, the conclusion of the Civil War at the end of the nineteenth century laid the groundwork for what would be called the "special relationship" between Great Britain and its former colony.[3] First, the conclusion of the Civil War gave the United States some military, political, and social stability, and the Union victory—with its abolitionist underpinning—meant that the policies of the two nations were also moving in the same direction. The conclusion of the Civil War also brought about increased travel between the two nations and opened up an exchange of goods, ideas, and people.

As the diplomatic relationship between the United States and Great Britain strengthened after the Civil War, contact between English and American women necessarily increased, resulting in a unique cross-cultural conversation about women and by women.[4] After the Civil War, American women began to travel to Great Britain and the European Continent with much more ease than had heretofore been possible. This was so much the case that Blanche McManus, an American travel writer, writing in 1911, declared, "The American woman needs no introduction abroad," and "All that Europe has to offer is hers on call, so long as she radiates that graciousness and appreciation which everywhere distinguishes her" (v). For McManus, the American woman is "gracious" and "appreciative," and these two qualities not only set her apart from her European counterparts, but they also make her welcomed and distinguished in her European travels. The implied differences between American women and European women—and by extension, American and European society—allude to how American women's travel writing often focused on differences and similarities between herself and her Old World counterparts.

American women were also interested in the differences between them and their British cousins. While on their travels, American women were often fascinated by, and more than a little critical of, the labor women undertook in the "Old World."[5] Lucy Bronson Dudley bluntly describes the situation of many women in 1895: "I have discovered in the old world three new beasts of burden,—women, cows, and dogs" (96). Certainly, what Dudley describes here is not only a gender issue, but a class issue as well. As an American woman travelling aboard, Dudley would have had more income at her disposal than any of the women she saw working the fields from her train car. Yet, despite Dudley's own class status, her ire here is focused on a society where women and women's work can be categorized alongside "cows and dogs." Dudley's frustrated, critical tone demonstrates another important facet of women's transatlantic travel: the ability to understand, critique, and possibly empathize with the position of women in England, Europe, and beyond.

In addition to how women were treated in the Old and New Worlds, the differences between American and European society also focused on the subtle yet distinctive differences between the manners and customs of the women themselves. McManus, for instance, discusses the differences in women's travel in 1911:

> [The Englishwoman] is in quite a different class from the restless-minded American who no sooner gets to a place than she wants to know "what there is to do." This phase does not bother the Englishwoman. To tell the truth, she has a clearer idea of what it is that she wants. She is either sketching in water colours, learning a language or busy occupying herself by studying the people, their literature or their mode of life [154].

Notably, these differences reside not in the particulars of the women themselves, but in the society in which these women live. It is not that American women are incapable of the kind of artistic acculturation that McManus describes, but rather European women seem more accustomed to this type of travel and entertainment. The American women, as relative newcomers to the European tour, want for "something to do" in a place that appears to them quite foreign. Thus, despite the claim that the Englishwoman "is in quite a different class from the restless-minded American," the differences drawn between American and English women appear to be distinctions of nationality and customs rather than anything particularly innate to the women themselves. Of course, the internalization of these national differences and how they are used to draw unwelcomed and unflattering distinctions between women is certainly at work in *Downton Abbey* as the two countesses vie not only for control over the household, but power within its micro-political hierarchy.

Like their American counterparts, British women were likewise fascinated by their travel to the States. Lady Jane Wilde, for instance, wrote around the turn of the century, "The first question propounded to a traveler on returning from a transatlantic tour is usually, 'What is your opinion of American women?' for, in truth, the American woman is by far the most important element in the social machinery of the States" (123). As part of the social "machinery," Wilde's description of American women in her essay entitled "American Women" is certainly a marked contrast to Dudley's account of European women being akin to "cows and dogs." Wilde's claim about women being imperative to the "machinery" of the States provides some insight not only about how American women were perceived by Englishwomen, but also about how Englishwomen perceived themselves. Wilde's assertion that American women are "by far the most important element" of American society casts a certain light on the authoress' own position within the British "machinery." Her implied criticism is that Englishwomen do not hold the same pride of place as do their American counterparts, and in praising the position of these women, she also suggests a possible model for Englishwomen who wish to be more substantive part of the British "machinery." A polemist and activist herself, Wilde's use of the word "machinery," suggests a political application and slyly argues that American women have the potential for political importance and persuasion that might be modeled by British women like herself. Wilde's insight into the politicized nature of the American woman will be of particular importance when applied to the two Countesses of Grantham and the power struggle over Cora's entailment. Wilde's comments, not unlike McManus or Dudley, demonstrate a keen awareness of the national difference between American and British women, and help to understand how transatlantic travel brought about an unprecedented discussion about the roles women play in the various machinery of their social spheres.

While the exchange of travelers contributed to a sense of shared cultural norms among the British and the Americans, their increased exposure to the world on the other side of the Atlantic also exposed implicit assumptions about the two nations and their peoples. For instance, an individual's reason for travelling across the Atlantic, according to historian Kathleen Burk depended on their national affiliation: "the British went to the United States as to a foreign land, in a spirit of adventure. Many Americans ventured to Britain in a spirit of pilgrimage, particularly an historical and literary pilgrimage, in a conscious return home" (300). Women's travel writing from the period certainly supports Burk's claim.[6] Writing in 1891, American Elizabeth Bisland describes, "Like the English sea, the English land swarms with phantoms—the folk of history, of romance, of poetry and fiction. They troop along the roads, prick across the fields, look over the hedges, and peer from every window" (195). Ella W. Thompson, writing around the turn-of-the-century, describes how American women "cast longing eyes at the door marked with the magical word 'Europe,' and it has opened freely enough when the husband said the 'Open, sesame'; it is only of late years that women have made the amazing discovery that they can say it themselves with like success" (10). For British travelers, America was a foreign, exotic, and wild with a landscape as untamable as its irascible inhabitants. For American travelers, Britain was a cultured, educated, and urban world where history, decorum, and progress reigned. In other words, America was Britain's exotic other, and Britain was America's cultural ideal.

Of course, such descriptions of the two nations suggest an implicit hierarchy drawn, interestingly, along what is usually considered nationalist lines: Britain is fashioned as the "us" to America's "them." While the "us versus them" rhetoric is usually reserved for nationalist and patriotic purposes, we see the authors of the travel writings themselves adopting positions as "others" and fashioning their self-portraits around this same understanding. McManus, for instance, views Englishwomen "in quite a different class" from Americans, it is by the British standard that American women, including herself, should be viewed and judged. Bisland and Thompson, moreover, see Europe as a "magical" world that is both different and more appealing than their own. Dudley certainly does not admire the way women are used as "beasts of burden," but even she is compelled to go to "the home of Shakespeare" where "all good Americans go" (55). Even Wilde who uses the American woman as a yardstick for the progress of British women does so in an effort to point out the British are falling behind their American counterparts in terms of progressive attitudes and politics when they should be many years ahead. Thus, while these authors can barely be considered a survey of women travellers working and writing during period of the Great Rapprochement, their words do speak to the attitudes and implicit prejudices held and shared by women on either side of the Atlantic. The attitude expressed in these writings, moreover, sheds light on how the "special" relationship between American and Britain was formed in part by these prejudices.

The implicit hierarchy between these two discourses, and indeed, much of inequality of America's relationship to Britain, can be traced to their colonial relationship and the particularly paternal language used to demarcate their roles and positions within this hierarchy.[7] Despite the rejection of this linguistic paradigm by the American Revolutionists, much of this parental hierarchy was still in place well into the nineteenth century.[8] Englishwomen were certainly not immune to this kind of parental inequity. Writing in 1922, Jane Louise Mesick describes nineteenth-century American women as "pale to eyes accustomed to look upon English roses," and much the same way a parent scolds a wayward child, she takes American women to task for their penchant for sweets and their subsequently poor dental hygiene; their inappropriately "flimsy" winter wardrobe; their "moral and intellectual degradation" through novel reading; and their physical modesty which renders them indistinguishable from prostitutes on the street (88–95). While Mesick certainly occupies an extreme example of how these cultural biases played themselves out in the perceptions of ordinary women, her insights do suggest an inherent predisposition for British sensibilities as she largely reiterates the same intangible hierarchies as Burk, Bisland, and Thompson employ in their writings. This perception of cultural superiority tinctured Anglo-American relationships, and becomes especially important in the way transatlantic marriages were viewed on both sides of the ocean.

The perception of cultural superiority tinctured Anglo-American relationships, especially when it involved transatlantic marriages. British partiality of their culture and society along with assumptions these travelers made about their destinations helps to explain their reaction to these marital transactions. Transatlantic marriages were an influential factor in the Great Rapprochement because such marriages helped to strengthen the underlying social, political, and historical ties between the two nations. The intermarriage of American elite with the British aristocracy meant that the period's movers and shakers were more than just business partners—they were in-laws. The intermarriage of these social elite meant that British and American politics were being drawn ever closer into alignment, setting the stage for what would become the great alliance between these two countries in World War I.

Throughout the 1880s and 1890s, British peers actively sought out American heiresses, and the period witnessed a rapid increase in transatlantic marriages.[9] Such marriages were popularly viewed as a kind of financial and social exchange between the two related nations. Writing around the turn of the century, Lady Randolph Nevill describes how such marriages "revivified" the British peerages in both "mind and pocket" and declared, "by the American girl we have been conquered" (33). With the "conquering" American girl came a deep and lasting impression that such marriages were, as Nevill begins her description, financially and socially "prudent" (33). Such a perception was only further reinforced by the gossip and scandal surrounding several of these high profile and seemingly loveless marriages.[10] Even if the reality of these marriages were far different from this perception, for the average Edwardian, these British-American marriages were seen as a kind of "gilded" prostitution. While many American wives reveled in their newfound social circles, others felt the acute pang of distance, exile, and otherness that comes with being a foreigner. For instance, despite her seemingly happy marriage to the Viceroy of India, Mary Cruzon, Baroness Curzon of Kedleston, declared, "50 years in a new country never alters your nationality and I shall never be an Englishwoman in feeling or character" (qtd. in Thomas 294). The Baroness, beloved and admired both in England and India, struggled to find her place in the rigid British hierarchy, finding, as many American women did, a very different way of life than the one they were accustomed.

Transatlantic marriages not only affected the financial and social climates of the Old and New Worlds, but they also influenced the politics and political goals of the two nations. While it would be impossible to parse out how exactly American wives influenced their British husbands' political views, it would be equally impossible not to suggest that these British-American marriages created a kind of cross-pollination between British and American diplomacy. Taking on this very issue, Richard Davis discusses the "pro–American" stance of several high-profile British peers who married American heiresses, and how these wives who "were accomplished political hostesses, all took a keen and well-informed interest in politics on both sides of the Atlantic, and all were their husband's political confidantes" (174).[11] The effect of American women in British politics, and the roles of transatlantic marriages in the British-American relationship at the beginning of the last century provides a unique framework for understanding the often complicated and conflicting relationship between the two female protagonists, Cora, Lady Grantham and Violet, the Dowager Countess. By tracing their relationship from its beginning in 1888 when Robert Crawley, Lord Grantham, and Cora wed to the alliance struck between Cora and Violet following the *Titanic* disaster in 1912, we will see how the changes taking place between the two women mirror the larger alliance of the Great Rapprochement and the inevitable pressure of testing that alliance in wartime.

Friends or Allies? War Comes to Downton Abbey

From the first frenzied moments of *Downton Abbey*, viewers are plunged into a world on the brink of collapse, and the show's creators seem intent on deconstructing the apparent isolationalism that has heretofore defined the Crawley family. Symbolized by the Abbey itself, viewers are left to reason that the walls of Downton have historically been used to not only keep the modern world at bay, but also to protect the sanctity of history. By the time the series begins in 1912, modernity, with its underlying drive towards globalization, has already forced its way into the Downton world in the guise of Thomas Edison's electric lights, Henry Ford's automobile, and perhaps most importantly, The White Star Line's RMS *Titanic*. After the Civil War, the exchange of goods, ideas, and people through transatlantic travel had laid the foundation for Great Rapprochement. For the denizens of Downton, however, the transnational yearning for such transatlantic travel would spell the end of their otherwise cocooned existence as the sinking of the *Titanic* forces them to break from tradition and form new allegiances. The world of Downton Abbey was becoming a global world whether the characters can recognize it or not. As viewer's watch the perfectly timed and organized world of the Abbey spiral wildly out of control, we see not only the slow and steady chipping away for the aristocratic Crawley family, but also the microcosm of British life that they have come to symbolize.

In the series, the importance of transatlantic travel and its effects on British and American national identities is highlighted in the very first moments of show when the Lord of Grantham, Robert Crawley, is notified that the family's heir apparent is believed to have been lost at sea after the tragic sinking of the *Titanic*. The specter of the *Titanic*, including all the ghosts aboard, continues to haunt the characters for the rest of the series. While transatlantic travel of this kind largely defined the Great Rapprochement, in the series, traveling across the Atlantic is not only costly to Crawley's way of life, but lethal. Examining the different responses to the sinking of the *Titanic*, Stephanie Barczewski argues that the fundamental difference between the English and American reactions is one of patriotism. American accounts of and responses to the sinking of the *Titanic* were less patriotic than their British counterparts because Britain "had more at stake than the United States," and Barczewski believes that the patriotic responses by the British were an attempt to bolster their own maritime reputation at a time when its historical prowess was being questioned (75, 76). The show uses the sinking of the *Titanic* not only as a pivotal plot device, but also as an immediate symbol of the decay of the inheritance and patrilineal system that had come to define British subjectivity in early twentieth century. This transatlantic disaster, moreover, is acts as foreshadowing for the shared suffering and loss between America and Britain during the World War I. The sinking of the *Titanic* is the show's first great tragedy, but it will not be its last.

In *Downton Abbey*, we see that it is not only Britain's maritime prowess being questioned but also the viability of the traditional aristocratic system writ large. Viewers are never allowed a moment's nostalgia about glory days of the landed gentry. This system, already in chaos before we formally meet any of the characters, is already a relic of a bygone era. The sinking of the *Titanic* on its maiden transatlantic voyage disrupts the entire inheritance system, and the reverberations of this failed voyage spark the show's central conflict: the debate over Cora's entailment.

While the tangled fiscal and legal languages shrouding the loss of Cora's entailment are certainly a topic of great concern among the show's characters, even more so is the tangled socio-historical reality behind Cora and Robert's marriage. In addition to the subsequent entailment, Robert and Cora's marriage provides viewers a glimpse into what the Great Rapprochement meant on a micro- social and economic scale. Central to the Great Rapprochement was the increase in transatlantic marriages, namely marriages between bankrupt English aristocrats, and *nouveau riche* American heiresses. This phenomenon attracted the show's creator, Julian Fellowes, to the project; according to an interview with *The Boston Globe*, Fellowes' reading of these American "buccaneers" or, "a group of monied East Coast American women who moved to England around the turn of the last century to marry into the aristocracy intrigued him. These women had the cash, and their British husbands had the breeding, the titles, and the real estate" (Muther).[12] Fellowes' interest in these marriages helps to explain why Cora and Robert's courtship and marriage takes place in 1888 at the height of when such marriages were *en vogue*.[13]

The pretense surrounding Cora and Robert's marriage, furthermore, is the subject of discussion, and the object of some ridicule, among the characters themselves. When confronting Robert about the issue of Cora's entailment, the Dowager Countess makes clear her criticism of the marriage, of Cora, and of the current situation:

> VIOLET: Twenty-four years ago, you married Cora against my wishes for her money! Give it away now, what was the point of your peculiar marriage in the first place?
> ROBERT: I were to tell you she's made me very happy, would that stretch belief?
> VIOLET: It's not why you chose her ... above all those other girls who could've filled my shoes so easily [1:1].

Violet's criticism of Robert is not necessarily a referendum on his rather utilitarian intentions in marrying Cora. After all, the Dowager Countess offers several very utilitarian suitors when it comes to the marriages of her granddaughters.[14] Rather, her issue with Robert is that having treated marriage as a fiscal transaction, he is unwilling to see it through to its logical conclusion. This *tête-à-tête* also suggests that the Violet's acrimony towards Cora is rooted primarily her in American breeding. Cora and Robert's "peculiar" arrangement has nothing to do with the fact that Robert married an heiress. As a member of the landed gentry, Robert was expected to marry within a certain social class, and certainly Cora's money placed in Robert's same social circles. Class, however, cannot trump Cora's American breeding, and it is this breeding that marks her as different from "all those other (English) girls" who could have "filled [her] shoes so easily." Cora and Rob-ert's marital and financial arrangement continues to haunt current familial relations, and while the United States and Great Britain have been enjoying the benefits from the Great Rapprochement, it is clear that Downton remains a house divided along national lines.

Such a beginning leads viewers to believe that the Dowager's Countess' disdain for her American daughter-in-law has been an ongoing family issue. Cora's Americanness sets her apart not only as an "other" but also as a lesser.[15] Grounded in the same social discourse about British superiority used in women's travel writing, Violet's own prejudices stem from what she views as Cora's inherent, flawed nationality.[16] The abiding nature of this national prejudice is constantly reasserting itself as characters berate Cora for what they see as her unsavory Americanness.[17] Unsurprisingly, many of these nationalist barbs come from Violet who views herself as the *grand dame* of British sensibility.[18] For instance, when Cora realizes that Mary will have a hard time marrying, she suggests sending her to New York to be with her American family to which Violet replies, "Oh, I don't think things are quite that desperate" (1:4). America, in other words, is only an option of last resort.

These implied hierarchies between America and Great Britain are also apparent whenever the Dowager Countess draws distinctions between British and American social mores. When Cora humorously berates the Countess saying, "I hope I don't hear sounds of a disagreement," Violet accuses, "What? Is that what they call discussion in New York?" (1:1). Violet's accusation calls into question not only Cora's understanding of proper social etiquette, but by drawing her critique along nationalist lines, Violet implies that Amer-icans and American culture are devoid of a proper social code. All of these examples speak to Violet's sense of British superiority rooted in what she believes is America's lack of history or identity. One example of this occurs when Cora queries about one of her daughter's suitors, "Is the family an old one?" Violet retorts, "Older than yours I imagine" (1:1). Perhaps most tellingly, the worst insult Robert says to his mother is to accuse her of having American tendencies: "Are you afraid someone will think you're American if you speak openly?" to which Violet replies, "I doubt it'll come to that" (1:3). Despite having been married to Robert and living in Great Britain for over twenty years, Cora's inherent Americanness continues to plague her relationship with Violet, setting her apart as other, different, and lesser.

Cora's Americanness, moreover, is constantly contrasted with Violet's inherent Britishness. If Cora is the consummate outsider in the show's premise, Violet is its ultimate insider. Interestingly, the series plays on the trope of the uptight British aristocrat, a trope that is itself quintessentially an American perspective of British pretentiousness. The series promotes Violet and Violet promotes herself as quintessentially British: witty, stoic, nostalgic, and fiercely patriotic bordering on a nationalistic narcissism. Violet shakes off criticism with witticisms coupled with a deep sense of self-confidence. Dismissing the stereotype about women as sentimental, Violet tells her Cora, "I'm tougher than I look" (1:1). Violet also fashions herself as supremely rooted in the past, and her nostalgia in the face of modernity becomes an important lens through which she understands her world and her identity. Violet sighs that she "hanker[s] for a simpler world" (1:3) and asks of dreadful swivel chair, "Why does every day involve a fight with an American?" (1:4). When faced with change, she bucks the very thought as was the case with the intro-duction of electricity: "I couldn't have electricity in the house. I wouldn't sleep a wink.

All those vapours seeping about" (1:1). Violet's strict understanding of herself and her world also informs the way she understands others.

Throughout the series, the Dowager Countess is portrayed as adhering to a tight code of social mores that dictate how she views Britishness in light of national otherness. In reference to the untimely—and Violet would say unseemly—death of Kamal Pamuk, Violet is applauded by this break of social etiquette: "Of course, it would happen to a foreigner. It's typical ... I'm not being ridiculous. No Englishman would dream of dying in someone else's house. Especially someone they didn't even know" (1:3). When pushed on the issue about how the English would be better behaved in the situation, the Dowager Countess flatly responds, "Well, I hope we're in control of something, if only ourselves" (1:3). Having the ability to control oneself and to exert that control even in the face of tragedy, disaster, chaos, or even death, according to Violet, is what it means to be British. It is this Britishness, marked by witticism, stoicism, nostalgia, and control, that will be tested with the outbreak of World War I where even the controlled and controlling Countess has to seek out new ways of defining herself in a new global landscape.

As war looms in the background, the two Countesses face their own war at home, namely the struggle over Cora's entailment. While divided historically and philosophically by an ocean, the two women find themselves on the same side of the war against Robert and his determination to keep Cora's money in the estate and out of their eldest daughter's hands. The seemingly unholy alliance between the British mother-in-law and her American daughter-in-law begins with what Cora calls "an absurd act of legal theft" (1:1). Despite Cora's argumentative tone, the Dowager Countess is determined that they should work together:

> VIOLET: My dear, I didn't come here to fight. Lord Grantham wanted to protect the estate. It never occurred to him that you wouldn't have a son.
> CORA: Are we to be friends, then?
> VIOLET: We are allies, my dear, which can be a good deal more effective.

Violet's insistence on the word "allies" suggests that while she and Cora are and will remain separate and disparate entities. They do share some common purpose and now, a common language. Their alliance also means that both parties must change their perception of the other even if that perception is limited to a quiet acceptance and steadfast respect.

This acceptance and respect occurs in subtle, substantive ways. When Violet learns of the gossip surrounding her eldest granddaughter's indiscretion with Pamuk, she goes to Cora who confesses to her how they dragged the body back to the guest room lest the dead man be caught in Mary's bedroom. Fearing that a war with her daughter-in-law is inevitable, the usually "prim" Violet casts off social decorum and asks for peace: "There's no need to be so prim. I come in peace. I confess I do not know if I would have had strength, mentally or physically, to carry a corpse the length of this house ... but I hope I would have done. [Cora smiles.] You were quite right. When something bad happens, there's no point in wishing it had not happened. The only option is to minimize the damage" (1:6). Violet's peaceful negotiations have the intended affect on Cora who is willing to recognize the importance of having a defined social code: "I know that you have rules, and when people break them you find it hard to forgive. I understand that and I respect it" (1:6). Cora's recognition of Violet's decorum and Violet's respect of Cora's resourcefulness suggests that the alliance between these two women is crucial to the survival of their family and their way of life. Yet another moment of crisis brings the two seemingly opposed women together and strengthens their alliance once more.

Cora and Violet's alliance, when viewed historically, both symbolizes and foreshadows the American-British alliance at the dawn of the first global war. Violet and Cora are positioned throughout the series as paragons, either wittingly or unwittingly, of their national heritages, British and American, respectively. As such, they are constantly positioned as foils of one another, and their differences highlighted by drawing larger upon national stereotypes. As national symbols, the alliance between the two Countesses foreshadows the transformation of the American-British "special relationship" into one of political, diplomatic, and militaristic activism. Violet's denial Cora's friendship is a signal of this transformation—what had heretofore been a relationship based on mutual interests and socio-historical ties.

The two countesses of Grantham symbolize the Great Rapprochement not only in their actions but in the very language they use to describe their "special relationship." Like the countesses, the Great Rapprochement had brought the two countries closer together politically, economically, and martially, but the nascent friends had yet to be tested in a way that would question its solvency. Violet's insistence on the word "allies" not only implies a diplomatic and political unity between the two previously warring factions, but also alludes to the same language used to describe the American-British relationship in World War I. Willing to set aside their historical differences, Cora and Violet, like America and Great Britain, must come together as allies, fighting for a common purpose and under a common understanding.

Friends and Allies: Downton Abbey and American Fandom

While the series plays with the historical realities facing the United States and Great Britain at the turn of the twentieth century, the transatlantic alliance between the two countesses of Grantham also might shed some light on the American fervor for a series, which on the surface, appears to be a distinctively and unapologetically British in nature. Since the show's debut, critics have posed the same question to the cast, crew, and even fans themselves: why have American audiences been overwhelmingly fascinated with what many view as a quintessentially British program?

The answers, it turns out, have been as varied as the actors. In an interview with the *Boston Globe*, Michelle Dockery believes that the popularity stems from its "classic and simple" execution in an entertainment culture that she describes as "gratuitous" (Muther).[19] Dan Stevens suggests that viewers can relate to the characters that are beginning to resemble their own modern lives: "They're starting to have telephones. They're starting to have cars.... They have electricity. It's still very different in many ways, but they're not riding around on horses wearing bonnets" (Muther).[20] While many of the cast and crew view their transatlantic audiences in similar ways, McGovern offers some perspective on the differences between English and American fan bases: "In America, there's an added *frisson* because the people who know about it feel like they've discovered it. There's an added passion that you have when you feel you own something that's only yours. (In London), *Downton Abbey* is in the papers all the time; people refer to something as 'very *Downton Abbey*' and everyone knows what you're talking about" (Puente).

McGovern's insight into the differences between "Abbeyites" sparks an interesting question: who "owns" *Downton Abbey*?

In many ways, both American and British fans "own" *Downton Abbey* in the sense that the series represents a crucial moment when the histories of these two nations were aligned. As a microcosm, the Crawley household represents the relationship between America and Britain at the turn of the twentieth century, and Cora and Violet, become the symbols of America and Great Britain, respectively. Upon meeting the two heads of household, we can see how the Great Rapprochement has influenced the two women's understanding of one another. Just as turn of the twentieth-century women described their transatlantic journeys and their impressions of their British and American counterparts, so, too, are Violet and Cora constructed from the same discourses of national otherness. Violet is the "phantom" of history, romance, poetry, and fiction that had so enchanted American Elisabeth Bisland.[21] Cora is Lady Randolph Nevill's "conquering" American woman, willing to drag a man's dead body across the house in order to save her daughter's and family's reputations. Yet despite these national differences, Cora and Violet form an alliance from the shared sense of identity, namely the identity of family, and through this transatlantic union, audiences, too, derive a shared sense of self.[22]

Certainly, this shared sense of self speaks to both the male and female members of the audience, but the portrayal of the countesses and their relationship sheds some light on why American and British women have been particularly taken with the series. Through Violet and Cora, the series' creators demonstrate how both British and American women had their hands in political matters. At a time when many women were frustrated by their societal, familial, and political roles, women like Violet and Cora demonstrate that many women were, as Lady Jane Wilde notes, "the most important element in the social machinery." American and British women viewers can imagine themselves sitting at the tea table—the war room of the time—discussing pressing personal matters that speak to the state not only of the household, but the nation writ large. During what has come to be known as an era primarily presided over by great men such as Woodrow Wilson, David Lloyd George, and Winston Churchill, *Downton Abbey* demonstrates that women were as much a part of the "allied" cause as their male counterparts.

It is this underlying, shared sense of identity can be traced back to the Great Rapprochement itself, which in many ways, is both a prominent and unseen specter in the lives of the Crawley family. The Great Rapprochement quietly instigates the marriage between Robert and Cora, and subsequently, drives the contentious relationship between Violet and Cora. It also subtly encourages the disastrous transatlantic journey of James and Patrick Crawley aboard the RMS *Titanic*, throwing the entire series into utter disarray. The Great Rapprochement also helps to bring about the alliance between the two Countesses, an alliance forged over tea, molded in tragedy and loss, and tested by an inter-family battle and a global war. Through this alliance, modern viewers from both sides of the Atlantic can claim "ownership" over a series that can be said to represent an Anglo-American history. And as old grudges give way to new coalitions on the series, the two countesses show modern audiences that in a time of global upheaval, it is important to know who are your friends and who are your allies.

NOTES

1. The diplomatic historian Bradford Perkins has referred to this period as the First Rapprochement and later as the Great Rapprochement in his works of the same names.

2. While scholars disagree about the defining moment of the period's beginning, the general consensus among diplomatic historians places the years of the First or Great Rapprochement in the two decades before the start of World War I. In general, historians place the beginning of rapprochement in the years between 1895 and 1898. For more, see Bemis, 446; Bourne, 340; Burk, 299; Campbell, introduction, and Perkins, *The First*, vii.

3. The phrase, "special relationship," is an allusion to a speech given by the British Prime Minister, Winston Churchill, in 1946 where he refers to "the fraternal association of the English-speaking peoples ... a special relationship between the British Commonwealth and Empire and the United States" (qtd. in Dumbrell 7). While this phrase appears much later than period discussed here, diplomatic historians use it to describe the historical relationship between the two countries that began with the Great Rapprochement. See Adams, 14 and 21; Burk, 299; and Campbell, *Unlikely Allies*, Introduction.

4. For more on the transatlantic women writing about women around the turn of the century, see Bisland, *A Flying Trip Around the World*; Dudley, *Letters to Ruth*; McCracken, *The Women of America*; McManus, *The American Woman Abroad*; Nevill, *Leaves from the Notebooks*; and Wilde, "American Women." See also Rapson, *Britons View America*, and Schriber, *Writing Home*.

5. Writing about the countryside between Antwerp and Brussels, Ella W. Thompson describes how "the fields are tilled almost entirely by women, whose faces are as wooden as their shoes" (112). Earlier in the nineteenth century, Evangeline, a pseudonym for A.E. Newman, expresses a similar sentiment as she describes a scene from her train car wherein she watched "women hard at work in the fields, bending beneath the pelting storm, or running hither and thither seeking shelter under the trees or in some little thatched hovel; alas! What perfect drudges women are!" (92).

6. Dudley, writing from London on July 1, 1895, describes how England, "black with age," compares to the United States: "I know there is no place like the United States of America, no flag like the stars and stripes, yet England is a garden, and London a desirable city. It was our mother, who tried to spank us in the last century; but the new version had even then commenced, for parents to obey their children, and she did not succeed" (20).

7. American Revolutionary thinkers, such as Thomas Paine, had been the first to reject the paradigm of Britain as parent and protector. In *Common Sense*, Paine rejects "the phrase of parent or mother country applied to England only, as being false, selfish, narrow, and ungenerous" (85).

8. Grund, a nineteenth-century social historian, refers to England as America's "guide and instructor," claiming: "The progress of America reflects but the glory of England; all the power she acquires, extends the moral empire of England; every page of American history is a valuable supplement to that of England" (416).

9. For more on the number of transatlantic marriages between the Civil War and World War I, see Temperley 82; Campbell, *Anglo-American Understanding* 9; Dunlap 37. It is important to note that many historians use *Burke's Genealogical and Heraldic History of the Peerage and Baronetage* to arrive at their numbers.

10. In *A Gilded Cage*, for instance, Folwer presents case studies of some of the more provocative scandals including Consuelo Yznaga who married the Eighth Duke of Manchester, Lily Hammersley and the Eighth Duke of Malborough, Consuelo Yznaga's granddaughter, Conseulo Vanderbilt, who married the Ninth Duke of Malborough, and Helena Zimmerman. Conseulo Vanderbilt wrote about her disastrous marriage in her memoir, *The Glitter and the Gold*. Her relationship with her mother, Alva, has been documented by Stuart in *Consuelo and Alva Vanderbilt*.

11. Specifically, Davis lists Viscount Lewis Harcourt who married Mary Burns; Lord Curzon of Kedleston who married Mary Leiter; Joseph Chamberlain who married Mary Crowninshield Endicott; and, "to a less extent," Lord Playfair who married Edith Russell (173). The marriage between Joseph Chamberlain, a British politician and statesman, and Mary Endicott, the daughter of the United States Secretary for War, William Crowninshield, provides an interesting example of how the political and diplomatic relationships between the two countries were mirrored in the private actions of their citizens.

12. The show's co-creator, Gareth Neame, corroborates Fellowes enthusiasm for the "buccaneering" Cora: "Cora was the first character who was Julian's purchase on this idea, and I think that's what got the flame going for him" (Muther). While the nature of the material Fellowes was referencing is unclear, the term "buccaneer" when applied to this situation most likely refers to Edith Wharton's novel *The Buccaneers*, which, like *Downton Abbey*, appeared as part of the Masterpiece Theatre series in the United States.

13. Violet gives us some insight into the chronology here when she says, "Twenty-four years ago you married Cora, against my wishes, for her money" (1:1). Since this speech takes place in 1912, we can discern that Cora and Robert courted and married in 1888.

14. When Violet discovers that Mary has slept with a man outside of marriage, she suggests what she believes is a practical solution: "Well, if she doesn't, we'll just have to take her abroad. In these moments, you can normally find an Italian who isn't too picky" (1:6). Again, such advice is drawn from certain historical and nationalist stereotypes.

15. Other characters also employ this nationalist prejudice as way to insult Cora. Brushing off her mother, Mary retorts, "You're American. You don't understand these things" (1:2). Robert, perhaps more lov-

ingly, reminds Cora that Downton is "in my blood and in my bones" and "it's not in yours" (1:2). Like Mary and Violet, he links it to an nationalist issue: "I can no more be the cause of its destruction than I could betray my country" (1:2).

16. It is interesting to note that Elizabeth McGovern is the only American in the cast and that she herself has been living in England after her own transatlantic marriage. Of this coincidence, McGovern states, "I've spent 20 years rehearsing the part … I do find myself bumping up against a culture that is in many subtle ways different to my own, and is a very interesting juxtaposition to me personally—and in this case, professionally" ("Elizabeth McGovern").

17. McGovern has also received some negative reviews based on what appears to be her Americanness. Siegel, from *Here & Now*, praises the entire cast except McGovern: "The one exception, though, is Elizabeth McGovern, an American-born actress who plays Lord Grantham's American-born wife and she is completely overshadowed by all the Brits."

18. Certainly, the series' writers intend to play with this idea further by introducing another American, Shirley MacLaine as Cora's mother, Martha Levinson, to play opposite to Violet.

19. McGovern agrees with her fictional daughter: "Now we have to contend with overstimulation and too many opportunities all the time, and too many decisions all the time. At *Downton Abbey*, everything is set. Everybody knows their place. I think people find it soothing" (Langmuir). Julian Fellowes has also pointed to the treatment of the upstairs, downstairs cast: "What makes it popular is we treat all the characters the same. We don't suggest that the 'upstairs' people are more important than the 'downstairs' people…. That was a decision that turned out to be right for the zeitgeist now" (Puente).

20. Hugh Bonneville agrees with Stevens: "It has a completely modern feel to it…. It's written in the style of 'The West Wing,' 'The Wire,' or [the long-running British soap] 'Coronation Street.' This has taken the best elements of the soaps, the best elements of costume drama, and the best elements of miniseries writing"(Muther).

21. American audiences do seem attracted to this idea of Englishness. Rebecca Eaton, the series' executive producer, describes the distinctively American fan base attraction to the show as rooted in national identity: "They're fascinated with the Englishness of it" (Puente).

22. Violet argues this very point when Cora confronts her about Mary's indiscretion and Violet's own strict social dictum. Violet says that Mary has "the trump card" because "Mary is family" (1:6).

WORKS CITED

Adams, Iestyn. *Brothers Across the Ocean: British Foreign Policy and the Origins of the Anglo-American "Special Relationship," 1900–1905.* New York: St. Martin's Press, 2005. Print.

Balsan, Consuelo Vanderbilt. *The Glitter and the Gold.* New York: Harper, 1952. Print.

Barczewski, Stephanie. *Titanic: A Night Remembered.* New York: Hambleton Continuum, 2006. Print.

Bemis, Samuel Flagg. *A Diplomatic History of the United States,* 4th ed. New York: Henry Holt, 1955. Print.

Bisland, Elizabeth [Wetmore]. *A Flying Trip Around the World.* New York: Harper and Brothers, 1891. *Google Books Search.* Web. 1 Aug. 2012.

Bourne, Kenneth. *Britain and the Balance of Power in North America, 1815–1908.* Berkeley: University of California Press, 1976. Print.

Brandon, Ruth. *The Dollar Princesses: Sagas of Upward Nobility, 1870–1914.* New York: Knopf, 1980. Print.

Burk, Kathleen. *Old World, New World: Great Britain America from the Beginning.* New York: Grove Press, 2007.

Campbell, Charles S. *Anglo-American Understanding, 1898–1903.* Baltimore: John Hopkins Press, 1957. Print.

_____. *From Revolution to Rapprochement: The United States and Great Britain, 1783–1900.* New York: Wiley, 1974. Print.

Campbell, Duncan Andrew. *Unlikely Allies: Britain, America and the Victorian Origins of the Special Relationship.* New York: Continuum, 2007. Print.

Davis, Richard W. "'We Are All Americans Now!' Anglo-American Marriages in the Later Nineteenth Century." *Proceedings of the American Philosophical Society* 2 (June 1991): 140–199. *JSTOR.* Web. 1 Feb. 2012.

Downton Abbey. PBS. 2011–16. Television.

Dudley, Lucy Bronson. *Letters to Ruth.* New York: 1896. *Google Books Search.* Web. 1 Aug. 2012.

Dumbrell, John. *A Special Relationship: Anglo-American Relations in the Cold War and After.* New York: St. Martin's Press, 2001. Print.

Dunlap, W.H. *Glided City: Scandal and Sensation in Turn-of-the-Century New York.* New York: William Morrow, 2000. Print.

"Elizabeth McGovern, Acting At an Intersection." 7 Jan. 2012. *NPR.* Web. 1 Aug. 2012

[Evangeline] A.E. Newman. *European Leaflets for Young Ladies.* Second Series. New York: John F. Baldwin, 1862. *Google Books Search.* Web. 1 Aug. 2012.

Fowler, Marian. *In a Gilded Cage: From Heiress to Duchess.* New York: St. Martin's Press, 1994. Print.

Hitchens, Christopher. *Blood, Class, and Empire: The Enduring Anglo-American Relationship.* New York: Nation Books, 1990. Print.

Langmuir, Molly. "*Downton Abbey's* Elizabeth McGovern on Season Two, Corsets, and What Cora Would Think of Her." *New York Magazine.* 6 Jan. 2012.

McCracken, Elizabeth. *The Women of America.* New York: Macmillan, 1904. *Google Books Search.* Web. 1 Aug. 2012.

McManus, Blanche. *The American Woman Abroad.* New York: Dodd, Mead, 1911. Print.

Mesick, Jane Louis. *The English Traveller in America, 1785–1835.* New York: Columbia University Press, 1922. *Google Books Search.* Web. 1 Aug. 2012.

Montgomery, Maureen E. *Gilded Prostitution: Status, Money, and Transatlantic Marriages, 1870–1914.* New York: Routledge, 1989. Print.

Muther, Christopher. "American Can't Get Enough of 'Downton Abbey.'" *The Boston Globe.* 8 Jan. 2012.

Nevill, Lady Dorothy. *Leaves from the Notebooks of Lady Dorothy Nevill.* Ralph Nevill, ed. London: Macmillan, 1907. *Google Books Search.* Web. 1 Aug. 2012.

Perkins, Bradford. *The First Rapprochement: England and the United States, 1795–1805.* Philadelphia: University of Pennsylvania Press, 1955. Print.

_____. *The Great Rapprochement: England and the United States, 1895–1914.* New York: Athenaeum, 1968. Print.

Puente, Maria. "Loyal U.S. Subjects Return to PBS' 'Downton Abbey.'" *USA Today Online.* 3 Jan. 2012.

Rapson, Richard L. *Britons View America: Travel Commentary, 1860–1935.* Seattle: University of Washington Press, 1971. Print.

Schriber, Mary. *Writing Home: American Women Abroad, 1830–1920.* Charlottesville: University of Virginia Press, 1997. Print.

Siegel, Ed. "'Downton Abbey' Delves Into Brewing Class Conflict in World War I." *Here & Now* 5 Jan. 2012.

Stuart, Amanda Mackenzie. *Consuelo and Alva Vanderbilt: The Story of a Daughter and a Mother in the Gilded Age.* New York: HarperCollins, 2005. Print.

Temperley, Howard. *Britain and America since Independence.* New York: Palgrave, 2002. Print.

Thomas, Nicola J. "Mary Curzon: 'American Queen of India.'" *Colonial Lives Across the British Empire: Imperial Careering in the Long Nineteenth Century.* David Lambert and Alan Lester, eds. Cambridge: Cambridge University Press, 2010. Print.

Thompson, Ella W. *Beaten Paths; Or, a Woman's Vacation.* Boston: Lee and Shepard, 1874. *Google Books Search.* Web. 1 Aug. 2012.

Wilde, Lady [Jane]. "American Women." *Social Studies.* London: Ward & Downey, 1893. 123–153. *Google Books.* Web. 1 Feb. 2012.

The Downstairs Domestic
Servant Femininity

COURTNEY PINA MILLER

The very first scenes within the breathtakingly beautiful Downton Abbey are not in its stunning library or its luxurious drawing room. Instead, our first glimpse inside the grand country estate is the servants' corridor, as then-scullery maid Daisy knocks on the housemaids' bedroom door. Daisy alerts Gwen and Anna that it is six o'clock in the morning and time to begin their days. As Anna stirs in her bed she groggily complains, "For once in my life I'd like to sleep until I woke up natural" (1:1). This scene cuts to an exchange between Mrs. Patmore and Daisy, as the former frantically shouts demands at the latter—a scene that will become all too familiar as the series progresses. Soon, a stern-looking Mrs. Hughes appears, grasping the keys to the property. She instructs Anna to give the dining room a "proper going over" and when she sees Daisy tending the drawing room's fire, she exclaims: "Oh, heavens, girl! You're building a fire, not inventing it…. Now, get back down to the kitchens before anyone sees you!" (1:1).

Within the first few minutes of the series' first episode, the core cast of female servants is introduced and the social hierarchy among the staff is clearly demarcated. Mrs. Hughes' instructions that Daisy remain unseen coincides with the strict rules of conduct that domestic servants were expected to adhere to, especially lower ranking servants like the kitchen staff. *The Servant's Behavior Book*, published in 1859, offers the following command to its specific servant audience: "Never let your voice be heard by the ladies and gentleman of the house except when necessary, and then as little as possible."[1] Of course, viewers of *Downton Abbey* will know that over the six seasons of this wildly popular series, we see the Crawleys' servant staff both adhering to and resisting this edict, especially its female members, who are often anything but reticent. This essay will examine and trace the figure of the female servant, with specific attention paid to the portrayals of Mrs. Hughes, Mrs. Patmore, Anna Bates, and Daisy Mason. This examination will, in particular, consider the ways in which the series depicts domestic labor as a social, spatial, and embodied force that shapes and determines certain understandings of post–Edwardian servant femininity. Perhaps one of the reasons why this series is so unique is its detailed look at the women beneath the aprons and below the stairs.

Through the series, these core four female servants play pivotal roles in the successful running of the estate. These women are responsible for keeping the home clean and the occupants' fed, and provide integral emotional support for the Crawley family and other

177

members of the staff alike. Mrs. Hughes and Mrs. Patmore are the perfect matriarchal duo in charge downstairs; Mrs. Hughes' calm, stoic, and assertive disposition complements Mrs. Patmore's flustered, bossy, and oftentimes cheeky demeanor. Anna and Daisy are youthful counterparts to the Housekeeper and Cook, who both take their work seriously, and are fiercely loyal and respectful workers. As the series progresses, the bonds among these women solidify as they negotiate health scares, proposals, marriages, deaths, issues with the law, among many other tribulations. This essay will sort through these varied plots, and examine the notable resilience that this cast of female servants demonstrates across the series' six seasons. In particular, this analysis will examine each female servant in detail by citing specific episodes which best showcase the women's quest for agency against a backdrop of fading Edwardian norms and radical modernization. The subsequent analysis reads each female servant as representing different archetypes of traditional and non-traditional femininity—*Mrs. Hughes as housewife; Mrs. Patmore as entrepreneur; Anna as sexualized woman; and Daisy as educated new woman*. What I will ultimately suggest is that although the series seemingly promises its viewers a look at the drastic changes between 1912 and 1925, the gendered expectations and realities for this core cast of female servants both shift and remain static in particular ways, for particular women. More importantly, what this essay examines is the way in which conflicting definitions of servant femininity drives the narrative below stairs. Although the series demonstrates a consistent concern for the quest of agency through its depiction of feminine labor, the unstable gender spectrum it presents, coupled with its adherence to normative conventions, ultimately undermines its progressive feminist potential.

Post-Edwardian Feminism and Domestic Service

Before closely reading the characters individually, it is important to consider the ways in which domestic service is historically situated. The series is set against the backdrop of a momentous historical era—the sinking of the *Titanic*, World War I and its ghastly aftermath, the rise of Britain's first Labor government, and women's fight for suffrage are just a few of the major events the series' plot and its characters must negotiate. And, while much of the series depicts the various proposals, marriages, and inheritances that the Crawley sisters face, similar occurrences happen below stairs, albeit on a different and less grand scale, as the cast of female servants must also face the difficulties of navigating the social conventions of a post–Edwardian world.

The work of Lucy Delap offers a critical insight into the complicated project of defining what post–Edwardian feminism (and anti-feminism) was and how we understand it today.[2] However, more relevant to the purposes of this essay, Delap's work is useful in outlining how domestic service at the turn of the century overlapped with many of the aforementioned gendered tensions. Delap is especially invested in the implications of the aphorism "knowing their place," which she argues, "was no longer simply a form of knowledge generated by the middle classes, but a form of self-fashioning and reflection on the part of the servants."[3] In fact, there were hierarchies *within* the servant class, "establishe[d] through rituals of naming, uniforms, and segregations of space and material culture."[4] This phenomenon is persistently demonstrated in *Downton Abbey*, as the members of the house staff (e.g., the Housekeeper and Lady's Maids) are often seen as socially superior to the kitchen staff (e.g., the Cook and the Kitchenmaids). Despite this divide, and despite the understanding that servants *know their place*, Delap asserts that twentieth-century female servants were *not* a silent class but were instead "articulate, vocal, and active" and the influence of the women's movement helped to empower them to contribute to the feminist cause.[5] The subsequent analysis will take these assertions seriously, and showcase that through its differing depictions of feminine labor and particular adherences to and deviations from gender norms, *Downton Abbey* is heavily invested in the plights and the triumphs of post–Edwardian female servants. The question of whether or not this translates into Mrs. Hughes, Mrs. Patmore, Anna, and Daisy all achieving empowered feminine agency will be the main task that this essay explores at length.

Mrs. Hughes: Housekeeper to Housewife

As she is the highest-ranking female servant, it makes sense to begin with a discussion of Mrs. Elsie Hughes. For the first few episodes of the series, Mrs. Hughes is depicted as a stern, yet compassionate leader downstairs. As Housekeeper, Mrs. Hughes' responsibilities include "ensuring that the duties of the female staff are discharged properly on a daily basis" and working closely with the Butler, who is "ultimately the arbiter of discipline for all."[6] It is easy to observe the respect the other servants and the Crawleys have for Mrs. Hughes—she is efficient, ethical, and trustworthy. Although she goes by the name Mrs. Hughes, it is important to remember that during this time, "Mrs." was a social title, not just a marital one. The title of Mrs. was given to women who governed subjects (i.e., employees or servants) or women who were skilled or educated.[7] Though she is unmarried, Mrs. Hughes reveals that in her youth she did receive a marriage proposal, which she ultimately turned down:

> Before I first came here as head housemaid, I was walking out with a farmer. When I told him I'd taken a job at Downton, he asked me to marry him. I was a farmer's daughter from Argyle, so I knew the life. He was very nice. But then I came here and I—I did well, and I … I didn't want to give it up. So, I told him no, and he married someone else [1:4].

What this admission reveals is that Mrs. Hughes deliberately chose a life in service, rather than a normative domestic life, because she found the work fulfilling. However, after decades of seemingly finding satisfaction with her work and with her life as an unmarried woman, Mrs. Hughes' ideas shift as her affection for Mr. Carson grows, and we begin to imagine her role in the series as more than just the Housekeeper.

Perhaps the first moment Mrs. Hughes begins to reevaluate her circumstances is when she sees Mr. Carson joyfully reacting to the news that she is cancer-free (3:3). Though Mrs. Hughes decided to keep her health scare a secret, telling only Dr. Clarkson and Mrs. Patmore, Mr. Carson senses something is wrong and tricks them both into telling him what is ailing Mrs. Hughes. When Mrs. Patmore shares the news that the tumor is benign, Mr. Carson joyfully sneaks away to polish the silver and Mrs. Hughes overhears him gleefully singing the nineteenth- century English folksong "Dashing Away with the Smoothing Iron."[8] The particular refrain Mr. Carson is heard singing is: "Dashing away with the smoothing iron, she stole my heart away," which brings a smile to Mrs. Hughes' face as the soundtrack music swells and the episode ends.

The Carson-Hughes relationship begins to blossom at the end of Series Four, when the servant staff have a day off at the beach and Mrs. Hughes persuades Mr. Carson to be a bit more adventurous and dip his toes in the water:

> MR. CARSON: Suppose I fall over?
> MRS. HUGHES: Suppose a bomb goes off, suppose we're hit by a falling star? You can hold my hand, then we'll both go in together.
> MR. CARSON: I think I will hold your hand. It'll make me feel a bit steadier.
> MRS. HUGHES: You can always hold my hand if you need to feel steady.
> MR. CARSON: I don't know how but you managed to make that sound a little risqué.
> MRS. HUGHES: And if I did? We're getting on, Mr. Carson, you and I. We can afford to live a little.

This playful exchange is perhaps the first moment in which the mutual affection between Mr. Carson and Mrs. Hughes is made legible on the screen. Mrs. Hughes' suggestion that Mr. Carson can hold on to her hand, both literally and metaphorically, is a sentimental moment that has been growing for many episodes, and the season ends with the tender image of the two of them walking hand in hand into the water. For the first time, we see a new dimension of Mrs. Hughes—the stoic housekeeper proves that she can be flirtatious, and perhaps even a little bit risqué (that is, according to Mr. Carson's rather conservative definition of the term). We see an attraction reciprocated, albeit modestly, in a way that suits the age and distinction of the two heads of staff, and Mrs. Patmore and Daisy exchange a quick glance of approval as the episode cuts to black. More importantly, though, we are left with the feeling that Mrs. Hughes is beginning to seriously reconsider what she wants for her future as an aging woman.

As in the previous two seasons, major developments in the Carson-Hughes romance are delayed until the end of Series Five, when Mr. Carson finally proposes to Mrs. Hughes—to her shock and delight:

> MRS. HUGHES: I'm not convinced I can be hearing this right.
> MR. CARSON: You are, if you think I'm asking you to marry me. Well?
> MRS. HUGHES: Well…. You could knock me down with a feather.
> MR. CARSON: And you're not offended?
> MRS. HUGHES: Oh, Mr. Carson…. I can assure you the very last thing in the world that I am at this moment is offended.
> MR. CARSON: You can take as long as you like—I won't press you. Because one thing I do know— I'm not marrying anyone else.
> MRS. HUGHES: Well, then. [She raises her glass to toast Mr. Carson]
> MR. CARSON: What exactly are we celebrating?
> MRS. HUGHES: We're celebrating the fact that I can still get a proposal at my age.
> MR. CARSON: And that's… it?
> MRS. HUGHES: Of course I'll marry you, you old booby. I thought you'd never ask [5:8].

Mr. Carson's romantic declaration feels quite out of character for the curmudgeon, and through it, we see an even more playful side to Mrs. Hughes than the scene by the sea. More importantly, this proposal reveals that Mr. Carson sees potential in Mrs. Hughes as a wife, not just a companion or co-worker. His concern that his proposal could some-how cause offense underscores his strict adherence to social conventions, especially the tradition that the Butler and Housekeeper of a prominent household remained unmarried and childless. Therefore, while a marriage between Mrs. Hughes and Mr. Carson might, on the surface, seem normative, it was actually quite a break from the traditions of the time. We also see Mrs. Hughes' proclamation that she has been long awaiting a romantic gesture from Mr. Carson; perhaps she assumed his traditionalist mindset would keep him from acting on the romantic feelings both characters have been harboring for some time.

While this long-awaited union seems to settle finally, a rather important facet of the marital arrangement causes Mrs. Hughes to have second thoughts, and 6:1 showcases frank (though veiled) discussions of sexuality in ways previously unexpected for the characters and the series. When Mrs. Patmore observes a sense of anxiety that has washed over the bride-to-be, she questions her in private and a hilariously awkward exchange between the two ensues. Though she accepted Mr. Carson's proposal, Mrs. Hughes admits to not having "fully considered … all the aspects of marriage" to which Mrs. Patmore replies, "I don't understand. What aspects? You know each other better than most couples at the start…. Oh, my Lord. You mean…?" While this exchange is comical for the discomfort it causes both women, a few important details are revealed. First, it is learned—though it is safe to say it was presumed—that both Mrs. Hughes and Mrs. Patmore are virgins. Mrs. Patmore remarks, "Well, there's nothing so terrible about it, is there? So they say. I wouldn't know, of course"—"it," of course, refers to sex, a word too indelicate for either woman to utter. We soon learn Mrs. Hughes' concerns for consummating her marriage have less to do with the idea of sexual intercourse and more about her own self-consciousness about her aging body (which is in a stage of "late middle age," as she declares it). When she contemplates that perhaps Mr. Carson would be okay with them living as close companions rather than lovers (or "like brother and sister," as Mrs. Patmore comically suggests), Mrs. Hughes admits, "I don't know what I want. Except not to feel embarrassed and absurd" (6:1). Mrs. Hughes' disgust with her aging body and her fear that it could not provide pleasure to Mr. Carson is the sole cause of her unease. She enlists Mrs. Patmore to act as a liaison between the two so as to negotiate and determine the "terms" of their marriage, and an *LA Times* review of the episode declares Mrs. Patmore, the "world's greatest friend" for agreeing (albeit reluctantly) to go along with this plan.[9]

After a first failed attempt at broaching the subject with Mr. Carson, who is endearingly oblivious to the content of her mission, Mrs. Patmore attempts to communicate the specifics of Mrs. Hughes' apprehensions to the naïve butler. Once he finally gets the point, he asks that she tell Mrs. Hughes that he indeed desires a "full marriage." Once Mrs. Patmore relays this message, Mrs. Hughes opens up to Mr. Carson and says, "I was afraid I'd be a disappointment to you. That I couldn't hope to please you as I am now. But if you're sure…. Well, then, Mr. Carson…. If you want me, you can have me. To quote Oliver Cromwell, 'warts and all.'" Mrs. Hughes' demonstration of her acceptance of her body and its sexual value showcases the peak of her feminine agency. While she initially fears that she could not offer sexual pleasure at her age and with the flawed state of her figure, Mrs. Hughes proclaims her body imperfectly perfect. This moment exemplifies a daring sense of empowerment and feminine liberation unexpectedly present in the union between the two eldest and presumable most conventional servants.

This sense of agency is echoed when Mrs. Hughes fights for the wedding reception that *she* wants—not what Mr. Carson or "the blessed Lady Mary" wants (6:2). In refusing to have the reception at Downton, she declares that she doesn't want to be a servant on her wedding day and that she wants her own wedding to be done in *her* own modest way. When Mr. Carson interjects that it is his wedding too, Mrs. Hughes retorts, "But I am the bride, we'll be doing it your way for the next thirty years, I know that well enough, but the wedding day is mine!" (6:2). While the location of the wedding reception might be seen as an insignificant detail when considering the fact that Mrs. Hughes is admitting Mr. Carson's dominance for the entire time they will spend married, the way in which she takes possession of the wedding day holds symbolic agential significance. From then on, we see Mrs. Hughes asserting her opinion in the marriage, and although Mr. Carson often remains the curmudgeon traditionalist, the Hughes-Carson union is one of respect and equality. The couple even decide to retain their original surnames (much to everyone's delight), and Mrs. Hughes eventually schools Mr. Carson on the challenges of being a proper housewife, after his demands and expectations get a little out of control. The scheme that Mrs. Hughes and Mrs. Patmore devise in order for Mr. Carson to gain "a new respect for the role of cook and bottle washer" (6:7) promises a lasting marriage full of mutual respect. Therefore, despite the fact that they are a "late-middle age" couple, their marriage is surprisingly modern, and it seems that Mrs. Hughes is sure to maintain autonomy despite her shift into the traditional feminine role of housewife.

Mrs. Patmore: Enemy of Modernity to Burgeoning Entrepreneur

Mrs. Beryl Patmore is perhaps the least traditionally "feminine" of all of the downstairs staff—she is often frantic, sometimes sweaty, and always bossy. Her sole responsibility as the Cook was "to deliver"—a task that required her to prepare meals "six times a day, plus elevenses and tea—in an often crowded kitchen in stifling heat produced by the huge coal-fired range that was kept lit all day."[10] As Cook, Mrs. Patmore is the "sole keeper of her kingdom and in charge of her own servants."[11] And, like Mrs. Hughes, Mrs. Patmore garners fierce respect from all of Downton's occupants. Also similar to Mrs. Hughes, Mrs. Patmore opted to forgo the normative path of marriage and children, to instead devote her life to service, something she excels at and finds fulfilling, albeit stressful. While housemaids and kitchenmaids often left service to marry, the likes of Mrs. Patmore and Daisy (if she chose to train as a Cook) would "remain in a kitchen for most of their lives"—Mrs. Patmore would stay at Downton "until old age force[d] her to leave."[12] It is surprising, then, that like Mrs. Hughes, Mrs. Patmore receives a marriage proposal late in life, from produce supplier Joseph Tufton. Mr. Tufton is "generous with compliments," and is overtly flirtatious, making remarks like, "I hope you don't mind my saying so, Mrs. Patmore, but in that blouse, you look as if you've just stepped out of *Vogue*." While Mrs. Hughes is skeptical of Tufton's interest in Mrs. Patmore—because of his brash demeanor and womanizing tendencies—the other servants, Thomas in particular, are more skeptical about the fact that a man could take an interest in her:

IVY: She's got a fancy man, I'm telling you.
ALFRED: Mrs. Patmore?
DAISY: Why not? She's a woman, isn't she?
THOMAS: Only technically.

Despite Thomas and Alfred's invalidation of Mrs. Patmore's feminine appeal, Mr. Tufton seems to find her extremely desirable and pledges his love for her multiple times (he "loves to be in love, any time, anywhere"). However, Mrs. Patmore slowly begins to realize that he is less attracted to *her* and more desirous of her exceptional cooking skills. After Mrs. Hughes tells her she saw him making passes at other women, Mrs. Patmore remarks, "God, I've never felt more relieved in all my life!… The more he said about how he liked his beef roasted, his eggs fried and his pancakes flipped, the more I wondered how to get away" (3:9). Whereas Mr. Carson seems to respect and desire Mrs. Hughes as a companion and lover, Mrs. Patmore's suitor seemingly reduces her to her labor value as a cook. Being the clever and strong-minded woman that she is, Mrs. Patmore detects this and seems to be just fine continuing to live on her own. While this choice adheres to the social conventions and expectations of a cook, Mrs. Patmore's refusal to be tied down to a man who only sees her as a servant demonstrates a notable sense of feminine agency, which is perhaps one of the reasons why others—namely the male servants—see her as markedly *un*-feminine.

Of course, another of Mrs. Patmore's most notable qualities is her staunch resistance to the rapidly modernizing world around her. Of all the characters, with perhaps the exception of Mr. Carson, Mrs. Patmore is the most hostile to change, and she resents new household appliances like electric mixers and refrigerators because she knows they have the capability of putting her out of a job. In *The Labors of Modernism*, Mary Wilson asserts that early twentieth-century servants "are relic[s] of a pre-capitalist society" and the emergence of innovative domestic technology began replacing the servant class that had maintained the homes of the upper classes. As a result of this social shift, Wilson argues that the "bustling, jolly, uniformed kitchenmaids, housekeepers, and cooks seem out of place in the modern world."[13] Mrs. Patmore is in constant battle with this tension between modernity and tradition, and in response to her fear of Baxter's electric sewing machine, Thomas cheekily remarks, "Mrs. Patmore is not what you'd call a futurist." In the same episode, Mrs. Patmore fights against the invasion of the modern age when Lady Grantham comes downstairs to insist on replacing the kitchen's icebox with a new, and more efficient solution—a refrigerator. When Lady Grantham asks, "Mrs. Patmore, is there any aspect of the present day that you can accept without resistance?" Mrs. Patmore whispers with all sincerity, "Well, My Lady, I wouldn't mind getting rid of my corset" (4:4). Therefore, although Mrs. Patmore is *not* a futurist, as Thomas says, it seems as though there are some traditions she is okay with letting go—she even considers buying a jar of horseradish instead of spending the time and energy to make it from scratch, even though she says this would be "cheating" (6:2). Despite the fact that Mrs. Patmore occupies the most conventionally feminine space of the home—the kitchen—it is her steady commitment to maintaining an effective and sustainable career that should be most noted.

Given her resistance to the modern world, it is surprising then, that of all the servant characters, Mrs. Patmore is the one who is most adequately prepared for her post-service life. After she inherits a sum of money from a deceased aunt, she decides to purchase a nearby cottage, renovate it, and operate it as a bed and breakfast. On the day it is finished, Daisy congratulates Mrs. Patmore, "Just think! It's finished and open for business. You are the owner of a bed-and-breakfast hotel!" Mrs. Patmore beams with pride as she explains to Andrew that she turned a bedroom into a bathroom and installed an inside privy ("Think of that!" Daisy exclaims) (6:7). Though much of her work takes places off screen (both Mr. Carson and Mrs. Hughes are amazed at how quickly it all comes together), her accomplishments impress the downstairs staff and family upstairs. However, when it is revealed that her first guests were adulterers and the local paper labels the bed and breakfast "a house of ill-repute," Mrs. Patmore is devastated. In an act of solidarity and gratitude for her loyal service, Lord and Lady Grantham decide to show her support by stopping by for a highly publicized visit. A photograph with the Crawleys in front of the bed and breakfast (6:8) ensures that regardless of whether or not she chooses to leave service, Mrs. Patmore will have the security of a successful business that is all her own. Moreover, it is interesting to note that, while Mrs. Hughes and Mr. Carson *and* Bates and Anna all discuss plans for opening their own hotels or bed and breakfasts in the future, Mrs. Patmore is the only one whose dream is realized within the series—and she does so without the help of a partner or spouse. This is particularly modern considering that women at this time were not even allowed to vote, which makes Mrs. Patmore's accomplishment as a sole female business owner all the more remarkable. Despite her persistent resistance to modernity, it seems as though Mrs. Patmore is emerging as a new modern woman and is in the best position to take care of her self whatever uncertainties the future may bring.

Anna Bates: A Body Violated, Normatively Recuperated

Almost the opposite of Mrs. Patmore, Anna Bates (née Smith) is petite, demure, and reticent. Anna is universally adored by everyone at Downton and offers friendship and compassion to all. When describing her to Baxter, Thomas memorably declares, "Anna is incorruptible so we have nothing in common" (4:4). The series begins with Anna as Head Housemaid, but she is eventually promoted to a proper Lady's Maid, a position of privilege and prestige. The job of the Lady's Maid is to be "on call for her mistress from the moment of waking until she retires to bed." Being "of good temper and reliability" are vital, as is "absolute discretion"[14] since the Lady's Maid is the faithful confidante of her mistress. Of all the characters in *Downton Abbey*, Anna is perhaps the most loyal and respected, and despite the many devastating traumas she endures, she remains a positive and considerate figure in the series. In fact, by Series Six, Lady Mary remarks, "no woman living has been put through more of an emotional wringer" (6:2) than Anna—a description that no viewer of the show would dare dispute. The many tragedies and traumas Anna faces occur alongside a solid and loving relationship with Mr. Bates. Initially, others ridicule her relationship with Bates, a man whose disabled body is often made the butt of both cruel and light-hearted jokes. Interestingly, it is *Anna's* body that undergoes the most throughout the series.

After Anna and Bates declare their mutual affection for one another, Anna patiently waits for Bates to secure a divorce from his first wife, Vera. When these proceedings are complicated by Vera's refusal of divorce, attempt at blackmail against the Crawley family, and eventual death, Anna remains a fierce advocate for Bates' innocence when he is convicted of murder, and eventually secures the evidence that absolves him of the crime. Vera's death, though it poses complications later, enables the couple to legally wed. Anna insists on the union, despite Bates' urging that she is deserving of a proper wedding, because she wants to have legal rights if he is suspected of being involved with Vera's death—a decision that Lady Mary describes as "a very brave decision" (2:8). Anna's unassuming courage is constantly highlighted throughout the series, and she quickly transforms from quiet and obedient, to a fiercely determined wife. Her transition from Anna Smith to Mrs. Bates is, at first, a secret (because it coincides with the Spanish flu epidemic that ultimately kills Lavinia Swire), but on their wedding night, Lady Mary arranges a guestroom for the newly minted Mr. and Mrs. Bates to share. The depiction of the marital and sexual union between Anna and Bates is a first for the series, as the two characters are shown as lying naked beneath the covers, gazing at one another. Mr. Bates playfully tells Anna that she's had her way with him and the two giggle in a moment of post-coital bliss. Anna literally and metaphorically lets her hair down, and this intimate moment demonstrates her transformation from a demure virgin to sexual woman and wife.

Of course, the Bates' happiness is not long-lived, as Anna is the victim of a vicious and graphic sexual assault by Mr. Green, a visiting valet accompanying Tony Gillingham. Many were critical of Fellowes' "particularly cold-blooded move"[15] to have Anna once again endure devastating pain and heartache, especially after the excruciating season in which Anna and Bates are separated when he is behind bars. While the actual rape scene is not depicted on screen, the before and after moments are brutal and violent and we hear guttural screams from Anna during the horrific assault. After the rape, Mrs. Hughes finds Anna hiding in a corner and the camera lingers on her violated body, which is bruised, bloodied, and disheveled. Her lip quivers as she later declares that she will kill herself if she becomes pregnant with her rapist's child. If this isn't enough to rip audiences' hearts out, Anna is imprisoned for allegedly murdering her rapist—she is literally shackled and placed behind bars—where we learn that when she was young, she endured sexual abuse from her stepfather. The abuse that Anna endures within the plot of the series amplifies the fragility of her stereotypically feminine character, which unsettled a great many viewers of the show. According to the BBC, ITV received sixty complaints after the sexual assault episode, which caused Julian Fellowes to defend his decision: "The whole point of the way we do things on *Downton* is we don't do them gratuitously," Fellowes told the BBC. "We are interested in exploring the resultant emotions and the effect these things have on people," he added, and he pointed out the attack took place behind closed doors, saying, "If we'd wanted a sensational rape we could have stayed down in the kitchen with the camera during the whole thing and wrung it out."[16] However, as Ronald Hyam and Lucy Delap observe, female servants were a "class of subordinate and sexually accessible women"[17] who had "no privacy, and may be observed at [their] most intimate moments"[18] by their employers. Katherine Byrne suggests that a more historically accurate portrayal of sexual abuse against female servants would have shown the perpetrator as a member of the aristocratic family, rather than have the attacker be "both a servant and an outsider," which enables the series to avoid "tackling any difficult questions surrounding predatory class relations."[19] Regardless of the intentions behind this narrative choice, Anna's rape transforms her body from virginal, to consummated, to "soiled" (4:4), perhaps challenging viewers' understanding of Anna's character and her role within the larger cast of female servants.

While it is true that Anna's body is policed and in distress during much of the series, she possesses an acute awareness of how her female form is under constant scrutiny. When Lady Mary requests that Anna purchase contraceptives on her behalf, Anna is initially horrified. However, after an embarrassing exchange with the pharmacy shopkeeper, who not only verifies that Anna is married but also curtly suggests abstinence as a birth control method, Anna changes her views. After Lady Mary asks if purchasing the contraception was a "ghastly" transaction, Anna explains, "I didn't know where to look. But when I thought about it afterwards it seemed unfair to punish me like that. Suppose I had eight children and didn't want any more? Wouldn't I have the right?… I feel like going back and ordering a baker's dozen" (5:2) After witnessing firsthand the unjust humiliation that a *married* woman had to face to purchase a contraceptive device, Anna is outraged. However, even though she seems to warm to the idea that women should have control over their reproductive rights, when Lady Mary asks that Anna hide the birth control with a copy of Marie Snopes' *Married Love*, Anna is reluctant. Though she seems to be in support of a *married* woman's right over her own body, Anna disapproves of Lady Mary's willingness to engage in unwedded sex. Despite her hesitation, Anna agrees and ominously says, "But I do feel I'm aiding and abetting a sin. I just hope I won't be made to pay" (5:2). This comment, in true Julian Fellowes fashion, serves to foreshadow even more trouble ahead for Anna.

When Anna and Bates are cleared of all wrongdoing in the murder case against Green, they mutually agree to put these horrors behind them and resume their life together. Yet, in what feels like a relentless refusal to offer the Bateses happiness, Anna is plagued by persistent miscarriages and the devastating fear that she is infertile. Later, when Anna confides in Mary about fertility struggles, she remarks, "It's almost funny really, given the service I once performed for you" (6:2) as though, perhaps, there is a causal relationship between her assistance in Mary's love tryst with Lord Gillingham and inability to sustain a pregnancy. More importantly, Anna's struggle with infertility is yet another way her feminine body functions as a burden to her and Bates' happiness. For example, when Bates suggests adoption, Anna does not think it to be a plausible solution:

> ANNA: You're tribal, Mr. Bates, and the tribe doesn't have a lot of members. You want your own child. No substitute will do.
> BATES: But what do *you* want?
> ANNA: See. You gave yourself away by not denying it.
> BATES: We must learn to be content as we are … which is easy for me.
> ANNA: But it's my fault, not yours, that I can't give you what you need [6:2].

Anna's reflection and assessment of her body's failure to produce a child underscores gendered expectations that persist to today—that if the female body is somehow unable to procreate, it is therefore broken or inadequate. Anna is found wiping away tears in the stairwell or bursting into emotion in the shoe polishing room at various points, and she harbors a growing resentment towards her body that seems to yet again stand in the way of her and Bates' happiness. However, with the help of Lady Mary, Anna's infertility issues are solved rather quickly and efficiently with a simple operation, and the series finale ends with her successful delivery of a son—a happy ending the entire household celebrates. By ending the series with the Bateses finally gaining a new "tribe" member, there is a suggestion that normative futurity somehow has the potential to recuperate Anna's body that has previously undergone duress. While this makes for a nice and tidy ending, its plausibility deserves a bit more scrutiny and skepticism.

Daisy: Reticent to Revolutionary

Of the four servant characters examined thus far, Daisy Mason (née Robinson) is the character who gains the most social mobility within the course of the series. The series' first episode depicts a young, slightly frantic scullery maid who scuttles between the kitchen and the bedrooms, lighting fires and scrubbing pans. Daisy's day would begin at 4:30 a.m. when she would awake "in the small, dark hours of the morning" and dress herself in a "hand-me-down corset, simple dress and apron" before creeping "around the family's bedrooms to light their fires."[20] A maid like Daisy in a prominent house was "the lowest of low." She would be young and "frightened out of her living wits if anyone from above stairs saw her, let alone talked to her. Her only aim was to get her job done quietly and quickly and out of everyone else's way."[21] Yet, as the series ends, Daisy is assistant cook to Mrs. Patmore, equipped with social and cultural capital that she gains through her acquisition of an education. However, despite the process of personal and intellectual maturation Daisy undergoes, she tends to be immature and sulky, especially when she doesn't get her way—characteristics that are especially heightened in the series' final season.

There are several occasions over the course of the series that Daisy's petulance irritates the staff and viewers alike. She often feels as though she is being mistreated and over-worked, and even stages a strike (after Thomas convinces her that she "withdraw her services" [3:1]) when she does not immediately get the promotion she requests. Her romantic life is also exhaustingly tumultuous—she has crushes on both Thomas and Alfred, neither of whom return her affections (but for different reasons), and she is on the receiving end of affection from fellow servant William Mason and Ethan Slade, a visiting American valet, but she doesn't love either of them back—or at least not in the ways they love her. The romantic drama occurring among the servant staff prompts Mrs. Patmore to aptly diagnose the situation: "You know the trouble with you lot? You're all in love with the wrong people" (3:5) Daisy's relationship with William is especially heart-wrenching given the fact that what she viewed as a platonic friendship ends with her being coerced (mostly by Mrs. Patmore) into marrying the dying soldier at his literal death bed. Against her better judgment, Daisy resolves to let William die believing she loved him back, something that haunts her for much of the subsequent episodes. Though Daisy takes on her dead husband's name, enjoys war widow's rights (though reluctantly), and eventually becomes heir to William's father's farm, the falseness of Daisy's marriage plagues her time and again.

Yet it is this marriage, however inauthentic it may be, that initiates Daisy's path toward education. Once Mr. Mason makes it clear that he wishes her to inherit his farm, Daisy begins to consider the importance of furthering her skills in mathematics, and Mrs. Patmore enlists the help of Miss Bunting to aid in Daisy's schooling. As a result of a new commitment to providing better education during the 1870s and 1880s, Daisy would have benefited from free compulsory education up until the age of ten and would be able to read and do simple arithmetic.[22] However, it is the possibility that she may have a future life outside of service that catalyzes Daisy's interest in bettering herself. Interestingly, Daisy's new desire coincides with the 1924 election of the Labor government, and as her political awareness grows, so does her confidence and eventual outspokenness. However, once Miss Bunting leaves town, Daisy struggles to find the motivation to continue her studies: "She gave me such confidence. She'd tell me how sharp I was, how quick" (5:6), she says. As she gains more insights into the political system in which she belongs, Daisy confronts feelings of disappointment in her government and her social position: "When I think about it, it seems to me that we're trapped. Held fast in a system that gives us no value and no freedom.... And now I'm wondering. Is it worth it me trying to better myself? What's the point?" (5:6). These kinds of poignant questions are central to her exploration of self in the series' final episodes.

Daisy's skepticism of the British political system collides with the unfair displacement of Mr. Mason as a tenant farmer, and what results is a bold public outburst in front of the Crawleys that nearly gets her fired (although Lady Grantham kindly convinces Mr. Carson that she deserves a second chance). However, when Daisy feels as though Lady Grantham isn't doing enough to offer Mr. Mason a secure tenancy, she resolves to confront her employer, although her fellow servants, especially Mrs. Patmore and Molesley beg her not to. This gesture is stalled, however, when the Crawleys reveal to Daisy that they *will* offer Yew Tree Farm to Mr. Mason after all. Yet, in typical Daisy-fashion, she feels conflicted—though she is happy that Mr. Mason's future is secure, she feels disappointment because she yearned to finally give the aristocracy a piece of her mind, and issue a complaint on behalf of the working class more generally. Her growing politicization is the exact opposite of the demeanor she has at the beginning of the series. The submissive scullery maid is surprisingly transformed into a thriving revolutionary, all because she was given the tools (by Mrs. Patmore and Ms. Bunting) to acquire the knowledge and the discourse that empowers her.

Yet, despite her political enlightenment and process of maturation, in the last few episodes of the series, Daisy becomes insufferable. For much of the last season, she is whiny, pouty, and annoying. The loyal and optimistic Daisy is gone, and a new and selfish Daisy emerges. If we are to forgive Daisy for her constant discourteous behavior towards Molesley, who replaces Ms. Bunting as her teacher and advocate, it is her deliberate sabotage of the growing relationship between Mrs. Patmore and Mr. Mason that feels unforgivable. It begins when Mrs. Patmore offers Mr. Mason a hot cup of tea, to which he replies, "It does me good to see a friendly woman bustling about the kitchen" (6:5), and she's quite pleased with the attention. Daisy scrutinizes the friendly exchanges between Mrs. Patmore and her father-in-law, and is very resistant of the idea that the two could become romantically (even platonically) close. In several of the final episodes of the series, Mrs. Patmore hints about wanting a man in her life, and she and Mr. Mason begin to demonstrate a mutual affection for one another. However, for some reason, this possibility irritates Daisy, who childishly thinks she should be the single center of *both* Mr. Mason and Mrs. Patmore's lives. She even goes so far as to throw away a note Mr. Mason sends Mrs. Patmore, as a way to prevent the courtship from blossoming—the epitome of her immature selfishness.

On the surface, this may seem as though Daisy is suffering from a kind of only-child syndrome, in which she yearns for the sole attention from her surrogate mother and father figures. However, could it be more complex than that? Through the course of the series, we see Daisy transform from shy to assertive as she begins to realize what she wants and demands that she be treated equally and respectfully. Daisy demonstrates a clear commitment to bettering herself, whether that be within the sphere of domestic service or beyond. While her various romantic failings may seem to be symptomatic of her girlish naiveté, perhaps her pattern of always falling for the "wrong" person, as Mrs. Patmore says, is more deliberate. Can we instead read Daisy as a burgeoning new woman, who is in control of herself and feels less inclined to define her feminine worth through the traditional path of marriage and children? If so, perhaps this is what she wants for her beloved mentor Mrs. Patmore, and a possible relationship with Mr. Mason could pose a threat to this way of life. However, despite her persistent resistance to traditional and normative femininity, the series ends by undermining the possibilities of Daisy and/or Mrs. Patmore as possessing the potential to exist as new modern women.

The Series Finale: Feminist Potential Overturned?

What the preceding sections illustrate are the various ways in which *Downton Abbey* carefully examines a complex set of feminine archetypes that post–Edwardian domestic servants negotiated. In their own ways and in varying degrees, each female servant is able to transcend the rigid conventions that both the historical context and the gendered labor system place on them. Mrs. Hughes successfully transitions from a long life as a single and successful housekeeper of a prominent home into the somewhat conventional role of wife. While this change is met with some complications, she settles into a happy marriage where she continues to hold onto the autonomy she enjoys as the female head of the household staff, and effectively manages to have success in both her home life and work life. Despite the grueling traumas Anna is forced to undergo, she too finds happiness with her husband and newly born child. While her demure and virtuous character is tested, Anna remains "incorruptible," as Thomas says, and enjoys a kind of moral restoration that successful procreation secures her. She even calls Mr. Bates "John" for the first time, as they cradle their newborn—a clear parallel with Mrs. Hughes and Carson calling each other "Elsie" and "Charlie," respectively, in some of their final pieces of dialogue in the series. These subtle shifts offer the suggestion of new beginnings and a farewell to the conventional past for the Carsons and the Bateses.

However, as for how the series leaves Mrs. Patmore and Daisy, there is an interesting divide between the house and kitchen staff. While Mrs. Hughes and Anna's endings feel just and organic, less can be said for how the series leaves Mrs. Patmore and Daisy. Despite seemingly being happily *un*married and enjoying modern feminine agency through their entrepreneurship and edification, the series ends with rather rushed suggestions of new relationships on the horizons for both Mrs. Patmore and Daisy. Though the "happy" ending is meant to be hopeful, it seems to raise more questions than it answers. Would Mrs. Patmore give up her successful bed and breakfast to live on the farm with Mr. Mason? Are Daisy's dreams and aspirations to leave service over once she pursues a relationship, and presumed marriage, with Andrew? A better question is why isn't it possible that these two women maintain "happy endings" as single women? Fellowes himself confronts the criticism of the saccharine ending: "I might be accused of a certain sentimentality in that, but you know I got very fond of them all and I felt I wanted them to have nice lives in the ether or wherever television characters go after the end of their shows."[23] Despite this justification, these romantic pairings feel sloppy and hasty, and work to undermine the notable successes and achievements Mrs. Patmore and Daisy acquire in the final season. In fact, I argue that the series' finale stands as the single episode that tempers the otherwise feminist bend the series seeks to promote for its female characters above and below stairs—a happy yet somewhat disappointing ending for characters who provided such strong and unique perspectives throughout the series.

When reflecting on the series as a whole, it is clear that each female servant oscillates along an uncertain spectrum of femininity. Mrs. Hughes defies her age and rank and pursues, what she discovers to be, a healthy and happy marriage. Mrs. Patmore initially resists the temptation of a proposal and creates an independent and self-sufficient future for herself, but then decides that having a man in her life *is* something she desires. Anna undergoes vast transformations from virginal, to married, to violated, to imprisoned, to infertile, to productive. And Daisy is promoted from the lowest ranks in the house, educates herself, all the while alienating co-workers and viewers alike, only to change her mind regarding her feelings for Andrew once he expresses interest in farm life. Domestic life and gender expectations for the cast of servants are in constant flux, and we are left with varying degrees of feminine agency and normative conclusions, that ultimately offer rather unsatisfying resolutions. It is interesting, then, to consider the very last lines of dialogue of the series, an exchange between Isobel and the Dowager Countess, as they toast the New Year (after all the "happy endings" are realized):

THE DOWAGER: It makes me smile, the way every year we drink to the future, whatever it may bring.
ISOBEL: Well, what else could we drink to? We're going forward to the future, not back into the past.
THE DOWAGER: If only we had the choice! [6:9].

If *Downton Abbey*'s primary focus is on how a Yorkshire estate and its occupants negotiate the post–Edwardian world, it is odd that virtually all of its characters are left adhering to conservative norms. If this is indeed the case, it seems as though, in the end, the Dowager's desires to revert to the past are in some ways realized for the women who serve her.

NOTES

1. Quoted in Mary Wilson's *The Labors of Modernism: Domesticity, Servants, and Authorship in Modernist Fiction*.
2. See Lucy Delap, "Feminist and Anti-Feminist Encounters in Edwardian Britain." *Historical Research* 78.201 (2005): 377–399. Web.
3. Lucy Delap, *Knowing Their Place: Domestic Service in Twentieth-Century Britain* (Oxford: Oxford University Press, 2011), 2–5. Print.
4. Ibid., 49.
5. Ibid., 8.
6. Justyn Barnes, *Downton Abbey: Rules for Household Staff* (New York: St. Martin's Griffin, 2014). Print.
7. Amy Louise Erickson, "Mistresses and Marriage: Or, a Short History of the Mrs," *History Workshop Journal* 78.1 (2014): 39–57. Web.
8. Tommy Reilly, Skaila Kanga, and James Moody, "Dashing Away with the Smoothing Iron," *British Folk-Songs* (Colchester, England: Chandos, 1987). MP3.
9. Meredith Blake, "'Downton Abbey' Season 6 Premiere Recap: Mrs. Patmore, World's Greatest Friend." *Los Angeles Times*, *latimes.com*, 4 January 2016. Web.
10. Jessica Fellowes and Matthew Sturgis, *The Chronicles of Downton Abbey: A New Era* (New York: Macmillan, 2012), 207. Print.
11. Ibid., 202.
12. Ibid., 207.
13. Mary Wilson, "Reading, Writing, Serving: The Threshold of Modernism," Introduction, *The Labors of Modernism: Domesticity, Servants, and Authorship in Modernist Fiction* (Burlington: Ashgate, 2013), 1–28. Print.
14. Barnes, 53.
15. Karen Valby, "TV's Tiresome Assault on Women," *Entertainment Weekly* 1301 (2014): 54. Print.
16. Sabrina Sweeney, "Downton Abbey Creator Julian Fellowes Defends Storyline," *BBC News*, Entertainment & Arts, 8 October 2013. Web.
17. Ronald Hyam, *Empire and Sexuality: The British Experience* (Manchester: Manchester University Press, 2004), 59. Print.
18. Delap, *Knowing Their Place*, 174.
19. Katherine Byrne, "New Developments in Heritage: The Recent Dark Side of Downton "Downer" Abbey," *Upstairs and Downstairs: British Costume Drama Television from The Forsyte Saga to Downton Abbey*, ed. James Leggott and Julie Taddeo (Lanham: Rowman & Littlefield, 2014),182. Print.
20. Jessica Fellowes, *The World of Downton Abbey* (New York: St. Martin's Press, 2011). Print.
21. Ibid.
22. Fellows and Sturgis, *The Chronicles of Downton Abbey*, 202.
23. Jace Lacob, "A Farewell to Downton Abbey with Julian Fellowes," podcast, *PBS.org. Masterpiece Podcast*, 6 March 2016. Web.

WORKS CITED

Barnes, Justyn. *Downton Abbey: Rules for Household Staff.* New York: St. Martin's Griffin, 2014. Print.
Blake, Meredith. "'Downton Abbey' Season 6 Premiere Recap: Mrs. Patmore, World's Greatest Friend." *Los Angeles Times. latimes.com.* 4 January 2016. Web.
Byrne, Katherine. "New Developments in Heritage: The Recent Dark Side of Downton 'Downer' Abbey." *Upstairs and Downstairs: British Costume Drama Television from The Forsyte Saga to Downton Abbey.* Ed. James Leggott and Julie Taddeo. Lanham: Rowman & Littlefield, 2014. 182. Print.

Delap, Lucy. "Feminist and Anti-Feminist Encounters in Edwardian Britain." *Historical Research* 78.201 (2005): 377–399. Web.

Delap, Lucy. *Knowing Their Place: Domestic Service in Twentieth-Century Britain.* Oxford: Oxford University Press, 2011. 2–5. Print.

Erickson, Amy Louise. "Mistresses and Marriage: Or, a Short History of the Mrs." *History Workshop Journal* 78.1 (2014): 39–57. Web.

Fellowes, Jessica, and Matthew Sturgis. *The Chronicles of Downton Abbey: A New Era.* New York: Macmillan, 2012. Print.

Fellowes, Jessica. *The World of Downton Abbey.* New York: St. Martin's Press, 2011. Print.

Hyam, Ronald. *Empire and Sexuality: The British Experience.* Manchester: Manchester University Press, 2004. Print.

Lacob, Jace. "A Farewell to *Downton Abbey* With Julian Fellowes." Podcast. *PBS.org. Masterpiece Podcast*, 6 Mar. 2016. Web.

Reilly, Tommy, Skaila Kanga, and James Moody. "Dashing Away with the Smoothing Iron." *British Folk-Songs.* Colchester, England: Chandos, 1987. MP3.

Sweeney, Sabrina. "*Downton Abbey* Creator Julian Fellowes Defends Storyline." *BBC News.* Entertainment & Arts, 8 Oct. 2013. Web.

Valby, Karen. "TV's Tiresome Assault on Women." *Entertainment Weekly* 1301 (2014): 54. Print.

Wilson, Mary. "Reading, Writing, Serving: The Threshold of Modernism." Introduction. *The Labors of Modernism: Domesticity, Servants, and Authorship in Modernist Fiction.* Burlington: Ashgate, 2013. Print.

"Education is for everyone"

Education and the American Dream

Katrin Suhren

Julian Fellowes' highly successful *Downton Abbey* is rife with the idea of social change. The first evidence for this preoccupation occurs as early as the pilot episode when Lord Grantham refers to the third-class passengers aboard the RMS *Titanic* as the "poor devils below decks ... on their way to a better life" (*Downton Abbey* 1:1). As Katherine Byrne notes, *Downton Abbey* is made specifically with a modern day audience in mind, which results in a combination of period drama and soap opera (311). While UK viewers criticize the show condescendingly for its anachronisms and shallowness, *Downton* is hugely popular in the U.S. (Miller 38). Arguably, a decisive factor in the series' success is the attention paid to detail when it comes to the accurate portrayal of the Edwardian society (Byrne 313). One important aspect of this accuracy is the depiction of social hierarchy emphasized by the show's creator:

> I think ... it is comforting for people to see a story about a period of British history when everybody had a station in life, whether it was as a footman or an earl. I'm not saying that's necessarily right, but everybody has a role to play in keeping this huge operation going, upstairs and downstairs, and for the most part they got along [Byrne 315].

While clearly stressing the importance of social order, there are a number of subplots in *Downton Abbey* which openly challenge this same order and instead foreground the possibility of social change.

The following essay seeks to explore these stories of social advancement by bringing them into connection with the issue of education. Just like social change, education is a recurring issue in the series and the overall message the show conveys in this context is that with a good education everything is possible. In the context of the series education is understood as the accumulation of knowledge and abilities as well as the active engagement with political matters. Following this observation, I establish a connection between the success of *Downton Abbey* among American audiences and the show's take on education, which essentially feeds the American dream of upward social mobility that is enabled through hard work and determination. The most compelling example for this message is given in the final season, when Mr. Molesley claims "education is for everyone" (6:8). In his speech to the children of the village school Molesley explicitly contemplates the idea of social mobility enabled through education, telling his students that "maybe one of you will run the country one day" (6:8).

Interestingly enough, a connection between the issue of education and America is brought forth by the series itself. When Lady Sybil regrets not having attended a "real school," the following dialogue ensues between Sybil, her mother, and her grandmother:

> DOWAGER COUNTESS: Why would you want to go to a real school? You're not a doctor's daughter.
> SYBIL: Nobody learns anything from a governess, apart from French and how to curtsy.
> DOWAGER COUNTESS: What else do you need? Are you thinking of a career in banking?
> CORA: Things are different in America.
> DOWAGER COUNTESS: I know. They live in wigwams.
> CORA: And when they come out of them they go to school [1:4].

In this exchange, Cora explicitly points to the American system of education as an example for modernity opposed to how educational matters are handled in England. This modernity is connected to Lady Sybil, who serves as a moral compass throughout all six seasons of *Downton Abbey*, which prompts the viewer to take Cora's side in this discussion. This early reference to America and the opportunities it offers already sets the theme for the series' emphasis on education as a means for social advancement while at the same time introducing American standards as a desired stance for the audience.

However, by contrasting the show's take on education and its impact with historically confirmed facts about the Edwardian period, it will become apparent that the significance ascribed to education is a message directed to a contemporary audience rather than a historically accurate description of the opportunities education offered to members of the working class at the turn of the century. Following this line of thought, this essay explores the interrelation between education and the possibility of social change depicted in *Downton Abbey* by tracing the development of three characters, namely Gwen Dawson, Daisy Mason, and Mr. Molesley that foreground the importance of education as an instrument for social change. By connecting the findings of my analysis to the ideology of the American dream I outline the relevance of this ideology for the series' success among the American television audience.

When it comes to the construction of American identity the concept of the American dream still plays a vital role. As Cyril Gosh notes, "not all people believe in its promises, [but] most people continue to think the Dream is either achievable or ought to be achievable" (1). Similarly, Jennifer Hochschild and Nathan Scovronick find that three-fourths of the American population answer in the affirmative when asked if they believe in the American dream (10). Considering these observations, it does not come as a surprise that Diana Ştiuliuc understands the dream as a cultural narrative which shapes the collective identity of the American people and thus regards it as the foundation of American culture (363–364). It is important to realize that this sustained influence of the ideology of the American dream stems from its specific structure: the American dream is a dualistic concept that draws on the determination and dedication of the individual on the one hand, and on a social framework of equality on the other. This means that as long as the government provides the conditions necessary for the achievement of success the individuals are on their own in terms of actually succeeding. In other words: "once the polity ensures a chance for everyone, it is up to the individuals to go as far and fast as they can in whatever direction they choose" (Hochschild and Scovronick 10).

As might be expected, there are various definitions of the term "American dream."[1] For example, Phillip Schlechty points to the possibility of upward social mobility as an integral part of the American dream (4), while Gosh emphasizes three constitutive elements of the American dream, namely equal opportunity, success, and individualism (33). Hanson and White also stress the important focus on equality of opportunity (8) and understand the American dream as a state of mind, "an enduring optimism" (4). As such, the dream is the idea of a life in which the status of a person at birth does not necessarily predetermine the course of the rest of their life: "Instead, one's own ability, god-given talent, and hard work determine what kind of life one gets to live" (Gosh 28). It is important to note that, according to the American dream, success should ideally be achieved through hard work, as opposed to good luck (Hanson and White 4). The most common definition of the American dream is found in President Clinton's 1993 speech to the Democratic Leadership Council: "The American dream that we were all raised on is a simple but powerful one—if you work hard and play by the rules you should be given a chance to go as far as your God-given ability will take you" (Hochschild 18).

In order to further specify the success typically associated with the American dream Hochschild points out that success can be measured in three different ways. She goes on to distinguish absolute, relative, and competitive success. While absolute success refers to a level of well being that is higher than it was at the outset and thus focuses on the development of an individual, relative success is based on comparison and means becoming better than someone or something else (16). Competitive success, on the other hand, is reached by achieving victory over another person (17). As Hochschild notes, the definitions of success she outlines have important normative and behavioral consequences. As such, they will serve as a useful means to describe the underlying aims of the *Downton Abbey* characters considered in this essay.

What all of the definitions of the American dream have in common is an emphasis on individual agency. It is in this context that education gains significance as a key factor for the access to the American dream. Hanson and White state that the American dream is explicitly linked to education, especially high school education, and refer to a survey from 1986 where 84 percent of the respondents named the ability to get a high school education as an important part of the American dream (9). Although iterations of the American dream change overtime, a strong focus on the attainment of education remains; consequently, a follow-up study from 2008 yielded similar results concerning the relevance of education (10). Schlechty, who understands the American dream as the dream of a society where every child has an equal chance to be successful, also expressly highlights the importance of education (4). He argues that a meaningful participation in the American life is enabled first and foremost through education and concludes that "education has ceased being merely a part of the American dream: *education is the key to the dream*" (5, italics in the original). In like manner, Hochschild and Scovronick stress the important role of public schools when it comes to ensuring the continuance of the American dream: "Public schools are where it is all supposed to start—they are the central institutions for bringing both parts of the dream into practice." (1).

This brief outline of the ideology of the American dream and its impact on American identity reveals two important insights. First, the American dream is still a concept that looms large and that is likely to create a strong response in an American television audience. Second, education appears to be a major factor for the achievement of the American dream, because it is tied to some of its key components, such as equality of opportunity, individual agency, and the importance of hard work. In the remainder of this essay I will use the concept of the American dream as a framework to analyze the development of

Gwen Dawson, Daisy Mason, and Mr. Molesley in order to underline how the individual stories of these characters cater to this concept and thus contribute to the exceeding success of *Downton Abbey* among the American television audience. These successful stories of advancement will then be compared critically with the historically confirmed situation concerning the access to education available to members of the working class at the turn of the century. Finally, the selected storylines will be contrasted with counter narratives of failed attempts of social change, which serve to underline the impact of the ideology of the American dream even further.

The first character to display an explicit interest in bettering her position is the housemaid Gwen Dawson, who is one of the central "downstairs" characters in Series One. When the head housemaid Anna discovers the typewriter Gwen bought for herself it is revealed that Gwen took a postal course in typing and shorthand. Although Gwen is aware of the fact that her family will frown upon her endeavor, she holds on to it: "Mum will think I'm getting above myself. But I don't believe that." (1:3). It is important to note, that the only information Anna needs in order to support Gwen, is whether she is any good at typing. As soon as Gwen confirms this, Anna is ready to accept her friend's wishes and becomes one of her most important allies by encouraging her and defending her decision against the other members of the staff whenever necessary. This short introduction of Gwen's storyline points out a number of important aspects. First, Gwen is willing to take her fate into her own hands, even if this means accepting a risk. After all, she spent almost all her savings on the typewriter and risks the anger of her family as well as the indignation of her co-workers. Second, she states that she is good at the job she chose for herself, which means that she is obviously following a talent. Finally and most importantly, the path Gwen embarks upon to accomplish her goal is that of education.

As might be expected, Gwen's plan does not go smoothly at first. Thanks to O'Brien the other servants discover the typewriter and, after forcing Gwen to explain herself, do not approve of her desire to leave service. Although she defends her wish of bettering her position in life at first, Gwen soon breaks down and voices her disillusionment in front of Anna and Mr. Bates: "I'm not going to be a secretary. I'm not going to leave service. I doubt I'll leave here before I'm 60. You saw their faces ... and they're right. Oh, look at me! I'm the daughter of a farmhand, I'm lucky to be a maid. I was born with nothing and I will die with nothing" (1:3). With this bleak statement, Gwen reiterates the notion of fixed positions in life which is diametrically opposed to the idea of the American dream. Interestingly, it is Mr. Bates—whose secrets of the past are still unknown at this point—who offers his support and who encourages Gwen to pursue her ambitions: "Don't talk like that. You can change your life if you want to. Sometimes you have to be hard on yourself, but you can change it completely. I know" (1:3). Bates' words explicitly point to the possibility of changing the course of one's life through determination and hard work. As such, they can be regarded as an almost perfect reiteration of the American dream, meant to confirm Gwen's decision to pursue a different career.

Of course, the downstairs characters are not the only ones who become aware of Gwen's ambitions. The news is met with the same mixed feelings upstairs as it was in the servant's hall. While the Dowager Countess is taken aback by the idea that someone would want to leave a good house like Downton in order to become a secretary and even ponders legal prohibition, Lady Sybil and Isobel Crawley welcome Gwen's initiative—especially Lady Sybil, who offers Gwen her support immediately: "I think it is terrific that people make their own lives" (1:3). This is of special relevance because it foregrounds the aspect of individual agency which can be linked explicitly to the idea of the American dream. Of course, Sybil does not only claim to support Gwen in front of her family, she truly does so. After all, it is Sybil who finds the first job opening for Gwen and who encourages her to apply, thus securing her the first job interview.

With this introduction of Sybil's help and support Gwen's storyline takes a turn that seemingly leads away from the importance of education. When her first interview gets cancelled because the company finds someone better qualified, Gwen is very disappointed. Considering her upbringing and her lack of experience, she believes that there will always be someone who is better suited for any job than herself. As might be expected, Lady Sybil is not willing to accept defeat and offers her ongoing support to Gwen. Eventually, she even applies for another position in Gwen's name, which leads to her first actual interview. However, Gwen receives a rejection letter almost immediately after, which leads to further discouragement. Gwen is ready to give up on her dream once and for all, stating that "[o]nly a fool doesn't know when they've been beaten" (1:5). Of course, Lady Sybil refuses to accept this and continues to encourage Gwen to follow her goals. These continuous attempts at encouragement and the stubbornness with which Sybil holds on to her plan finally lead Gwen to point out what she believes to be the crucial difference between Lady Sybil and herself: "See, you don't get it. You're all brought up to think it's all within your grasp, that if you want something enough it will come to you. But … we're not like that. We don't think our dreams are bound to come true because … because they almost never do" (1:6). This proves significant because it is the first time that Gwen refers to her ambition as a *dream*. Furthermore, it is another example of Gwen's belief in her fixed position on the social scale that prevents her from ever leaving service. It is important to realize that in her response to this speech Lady Sybil expressly makes Gwen's dream her own: "Your dream is my dream now. And I'll make it come true" (1:6). The fact that Sybil takes up responsibility for Gwen's future as a secretary seems to undermine the notion of individual agency that appeared to be of vital importance to this storyline at the outset. While Gwen took the first step to a brighter future herself by seeking out an education, the final accomplishment of her dream appears now to be explicitly linked to Sybil and the possibilities that her privileged social status offers.

Lady Sybil does not have to wait long for an opportunity to pursue her quest of helping Gwen. When a telephone is installed at Downton, she overhears Mr. Bromidge, the owner of the telephone company, complain about his difficulties in finding a secretary. Of course, Sybil immediately takes her chance and claims to know the perfect candidate for the position, without revealing, however, that Gwen is working at the Abbey. When Gwen never gets any response to her application Sybil approaches the subject with Mr. Bromidge on his next visit. Confronted like this, he admits that he was put off by the fact that Gwen could not list any experience of hard work and that Sybil's reference was not enough to convince him of her suitability for the position. As soon as Sybil explains that Gwen works as a housemaid at Downton Abbey and that she was afraid to list that kind of job as past experience, Mr. Bromidge readily agrees to meet with Gwen and to test her abilities. Remarkably, he does not see Gwen's position as a housemaid as a reason not to hire her. Rather on the contrary, he points out that his own mother was a housemaid and that he values the experience attached to a position like that: "They know about hard work and long hours, that's for sure" (1:7). The interview goes well and shortly after, Gwen learns from Tom Branson and Lady Sybil that she has been offered the position.

Although the penultimate episode of Series One gave the impression that Gwen could only be successful through the help of Lady Sybil, in the end it is her own achievement that guarantees her the first job in business. Apparently, Mr. Bromidge is less impressed by Sybil's reference than he is by the fact that Gwen indeed knows the meaning of hard work. In addition to that, Sybil is not present during the interview and it is therefore solely Gwen's skills that convince Mr. Bromidge of her potential. All things considered, Gwen's success and her story can be understood as a first example of the embodiment of the American dream in *Downton Abbey*: Gwen uses her "god-given talents," follows her dream (albeit with the help of Lady Sybil), and is finally able to achieve it through hard work and determination. The determining factor enabling this success, however, is Gwen's decision to educate herself in order to pursue her talents as far as possible.

Gwen's story appears to be a loose end until the final season of the series, where she returns to the Abbey as a guest of Lady Rosamund. Gwen, who is a married woman now and introduced as Mrs. Harding, supports a women's college that Rosamund takes an interest in. While Gwen avoids revealing herself to the family as a former employee, she does indeed tell them about her career. In this context, she points out that she did not have any higher education and that she worked at a telephone company first, which she eventually left to move into local government. In this position she met her future husband, who is now the treasurer at the women's college Gwen is associated with. With regard to Gwen's story it is remarkable that she, despite having achieved so much, still believes she could have made even more of her life: "If I had more education, I might have gone further" (6:4). Here, she explicitly stresses the importance of education for her advancement, while at the same time highlighting the fact that she could have had even more opportunities. If her storyline in Series One seemed to rely on good fortune and Lady Sybil's commitment, Gwen now foregrounds the relevance of education for the path she chose and the possibilities it offered. What is even more, she does not only focus on her own life but transfers the importance of education on others, especially working class women: "We can't afford to waste working women by not educating them" (6:4).

After Thomas Barrow exposes Gwen's past as a housemaid at Downton Abbey to the family and Gwen's husband, she again becomes the center of attention. Particularly Isobel is impressed with Gwen's development and calls it a true "twentieth century story" (6:4), thereby pointing out the singularity of her success. Naturally, not all of the upstairs characters are sympathetic towards Gwen's ambitions, causing her to justify herself:

> GWEN: I didn't' want to be in service my whole life, that's all.
> ISOBEL: So you found an opportunity and took it. Brava! [6:4].

Only at this point does Gwen reveal the important role Lady Sybil played in her advancement, by admitting that it was not her who found the opportunity for her first job, but Sybil. Of course, this revelation initiates the reminiscence of Sybil and her kindness. It does not, however, diminish the impression that Gwen achieved her position by herself, especially if we keep in mind the forceful speech she delivered earlier on the importance of educating the working class.

As can be seen, in her final appearance in the series education is at the center of Gwen's storyline once more. Not only does Gwen herself emphasize the pivotal part that education played in her success, she is convinced that she could have done even better had she not been limited by a lack of higher education. Using Hochschild's terminology,

Gwen's advancement can be classified first and foremost as an example for absolute success: By Series Six of *Downton Abbey* she is considerably better off than she was at the outset. However, in the reactions of her former fellow servants we can also detect traces of relative success. Thomas, for example, begrudges Gwen her "luck," as Mr. Bates calls it, and tries to harm her by exposing her past to the family. Another character that reacts strongly to Gwen's return is Daisy, who takes it as an opportunity to reflect upon her own life: "Look at Gwen. She's thrown off the yoke of service to make a good life. What am I doing with mine?" (6:4). Even in later episodes, Gwen continuously serves as reference whenever the idea of social advancement is discussed. All in all, Gwen's story sets the tone for the series' take on upward social mobility because her development already showcases the possibilities attached to and offered by education.

The second character in *Downton Abbey* who realizes the importance of education is Daisy Mason. Whereas Gwen only appears in a total of eight episodes, Daisy is a recurrent character in all six seasons of *Downton Abbey*. However, the plotline focusing on Daisy's interest in education and the development triggered by this interest is only introduced in Series Five. Until the end of Series Four, Daisy is mainly depicted as a simple-minded and naïve kitchen maid, afraid of electricity and is not to be seen upstairs under any circumstances. Unsurprisingly, she is easily manipulated and readily surrenders her own opinion to those of others. In Series One her infatuation with Thomas Barrow causes her to lie to Mr. Carson in order to frame Mr. Bates for a crime he did not commit. Notwithstanding her naivety, Daisy already displays a sense of missed opportunities in these early episodes, stating, "I've been nowhere and done nothing" (1:4). Even if she does not follow this insight at this point, it already foreshadows the development her character will undergo in later seasons. Although Daisy starts to take a stance for her own interests during Series Three and Series Four, she remains a rather naïve girl without any specific ambition. As such, she continuously values personal relationships over her professional advancement. Maybe the best example for this lack of professional ambition is her refusal to go to America as a cook for Mr. Lavinson at the end of Series Four, an opportunity that passes to Ivy instead.

The most remarkable part of Daisy's development, then, begins with her interest in education first mentioned in Series Five. This interest is sparked when Downton's housekeeper Mrs. Hughes brings news of a neighboring manor house which is run with a dramatically reduced staff. When Daisy asks what has happened to the servants who worked there before, Mrs. Hughes tells her that they left in order to work at factories because they prefer the working conditions there. This information causes Daisy to wonder if she and Mrs. Patmore will ever leave service. Mrs. Patmore reminds her of her father-in-law and his farm, pointing out the opportunities it holds in store for her should she ever wish to change her position. However, Daisy doubts that she will be able to make a life for herself at the farm, because she does not know anything about accounting. Therefore, so she believes, it will be impossible for her to adjust to a new life that requires more of her than the domestic duties of a kitchen maid.

Although Daisy does not believe in her capabilities, she begins to study arithmetic in order to improve her insight into accounting. The main reason for this effort is, as she confesses to Mrs. Patmore, that she wants to be a grownup and take on responsibility for her own life. Unlike Gwen, who embarked on her journey towards a different future with a clear set goal in mind, Daisy seems to be interested more in personal development. Nevertheless, in choosing to educate herself, she follows a path similar to Gwen. Just like

Gwen, Daisy identifies her lack of education as the decisive factor holding her back and attempts to correct this shortcoming through self-education. Unfortunately, her studies progress only slowly and Daisy finds it impossible to wrap her mind around mathematics. Her frustration induces Mrs. Patmore to approach Lady Rose, who engages herself at the village school, in order to ask for a tutor to help Daisy with her studies. Miss Bunting, who has already been presented as a force of modernity in the previous season, agrees to tutor Daisy and immediately recognizes her potential. As soon as the first lesson is over, Miss Bunting points out that Daisy will prove "a talented mathematician" (5:2). In the wake of her tuition, Daisy is amazed to realize that she suddenly understands everything and wonders how her life might have turned out if she had had a teacher like Miss Bunting when she was at school.

The impact this realization has on Daisy as a character is remarkable. She discovers her talent and her ability to learn, a perspective that is diametrically opposed to the assessment of her competence she voiced at the beginning of the season. Her impressive progress makes her think about sitting for an exam at the village school as soon as possible and even leads her to consider taking her studies further than mathematics, much to Mr. Carson's dismay. He is skeptical about Daisy's newfound ambition, because he doubts that all the extra work she is taking on will prove "necessary for [her] place in the scheme of things" (5:3). In this statement Carson, who can be understood as an embodiment of conservatism, displays his belief in the validity of fixed positions within a society. Daisy is, however, encouraged by Mrs. Hughes, who advises her "to go as far in life as God and luck allow" (5:3). Daisy apparently follows this advice and soon broadens her interest to topics such as history and politics. This development does not go unnoticed by Mrs. Patmore who remarks that "studying mathematics is one thing; she's studying to be a revolutionary now" (5:4), which concisely sums up the change in Daisy's interests and in her outlook on life.

How profoundly Daisy has changed on a personal level is put into words when she and Mrs. Patmore are called upstairs during a dinner in order to solve a dispute between Lord Grantham and Miss Bunting. Daisy apologizes if her studies have interfered with her work in the kitchen but immediately goes on to praise Miss Bunting for changing her life: "Miss Bunting has opened my eyes to a world of knowledge I knew nothing of. Maybe I'll stay a cook all my life, but I have choices now, interests, facts at my fingertips. I'd never had any of that if she hadn't come to teach me" (5:3). Daisy clearly recognizes the opportunities that opened up for her once she had access to education. This does not only change the way she thinks about herself, but more importantly how she interacts with other characters. While people she looked up to easily influenced Daisy in earlier seasons, she now takes on responsibility and stands up for them. This development can best be seen in her relationship with Mrs. Patmore, who serves as a mother figure for Daisy throughout the series. Noticing Mrs. Patmore's distress about that fact that her nephew Archie, who had been shot for cowardice during World War I, is to be excluded from his home village's war memorial, Daisy sticks up for her and encourages her to protest to the war office. When Mrs. Patmore is reluctant and points out that she would not know how to write such a letter of protest, Daisy instantly offers to write the letter for her, arguing that if enough people protest this might change the rules. This short exchange between Daisy and Mrs. Patmore is remarkable for two different aspects. On the one hand it is an important indicator for Daisy's newfound belief in her own strength and abilities. On the other hand, it points to the power of the people which Daisy begins to grasp and which can be traced back to her contact with Miss Bunting. Mrs. Patmore, who recognizes Daisy's personal growth, associates this change with her learning. Thereby, she points out the important influence the lessons with Miss Bunting have on Daisy and thus confirms the observations made so far.

Considering the huge impact Miss Bunting's presence has on Daisy's personal development it does not come as a surprise that she is devastated about her teacher's decision to leave the village in order to take on a new job. She voices this anger openly, once again proving how much she has changed and how little is left of the shy and impressionable kitchen maid she was introduced as at the beginning of the series. In her leaving remarks, Miss Bunting explicitly asks Mrs. Patmore to ensure that Daisy does not give up her interest in education: "Don't let Daisy give up her studies, she's got potential" (5:5). The fact that Daisy leaves her downstairs domain in order to approach Tom Branson about Miss Bunting's decision is further proof for how much she has grown. Including him in her own peer group she voices one of her newly acquired political views, stating, "We're the future, they're the past" (5:5). This exchange between Daisy and Branson marks the first moment where Daisy explicitly expresses her political views towards a member of the family (albeit an assimilated one), thus indeed proving the revolutionary force that Mrs. Patmore already suspected her to be.

After Miss Bunting's departure from the village, Daisy is more devoted to her studies than ever, because she does not want the let down her former teacher—who was after all the first person who truly believed in her capabilities beyond her work in the kitchen. Nevertheless, she soon has to face the fact that it is much harder on her own. Even though Mr. Molesley offers his help, Daisy feels left alone and gradually loses sight of her goals. This discouragement is intensified when the newly elected labor party fails to accomplish the things Daisy had hoped for. This political development results in an increasing disillusionment on her part, which finally causes her to not only doubt the effectiveness of the party but the point of her attempt at educating herself as well. She feels "trapped, held fast in a system that gives us [the working class] no value and no freedom" (5:7). In an attempt to rekindle Daisy's interest in education Mrs. Patmore and Mr. Molesley engage her father-in-law Mr. Mason, whose wish for Daisy to join him on his farm was the initial reason for her to take an interest in education at all. Of course, Mr. Mason proves a reliable ally and voices a remarkable creed in favor of education as soon as he is faced with Daisy's doubts: "Education is power. Don't forget that. There's no limit to what you can achieve. If you'll only give a year or two to mastering those books.... There are millions out there who could have done so much, if they'd only been given an education" (5:7). In this surprisingly modern speech, Mr. Mason points to the personal agency education offers to everyone who has access to it, while at the same time expressing the wasted potential of those without such an opportunity. Of course, Daisy obliges to the wish of her father-in-law and takes up her efforts with new energy.

Once she is exposed to art and culture in London Daisy thrives even more. She realizes that the opportunities provided by a city like London, such as art and literature, are not reserved for the upper class but accessible for her as well. As a consequence, she considers handing in her notice in order to find work in London and continue her studies there. However, as soon as she realizes how hurt Mrs. Patmore is by this decision, she changes her mind and resolves to stay at Downton at least until her exams. This willingness to subordinate her wish for change to her personal relationships once more emphasizes the observation that Daisy's plotline focuses on her personal development rather than on a specific ambition on her part. Nevertheless, Daisy pursues her studies further in Series Six and receives support from the staff as well as the family. Even Mr. Carson, who admits to being skeptical at first, voices his approval and wishes her luck when her exams finally come up. Likewise, Mrs. Hughes admires her for taking a second chance and refers to Gwen's visit as proof that anything is possible when the staff discuss Daisy's future (thereby confirming my previous observation that Gwen's story serves as a point of reference in connection to social advancement). Of course, it does not come as a surprise that Daisy passes all of her papers with high marks and receives the praise of the village school's headmaster.

In the final season of *Downton Abbey* Daisy appears as a strong young woman who is not afraid to stand up for her own interests and for the people she loves. However, the development of her character takes a turn that serves to put her academic achievements into the background. While it is true that she finally finds her own voice and does not shy back from expressing her opinion as she used to, she frequently causes trouble with that. The most obvious example for this is her attempt to save the tenancy of her father-in-law by approaching and confronting the new owners of the land. Instead of making them see her point (that Mr. Mason gave his whole life to the farm and deserves to be kept on as a tenant) she alienates the new owners and thus ensures that he indeed loses his farm. This new side of Daisy's character is underlined by nicknames such as "Guy Fawkes" and "Madame Defarge" given to her by Mrs. Patmore, which highlight the revolutionary but at the same time destructive energy Daisy displays in the final seasons of *Downton Abbey*.[2] As can be seen, this development removes the focus of Daisy's storyline from the possibilities offered by education. Furthermore, by foregrounding the difficult romantic relationship between Daisy and the footman Andrew, the importance of her studies become even less important. By the series finale it is not quite clear anymore why Daisy took her exams in the first place and there is nothing left of her plans to leave for London once she completed her studies. In addition to this, Daisy is now preoccupied and unsatisfied with her appearance, referring to herself as a "frump" (6:9). At the end of the finale episode she reveals her decision to move into Mr. Mason's farm, hinting at a possible future with Andrew, who always insisted that he dreamed of becoming a farmer one day. In this sense, Daisy continues her life as a domestic servant.

Despite the fact that, strictly speaking, Daisy's story is not one of social advancement, her development is probably the most remarkable of the series. The subplot concerning Daisy and her quest for education concentrates on the personal growth triggered by her lessons and not so much on the issue of upward social mobility. Still, it is the idea of leaving service that provides the first impulse for her interest in education and she indeed manages to achieve the goal she set for herself, as she matures into a young woman who is not afraid of taking responsibility for her own actions. As such, she is the character in *Downton Abbey* who voices the injustice of the English class system in all openness. She considers the Crawleys as representatives of a system that represses the members of the working class like Mr. Mason and she strongly disapproves of that. Considering this, it is no coincidence that the subversive energy Daisy embodies has to be contained by removing the emphasis of her storyline from her revolutionary views and transferring it to her romantic relationship with Andy.

While Daisy can be less obviously described as a realization of the American dream her story does indeed put forth important aspects of the ideology captured by the dream. Voicing a demand for equality among all strata of society, Daisy expresses one of the key components of the American dream, thereby underlining the relevance of the concept once more.

Mr. Molesley is the final character that plays a significant role with regard to the portrayal of education. His storyline is most obviously modeled after the ideals of the American dream, at least with regard to the events of Series Five and Series Six of *Downton Abbey*. Molesley is introduced in 1:2 as the butler of the new heir to Downton, Matthew Crawley. During the first series he predominantly serves as an indicator for Matthew's increasing adaptation to his new upper class life (Byrne 317–319). However, after Matthew's death in the Series Three finale, Mr. Molesley loses his job as valet and quickly moves down the social scale. As a consequence, his storyline for Series Four revolves on this downward path and his unsuccessful attempts to secure an adequate position for himself in service.

Although Molesley places a number of advertisements looking for a suitable job after the tragic accident he is ultimately forced to leave the Abbey and to move back in with his father. His decline goes so far that he even has to work as a simple laborer, mending streets and filling in as a deliveryman. When the opportunity arises, he reluctantly returns to Downton as a stand-in footman, but he continues to point out that he has "come down in the world" (4:3). His disappointment with the course his life has taken is especially apparent when the Dowager Countess voices her delight in seeing Mr. Molesley back at the Abbey:

> Dowager Countess: They can't keep a good man down.
> Mr. Molesley: On the contrary, milady, that's exactly what they can do [4:3].

Molesley is very aware of the fact that returning to Downton as a footman is below his qualification and his talents, which is the reason why he hesitates when Mr. Carson offers him a long-term job as a replacement for Alfred.[3] Molesley believes that taking on a "permanent inferior job" (4:5) would determine the ultimate acceptance of his downfall. But in view of the fact that he has no other options, he finally agrees to Carson's offer. All things considered, Mr. Molesley's plotline in Series Four serves mainly to outline him as an unlucky person who somehow always misses his opportunity to get ahead. However, his budding relationship with Mrs. Baxter already hints at the possibility of a future advancement because she keeps reminding him that even though he has been dealt a difficult hand in life, he can always "climb up again" (4:8).

Molesley's opportunity to pursue his true interests arises when Miss Bunting decides to leave the village. Noticing how Daisy struggles to keep up her studies on her own, Mr. Molesley offers his help. His interest in literature had already been hinted at in the second season, when he bought a book for Anna to read and discuss with him. In a conversation with Daisy he now reveals his deeply ingrained passion for education and learning and admits that he dreamed of becoming a teacher when he was younger. When Daisy asks him why he does not pursue that career now, he immediately rejects the idea: "No…. I've missed it" (5:6). This disillusionment and the experience of missed chances is a recurring theme in connection to Molesley, who points this out himself in the following exchange with Mr. Carson:

> Mr. Carson: As is it, you've missed your chance.
> Mr. Molesley: As I generally do [4:5].

Even though Molesley feels that his chance of pursuing his dreams has passed, he is very eager to help Daisy get on with her studies. While she used to concentrate on mathematics and history when she was studying with Miss Bunting, Mr. Molesley tries to interest her in literature, introducing her to novels like *Vanity Fair*.[4] Mrs. Patmore is impressed by his dedication and observes that he obviously "missed out on [his] vocation" (5:7). By pointing this out, Mrs. Patmore feeds into the impression of missed opportunities that Molesley himself keeps referring to.

Mr. Molesley continues to help Daisy with the preparation for her exams in the final season of *Downton Abbey*. He even approaches Mr. Dawes, the headmaster of the village school, about Daisy's examination and procures old exams papers for her to study with. More importantly, however, by doing so he catches Mr. Dawes' interest. The headmaster is surprised to learn about Molesley's capabilities when they go over the examination papers together. When Molesley praises Daisy's progress during the wedding of Mr. Carson and Mrs. Hughes, the headmaster strikes up a conversation with Molesley that captures the relevance the latter places on education and the opportunities it offers to those lucky enough to be exposed to it:

> Mr. Dawes: I think she'll do *you* credit, Mr. Molesley. You seem to have been an excellent influence in all this.
> Mr. Molesley: Well, I believe that education is the gate that leads to any future worth having.
> Mr. Dawes: Have you missed your vocation?
> Mr. Molesley: I've missed everything, Mr. Dawes. But Daisy doesn't have to [6:3, my italics].

This conversation not only once more highlights Molesley's disappointment with the course of his life, but also stresses his view on education as a means for advancement. For him education is the best, if not the only way, to ensure the chance to follow ones dreams—an opportunity that he feels he himself has missed, but that he wants Daisy to have nonetheless.

When Daisy's exams finally come up Mr. Dawes offers Molesley the opportunity to take a test himself. The headmaster is impressed with Molesley's "respect for education" and his "enthusiasm" (6:6) and wants to make use of his potential if possible. In order to do so, he proposes to devise a test on general knowledge to get a better idea of Molesley's abilities. The results of his examination are so overwhelming that Mr. Dawes offers Molesley a teaching position at the village school right away: "Mr. Molesley, I'd be very glad if you would join the teaching staff at the village school … I'm impressed, Mr. Molesley. There are Oxford and Cambridge graduates who know far less than you do. You should be proud" (6:7). Mr. Dawes attests Molesley a level of knowledge comparable to that of a university student. Although the teaching position offered to him is only a part-time engagement, this development clearly marks the moment where Molesley receives the reward for the hard work he put into educating himself throughout his life. By taking on five classes as a teacher for history and English literature, Molesley is finally given the opportunity to pursue the career he always envisioned for himself.

However, his working-class students do not react well toward him at first: they make fun of him and refuse to pay attention to what he is trying to teach them. It is only after Molesley reveals his humble background as a servant that he succeeds in capturing their attention. Obviously, the fact that he is a servant establishes a contact on equal footing between the students and Molesley which ultimately enables him to deliver the most important speech the series has to offer with regard to education: "You must never think that education is only for special people, you know, for clever people, the toffs. Education is for everyone. […] I never gave up on learning, do you see? I read as much as I could and I taught myself. And I hope to be able to teach you, maybe give you the shortcut I never had" (6:8).

This speech is remarkable for a number of reasons. First of all, it once more emphasizes the importance of education as the enabling factor for personal and professional success. Even though Molesley had to leave school at the age of twelve, he pursued his interest in education and thus ultimately obtained the opportunity to follow his true calling. Second, it highlights the idea of equality when it comes to education. Molesley points out in all clarity that education is not reserved for the aristocracy but that everyone should have equal access to knowledge and the possibilities connected to it. This last point is underlined further by the fact that Molesley's speech is framed by a classroom discussion on the divine right of kings, which is a theory of authority that can easily be regarded as the embodiment of class difference. The scene is opened by Molesley's suggestion that one of his students "might run the country one day" and ends with his remark that "kings are like anyone else" (6:8). Just like Daisy did before him, Molesley expresses the idea of equality among all parts of society that should result in a world where everyone is given an equal chance to succeed, be it the daughter of a servant or the son of an earl. By doing so, Molesley fulfills what Hochschild & Scovronick recognize as one of the central responsibilities of schools: he strives to raise awareness for a sense of equality among his working-class students, thereby laying the groundwork for a future generation whose identity and ambitions are shaped by that idea.

Of course, Mr. Molesley's final reward comes in the last episode when he is offered a permanent position as a full-time teacher and moves out of Downton and into his own cottage. With this outcome his story comes close to the "rags to riches" stories often associated with the American dream. During the first four seasons of *Downton* the series depicts his downfall from a respectable position as a butler to that of a menial worker. Molesley's luck only turns in Series Five and this turnaround is explicitly connected to his interest in education. Unlike Gwen and Daisy he manages to better his station in life without external assistance (except, of course the support he receives from Mr. Dawes). Furthermore, his story places a very strong emphasis on his personal agency, because it is stressed time and again that Molesley is self-taught and thus achieved his goal purely through his own hard work and determination. In the terminology of success suggested by Hochschild, Molesley's is an absolute success, because he clearly ends up in a position that is much better than the one he started out in.

As has been noted at the beginning of this essay, the idea of social change is present in *Downton Abbey* from the first episode onwards and it is considered from a wide variety of angles. In the first episode of the series Mrs. Hughes asks Mr. Carson if he ever considered taking a different path: "Do you ever wish you'd gone another way? Worked in a shop or a factory?" (1:1). While Mrs. Hughes' questions embody the wish for a past lived differently, stories such as Gwen's and Mr. Molesley's depict the actual realization of upward social mobility.

However, the reality concerning the possibility of members of the working class, especially women, to move up the social scale was rather different. As Pamela Horn asserts when it comes to the elementary education of girls "the picture was, on the whole, a depressing one" (79). It was believed that a woman's place was in a home, either as housewife and mother or as a domestic servant (74). As a consequence, the education of girls was believed to be less important and thus the curriculum for girls focused on domestic skills rather than academic achievements (72). Although boys and girls alike were supposed to be taught the three R's (reading, writing, and arithmetic) the expectations toward female pupils were much lower, especially when it came to arithmetic: "Small wonder that girls' numeracy skills were often so weak" (76). This circumstance is reflected rather accurately in the character of Daisy Mason who claims she was "rubbish at numbers in school" (5:1). Thus, Daisy's storyline as well as those of Gwen and Molesley depict the wish for a more extensive education that, as Jonathan Rose points out, was widespread among the working-class at the turn of the century (135).

While the subplot concerning Daisy and her thirst for knowledge seems a conceivable (albeit glorified) storyline, Gwen's advancement from a housemaid to a secretary and finally even to a government employee is much less likely. Horn highlights the limited access women had to education in the late nineteenth century, an observation which especially concerns daughters of farmers, like Gwen (77). Horn evaluates the data collected in the 1901 census and concludes that "only the most determined minority of working-class girls were able to obtain, through education, entry to jobs which allowed them to compete equally with men and to develop their individual talents and skills to the full" (82).

Against this historical backdrop the ease with which Gwen masters her postal course in typewriting appears rather unlikely. In addition to that, her endeavor would probably have been complicated by her physically exhausting work as a domestic servant, which very likely left little time for private matters. A similar observation holds true for Mr. Molesley, whose plotline in Series Five and Six is clearly modeled after the concept of the American dream. Having been forced to leave school at the age of twelve in order to support his father financially, he continues to educate himself on his own account. This endeavor proves so successful that the headmaster of the village school attests him an education equal—if not superior—to that of Oxford and Cambridge graduates. While it may be believable that a domestic servant continued to pursue an interest in history and literature sparked by his elementary education the assumption that the results would surpass those of the country's educational elite seems highly unlikely. This observation is supported by the fact that public schools in the second half of the nineteenth century (which is when Molesley would have attended school) concentrated mostly on the conveyance of the three rudiments of education. Aside from that, the focus was on raising decorous young men, as Adonis and Pollard emphasize: "Knowledge of manners, not maths, was the demand of the era, and public schools were there to provide it" (40). It seems, then, that *Downton Abbey*'s take on education and the possibilities it offers to members of the working class is not a historically accurate depiction of the circumstances people like Gwen and Mr. Molesley would have faced. Rather, it caters to a contemporary understanding of the relevance of education and foregrounds the opportunities connected to it.

The three subplots considered are certainly not the only storylines in *Downton Abbey* that focus on social advancement. In order to underline the significance of the ideology of the American dream on the events of the series even further, I would like to briefly consider two characters whose stories function as counter narratives to the successful depictions presented through Gwen, Daisy, and Mr. Molesley.

The first example is Thomas Barrow, cast as one of the series' main antagonists and deeply dissatisfied with his position as first footman. But unlike Gwen, he does not have a specific future in mind and thus tries a range of tactics in order to better his position. Anticipating the outbreak of World War I, Thomas joins the medical corps in an attempt to avoid combat.[5] When this attempt fails, he deliberately gets himself shot in the hand to guarantee his return from the front. Thomas comes back to Downton as a medical officer and is even put in charge of running the house when the Abbey is turned into a convalescent home for officers for the duration of the war. In this position, he is no longer answerable to the firm hierarchy he resents so much, thus seemingly overcoming the boundaries imposed on him by his social class (Byrne 324). Compared to the other members of the staff he consequently describes himself as "the one that got away" (2:2). This advancement, however, is by no means permanent. As soon as the war ends, Thomas finds himself unemployed and in the need for a future. He seeks this future in business, by exploiting the post-war need for supplies and engaging in black-market activities. When this endeavor fails, Thomas is left with no other opportunity but to return to the Abbey and to a life of service.

Thomas' plotline in Series Two serves as a counter narrative to the successful stories of social change discussed in the first part of this essay. However, instead of calling the possibility of social advancement into question, Thomas' failures rather underline the validity of the American dream-ideology. It appears that only change achieved through industriousness and hard work is permanent. Opposed to that, Thomas tries to change his station in life through cunning, manipulation, and borderline criminal activities.[6] To recall the definition of the American dream offered by President Clinton, Thomas does not "play by the rules" but on the contrary frequently breaks them. Furthermore, the success that he is after is an embodiment of competitive success which means that he strives to achieve victory over others (Hochschild 18). The fact that this behavior is clearly not rewarded is significant and serves as a reassurance of the ideal captured by the American dream and the representation of this ideology within the fictional world of *Downton Abbey*.

Another example of such a counter narrative is discernable in the subplot that focuses on the housemaid Ethel. When Ethel arrives at Downton at the beginning of Series Two she brings with her an air of anticipation. She is confident that the war will change the structure of society, for the working class as well as for the aristocracy. Just like Thomas, Ethel wishes for social advancement and openly voices her discontentment with being in service: "In the end, I want to be more than just a servant" (2:1). Significantly, her role model is the American silent movie actress Mabel Normand, whose life was affected by scandals (Sherman 24–28) and who "was nothing when she started" (2:1). When Downton is turned into a convalescent home for wounded officers Ethel flirts with one of the patients and is eventually dismissed by Mrs. Hughes for having an affair. In the end, Ethel's attempt to better her position in life results in an illegitimate child and ultimately forces her into prostitution in Series Three. Just like Thomas, Ethel chooses to seek a better fortune through questionable methods and fails bitterly, thereby strengthening the series' focus on opportunities acquired through hard work and personal dedication. This observation is underpinned by the fact that Ethel fills in the vacancy resulting from Gwen's successful attempt at bettering herself. Seen from this angle, Ethel can be understood as a negative foil to Gwen's advancement, thereby reinforcing the workings of the American dream.

The counter narratives provided by characters such as Thomas and Ethel confirm the observations made in this essay—both when it comes to the attitude most promising for a successful social change and the relevance of education as a means for this success. When Thomas is finally considered for the position as the new butler of Downton Abbey due to Carson's impairment the latter highlights the training Thomas received during his employment at Downton as the most convincing proof for his suitability to the task. Throughout the second half of the final season Thomas had time and again highlighted learning experiences offered to him by Mr. Carson as well as by Lord Grantham. The positive outcome of Thomas' storyline, then, is also connected to his newly acquired willingness to learn and to truly better himself, which once more underlines the principles of the American dream: as soon as he is willing to "play by the rules," he is rewarded.

This essay has argued that the depiction of those storylines in *Downton Abbey* influenced by the issue of education are—in varying degrees—modeled after the ideology of the American dream. Gwen and Daisy as well as Mr. Molesley follow their "god-given talent" (Gosh 28) and use it in order to improve their station in life. In the case of Daisy this means a personal development that ultimately molds her into one of the distinctly modern characters with a modern understanding of society, while Gwen and Mr. Molesley pursue their professional ambitions and manage to leave service. It has become evident that the characters considered are enabled to pursue their dreams because of the possibilities education creates for them. This interrelation between education and social advancement lies at the core of the American dream and is therefore bound to resonate with American audiences. Seen from this angle, the trajectories of the central characters considered showcase the relevance of a concept deeply rooted in the minds of American viewers. Thus, *Downton Abbey* helps to validate and confirm the belief in an ideology which is of significant importance to the construction of American identity.

NOTES

1. There is debate about the origin of the term "American dream." Hanson and White argue that the idea of the dream can be traced back to the Declaration of Independence (1), while Cullen draws parallels between the Roman republic and empire and the ideology of the American dream (17–26). However, while the origin of the concept itself remains uncertain, it is generally agreed that the term became popular through the work of James Truslow Adams, who introduced it in 1931 in his *Epic of America* (Gosh 29).

2. There are a number of references to Guy Fawkes in *Downton Abbey*, and each time he is used as an example for an attempt at revolution that went horrible wrong and that was rightfully punished. The reference to Madame Defarge, one of the central villains in Charles Dickens' *A Tale of Two Cities*, falls in line with further mentions of the French Revolution that all highlight the destructive aspects of that period of upheaval.

3. The most obvious symbol for his decline is the fact that he has to wear white gloves that identify him as a footman. In Series One Isobel mistakenly suspects Molesley to suffer from erysipelas and advises he should wear gloves at all times. His reaction to this suggestion is one of pure bewilderment and refusal: "I couldn't wait a table wearing gloves. I'd look like a footman" (*Downton Abbey*, 1:4).

4. This is another indicator for the emphasis the show puts on stories of social advancement because Becky Sharp, the protagonist of Thackeray's novel, likewise attempts to better her position in life. Of course, Becky does not choose the path of education, but the mentioning of *Vanity Fair* again draws attention to the issue of upward social mobility.

5. Byrne argues that Thomas uses the outbreak of the war as an opportunity for social advancement (323). While the characters considered so far all create opportunities for themselves, Thomas uses an outward impulse as a welcome starting point for bettering his position, which already sets him apart.

6. A first example for such a failed attempt is presented as early as the first episode, where Thomas tries to blackmail the Duke of Crowborough after the latter refuses to hire him as his valet.

WORKS CITED

Adonis, Andrew, and Stephen Pollard. *A Class Act. The Myth of Britain's Classless Society*. London: Hamish Hamilton, 1997. Print.

Beach, J.M. "The Ideology of the American Dream: Two Competing Ideologies in Education, 1776–2006." *Educational Studies* 41 (2007): 148–164.

Byrne, Katherine. "Adapting Heritage: Class and Conservatism in *Downton Abbey*." *Rethinking History* 18 (2014): 311–327. Print.

Cullen, Jim: "Twilight's Gleaming: The American Dream and the Ends of Republics." *The American Dream in the 21st Century*. Eds. Sandra L. Hanson and John Kenneth White. Philadelphia: Temple University Press, 2011: 17–26. Print.

Gosh, Cyril. *The Politics of the American Dream. Democratic Inclusion in Contemporary American Political Culture*. New York: Palgrave Macmillan, 2013. Print.

Hanson, Sandra L., and John Kenneth White. "Introduction: The Making and Persistence of the American Dream." *The American Dream in the 21st Century*. Eds. Sandra L. Hanson and John Kenneth White. Philadelphia: Temple University Press, 2011: 1–16. Print.

Hochschild, Jennifer L. *Facing Up to the American Dream: Race, Class, and the Soul of the Nation*. Princeton: Princeton University Press, 1995. Print.

Hochschild, Jennifer L., and Nathan Scovronick. *The American Dream and the Public Schools*. Oxford: Oxford University Press, 2003. Print.

Horn, Pamela. "The Education and Employment of Working-Class Girls, 1870–1914." *History of Education* 17 (1988): 71–82. Print.

Miller, Laura. "Sweet Valet High: The American Love Affair with *Downton Abbey*." *New Statesman* 142 (2013): 38–40. Print.

Rose, Jonathan. "Willingly to School: The Working-Class Response to Elementary Education in Britain, 1875–1918." *Journal of British Studies* 32 (1993): 114–138. Print.

Schlechty, Phillip C. "Schooling, Business, and the New American Dream." *Business Horizons* 36 (1993): 3–8. Print.

Sherman, William Thomas. *Mabel Normand: A Source Book to her Life and Films*. Gun Jones Publishing, 2006. Web.

Ştiuliuc, Diana. "The American Dream as the Cultural Expression of North American Identity." *Philological Jassyensia* 7 (2011): 363–370. Print.

Umstead, R. Thomas. "Historical License." *Multichannel News* 34 (2013): 10–11. Print.

"We're all in this together!"

Big Society Themes

GILL JAMIESON

It's no coincidence that *Downton Abbey* aired at a time when the political environment in the UK was dominated by the first coalition government since the Second World War, formed in an uneasy alliance between the Conservatives and Liberal Democrats. As Atkinson, Robert and Savage point out, this was a government committed to cutting public spending, reducing the deficit and encouraging self-reliance and social responsibility, underpinned somewhat controversially, by a "rhetoric of fairness" (14). In a manifesto subtitled "Freedom, Fairness and Responsibility" ("The Coalition: Our Programme for Government," Cabinet Office 2010), social mobility, self-sufficiency and David Cameron's notions of a "Big Society" would take precedence: "You can call it liberalism. You can call it empowerment. You can call it freedom. You can call it responsibility. I call it the Big Society."

It is against this backdrop that we should contextualize *Downton Abbey*. The series presents a lavish portrayal of Edwardian England in which competing discourses of affluence and austerity are explored through a "structured narrative of modernity" (Nava 2). Longstanding debates about the heritage industry (see for example, Hewison; Higson; Monk) recognize the country house setting as a familiar trope in heritage drama in which the strictures of class and social mobility are navigated and exposed. Although some critics would dismiss the series as a nostalgic fantasy, others have recognized its deeper significance. Jennifer P. Nesbitt argues in a recent critique: "*Downton Abbey* continues a tradition of using historical, or costume, drama to reflect on contemporary social conflicts from a (safe) distance" (253). The tendency to interpret the series as a comment on the present is certainly not new; indeed this approach continues the long-standing debate about the significance of the heritage industry as an "emollient," as Robert Hewison noted in a seminal account of the heritage industry: "the nostalgic impulse is an important agency in adjustment to crisis, it is a social emollient and reinforces national identity when confidence is weakened or threatened" (Hewison 47).

Katherine Byrne's reading situates the series in a post-heritage landscape and she too is mindful of the various ways in which it continues to resonate for a contemporary audience. Byrne acknowledges the parallel with the contemporary political scene in her analysis:

Perhaps what is most "post-heritage" about this series then, is the post-modern way it blurs the lines between real life and fiction—to the extent that, due to its focus on money and privilege, the Coalition in power from 2010–2015 has been nicknamed "the Downton Abbey government" [Freeland in Byrne 8].

However, despite the consensus that the series often articulates contemporary anxieties, critical accounts tend to stop short of a detailed engagement with the political rhetoric of the Coalition. This essay therefore proposes the first detailed examination of the series in light of coalition political philosophy and policy during that pivotal five-year period. Extending the work of Bryne, Tincknell and Nesbitt in particular, I discuss the various ways in which the series intersects with and frames, contemporary public debates in the UK about spending, consumption, equality, welfare provision and personal responsibility.

One of the remarkable parallels between the series and the contemporary political arena is the fact that the narrative world of the series from Series Two to Four covers the period when the UK was governed by a coalition government with the Liberal Democrat Lloyd George as Prime Minister (1916–1922). This momentous period in British history encompassed the Great War and the beginnings of welfare provision in the UK. Lloyd George is regarded as one of the most important political figures of the twentieth century in terms of laying the groundwork for the Welfare State (Gilbert; Toye; Fraser; Hattersley). Therefore, it seems particularly apt that the narrative of *Downton Abbey* often involves the re-evaluation of welfare provision at precisely the same time as these issues are being debated publically in the UK today.

Although there is much to support the view that ideologically the series "shores up a deeply conservative model of gender and class" (Tincknell 778), and a "misty-eyed nostalgia for England's class structure" (Nesbitt 253), according to series creator and writer Julian Fellowes, the Grantham family are liberal in their outlook, although he hesitates to describe them as liberal in a political sense:

> I think we present the Granthams as a liberal family, socially. Not particularly liberal, politically. On the whole, it has been a feature that liberalism was more to be found at the upper end of the aristocracy, socially, than it was in the middle classes. Because they were more traveled, they were more sophisticated, they were more educated. It was a much broader-looking culture [Fellowes, interviewed by Dave Itzkoff].

The Granthams are for all of their railing against social change, the same kind of Conservatives who would gravitate to Lloyd George, even as they appear to often represent a "demagogic Torysim" (Gilbert 1058) which would foment Liberal radicalism. Fellowes' distinction between the social and the political manifestation of liberalism is very revealing of political nuances; arguably borne out of his own understanding of the complexities of the British political arena, and one knowledgeable of the spectrum of views contained in each political party. As Beech notes, there are contradictory strands in every political party in the UK and in the run up to the election campaign of 2010 both the Conservatives and the Liberals "rebooted" their own brand of liberalism (Beech and Lee 2). The prevailing view that the series is archly conservative in its politics, therefore, needs to be re-evaluated in light of these shifts. Truncknell's analysis for example, tends to stress the conservative currents within the narrative at the expense of the liberal tendency, when in reality these two tendencies co-exist within a rebranded Conservative party and as a consequence of the new political reality of a coalition government seeking a "broad church" consensus. Although it is tempting to read the sly asides to the Liberals in the series as evidence of anxieties around the impact of the Coalition, repeatedly and overtly debunking the Liberal viewpoint particularly when aired by popular and much-loved characters makes it seem like a Tory "stich-up." However, the Liberal pathway is the one that inevitably prevails as a narrative outcome. When the Dowager Countess remarks in typically caustic fashion to Mary that Matthew's love interest Lavinia Swire and therefore Mary's rival for Matthew's affections, "knows those damned idiot liberals on the front bench" (2:3), we are invited to laugh at the current political situation. How could this *not* be a thinly-veiled attack on the Liberals in the contemporary coalition? Arguably, at the same time, we are laughing at Violet and her outmoded and preposterous assertions of conservatism. Could it be that despite those assertions the audience knows she is really a soft-hearted liberal deep down?

Downton's exploration of contradictory impulses is arguably what gives it its great dramatic momentum. Similarly, the British political system is famously built around the cut and thrust of adversarial politics, with the spectacle of debate in the House of Commons as thrillingly dramatic as any dinner party scene in *Downton Abbey*. On the surface it seems a polarized environment, but in reality each party encompasses a spectrum of viewpoints, and finding the consensus to lead and govern the key objective. David Cameron's vocal endorsement of liberal conservatism would be an astute maneuver paving the way for an alliance with the Liberal Democrats following the hung parliament in 2010. Cameron's speech of 11 September 2006 at the British-American Project (Seldom and Finn), is suggestive of a centrist position that is not dissimilar to that endorsed in *Downton Abbey*:

> I am a liberal conservative, rather than a neo-conservative. Liberal—because I support the aim of spreading freedom and democracy, and support humanitarian intervention. Conservative—because I recognise the complexities of human nature, and am sceptical of grand schemes to remake the world.

My argument is that the liberal conservative viewpoint is the one which carries the day in the series, a departure from the view that the series is an uncomplicated exponent of traditional conservatism. Although many characters express concerns about the preservation of tradition in the narrative, this is shown to be an objective best achieved through adoption of the confluence of a liberal conservative ideology in which social responsibility and self-sufficiency frames an investment in a compassionate community as the bedrock of a "good society." This parallels the outcome of the 2010 General Election in which the resulting coalition between two ideologically opposed parties (as Finn points out), ensured stability by providing a majority in the House of Commons and a mandate to govern based on a re-evaluation of both parties' political manifestos. According to Quinn, this was a coalition in which the Liberal Democrats did considerably better on a number of key policy issues as the coalition pursued a broadly centrist policy. Subsequently, I believe it is possible to argue that the liberal view is the one that dominates and prevails in *Downton Abbey*.

"Big Society" versus "Big Government"

Tracing the origins of the idea of the Big Society, Antje Bednarek maps out the complex set of expectations around the idea and explains why it came to dominate David

Cameron's political manifesto. One of the cornerstones of traditional Tory thinking revolves around a belief in charity as the responsibility of family, church, and the wider community. It is not something dispensed by government. Bednarek's analysis links the evolution of the term "Big Society" to "Cameron's belief in compassionate Conservatism" (O'Hara 48). Cameron emerges as an exponent of a new type of conservatism that maintains its ideological roots in "traditionalism" by stressing personal and social responsibility. However, in order to build the Big Society it is necessary to appeal to the electorate. This has to be placed within a contextualization of the public perception of the Conservative Party in the UK, which would be described somewhat infamously as "the nasty party" by one of its own members, Theresa May, during her tenure as Party Chairwoman in 2003, before she would go on to serve in government as Home Secretary and latterly as Prime Minister. The notion that the Conservatives were a party lacking compassion for the vulnerable following a lengthy period of Conservative government (first under Margaret Thatcher, then under John Major), resulting in thirteen years of opposition and the widespread belief that they were unelectable, led to deliberate (and sometimes laughable) attempts to counter this widely-held view at the same time as the party would adopt increasingly austere policies with regard to welfare provision and the deficit. These attempts would become a characteristic of David Cameron's leadership. For example, in 2006 he would make a somewhat notorious speech to the Centre for Social Justice encouraging conservatives to "hug a hoodie" in an overt attempt to rebrand the party as the one which would care for the disenfranchised. Tonally this ideological shift fits perfectly with *Downton* in the sense that the comedic potential of storylines and situations is often yoked from the most conservative characters coming round to accept or even advocate "leftish" views. Cameron's "hug a hoodie" moment is the equivalent Violet Grantham expressing a fondness for street children. This is why, when we laugh at Violet's caustic remark about Liberals on the front-bench cited earlier, I believe we are laughing because we know she too is a liberal at heart.

The idea that charitable giving and compassion, both explored at great length through the various narrative arcs of *Downton*, are core ideals promoted in Cameron's Big Society is a deliberate strategy aimed at limiting the need for state funded intervention, or "Big Government" as Cameron would describe it. He would address this idea explicitly in his Commons tribute following the death of former Conservative Prime Minister Margaret Thatcher in 2013:

> Though it seems absurd today, the state had got so big that it owned our airports and airline, the phones in our houses, and trucks on our roads. They even owned a removal company. The air was thick with defeatism; there was a sense that the role of government was simply to manage decline. Margaret Thatcher rejected this defeatism. She had a clear view about what needed to change.

Downton Abbey privileges charitable giving as the preferred course of action from the more fortunate to the less fortunate. Perhaps the most overtly charitable character in *Downton* is Mrs. Crawley, who from her first appearance in the series is committed to sometimes radical notions of reform in which volunteering for the betterment of the local community brings her into frequent conflict with other members of the family, notably the Dowager Countess. The two frequently spar over ideas and values. It is significant that Mrs. Crawley is middle class, which ensures an ideological polarization with upper class Violet Grantham. However, despite their obvious polarities the two women are not dissimilar in their acts of charity. Moreover, the working class characters precipitate their charitable acts, such as in Series Four, when Bates and Mrs. Hughes contend with the plight of Grigg and Molesley. Mrs. Hughes finds Grigg, a former music hall partner of Mr. Carson's, living in a workhouse (an example of a much-maligned form of state-run charity); when she asks recently bereaved Isobel Crawley to take him in, Isobel does so and secures suitable employment for him in Belfast to get him back on his own two feet. When Molesley loses his position following the death of Matthew in Series Three he finds it hard to secure suitable alternative employment; he ends up doing casual manual labor and acting as a delivery "boy" for Bakewell's. His fall from the prestigious position as valet results in the self-deprecating quip "I'm having my career backwards" (4:3). When Anna is troubled by his plight, Bates approaches the Dowager for help and then contrives to give him £30 under the pretext that he is merely repaying an old debt (a ruse designed to safeguard Molesely's pride). Both examples illustrate the collective charitable effort and the role of Isobel and Violet in these efforts. These examples also illustrate the pivotal role of the working-class characters in making charitable acts an acceptable outcome within the narrative. Additionally, the distinction between the two examples, in that Isobel sources suitable employment for Grigg and empowers him in the process whereas Molesley still has to find suitable employment, is arguably the more desirable outcome, one commensurate with the Liberal Conservative policy of self-sufficiency. That's not to say that the course of action taken by Bates is wrong; it merely acknowledges that giving money away and running up debt is hardly sustainable in the long run. However, Molesley is a popular character and he has an interesting story that involves him diversifying and adapting (or modernizing). His decision to retrain as a schoolteacher in Series Six demonstrates that the changes he has endured have a potentially positive outcome in taking him into a different professional sector of employment.

The most conservative characters often practice compassionate conservatism, or liberal conservatism. These are the characters who behave with the most tolerance although they would not necessarily describe themselves as liberals; they do, in fact, advocate liberal paths in order to sustain and preserve Downton through subtle acts of modernization. Therefore it is Violet, often perceived to be the archconservative of the narrative, who gives Bates the money to give to Molesley. It is Violet who arranges for former maid Ethel to take up a position in a respectable house closer to where her illegitimate son is being brought up by the Bryants in Series Three. And it is Violet who ensures a positive outcome by inviting Mrs. Bryant to speak directly to Ethel about possible regular access to the boy. It is also Violet who instigates Sybil and Branson's return to Downton after they have eloped when she secretly pays their fares, and it is Violet who will suggest Thomas for the important position of agent when the current agent summarily resigns due to Matthew's plans for reform in Series Three. Finally, it is Violet who arranges for Lady Mary to shadow Branson on his rounds so that she can learn the business of the estate when it is revealed that she is Matthew's sole heir in Series Four.

The trajectory of the narrative in Series Three around the development of the character of Thomas Barrow from largely unsympathetic schemer into a character the audience cares about reflects the viewpoint of mildly tolerant consensus. This particular storyline is discussed at length by Nesbitt, as an "unconsciously political" narrative in which, she cites Jonathon Dollimore's work on cultural representations of homosexuality to argue that Barrow's 'sexual dissidence' is ultimately contained within the narrative. When Thomas misconstrues Jimmy's friendship for romantic interest and makes a badly judged pass, witnessed by Albert, he jeopardizes his position in the household.

Homosexuality at that time was illegal and would not be decriminalized in England, Scotland and Wales until the Sexual Offences Act of 1967 was passed, following the publication of the Wolfendon Report which was a committee established by the Conservative Government in 1957 to examine the case for the decriminalization of homosexuality and prostitution.

Although Jimmy is keen to let the matter rest, he is manipulated by O'Brien into pursuing Thomas' dismissal with Carson who reluctantly agrees to this dismissal without a reference to stop Jimmy going to the police. In agreeing not to provide a reference, Carson exposes Thomas to the vagaries of misfortune in a manner not dissimilar to that experienced by Ethel in Series Two when Mrs. Hughes dismisses her for engaging in sexual activity with the army officer convalescing at Downton as part of the rehabilitation program organized by Mrs. Crawley. Although Hughes can't know it at the time, her decision to dismiss Ethel without a reference leads to her turning to a life of prostitution: a form of sexual dissidence that marks her out as unsuitable for motherhood until she is "rehabilitated" by Isobel and Violet with their respective solutions to her situation (for Isobel that involves giving her a job; for Violet it means making sure she gets a job closer to her son). The audience is already in possession of Ethel's cautionary tale when Carson dismisses Barrow without a reference: therefore there can be no doubt that his future is dire.

To compound matters, Carson's comment to Barrow, "You have been twisted by nature into something foul" (3:8) marks the scene with a measure of homophobic violence which is nevertheless Carson's own attempt at charitable compassion, one in which he absolves Barrow of responsibility for his "deviance." Barrow's stoicism is evident when he responds with great dignity, "I am not foul," arguably the moment the audience begins to "root" for him as a character. Although Carson is quite reluctant to take the matter any further, his hand is forced by Jimmy who says, "I ought to report him to the police.... I know today's thinking is much more liberal." At this point Carson erupts as if he has been smeared with something quite unthinkable: "Just a minute, I've never been called liberal in my life and I don't intend to start now." Surprisingly, it is Bates who intervenes on Barrow's behalf to persuade Lord Grantham that the matter has been blown out of all proportion and to retain him on the staff. This is a significant moment in the narrative in that it demonstrates a commonality between two previously opposed characters: Bates and Barrows have been staunch opponents throughout the first three Series. This moment occurs when Bates has just been released from prison where he languished, falsely accused of murdering his wife. Now happily married to Anna, he explains his new found compassion for Barrow: "I know what it is like to feel powerless, to see a life slide away and there is nothing you can do to stop it." This absolutely echoes Cameron's belief that a good society works to counter feelings of powerlessness by instilling a belief in self-determination. Moreover, the fact that Bates intervenes following his stint in prison, reconnects us to the "hug a hoodie" ethos as the context for that intervention by David Cameron was similarly one motivated by a desire to decriminalize a sector of the population that had been disenfranchised. The message then is that Thomas Barrow is blameless and deserving of compassion. This is reinforced when Lord Grantham, possibly the most conservative character after Carson and Violet, laughingly dismisses the furor over the open-secret of Barrow's sexuality with the quip "If I roared every time someone tried to kiss me at Eton I'd be hoarse." Bates' criticism of Jimmy when he reports the matter to Carson in which he effectively exhorts him to "man up," asking him, "Why do you have to be such a big girl's blouse about it?" suggesting that it is Jimmy, rather than Thomas, who is emasculated by a lack of tolerance and a willingness to pursue a vindictive course of action.

Barrow's story resonates during the contemporary period most obviously in relation to the debate around same sex marriage. This debate would gather pace during the first term of government for the Coalition. Indeed, the Conservatives would put this issue on the agenda in the publication "Contract for Equalities" in 2010 which would include the line "We will also consider the case for changing the law to allow civil partnerships to be called and classified as marriage," and the Liberal Democrats under Nick Clegg were also firm advocates for passing legislation. So this is a very real debate that would culminate in an amendment (but not a free vote in the House of Commons), passed in July 2013 and formally introduced in March 2014. Again, the on-going metanarrative of the transformation of the Conservative Party deserves special mention here. The Contract for Equalities' publication marks an important re-evaluation of the Tory position on gender and sexual equality following the Conservative Government of Margaret Thatcher, an administration which did not have a particularly tolerant or enlightened opinion of homosexuality, having introduced the notorious Clause 28 which prevented the promotion of homosexuality in schools in England, Scotland and Wales. This unpopular piece of legislation would be repealed in 2003 by the then Labour government and a little earlier in 2000 by the devolved Scottish Parliament.

"The state is your servant, never your master": Social Capital and Service in Downton Abbey

The view that the message of *Downton Abbey* is "that all classes must pull together in order to survive hardship" (Byrne 94) echoes David Cameron's belief that "we're all in this together" (2009). This is what Cameron alludes to when he made he made that speech at the Conservative Party conference in Manchester. He would aim for a deeply personal tone, saying, "I am not a complicated person. I love this country and the things it stands for. That the state is your servant, never your master. Common sense and decency. The British sense of community." Peter A. Hall defines social capital as "the propensity of individuals to associate together on a regular basis, to trust one another, and to engage in community affairs." The great advantage of the country house estate setting is that it provides opportunities for many different kinds of interaction or association across the different class groups. It is therefore the perfect environment to explore social capital as the community and meeting place for disparate groups is assured in the social setting.

Social capital is also assured through the management of leisure time which serves the purpose of ensuring different social classes mix in informal settings in a manner that would not otherwise be permissible. The final episode of the third series culminates in the quintessential English pastime of a cricket match between the estate and the village, in which Lord Grantham plays for the estate although according to Edith he "owns both." Getting everyone to pull together to make their own small contribution, much as it did in the previous series in regards to the war effort, leads Grantham to cajole a reluctant Thomas, "we all have to do what we can do." This results in the pleasing outcome of a diverse group (and the key here is in their diversity) including dissident Irish Republican

Thomas Branson, middle class Matthew, Lord Grantham himself, and the servants, including the most skilled player of Barrow who has just been "outed" as a homosexual.

Although the world of Downton is very far removed geographically from the trenches of the First World War, Series Two begins literally in the trenches before shifting to sustain a focus on the estate. The huge cost of the military campaign embodies an idea of service that preoccupies this particular series and persists to this day as the ultimate sacrifice that any individual can make for their country. It is evident in Grantham's desire to serve at the front with his regiment and in his disappointment when he realizes his appointment is only symbolic. It extends to the women of Downton all seeking out appropriate ways to make a contribution to the war effort, from Sybil's work in the cottage hospital, to the giving up of space in Downton itself to house recuperating officers. And most poignantly, it extends to the far from symbolic sacrifice made by William, the young footman who dies during the campaign. Service, although enshrined in the life of the servant, also encompasses the upper class characters explicitly—to become something that everyone in society can and should commit to. This is one of the cornerstones of Cameron's "Big Society" idea: volunteering becomes the norm rather than the exception and the upper echelons of society in Downton, although initially reluctant, have to accept this is a new reality.

The establishment of a weekly soup kitchen in the Crawley house by the servants combines the collective and the individual response to the hardships of war. The soup kitchen serves wounded and destitute men who have returned from the trenches. This resonates with the experience of hardship during the current climate of austerity and recession, when many people are struggling to make ends meet. One of the consequences of the drive to reduce the deficit (the number one priority of the Coalition) has been a scaling back of benefits coupled with the rising cost of living, leading to food banks appearing in the UK as an additional means of support for struggling families and indeed veterans returning from conflict zones such as Iraq and Afghanistan. When O'Brien misconstrues the appropriation of food from Downton's kitchen she seeks to profit from the knowledge for personal gain, when in reality the food is being taken from the army for returning soldiers on Mrs. Bird's initiative, aided by Mrs. Patmore. Cora's concern that this will be perceived as misappropriation of funds leads her to insist Downton's own food supply is used in future and she then goes on to personally serve the soldiers herself. Although the servants take the lead it is a course of action sanctioned by Cora ensuring once again, a consensus of opinion is achieved.

The intersection between public and private charitable acts of compassion is also evident in the setting up of the cottage hospital which of course predates a national health service in the UK. Byrne argues that the preoccupation with welfare in the series coincides with anxieties about provision both in the UK and the U.S.:

> The NHS's role has been the subject of debate and dispute in Britain and major reform is constantly on the political agenda of the Conservative-led Coalition government committed to public spending cuts. In the same period, the Patient Protection and Affordable Care Act, more usually known as "ObamaCare," has brought about the most extensive changes to healthcare in America since the 1960s, and has caused much controversy in the United States [Byrne 76].

This preoccupation is highlighted in the narrative through the numerous medical emergencies and crises, from Mrs. Hughes dealing with a possible breast cancer diagnosis, to Mrs. Patmore's eye operation in the early Series, to Lord Grantham's spectacular collapse over the dinner table due to a perforated ulcer in Series Six. Healthcare is an abiding concern of all of the characters. Mrs. Crawley's "powerful pivotality," to borrow an expression used by Quinn et al. to describe the key position of the Liberals following the General Election in 2010, which some construe as meddling, reflects in actuality the increasingly influential role of female medical practitioners of the era, women such as Dame Janet Campbell whose experience of the Boer War would lead to pioneering work in ante-natal care in particular.

Lady Sybil's death in Series Three is the most tragic consequence of a breakdown in consensus in the estate: the single greatest rupture of social capital in the series. The medical reason for her death following childbirth, is given as eclampsia, a condition not uncommon during the Edwardian era and one which would prove fatal given the lack of sophisticated medical resources of the modern era. However, in examining the storyline of Sybil's tragic death again, it could be argued that it represents a moment when the investment in community, commonality and consensus literally falls apart as Sybil struggles to breathe surrounded by her family and other members of the community. Sybil does not lack for healthcare provision, in fact she has on hand two physicians to manage her care: one an eminent physician, titled, who advocates non-intervention and the other the ordinary village doctor who has known Sybil all of her life and who advocates a medical intervention in a hospital setting. With historical hindsight we know that the village doctor is correct, but it is the eminent physician who prevails with Robert's backing, and of course Sybil dies shortly after giving birth. Sybil dies because fundamentally there is a breakdown in trust between Robert and Cora and between Robert and Doctor Clark (following his misdiagnosis of Matthew's condition in the previous series). When Robert and Cora disagree there is extreme disharmony, as is also the case when below stairs surrogates Carson and Mrs. Hughes disagree.

The effective management of a great estate to ensure longevity and sustainability is the overwhelming preoccupation of the series from its inception. Although the country house estate environment clearly presents challenges for all involved in its upkeep and smooth running, the on-going challenge of sustainability, which would form one of the main narrative plotlines in Series Three in particular, taps in to contemporary debates around growth, profitability and "big government." Trust between husband and wife and indeed between social classes is necessary in order that consensus and harmony be achieved. Throughout the series it is often Robert who is inclined to withhold trust as he does in Series Three when he rejects Matthew's planned reforms for the estate, "we must invest and cut waste," a view supported crucially by Thomas and Mary (therefore all classes are in agreement) and they are finally endorsed by Cora who tells Robert, "we must ensure the estate as a place of employment." An emotional Robert responds by accusing Cora of taking sides against him but it is clear that Robert's credibility as a manager has been undermined by the loss of Cora's fortune earlier in the series. Indeed he implores Matthew to consider investing in a Ponzi scheme—this is a historically factual scheme that would become a notoriously fraudulent enterprise in which many UK investors would lose their fortunes. Robert is a reckless manager: high stakes and high risk.

The impossibility of sustaining Downton on the old economic model favored by Lord Grantham is sharply exposed is Series Three when Grantham's investment in the Grand Trunk Railway using Cora's fortune is found to have been a bad investment, bringing the estate to the brink of ruin. This is exactly the kind of risk-taking with expenditure/capital that the current economic climate disdains. The backstory (it is a Canadian investment) is significant—an aspect which would remind the audience that the flow of capital is global and precarious. Although the investment is only briefly mentioned as the pretext for crisis at Downton (will they lose the estate?), it is a venture, which would end with bankruptcy and the nationalization of the Canadian rail networks—an outcome that would surely appall any Conservative. Avoiding bankruptcy, maintaining growth and sustaining a healthy credit rating are the dominant concerns of the Coalition. Matthew urges strategic investment, particularly in the farming side of the business, left to stagnate by Lord Grantham and his agent Jarvis. Matthew brings to the management of the estate a degree of entrepreneurialism that stems from his middle class background.

"Work is pleasurable and rewarding (as long as there is 'a clear chain of command')"

One of the singular themes promoted through the narrative of the series is the belief that "employment" is aspirational on multiple levels. This is a core ideal that resonates with the rhetoric of the Big Society and might be regarded as the cornerstone of policies based around advocacy of personal responsibility. In *Downton Abbey* everyone takes pride in their work from the employee on the lowest rung of the ladder to the highest, and everyone has their métier; it is idleness that is to be feared and distrusted. This extends even to Cora, Edith, Lady Mary and the Dowager Countess—all representatives of a class defined as 'ladies of leisure' who nevertheless find fulfillment in occupation. The overwhelming message of the series is that work is desirable and fulfilling.

People also fear losing their job and this is certainly a fear that resonates during the current economic climate following the collapse of the financial crisis of 2007–2008 and the global recession. When Mrs. Patmore says to Mrs. Hughes in 4:1 on the subject of the new blender already mastered by the much younger Daisy, "it makes her part of the future and me part of the past," she is expressing the same anxiety that plagues many people about the pace of change and the stability of the economy.

A global conflict such as war, and on a scale never seen before, provides an opportunity to explore directly the idea of change on multiple levels. Change is perceived by many of the characters as a threat to stability and tradition, a disruption of the status quo. The potential to disrupt order has moral and ideological implications and is alluded to by Carson (2:3) when he expresses the hope that "a chain of command will be sorted out soon" to make sense of this new reality (Downton being turned into a convalescent home). The idea of hierarchy in which decisions are taken by the right people is eerily reminiscent of Cameron's own words in his party conference speech in which he said back in 2009 (before the general election), "We need a clear chain of command that flows right from the top"; the manor house is a stratified environment and the staff obsess on the nuances of any given role, the distinction between footman and first footman or under butler and head valet (3:8), borne out in Series Three, when the battle lines are drawn between Alfred and Jimmy over who has seniority; in other words, who should carry the meat and who should carry the vegetables into the dining room? The importance of maintaining a clear chain of command is constantly stressed as a principle upon which longevity and continuity will be assured.

Although the strictly stratified world of Downton is, of course, based on class, this is not predicated on notions of inequality but on ensuring equality and fairness. Social mobility is permissible when earned and achieved on merit: any advancement attained through other means is problematic as can be discerned with Barrow and Branson. When Barrow is promoted to Sergeant to oversee the running of the convalescent home at Downton, he is promoted out of the natural order and above his station, having contrived an injury, his resultant manner is overbearing and he is reprimanded by Clarkson. Branson's advancement comes through marriage to Sybil but his assimilation within the family is not without difficulty. The social faux pas committed by Branson during the house party in 4:3, when he calls a Duchess "Your Grace," leads to a rebuke from Violet which ends with a putdown that pokes fun at her own class: "If you are looking for logic don't look for it in the English upper classes." This immediately precedes a serious blunder by Branson when he addresses Barrows informally as "Thomas." He is sharply reminded that "it's Barrow now." This presents the perfect snapshot of the often unwritten rules that underpin order in the Downton world, and crucially: these rules work both ways. Both men eventually gain acceptance and promotion that is crucially underpinned on merit: Barrow will finally achieve his career aspirations to take over from an ageing Carson in the final episode of the series. It is clear that he has earned his place and the progression appears natural. Branson also prevails to become a fully accepted member of the family: his great love of Sybil and his ideas for the running of the estate ensure that he too has his place.

"How little we know our parents":
Parents as Enablers

Cameron's conference speech draws to a close with a reflection on fatherless children: "And I know there are children growing up in Britain today who will never know the love of a father. Who are born in homes that hold them back." There's no shortage of children in the series who will not know the love of a father (or mother for that matter in the case of Sybbi) and this raises the specter of the rising cost of single-parent families and "blended" families that are an increasing part of contemporary UK society. The concern David Cameron expresses about the decline in family values and the erosion of firm notions of parental responsibility, as Val Gillies points out, cements an emotional investment in a traditional idea of family which remains at the heart of conservative ideology: "family remained the symbolic lynchpin of communities" (Gillies 91). Gillies goes on to argue that the drive to "control and regulate the conduct of parents" becomes an abiding concern of the Coalition. The arrival of Sybil, George and Marigold (Edith's illegitimate child with Strallan) in the nursery suggests that the family at Downton is anything but traditional; however, the expectations around parental responsibility *are* traditional: Edith, for example, must "step up" to being Marigold's guardian and provide her with the opportunities she herself is making possible through her work as a magazine editor. Bringing Marigold to Downton reverses the situation faced by Ethel when she gives her son to the Bryants to be brought up in material comfort. Leaving Marigold with the good farming family would have provided a good upbringing, and there is no doubt the family would have loved Marigold. But this would have in many ways been a tragic outcome for both Edith and Marigold, and not just on emotional terms: Edith has to accept responsibility for Marigold in order to fulfill her place as one of the most liberal conservative characters in the series.

The world of Downton can hardly be accused of holding its children back: Mary, Edith and Sybil all have access to the kind of privileges that ordinary people can only dream about. However, they are nevertheless constrained by their class and each must assert their independence in their own ways. Although there are many occasions when Cora and Robert disagree with their children and indeed, *over* their children, they nevertheless invariably allow them to choose their own paths and make their own mistakes. Even when they are being bad parents (and this rarely applies to Cora), there are other surrogate role models to rely on, as is the case in Series Four when Mary turns to Carson for emotional support rather than her very 'buttoned up' father who seems to be encouraging her to suppress her grief at the death of Matthew, and yet he allows her to wallow in inactivity which means she cannot move on. In a moving scene in 4:1 when Mary breaks down completely, Carson embraces her and reassures her that she can rejoin the land of the living. The coalition recasts parents as enablers, making it possible for children to achieve and to serve.

A Special Relationship?

Ever since Winston Churchill described "the special relationship" between the U.S. and the UK in 1946, successive governments have been obsessed with proving this relationship persists to this day. The Coalition government of 2010 is no exception. When Mary and Violet try to borrow from Cora's wealthy American mother Martha Levinson to bail the family out and prevent them from losing the estate, she declines on the basis that her money is tied up in the U.S. estate. Violet even uses the expression "special relationship" to describe the bond between the Crawleys and the Levinsons (3:2).

Cameron addresses the concept of the special relationship in emotive terms following a lengthy and personalized account of his response to the events of 9/11 and the threat of terror on an unprecedented scale:

> I and my party are instinctive friends of America, and passionate supporters of the Atlantic Alliance. We believe in the alliance for both emotional and rational reasons. Emotional—because we share so much. A set of values and beliefs about the world—a common language, common institutions, and our common belief in individual liberty.... So when it comes to the special relationship with America, Conservatives feel it, understand it and believe in it.

Is Martha's refusal to bankroll Downton a betrayal of this special relationship or simply a reality check in which "wealth" is shown to be largely symbolic? When the wealthy have just as much trouble accessing funds as other social groups, and this certainly seems to be the abiding message of Series Three, the impact of austerity and recession affect all social groups without prejudice.

Conclusion

Although the Coalition would mark the pinnacle of Nick Clegg's leadership in bringing unforeseen and unprecedented political influence at a time when the Liberal Democrats were the third party in the UK, ultimately it also inaugurated a period of unpopularity as core supporters and potential supporters recoiled at the cost of the alliance (for example, having to accept policies such as the introduction of tuition fees which they had staunchly opposed during the election campaign). The parallels with the declining fortunes of the Liberals of the Edwardian era following the Lloyd George Coalition, is particularly ironic in this context. The 2015 election would return the Conservatives to a majority government and the Liberal Democrats would be virtually wiped out as a political force in the UK. This happened to coincide with the end of *Downton Abbey* that would cease production after six seasons. However, I don't regard this as an outright rejection of liberal thinking; rather I see it as evidence of the Conservative party's more successful "reboot," one in which they managed to assimilate liberal political ideals alongside traditional Tory party values focused on family, social responsibility, self-sufficiency and community. The Big Society idea might have been met with some skepticism by some sections of the press, but it is an idea almost perfectly expressed in the dramatic cut and thrust of the series.

WORKS CITED

Atkinson, W., S. Roberts, and M. Savage, eds. *Class Inequality and Austerity Britain: Power, Difference and Suffering*. Basingstoke: Palgrave Macmillan, 2013.

Beech, M. "The Ideology of the Coalition: More Liberal Than Conservative." In Matt Beech and Simon Lee, eds., *The Conservative-Liberal Coalition Examining the Cameron-Clegg Government*. Basingstoke: Palgrave Macmillan, 2015.

Bednarek, A. "Responsibility and the Big Society." *Sociological Research Online* 16:2 (2011). Available at: http://www.socresonline.org.uk/16/2/17.html. Date accessed: 4/2/16.

Byrne, K. *Edwardians on Screen: From Downton Abbey to Parade's End*. Basingstoke: Palgrave Macmillan, 2015.

Cameron, D. Speech delivered at the Centre for Social Justice, 20 July 2006. Available online: http://news.bbc.co.uk/1/hi/5166498.stm. Date accessed: 6/6/16.

Cameron, D. Speech delivered at the Conservative Party Conference in Manchester, October 2009. Available at: http://www.theguardian.com/politics/2009/oct/08/david-cameron-speech-in-full. Date accessed: 6/6/16.

Cameron, D. Tribute to Margaret Thatcher delivered in the House of Commons on 10/4/13. Available online at: http://www.theguardian.com/politics/2013/apr/10/margaret-thatcher-tributes-david-cameron-speech. Date accessed: 1/6/16.

Cameron, D. "Big Society speech" delivered in Liverpool 19 July 2010. Available online at: https://www.gov.uk/government/speeches/big-society-speech. Date accessed: 4/2/16.

Conservative Party publication "A Contract for Equalities." Available online at: http://www.lgbtory.co.uk/sites/www.lgbtory.co.uk/files/conservative_party_contract_for_equalities_2010.pdf. Date accessed: 2/6/16.

Conservative & Liberal Democrat Manifesto. *The Coalition: Our Programme for Government*. Cabinet Office, 2010.

Finn, M. "The Coming of the Coalition and the Coalition Agreement." In Anthony Seldon and M. Finn, eds., *The Coalition Effect 2010–2015*. Cambridge: Cambridge University Press.

Fraser, D. *The Evolution of the British Welfare State: A History of Social Policy since the industrial Revolution*. Basingstoke: Palgrave Macmillan, 2009.

Gilbert, B.B. "David Lloyd George: Land, the Budget, and Social Reform." *The American Historical Review* 81:5 (December 1976), pp. 1058–1066.

Gillies, V. "Personalising Poverty: Parental Determinism and the Big Society Agenda." In W. Atkinson, S. Roberts, and M. Savage, eds., *Class Inequality and Austerity Britain: Power, Difference and Suffering*. Basingstoke: Palgrave Macmillan, 2013, pp. 90–110.

Hall, P. "Social Capital in Britain." *British Journal of Political Science* 29:3 (1999), 417–461.

Hattersley, R. *David Lloyd George: The Great Outsider*. London: Little, Brown, 2010.

Hewison, R. *The Heritage Industry: Britain in a Climate of Decline*. London: Methuen, 1987.

Higson, A. "The Heritage Film and British Cinema." In Andrew Higson, ed., *Dissolving Views: Key Writings on British Cinema*. London: Cassell, 1996.

Itzkoff, D. "Julian Fellowes on Viewer Criticism and 'Downton Abbey's' Future." 2014. Available online: http://artsbeat.blogs.nytimes.com/2014/02/23/julian-fellowes-on-viewer-criticism-and-downton-abbeys-future/?_r=0. Date accessed; 1/6/16.

Leggot, J., and J. Taddeo, eds. *Upstairs and Downstairs: British Costume Drama from The Forsyte Saga to Downton Abbey*. London: Rowman & Littlefield, 2015.

Nava, M. "Modernity's Disavowal: Women, the City and the Department Store." In Mica Nava and Alan O'Shea, *Modern Times: Reflections on a Century of English Modernity*. London Routledge, 1996, 38–76.

Nesbitt, J. "The Absent Presence of Virginia Woolf: Queering Downton Abbey." *The Journal of Popular Culture* 49:2 (2016).

May, T. Speech delivered at the Conservative Party Annual Conference in Bournemouth, 7 October 2002. http://www.theguardian.com/politics/2002/oct/07/conservatives2002.conservatives1. Date accessed: 1/6/16.

Monk, C. "The British Heritage Debate Revisited." In C. Monk and Amy Sargent, eds., *British Historical Cinema*, 176–198. London: Routledge, 2002.

O'Hara, K. *After Blair: David Cameron and the Conservative Tradition*. Cambridge: Icon Books, 2007.

Quinn, T., J. Bara, and J. Bartle J. "The UK Coalition Agreement of 2010: Who Won?" *Journal of Elections, Public Opinion and Parties* 21:2 (2011), pp. 295–312.

Tincknell, E. "Dowagers, Debs, Nuns and Babies: The Politics of Nostalgia and the Older Woman in the British Sunday Night Television Serial." *Journal of British Cinema and Television* 10.4 (2013): 769–784.

Toye, R. *Lloyd George and Churchill: Rivals for Greatness*. London: Pan Books, 2008.

About the Contributors

Rachel L. **Carazo** is earning a graduate degree in English from Northwestern State University and undergraduate degrees from Southern New Hampshire University. She is the author *The Vaïndrian Queen*, the first novel in a fantasy series.

Elizabeth **Fitzgerald** is an adjunct professor of English at Carroll Community College and Cecil College. In her composition and literature courses, she frequently draws connections between literature, writing, and pop culture.

Jennifer **Harrison** is a professor in the Humanities & Social Sciences Department at Kaplan University. She specializes in nineteenth-century American women's history, art and humanities, and pop culture.

Ellen **Hernandez** has taught in the Academic Skills English Department of Camden County College since 1989. She has taught and tutored in secondary English and mathematics and run remedial reading and writing labs in New York and New Jersey.

Gill **Jamieson** is a senior lecturer in filmmaking and screenwriting in the School of Media, Culture and Society on the Ayr Campus of the University of West Scotland. She teaches courses in British and American television drama and cinema, Asian cinema, screen adaptation and popular culture.

Gayle Sherwood **Magee** is a professor in the School of Music at the University of Illinois, Urbana-Champaign. She writes and teaches on American music since the late nineteenth century, including contemporary music and film music.

Mary Ruth **Marotte** is a professor of English at the University of Central Arkansas, where she specializes in women's studies and critical theory. She also serves as the Executive Director of Arkansas Shakespeare Theatre, the state's only professional Shakespeare theater.

Courtney Pina **Miller** is a doctoral student at Brandeis University. She studies transatlantic modernist literature, working class characters and spaces, critical race theory, and white trash culture and servant characters in literature, television and film.

Joy E. **Morrow** teaches introductory writing and conversational English courses in Japan. Her areas of research interest are Victorian literature, Irish literature at the beginning of the twentieth century and cultural studies.

Jennifer Poulos **Nesbitt** is an associate professor of English at the York Campus of Penn State University. Her teaching areas include British literature, feminism, and postcolonialism.

Anthony Guy **Patricia** is an instructor of English at Concord University in Athens, West Virginia. He teaches freshman composition and world literature as well as special topics courses on Shakespeare and film, Tennessee Williams, and Harry Potter.

Michael **Samuel** is a doctoral candidate at the University of Leeds. His research analyzes the relationship between heritage film, tourism and historical buildings.

Katrin **Suhren** has presented papers on various aspects of Shakespeare and his plays at conferences in Germany, Austria and the United Kingdom. Further research interests include education in literary and popular cultures, ecocriticism and young adult literature.

Scott F. **Stoddart** is the dean of the College of Arts and Sciences at Saint Peter's University, where he is also an associate professor of English. He teaches courses in American literature, cinema studies and musical theatre history and has published widely on these topics.

Melissa **Wehler** is the dean of Humanities and Sciences at Central Penn College. Her publications include essays in a variety of edited collections where she discusses topics including the gothic, feminism, performance and culture.

Index

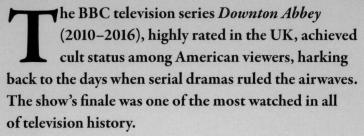

The BBC television series *Downton Abbey* (2010–2016), highly rated in the UK, achieved cult status among American viewers, harking back to the days when serial dramas ruled the airwaves. The show's finale was one of the most watched in all of television history.

This collection of new essays by British and American contributors explores how a series about life in an early 20th century English manor home resonated with American audiences. Topics include the role of the house in literature and film, the changing roles of women and the servant class, the influence of jazz and fashion, and attitudes regarding education and the class system.

SCOTT F. STODDART is the dean of the College of Arts and Sciences at Saint Peter's University in Jersey City, New Jersey. He has written about culture, literature and the arts on such topics as F. Scott Fitzgerald, Stephen Sondheim and the Coen brothers. He is a host of the Sundance television series *Love/Lust* and a contributor to the PBS series *American Icons*.

Front cover images © 2018 iStock

McFarland